NICK
MALGIERI'S
PERFECT
PASTRY

NICK
MALGIERI'S
PERFECT
PASTRY

MACMILLAN PUBLISHING COMPANY
NEW YORK

COLLIER MACMILLAN PUBLISHERS
LONDON

Macmillan Publishing Company
866 Third Avenue, New York, NY 10022
Collier Macmillan Canada, Inc.

Library of Congress Cataloging-in-Publication Data
Malgieri, Nick.
Nick Malgieri's perfect pastry.
p.   cm.
Includes bibliographical references.
ISBN 0-02-579251-2
1. Pastry. I. Title. II. Title: Perfect pastry.
TX773.M238   1989
641.8'65—dc20   89-12954   CIP

Macmillan books are available at special discounts for
bulk purchases for sales promotions, premiums, fund-
raising, or educational use. For details contact:

Special Sales Director
Macmillan Publishing Company
866 Third Avenue
New York, NY 10022

10 9 8 7 6 5 4 3 2 1

Printed in the United States of America

37/08588

For Albert Kumin, my teacher,
and all my students.

ACKNOWLEDGMENTS

On New Year's Eve, 1984, I was visiting my old friend Sandy Leonard in Cambridge, taking a few days off after the busy holiday season at the Board Room Club. Late in the day I received a call from Joseph Viggiani informing me that his friend and colleague, Sturgess Spanos, knew an editor from Bobbs-Merrill who was interested in acquiring some cookbooks. Early in 1985, I met Cornelia Guest, the editor, and we initiated the process that has resulted in this book. Shortly thereafter Bobbs-Merrill was acquired by Macmillan and John Woodside became my editor. John's patience is enormous and his keen sense of order and continuity have made my techniques and recipes into a book. Thanks, John.

Bonnie Tandy Leblang, my copy editor, went over the manuscript with infinite care, noting every tiny inconsistency and pointing out every instance where more explanation was needed, and still managed to survive with her sense of humor and sanity intact. She deserves the greatest praise.

There are many other people to thank: Susan Cohen, my literary agent, has been enthusiastic, helpful and always easy to reach, a great virtue in her busy field. I owe a lot to Anne Casale who introduced me to Writer's House, Susan's agency.

Special thanks are due to Ceri Hadda. In the actual planning, research and writing, Ceri has contributed an incredible amount. We first worked together on recipes I needed to revise for classes, and I could see immediately that she had a genuine understanding and appreciation of the material. From then on, we spent many hours together, planning the chapters, brainstorming for recipe ideas, testing, writing, revising and generally working ourselves silly. Ceri has been involved with every aspect of this book, including the photographs in the text; she has worked weekends, nights and even through the night to help make this book a reality.

Don Kushnick did the photographs in the text, spending most of his free time over the course of several months focusing on dough and buttercream. His judgment and experience saved many a shot from ambiguity. Don's patience, kindness and generosity, as well as his most dry wit, made the photography sessions a real pleasure. I was fortunate that such a busy and sought-after photographer did this immense job out of friendship.

Richard Felber, who took the photograph for the cover, is a joy to work with. We had many a laugh during the day of shooting for the cover, although I don't think I could have rearranged the desserts on the table one more time! A real perfectionist, Richard has an accurate eye for detail—he loves to make food look beautiful on paper.

Mary Wamby and Alison Radin tested many of the recipes, noting quantities, baking times and results with minute detail. Alison spent an entire day in the kitchen verifying the weights of the volume measurements of the ingredients and preparing a table that we could work from to write the recipes. They are both devoted friends.

Another dear friend, Peter Madden, started typing the manuscript; Peter worked long and odd hours, putting up with all the retyping necessary every time a change had to be made in the text. Suzy Madden joined us shortly thereafter, and helped type and research the fruit section. Jacqui Henitz typed several chapters on her word processor until I acquired one of my own. From then on we all typed, printed and edited, with many urgent phone calls to Gaynor Grant, my friend, colleague and resident computer expert from Peter Kump's New York Cooking School.

Ramon Castillo and Barbara Lind helped during the photography sessions at Don's and Richard Simpson contributed his inexhaustible energy and humor during the cover shoot. Students in my Fall 1988 Intensive Pastry Course at Peter Kump's also assisted in preparing the desserts for the cover.

Emory Thompson of White Lily Foods helped me verify the flour and gluten information. Carole Walter and I had many long conversations about measuring flour and determining its protein content. Carole has always been unstinting in her generosity, sharing information from her vast baking experience.

Moral support came from my ever-wonderful parents, Ann and Nufre Malgieri, and good friends like Sandy Leonard, Miriam Brickman, Marilyn Fine, Peter Fresulone, Jeanne Kahn and Peter Kump. Peter generously provided space at his school whenever necessary for testing and preparation of food for photography. His continual encouragement has helped me immeasurably.

Pat Soller Bartholomew recommended me for my first teaching job, more than ten years ago. She, along with so many others, played a part in this book and I give them my heartfelt thanks.

CONTENTS

FOREWORD

For me cookbooks fall into many categories. Some are definitive reference books like *The Joy of Cooking* or Diana Kennedy's *The Cuisines of Mexico,* some are personal cookbooks in which I look for special recipes, others are by cooks or cooking teachers that I peruse for new techniques—to find out if they've discovered anything new or different. I like to browse through some cookbooks because of the anecdotes included with the recipes, then there are the coffee table cookbooks, mainly for looking.

I've known and worked with Nick for many years. In New York City he's known as the city's leading pastry teacher, a reputation that is slowly building around the country as he tirelessly travels giving classes. In picking up his book I expected something special; I wasn't disappointed.

Nick has sterling credentials and has proven himself both as a professional as well as a teacher. When someone is a consummate professional with training, knowledge and a thorough background, and who day in and day out spends his time not only creating the most stunning desserts but also teaching them—the result is a cookbook that can be a reference, an inspiration and a self-instructional guide.

Nick is one of those rare people who is as comfortable in the professional world as he is teaching. And he is blessed with lots of patience as well as the talent to be able to make complicated procedures crystal clear to his students. You should see the results of his efforts! In a few short weeks he has students turning out the most glorious desserts imaginable, not only attractive to the eye, but tasting just as good as they look. His students are heading, and working in, the pastry kitchens of some of the greatest restaurants in New York City. Others are happily and effortlessly at home stunning their friends with their latest creations.

This book has it all. His tricks, his secrets, his techniques that really work. It is loaded with his new ways of achieving results with less effort—using techniques he has developed over the years that help to simplify complex processes. Nick doesn't do things in a harder, "authentic" way if he can achieve the same—or even better—results with new equipment and less work. He never sacrifices quality for expediency. He is a true professional's professional.

This book is one of the finest, if not the finest, of its kind, one that you will refer to constantly. It will join that inner circle of cookbooks that you really trust and use. This book is about the best thing you can do if you can't study with Nick. Read it with pleasure, use it with success and I know that you'll be sharing enviable times with your friends savoring your own delectable creations. Enjoy.

Peter Kump

NICK MALGIERI'S PERFECT PASTRY

1

BEFORE YOU START

During the past ten years I have had the pleasure of teaching thousands of people how to prepare desserts and pastries. Some have had professional aspirations—young people seeking careers as pastry chefs, mature people looking to change from careers that they no longer found fulfilling. Some have already been launched in careers as pastry cooks and chefs and wanted to learn new skills to improve the quality of their work.

The great majority of students, however, has been made up of *amateurs.* I use the word in the original sense, to indicate those who pursue a particular interest out of love for it. Some have been accomplished home cooks who never had the courage to attempt desserts. Others have been experienced home bakers who have shared as much knowledge with me as I have been able to impart to them.

The one thing that all students have had in common is a desire to learn the how's and why's of baking, rather than individual recipes. In written evaluations made after each course, students have overwhelmingly praised the emphasis on technique—the explanation of *how* different processes should be accomplished and *why* they work one way and not another.

I have always approached teaching as an explanation of techniques. Each class may be devoted to one principal technique—puff pastry preparation, for example—and the different finished products that may be prepared from it. Many courses have had a more specific orientation, such as Viennese, Italian or traditional French pastry making. But the emphasis has always been on the same important point: The recipe for a particular finished product, no matter what tradition it may spring from, is always composed of a collection of different techniques.

In all of the recipes in this book, emphasis has been placed on the exposition of technique. Although the recipes may stand alone, each represents a particular technique or set of techniques that once fully mastered can be used to create new recipes. To reinforce this point, I have also included variations and suggestions based on the recipes.

The book begins with an explanation of

equipment and the nature of ingredients. Using the proper equipment always makes it easier to accomplish whatever work is necessary more efficiently. Knowledge of the nature and properties of ingredients makes it possible to handle them suitably and prevents disasters brought on by substituting incompatible ingredients.

The techniques presented begin with the most simple—measuring ingredients—and build in complexity through creams, custards and meringues. From there on, each chapter treats a particular basic type of dough or batter and shows the many different forms it may take as finished desserts. The final chapter, devoted to decorating techniques, shows all the "tricks" for professional-looking presentations. All the flourishes that turn a dessert into a beautifully finished creation are presented in detail.

Although the techniques in this book tend to build in complexity, it is certainly not necessary to complete every previous technique and recipe before attempting one that appears later in the book. Each recipe stands alone, with sufficient instructions for its particular preparation. It is a good idea to review in full the techniques for the components used in a recipe before preparing it, but short explanations of all techniques are included to eliminate endless cross-referencing and page-turning. If more detailed instructions are required, simply refer back to the complete explanation of the problem technique. **In recipe variations, if an ingredient can be substituted for another, it is understood that the quantity is the same unless otherwise specified.**

The number of pans used to prepare the recipes has deliberately been limited to several easy-to-obtain sizes, most of which can be found in any hardware or department store. The ingredients, except in a very few cases, are easy to find in any supermarket. For readers interested in special equipment or ingredients, a list of sources appears at the end of the book.

The quantities that the recipes yield are not arbitrary. The yields of all fillings, whether they be Bavarian creams or buttercreams, are geared toward the finished products in which they will be used. This feature also makes it easy to create new desserts at will, since the different components used will be in the right proportion to each other.

The material presented here is a distillation of all my experience in preparing pastries and desserts from the past fifteen years. It is my hope that this work will be used by home bakers and professionals alike, functioning as a reference manual that will explain techniques not fully treated in other books on the subject.

EQUIPMENT

The right equipment for each recipe eases preparation and minimizes the chances for failure. Each recipe includes information on appropriate equipment needed; wherever possible, alternatives (such as different pan sizes) are also given. Obviously it is not necessary to acquire every piece below before attempting one of the recipes, but preparation will be easier and less time-consuming with the right tools.

Hand Tools

Knives

Buy the best knives available and they will last a lifetime. So many tasks in dessert making are accomplished more easily and more accurately with the help of a strong, sharp knife. Knives with stainless steel blades are best because, unlike carbon steel blades, they do not react with the acidity of fruit.

Look for full-tang knives—ones where the blade and handle are one continuous piece of metal with the wooden handle riveted on. These are less likely to come loose from their handles than cheaper knives where the blade only partially extends into the handle.

Store knives in a dry place, making sure that they are perfectly clean and dry before putting them away. A knife rack is helpful in preventing damage to the points. Use a *carborundum stone* for sharpening, or have knives professionally sharpened every six months or so, depending on use. A *steel* helps to keep the knife edge in good shape between sharpenings.

PARING KNIFE. I prefer a paring knife with a 3-inch blade. Tasks like peeling apples or cutting other fruit are less awkward with the small blade.

CHEF'S OR CHOPPING KNIFE (also called a *French knife*). This knife is used for simple chopping or cutting of ingredients such as nuts or chocolate. The length of the blade depends entirely upon the user. I like an 8- to 10-inch blade. People with smaller hands prefer a shorter blade since the knife is lighter to hold and easier to balance.

SERRATED KNIFE (BREAD KNIFE). The serrated knife is primarily used for cutting cakes into layers, trimming layers and cutting finished cakes. Since the blade has teeth rather than a straight edge, the knife cannot be easily sharpened if it becomes dull. To maintain sharpness, try to avoid cutting through anything that will ultimately push the knife blade against a hard work surface. *Never* cut paper, cardboard, chocolate or anything resistant with a serrated knife. A 12-inch blade is best since it will cut through most layers easily.

Metal Spatulas

Spatulas are used for many different purposes in dessert and pastry making, so an assortment is a necessity.

STRAIGHT SPATULAS. These are used for finishing cakes and transferring finished cakes and pastries. Those with 8- to 12-inch blades, about 1½ inches wide, are best.

OFFSET SPATULAS. With blades offset an inch or so lower than the handle, these come in very small (3-inch blade) and large sizes (8- to 12-inch blades). They are most useful for filling and finishing cakes which must be flat and straight, as well as for spreading batters in pans.

Bench Scraper

This tool has a rectangular stainless-steel blade—usually 3 × 5 inches, and a rectangular wooden handle. Indispensable for working with dough, it is used for keeping the surface free of stuck dough as well as cutting through thick pieces of dough. A corne, de-scribed later, also works.

Pastry Wheel

For cutting dough into strips and trimming large pieces of puff pastry, a sharp, metal pastry wheel gives straight, accurate results. It is available in straight and serrated versions. Use the serrated wheel for sweet doughs only; it might seal the puff pastry or flaky dough layers together. Pastry wheels are also useful for decorative work like cutting marzipan and chocolate ribbons.

Vegetable Peeler

A swivel-bladed peeler, like the one used for potatoes, is useful for peeling fruit and making chocolate shavings.

Melon Scoop

I like to use a scoop for coring apples and pears after they have been halved. I find this more accurate and less wasteful than using a corer or knife.

Zester

This removes the zest from citrus fruit in long, thin strands. Look for a zester that has sharp openings on the top and a well-attached handle.

Stripper

Used to remove 1/4-inch strips of rind from citrus fruits, the stripper makes decorating citrus slices or wedges a simple technique.

Choose a stripper with the same qualities as a zester.

Grater

A box grater has four or six sides with sharp openings of different shapes and sizes. I avoid those openings which resemble nail holes and prefer to use the openings which are set into the grater at an angle, so that delicate materials such as citrus zests do not stick in them.

Wooden Spoons and Spatulas

Boxwood spoons and spatulas are best since the wood is hard and less likely to splinter. An assortment of graduated sizes is good, from 8 to 12 inches long. Wooden spatulas have a straight bottom edge and are best for stirring mixtures likely to scorch while cooking since the flat edge covers the bottom of the pan more easily than a round one.

Rubber Spatulas

The professional type with a hard plastic or rubber handle is best. They range in length from 8 to 14 inches. An assortment of different sizes is recommended.

Rubber or Plastic Scraper

Sometimes called a corne since it was previously made from horn, this is useful for scraping the inside of a mixing bowl, filling a pastry bag, or smoothing a batter or filling with the flat edge.

Wire Whips (Whisks)

The thin-wired whips are best for most purposes. Usually called *piano wire whips,* their flexible wires are best for incorporating mixtures that are not too dense. A small (8-inch) and large (12-inch) whip are usually sufficient. For beating cream and egg whites by hand, a *balloon whip,* with a wide spherical space in the middle, incorporates air more quickly than a more narrow whip.

Strainers

Several different round-bottomed strainers with very fine to coarse mesh are useful for sifting dry ingredients, straining liquids and removing seeds from purees. A conical mesh strainer, called a *chinois* in French, is also good for large quantities of liquids such as Crème Anglaise and thin glazes.

Food Mill

Mostly outmoded by the food processor, this tool is still useful for making purees and removing the seeds from mixtures such as raspberry purees.

Rolling Pins

A straight boxwood pin, about 16 inches long and 2 inches in diameter, is a good all-purpose rolling pin. For heavier work such as large batches of puff pastry, a 14- or 16-inch ball-bearing pin is useful. There are also heavy, ball-bearing rolling pins of heavy plastic with a channeled surface for puff pastry and other layered doughs. I have never found this type necessary or helpful.

Brushes

Flexible natural bristle brushes are used for applying egg wash, glazes and syrups to desserts. A range of sizes from ½ inch to 3 inches in width is useful.

Vessels

Bowls

Stainless steel bowls in graduated sizes—from 1 to 6 quarts—can hold different parts of the same recipe and be used for mixing as well. Pyrex bowls come in graduated sets and are useful as well as inexpensive. A *copper bowl* should be used *only* for beating egg whites. The copper can react with fat and produce mildly toxic results.

Measuring Tools

Glass measuring cups in 1-, 2- and 4-cup sizes are good for liquids. Stainless steel dry measure cups in ¼-, ⅓-, ½-, 1- and 2-cup sizes are best for dry ingredients. Standard metal measuring spoons in ¼-teaspoon, ½-teaspoon, 1-teaspoon and 1-tablespoon sizes give accurate measurements for small quantities. Some sets also include a ⅛ teaspoon and a ½ tablespoon. Although the ⅛ teaspoon is sometimes called for, the ½ tablespoon measure is easily confused with the 1 teaspoon measure and is better discarded to prevent mishaps.

Saucepans

Enameled iron pans are good for dessert preparations because of their nonreactive interiors. Try to avoid aluminum pans and all-stainless pans. The aluminum may discolor acid or egg yolk preparations. All-stainless pans heat very unevenly. Aluminum pans lined with stainless are good choices since they combine the even heating of aluminum with the nonreactive property of stainless. Pans useful for different recipes include 1-, 1½-, 3- and 4-quart ones. Copper pans lined with tin or nickel give excellent results, but unfortunately are expensive. Choose very heavy pans in copper for best results.

Baking Pans

Baking pan sizes are kept to a minimum in the recipes to avoid purchasing many different pans with limited uses.

CAKE PANS. For baking the cake layers, as well as for making the molded cakes, a 9- or 10-inch diameter × 2½- to 3-inch deep springform pan is used for all the recipes. I prefer the straight-sided American version (available in hardware stores) over the imported type which flares out slightly at the top, making an awkward shape in a molded cake. In recipes for layer cakes, a 10-inch diameter × 2-inch deep pan may be substituted. Be careful not to use this pan in preparing the layer for a molded cake, since the layer will be too wide and shallow.

TART PANS. The French fluted-edged, tinned, removable-bottom pan is used in all the tart recipes. The 9½- or 10-inch size will work well for all the tart formulas.

PIE PANS. A 9-inch Pyrex pie pan is used for all the pies. The glass makes it easier to see the degree of doneness on the bottom crust and the glass heats better than metal, assuring a well-baked bottom crust. **If metal pans are used, the oven temperatures given in the pie recipes should be increased by 25°F.**

COOKIE SHEETS. A cookie sheet is useful for baking items like sponge fingers or palmiers as well as for holding pieces of dough or whole cakes in the refrigerator. Sheets with three open ends can also be used as spatulas, moving large pieces of dough which may have stuck to the work surface.

BAKING PANS. Sometimes called jelly-roll pans, these rectangular baking pans range from 10 × 15 inches to 12 × 18 inches. Either may be used in the recipes. The 12 × 18-inch size is the same as a commercial half-sheet pan available at restaurant supply stores. Made of heavy-gauge aluminum, it is less likely to warp in the oven than lighter pans. Rectangular cake layers baked in the larger pan will be somewhat thinner, but not enough to affect the result of the recipe.

ROASTING PAN. Useful for preparing Sugared Almonds or toasting nuts, the higher sides make it easier to stir without having the nuts spill in the oven.

Machinery

Electric Mixers

Instructions have been included for both hand mixers and table-model mixers in all the recipes. The balloon whip and paddle attachments of the table-model mixer are more efficient for aerating and mixing. A hand mixer will do almost as well, but usually increases the mixing time by about 50 percent.

Low speed on an electric mixer is the first setting; medium, the one that falls between the lowest and the highest; and high, the highest.

Food Processor

By now the food processor has become a standard piece of kitchen equipment. To substitute for it, use a hand-held nut grinder or blender for grinding nuts (a little at a time). Or for making purees use a food mill or blender.

Oven

All recipes have been tested in a home oven. Every oven differs slightly and an oven thermometer will help to gauge the accuracy of the thermostat. Be sure to notice hot spots; moving pans around in the oven during baking, alternating them side to side and from bottom shelf upward and vice versa, can make up for any excessively hot areas. When baking something in the bottom shelf, check that it is not coloring too deeply on the bottom. If so, insulate the bottom by sliding another pan under the baking pan being used.

Decorating Equipment

Pastry Bags

I prefer plastic-coated canvas bags. Remember to snip the narrow end of a new bag to allow the end of the tube to protrude sufficiently. Wash bags with soap and water and turn them inside out after each use; stand them upright to dry. Every few weeks, machine-wash the bags with other kitchen wash, using detergent and bleach, to prevent them from becoming rancid from accumulated traces of fat. An 8-inch bag is good for piping small amounts of whipped cream or buttercream; 12- and 14-inch sizes are good for pâte à choux and fillings.

Decorating Tubes

There are hundreds of different shapes of tubes or nozzles used for decorating. The first is *a plain tube with a ½-inch opening* for most general piping (pâte à choux, meringue, ladyfingers); then *a star tube with a ½-inch opening* for whipped cream and meringue. The best star tube for piping whipped cream and meringue has six or eight large triangular teeth and is open at the end. Teeth that are too small, too numerous and too close together will not make a sufficiently deep impression in soft materials like whipped cream and meringue, although they are excellent for firmer mixtures like buttercream and whipped ganache. *A small plain tube with a ¼-inch opening* is useful for filling choux and piping thin lines of buttercream or ganache. A Saint-Honoré tube, like a plain tube with a V-shaped cut on the side near the top opening, pipes neat, decorative egg shapes.

Decorating Comb

This is a thin piece of metal or plastic, usually triangular, with serrated edges like saw teeth. Draw the comb gently across the top or side of a cake to leave a grooved pattern on the surface. For cake tops, the same thing can be accomplished using the edge of a serrated knife.

Blowtorch

I often use a butane torch, available for under twenty dollars at a hardware store, to color meringue or caramelize the top of a sugar-dredged dessert, such as a Mille Feuille. Since the torch emits a powerful flame when lit, it poses a considerable safety hazard, and I have not included it in the instructions for meringues and caramelized sugar tops in the recipes that use those finishes. If you wish to try using a torch for those purposes, observe the following rules:

- Always point the torch away from you.
- Always strike the match for lighting the torch before turning the valve that emits the gas.
- Only open the valve a small amount, to make sure that the initial flame will not be too large. After lighting the torch adjust the flame.
- Always turn off the torch before placing it down, even if you need to continue later. It is safer to light the torch again than to risk starting a fire.
- When using the torch, hold it pointing away from you, with the tip of the flame about 2 inches away from the dessert. Move the torch back and forth over the area to be colored, moving to a new area after the area has colored.

MEASURING

With the best ingredients and a well-tested recipe, it is still important to measure accurately to ensure consistent results. Professional bakers and pastry chefs use a scale for dry ingredients like flour and sugar. The weight of the ingredient will always remain the same, even if it is compacted. I have listed the weights of all dry ingredients in each recipe, but since the most common system for measuring ingredients at home is with measuring cups, I have also given volumes. Measurements for solid ingredients always purchased by weight, like chocolate, are given by weight. Eggs are usually measured by number as opposed to weight or volume. **In this book, all eggs called for are large.**

The following rules will help to make volume measurement as accurate as possible.

1. Always make sure that dry ingredients are not compacted before measuring. Pour flour, cake flour, cocoa powder and other finely milled ingredients from the package into a bowl or canister and stir to aerate before measuring.

2. Always use level-measure cups for measuring dry ingredients. These usually come in nested sets and give the correct measure when filled to the top.

Scoop up the ingredient and level off the top with a straight implement. Do not shake the ingredient in the cup to level it because this will compact it.

3. To measure small quantities of dry or liquid ingredients, use a set of level-measure spoons.

4. Larger quantities of liquid ingredients are measured by volume in liquid measure cups. The best are made of glass to allow easy reading of the quantity in the cup. It is useful to have several and these are available in 1-cup, 2-cup, and 4-cup sizes. Larger liquid measure cups tend to be less accurate for small quantities.

MIXING

The ability to distinguish among the different techniques of mixing ingredients into doughs, batters and creams can make a dramatic difference in the results of those preparations. Although stirring, creaming, whisking, whipping, and folding are closely related, each demands specific techniques for efficient use.

Beating is a general term. I prefer to use the term *creaming* for beating butter and for beating other ingredients into it, *whisking* for beating eggs or cream by hand and *whipping* for beating eggs, cream or other ingredients by machine.

Stirring

Mixing ingredients together with a wooden or metal spoon or a wooden or rubber spatula is stirring. Avoid flatware for stirring since it tends to be too small for large quantities of ingredients. Hold the spoon or spatula like a pencil. Quickly stir clockwise in a circular motion scraping the bottom of the bowl until the ingredients are smooth.

Whisking

Hand beating with a wire whisk is whisking. Used to incorporate air into egg mixtures or cream and to mix ingredients together, this technique uses a vigorous stirring motion.

When whisking sugar into eggs or keeping an egg and sugar mixture moving in a bowl over simmering water, hold the whisk like a pencil and move it in a circular motion, at a moderate speed, being sure to scrape the bottom of the bowl.

To whisk air into a mixture, wrap your hand around the handle of the whisk as though grasping the handle of a heavy pan. Tilt the bowl toward the whisk, holding the top of the bowl with the other hand. Move the whisk in a circle almost perpendicular to the work surface with the end of the whisk in the bottom of the bowl. This technique allows for maximum air absorption and may be used for whipping cream as well as eggs or egg whites. Be sure to choose a large round-bottomed bowl for this.

Whipping

Incorporating air into ingredients by machine is whipping. A medium speed is often used so delicate preparations like cream and egg whites do not overwhip as they might on a high speed. Use high speed for such processes as egg foams for Génoise batters and incorporating sugar into egg whites.

With a rotary hand mixer, move the mixer in a circular motion in the bowl closely watching the density of the material being whipped to prevent overwhipping. With a table-model mixer, use the balloon whip attachment and watch closely. Stop the mixer occasionally to check the consistency to prevent overwhipping.

Folding

Using a flexible rubber spatula to incorporate ingredients into an aerated mixture so that it retains the most air possible is folding.

The three most common circumstances in which folding occurs are:

1. Folding whipped egg whites into a batter so the air in the egg whites will expand during baking to leaven the batter.

2. Folding whipped cream or a cooked meringue into a preparation such as a mousse or other filling to lighten it.

3. Folding dry ingredients into the egg foam of a Génoise batter or into beaten yolks or whites in other batters to retain maximum aeration.

Fold by scraping the flat side of the blade of a flexible rubber spatula from the inside of the bowl on one side through the ingredients, being careful to scrape the bottom, and allowing it to emerge on the opposite side of the bowl. Revolve the bowl so that the spatula enters and emerges at a different point every time it passes through the ingredients. Scraping the bottom of the bowl with the spatula every time it passes through is important since the heavier ingredients have a tendency to fall to the bottom of the mixture. Scrape the side of the bowl several times to ensure that no ingredients cling there.

To fold egg whites into a batter, stir about one quarter of them into the batter to lighten it. Although this causes some loss of air, it lightens the batter sufficiently so that when the remaining whites are folded in, little air will be lost. Without first lightening the batter, the density of the batter might crush the air from all the whites.

When folding whipped cream into another preparation, do not overmix or the cream may become coarse and separated, ruining the texture of the dessert.

To fold dry ingredients into batters, proceed very quickly, since the friction from the granules being folded into the aerated mass will always dissipate some of the air. If the batter stands too long, it will lose more air and probably not retain enough to leaven.

2

BASIC INGREDIENTS

A fine dessert is only as good as its ingredients. Technique cannot turn substandard or inappropriate ingredients into a superior product. Therefore, it is crucial to know how to judge ingredients and their quality. The higher the quality, the better the results, both in terms of recipe performance and flavor. The following chapter provides the criteria for judging freshness and indicates which ingredients are best for particular uses.

Dairy products, sugar, and flour are the building blocks of pastry making. In addition to contributing their own intrinsic flavors, these ingredients form the foundation for the flavorings, nuts and fruits that add nuance to pastries. The chemical structures and properties of these basic ingredients influence their behavior in cooking. That is why it is necessary to become familiar with the ingredients themselves before learning the pastry techniques that rely upon them.

Dairy products such as butter, eggs and cream are the only basic ingredients that have a time-limited shelf life and require refrigeration. As such, they must be handled particularly carefully to provide best results. Dairy products contain fat which adds rich complexity and tenderness to desserts and pastries.

Sugar provides body and texture, besides contributing its obvious sweetness. It is the sugar in meringue that enables the egg whites to retain the air that is beaten into them. In another recipe, the sugar might result in a crisp, shiny exterior. Sugar can be used in many ways. Added little by little to eggs, egg yolks or egg whites, the sugar provides stability. Dissolved in water to form a syrup, the sugar becomes a basic sweet liquid that can be mixed with flavorings to add taste and moisture to cakes and pastries. Cooking the syrup transforms it still further. Basic cooked syrup is beaten into beaten egg yolks, cooking and thickening them to form the base for butter-cream. Cooking the syrup to an amber, caramelized stage gives it a nutty flavor and crackly texture.

How flour is used determines the type of flour called for in a recipe. A delicate, shattery puff pastry, for example, requires a flour that won't cause the dough to toughen but will be flexible enough to expand with the steam from the butter trapped within it.

Thickeners like cornstarch and gelatin bind other ingredients together, holding them in suspension and preventing them from separating back into their individual parts.

Familiarity with the basic ingredients and their properties will help elucidate the pastry techniques that use them. Once you understand how an ingredient will behave, the right way to use it will be all the simpler.

Dairy Products

Milk and its derivatives, butter, milk, cream, sour cream, yoghurt and cheese, make up the dairy ingredients. Although goats, sheep and other animals are often sources of dairy foods in other cultures, the dairy industry in the United States is based on cow's milk. Even though goat's milk and cheese are becoming more popular here, baking still relies almost solely on those dairy products produced with cow's milk.

Milk

Fresh whole milk is a major ingredient in the production of Crème Anglaise and pastry cream. Although virtually all milk is pasteurized today, "fresh" milk refers to milk neither ultra-pasteurized nor ultra-high temperature (UHT) processed. Regular pasteurization involves heating the milk at 161°F for 15 seconds. The other two methods heat the milk at 280°F for at least 2 seconds. Ultra-pasteurized milk is packaged like pasturized milk and requires refrigeration. UHT milk is vacuum packed in sterilized containers and stored at room temperature until opened. While greatly increasing the refrigerated shelf life of the milk, it also imparts a "cooked" flavor to it.

Milk is made up of about 87 percent water combined with 13 percent solids. The solids consist of milkfat and nonfat solids such as protein, minerals and carbohydrates. It is the percentage of fat which determines whether milk is designated whole, lowfat or skim. **All recipes in this book use whole milk, which contains not less than 3.25 percent milkfat.** Usually the milkfat is evenly dispersed throughout the milk as a result of homogenization: The milk is passed through very tiny openings, breaking the milkfat into small particles that will not resolidify and float to the top of the milk as a layer of cream.

Whenever milk is heated on its own (as opposed to in combination with cream or sugar), it must never be allowed to boil, or some of its protein will coagulate and form a skin. Instead, it should be gently heated in a heavy saucepan *just* until bubbles form around the side of the pan and steam begins to escape.

Cream

Cream is that portion of unhomogenized milk that floats to the top, due to its high fat content. It is separated from the milk before or after pasteurization.

Like milk, cream is categorized according to the percentage of fat in it. To comply with the levels established by federal regulation, dairies may add milk to the cream to achieve the proper fat-to-liquid ratio.

HEAVY WHIPPING CREAM. Referred to as heavy cream in some parts of the country, this cream contains not less than 36 percent milkfat. This level of fat is important because it provides rich flavor, and contributes to the cream's desirable boiling and whipping properties. Because the protein molecules are buffered by a high level of fat molecules, they are not likely to coagulate when the cream is boiled. This is crucial to the preparation of custards and ganaches.

This same high level of fat provides stability when heavy cream is whipped. When air is beaten into the cream, fat globules stick together, forming a stabilizing network to support the air bubbles. **Unless otherwise specified, any mention of cream in this book refers to heavy whipping cream.**

LIGHT WHIPPING CREAM. Light whipping cream has a lower milkfat content (30 to 36 percent) than heavy whipping cream but can still be whipped.

LIGHT CREAM. Also known as coffee cream or table cream, this is cream with 18 to 30 percent milk fat.

HALF AND HALF. A blend of milk and cream with a total milkfat content of 10.5 to 18 percent.

Cream is available pasteurized and ultra-pasteurized. As with milk, ultra-pasteurization imparts a "cooked" flavor to cream.

Because it is a delicate dairy product, cream must be kept well chilled at all times to prevent spoilage. Chilling is also necessary to prevent separation when heavy cream is to be whipped.

Cream keeps for at least a week in the refrigerator. It should not be frozen since freezing alters the texture.

Butter

Unsalted butter is widely used in the preparation of pastry doughs, cake batters and buttercreams.

Made from pasteurized cream mechanically churned to separate the fat granules from the liquid buttermilk, butter is required by federal law to contain a minimum of 80 percent milkfat. The remaining 20 percent is predominantly water mixed with milk solids. Salt and natural coloring may also be added.

Butter is graded on the basis of flavor, body, color, and saltiness (when appropriate). U.S. grade AA butter has a sweet aroma and flavor, with a smooth creamy texture. Since it is made from the highest quality fresh cream, it is the grade to look for when buying butter.

Unsalted "sweet" butter has been used in the preparation of all recipes in this book. It is preferable to salted butter for several reasons: Salt levels in butter may vary, thus affecting uniformity of taste; salt preserves butter but may also mask off-tasting butter; salted butter has a higher water content than unsalted butter.

Do not use whipped butter in baking. Again, variables in the amount of air incorporated into butter would affect the final outcome of any baked item.

Always keep opened butter, wrapped, in the butter compartment of the refrigerator to avoid transfer of flavors from other foods. Unopened butter keeps for several weeks stored in a refrigerator at 39°F or lower. For longer storage (up to 9 months), wrap each package of butter with plastic wrap or foil and freeze at 0°F or lower. Higher freezer temperature will shorten freezer time.

Creaming

Creaming is the action of beating butter until it is soft and light. Cream butter by hand by beating it vigorously with a wooden spoon. To make creaming easier, allow the butter to soften slightly at room temperature or heat a bowl very quickly over warm water before placing the butter, cut into small pieces, in it.

With a rotary hand mixer, cream butter on medium speed, moving the mixer in a circular motion, rather than holding the mixer in one place. With a table-model mixer, use the paddle or flat beater and set the mixer at medium speed. When creaming by machine, stop the mixer and scrape the sides of the bowl often to ensure even results.

Sugar is often added to and creamed with the butter. Cream at medium speed until the mixture "whitens," signifying the sugar has dissolved somewhat and the mixture has absorbed air.

Sour Cream

At one time prepared at home by allowing cream to sour at the back of the kitchen range, today's sour cream is carefully monitored at all stages of processing.

After pasteurizing (which kills harmful bacteria, aids the growth of bacteria later on and promotes homogenization), cream is subjected to a dual homogenization process.

Cream is "squeezed" at extremely high pressures, rendering its milkfat particles so small they remain in suspension, rather than separating from the liquid whey. This process is repeated, yielding a very thick, smooth product.

Once homogenized, the cream is inoculated with any of several bacteria for acid and flavor. These bacteria starters are stirred into the cream, then left to incubate or ripen. During this period, some of the cream's lactose (milk sugar) converts to lactic acid, giving the characteristic taste.

The ripened sour cream is chilled and then aged 12 to 48 hours before being sold. Once purchased, sour cream should be refrigerated, covered, at 40°F. This temperature, coupled with the sour cream's acidity, inhibits the growth of harmful bacteria. Although refrigerated sour cream keeps for about a month, optimum freshness lasts only for a few days after purchase. Since sour cream does not freeze well (it will separate), it should be bought only in quantities that can be used in a short period of time.

Crème Fraîche

Increasingly available in the United States, Crème Fraîche is similar in flavor and texture to sour cream. Because it has a higher fat content, it can be whipped whereas sour cream cannot. Crème Fraiche, prepared at home, will not be as thick as the commercial versions.

CRÈME FRAÎCHE

How thick and tangy this cream becomes depends on how long you leave it at room temperature and how high the temperature is. Monitor it carefully for maximum thickening without developing excessively sour flavor.

Crème Fraîche is wonderful as an accompaniment to fruit and berries; a few tablespoons added to heavy whipping cream gives the cream a slight tang and firmer texture.

1 CUP HEAVY WHIPPING CREAM
1 TABLESPOON BUTTERMILK

In a small saucepan over low heat, warm the cream to just lukewarm, about 100°F. Remove it from the heat, stir in buttermilk thoroughly, and pour the mixture into a clean 1-quart bowl. Cover tightly with plastic wrap and allow it to stand in a warm place (70°F to 80°F) about 12 to 18 hours, until the mixture is slightly thickened. Stir to an even consistency, cover with plastic wrap, and refrigerate.

Holding. Keep the Crème Fraiche refrigerated for up to 1 week.

Yield. About 1 cup

Buttermilk

Buttermilk is used as an ingredient in doughs and batters where its tangy flavor will enhance the end product. Buttermilk does not contain butter. Although its name is derived from its history as a by-product of buttermaking, most buttermilk available today is fermented from milk mixed with bacterial cultures.

Buttermilk is produced like yoghurt and sour cream. The buttermilk base is usually grade A lowfat or skim milk; nonfat dry milk is often added to skim milk to promote thickness.

The milk, which is usually salted, is pasteurized to destroy harmful bacteria, then cooled and inoculated with selected bacterial cultures. These bacteria incubate for approximately 12 to 14 hours, allowing some of the milk's lactose to turn to lactic acid. When the acid and flavor balance is correct, the milk is stirred to break up any curd that has formed, then further cooled to halt fermentation.

For maximum keeping and flavor qualities keep buttermilk refrigerated. Because of its high acidity, it will keep for up to 2 weeks after purchase, although optimal use is within the first week.

Cheese

Valued for its flavor, which can be sweet and mild or piquant and assertive, and for its richness, cheese is often a component of fillings and pastry doughs. Once a primarily domestic product with haphazard results, cheese is now scientifically prepared.

Although there are literally thousands of cheese varieties, they all begin in the same way: as milk treated with enzymes or bacteria, and sometimes heat, to separate it into curds and whey. What is curdled at this primary stage (cow's or sheep's milk, skimmed milk or milk that has been mixed with cream to increase its fat content) and how it is curdled (with rennet or starter, heated before or during inoculation or not at all) determines the cheese produced.

After the curd is cut or broken up, it is

drained and sometimes salted. At this point, fresh cheeses such as ricotta and cream cheese are ready for use.

Cured cheeses go through more processing. The drained curds are stirred, then ripened in temperature- and humidity-controlled environments for very specific amounts of time. Different curing agents, added alone or in combination into or on the cheese include bacteria, enzymes, molds and yeast.

All cheeses should be refrigerated. In general, soft and fresh cheeses need to be consumed within days of purchasing, while hard cheeses will keep longer. Always directly cover cut surfaces to prevent drying out.

Some hard cheeses such as Parmesan and Gouda freeze well. Cut the cheese into ½ pound or smaller pieces and wrap tightly in a moisture-proof wrapper. Quick freezing (at 0°F or less) and slow thawing (in the refrigerator, if possible) seems to be the best method for maintaining a cheese's quality. Once thawed, the cheese should be consumed as quickly as possible. Because freezing alters the texture of fresh cheeses like cream cheese or ricotta, it should be avoided.

The following cheeses are used most often in the baker's repertoire:

CREAM CHEESE. Made from cream and milk, cream cheese is an unripened cheese with a rich, buttery flavor. It is the principal ingredient in cheesecakes and cheese fillings.

Although most cream cheese is stabilized with gum arabic, unadulterated varieties are available. Their lighter, more crumbly texture is well worth the extra price.

Since cream cheese is quite perishable (and should never be frozen), only buy as much as is needed for a particular purpose.

Whipped cream cheese should not be substituted in a recipe, since its higher air content would alter the final product.

FARMER CHEESE. Farmer cheese is drier and firmer than other fresh cheeses like cottage and pot cheese. Like them, it is produced from whole and skim milks. It has a mild, slightly acidic flavor. Because of its low moisture content, farmer cheese is an ideal filling ingredient.

As with other fresh cheeses, farmer cheese should be used within a few days of purchase.

RICOTTA. A fresh cheese of Italian origin, ricotta is used in fillings much the same way farmer and cream cheeses are used. Although its texture is similar to cottage cheese, ricotta is usually less watery, with a close, grainy texture.

In Italy, ricotta is made from the coagulable substances in whey, the by-product of other cheeses. In this country, the whey is mixed with whole or skim milk.

If freshly made ricotta is available (as it is in most cities with an Italian area), it is incomparably better than the packaged variety—sweeter, creamier, less watery and fresher tasting.

GRUYÈRE. Prepared in the cantons of Fribourg, Neuchâtel and Vaud in Switzerland, Gruyère is a firm cheese with an ivory color and a brown rind. Although similar to Emmenthal cheese, Gruyère has smaller holes, a slightly higher fat content and a nuttier flavor, likened to that of hazelnuts.

Because it is a good melting cheese, Gruyère is used in the preparation of Gougère

(Pâte à Choux flavored with cheese), and other baked hors d'oeuvre.

EGGS

Probably the most versatile of a baker's ingredients, eggs are primary in the production of cakes, custards, buttercreams and such pastries as Pâte à Choux.

Whole or separated, eggs perform many tasks: they *bind* together other ingredients like flour, sugar and butter in a cake; they *act as leaveners,* sometimes on their own, as in génoise cakes or soufflés, other times in combination with chemical leaveners like baking powder; they *enrich* foods, rendering them moist with a golden color; they *thicken* mixtures like custards and buttercreams; they *emulsify* liquids, holding fats in suspension so that ingredients hold together rather than separate; and they *glaze* pastries and doughs.

Eggs are categorized by grade and size. Grade is based on the inner and outer quality of the egg, while size is determined by the average weight per dozen eggs. **All recipes in this book use large eggs** (24 ounces per dozen). Grades AA, A and B have the same nutritive value.

There is no difference in quality or nutrition between brown and white eggs, nor between eggs with deep golden or pale yellow yolks.

When selecting eggs, choose those that have clean, uncracked shells. Store eggs large-end up in their cartons in the refrigerator for maximum keeping quality (up to 5 weeks). Because eggs absorb odors, they should be kept away from strong-flavored foods.

Egg whites can be stored covered, in the refrigerator, up to 10 days. Yolks should be carefully covered with water in a covered container before being refrigerated up to 2 days.

Egg Whites

Egg white, or albumen, makes up about two thirds of the total weight of the egg, providing over half the total protein. Egg white is often used to aerate, bind and, to a lesser extent, emulsify preparations.

When whipped, egg whites increase in volume six to eight times. When incorporated into a batter, the entrapped air provides leavening during baking. Room temperature egg whites whip up more quickly.

Egg Yolks

Egg yolk makes up about one third of the total weight of the egg. Containing all the fat and a bit less than half the protein, the yolk provides richness, a golden color and a tender texture to preparations. The yolk can also emulsify mixtures due to its lecithin content.

Separating Eggs

Cold eggs separate better than warm ones because the egg white is more viscous. Although egg separators come in and out of vogue every few years, it is better to separate eggs by hand. Keep the yolk and white intact. If the yolk breaks and even a small amount enters the white, the white will not be usable for whipping. The presence of fat in whites prevents them from absorbing air.

Sometimes, despite all precautions, a yolk will break. Since this is possible it is better to separate eggs one at a time into an intermediate vessel to prevent ruining an entire batch of whites.

Use three small bowls or cups. Crack the egg on the rim of the first bowl. Hold the egg rounded-side down over the bowl. Remove the top half of the shell. Most of the egg white will run out of the egg and fall into the bowl. Pass the yolk gently into the other half of the shell. Most of the remaining egg white will run into the bowl. Slide the yolk into the second bowl and pour the white from the first bowl into the third. Continue in this fashion with the remaining eggs.

If one of the yolks breaks, it will only ruin one egg white. If this happens, discard the yolk-stained white. If only a small speck of yolk enters the white, you can use a shell to scoop the yolk out of the white.

Egg Wash

Eggs are used to adhere layers of pastry and to enhance the appearance of baked pastry by giving it a deep golden color and a bright sheen. There are many formulas for egg wash, most of which dilute the eggs with water, milk or cream. I prefer to use a whole egg for adhering pastry and a whole egg plus an extra yolk for glazing. The extra yolk helps produce a richer pastry color. I add a pinch of salt, then whisk the eggs in a bowl until they are very liquid. The salt helps the eggs liquefy. A viscous egg wash is difficult to brush on the pastry in a thin, even layer, and clumps of egg white can harden and burn as the pastry bakes.

SUGAR AND OTHER SWEETENERS

Sucrose, or granulated sugar, is a disaccharide—complex or double sugar—as opposed to a monosaccharide—simple or single sugar—like glucose.

During sugar production, sugar cane is ground, then pressed to release its juice. This liquid is heated and centrifuged, to produce sugar and molasses. The sugar is redissolved and purified with granular carbon, which is then filtered out along with the impurities it traps. Once purified, the sugar is processed to form crystals. The crystals are dried to remove any remaining moisture. Finally, the sugar is passed through a succession of sieves to separate the coarse from fine crystals.

Sugar is hygroscopic, that is, it absorbs water. Therefore, it should be stored as airtight as possible. It will last indefinitely if properly stored.

Granulated Sugar

Besides adding sweetness to baked products, granulated sugar provides structure (as in egg foams and meringues), helps to retain moisture and contributes tenderness. It also aids in crust color and formation because it caramelizes during baking. **All recipes in this book use granulated sugar, unless otherwise specified.**

By scooping and leveling 1 cup of sugar, its weight is 7½ ounces.

Add granulated sugar gradually to most preparations, especially to egg mixtures. Unbeaten egg yolks to which sugar is quickly added may lump and "burn," a phenomenon in which sugar absorbs so much of the yolk liquid on initial contact that the remaining yolk components harden, preventing the sugar from dissolving completely. When you beat egg whites with sugar, a large quantity of sugar falling on the egg whites at one time can force air out of them.

Superfine Sugar

Superfine sugar is made of the finest crystals produced during the final sifting process. It dissolves easily in cold liquid. Superfine sugar has limited uses in the recipes in this book.

Confectioners' (Powdered) Sugar

Also known as "10X" sugar (because it is approximately ten times finer than granulated sugar), confectioners' sugar is ground to a powder. In the United States, it contains 3 percent cornstarch to prevent caking. For this reason, **never use confectioners' sugar in any kind of cooked sugar solution,** since the cornstarch might burn.

Confectioners' sugar is used in uncooked preparations, where granulated sugar would produce a grainy texture. It is also dusted on certain baked products, as a simple decoration.

To eliminate lumps that often form in confectioners' sugar, sift it prior to use.

Cube Sugar

Sugar cubes are produced by molding moist crystallized sugar. After molding, the cubes are dried to retain their shape. Cube sugar is sometimes used in sugar cooking because the absence of freestanding crystals inhibits recrystallization.

Molasses

This dark, highly flavored syrup is a by-product of the initial stages of sugar refining: After the cane juice has been concentrated, the sucrose crystals formed are coated with murky brown liquid. The crystals are centrifuged, leaving the liquid, or molasses.

Molasses is used for its pungent flavor, as well as for its moisture and the color it imparts.

Brown Sugar

Brown sugar is made from liquid sucrose blended with molasses before crystallization; the molasses coating remains on the subsequent crystals, providing moisture and flavor. The degree of molasses added determines the classification of light brown or dark brown sugar.

Brown sugar has a tendency to collect air between its crystals. For proper measuring, pack it firmly.

Although brown sugar is moist and compact because of its molasses content, it can dry out and harden if left uncovered. To avoid this, keep brown sugar tightly covered, preferably in a plastic bag, in a cool place— the refrigerator if you have room.

Granulated brown sugar eliminates the problem of dehydration. In measuring, it is equal in volume to moist brown sugar.

Honey

Many very old recipes call for honey as a sweetener, since its use predates the introduction of refined sugar.

Produced by certain bee species for food,

honey is derived from the nectar of flowers, as well as from the fluids of other nonflowering plants. The flavor of honey is influenced by the predominant plant tapped by the bee—whether it is orange blossom, lavender, clover, pine or another plant.

Once extracted from the comb, honey is heated, refined and strained.

Honey is best used in recipes where its distinctive flavor will enhance, rather than overpower, a baked product. In addition to flavor and sweetness, honey is valued for its ability to retain moisture, thus extending the freshness of baked goods.

Store honey in an airtight container in a cool place to minimize crystallization. (When crystallization occurs, the honey is prone to fermentation and spoilage.) If your cupboards are very warm or if the honey will be stored for a long time, keep it refrigerated. Liquefy both crystallized and refrigerated honey *each* time you use it, by heating the jar of honey in a pan of hot water.

Corn Syrups

After starch is extracted from corn, it is treated with enzymes to produce corn syrup. Light corn syrup is clarified and milder in flavor than darker corn syrup, which contains a proportion of molasses for color and flavor.

Corn syrup is sometimes used as a glaze, producing a transparent, varnishlike sheen. It is also added to sugar syrups which will be cooked to temperatures beyond the boiling point—as in certain icings and confections— to control crystallization. Here, the corn syrup interferes on a molecular level with the production of sucrose crystals, thus preventing graininess. In this role, corn syrup and

other interferants are sometimes referred to as "grease" in confectioners' terminology.

When mixtures of corn syrup and sugar are heated beyond the boiling point, stirring must be kept to a minimum; excess agitation may nullify the effect of the corn syrup and cause crystallization to occur after all.

Maple Syrup

Maple syrup is the concentrated sap of the sugar maple tree. It is made by boiling down the sap to up to one fortieth of its original volume and skimming the impurities. The resulting amber to brown syrup is principally used to impart its unique flavor to baked goods.

When purchasing maple syrup, only select pure syrup, as opposed to maple-flavored syrup. Once opened, store it in a nonmetallic container in the refrigerator.

SYRUPS AND GLAZES

Syrups are solutions of sugar and liquid, usually made by heating the two ingredients together. Syrups can be used to cook fruit or moisten cakes, or be transformed into icings and glazes, such as fondant or caramel. Once prepared, thin sugar syrups may be flavored with liqueurs, fruit juices, spices or extracts.

Heavier syrups, like those used to prepare glazes, are supersaturated solutions in which the quantity of sugar is greater than the quantity of liquid. These syrups usually contain an acid like lemon juice which helps to prevent crystallization. They are cooked to temperatures higher than the boiling point. As the temperature increases the syrup becomes denser due to the evaporation of water.

POACHING SYRUP

This thin syrup is suitable for cooking hard, stone or dried fruit. Quantities given can be used for approximately 2 pounds of fruit.

3 CUPS WATER
1 CUP SUGAR, ABOUT 7½ OUNCES

Mixing. Combine the water and sugar in a 2-quart saucepan.
Cooking. Place over medium heat. Cook, stirring occasionally to aid in dissolving the sugar crystals, until the mixture comes to a full rolling boil. Remove from heat.
Holding. Cool to room temperature. The syrup may be refrigerated up to 10 days in a covered jar or plastic container.

Yield. Approximately 3 cups

MOISTENING SYRUP

This thin syrup is used to moisten cake layers for layered and rolled cakes. A moistening syrup always has flavoring—liqueur, fruit juice, vanilla or other extracts—added to it immediately before using. Quantity is sufficient for a 9- or 10-inch cake.

½ CUP WATER
¼ CUP SUGAR, ABOUT 1¾ OUNCES

Mixing. Combine the water and sugar in a 1-quart saucepan.
Cooking. Place over medium heat. Cook, stirring occasionally to dissolve the sugar, until the mixture comes to a full rolling boil. Remove from heat.
Holding. Cool to room temperature. The syrup may be refrigerated up to 10 days in a covered jar or plastic container.

Yield. Approximately ½ cup

To flavor the moistening syrup, add 2 to 3 tablespoons of liqueur or fruit juice to it just before using. If using an extract, such as vanilla, 2 teaspoons is enough. In every recipe that requires this syrup, the type and quantity of flavoring are specified.

COOKED SUGAR SYRUP

Although the previous two syrups are brought to a boil, the term "cooked sugar" refers to a syrup cooked to a temperature beyond the boiling point. In French, the syrup is said to be *entrer en cuisson* or to "begin cooking," signifying the start of concentrating the syrup to a greater density. A cooked sugar syrup has a wide range of uses: Fondant and caramel are prepared from it, and it is added to egg whites in preparing Italian Meringue.

The chart on page 22 identifies each stage

by its traditional name and temperature and also gives the principal uses.

2/3 CUP WATER

2 CUPS SUGAR, ABOUT 1 POUND

1/4 TEASPOON CREAM OF TARTAR OR 1
TABLESPOON LIGHT CORN SYRUP

Mixing. Combine all the ingredients in a 1½-quart saucepan.

Cooking. Place the pan over low heat and stir the syrup with a clean wooden spoon to dissolve the sugar crystals. As the syrup approaches boiling, wipe the inside of the pan with a clean brush dipped in cold water to remove any sugar crystals.

Removal of these crystals is important because even one might seed the syrup and cause it to recrystallize. The cream of tartar or corn syrup will also help prevent this.

At the boiling point, the syrup may foam up in the pan because of slight impurities in the sugar. Skim off any gray foam from the surface of the syrup with a spoon.

Cover the pan and allow it to boil for 2 minutes. The steam that accumulates will prevent any further crystals from forming on the sides of the pan.

Uncover the pan. Insert a candy thermometer and cook the syrup to the temperature necessary for the specific preparation.

Yield. About 2 cups, 1 pound

Glazes

Glazes are used to impart a smooth, shiny coating to the outside of a dessert, giving it an attractive appearance and sealing its surface

STAGES OF SUGAR COOKING

Stage	Temperature	Use
soft ball	238°F–240°F	Fondant; Italian Meringue
hard ball	250°F–260°F	confections (taffy)
soft crack	275°F–280°F	
hard crack	300°F–310°F	glazing; decoration (pulled and spun sugar)
light caramel	325°F–340°F	glazing
dark caramel	345°F	flavoring syrups; diluted caramel

to prevent moisture loss. Often made from Cooked Sugar Syrup, some glazes utilize a thin syrup in combination with other ingredients, like chocolate. Others are made from jellies or preserves and are used for glazing fruit on tarts.

Most glazes should be prepared immediately before being poured. Otherwise, the glaze's texture may change on standing and cooling, making it difficult to pour.

HARD CRACK GLAZE

Used for imparting a colorless, transparent sugar glaze to the outside of some pastries, a Hard Crack Glaze can also be used for dipping fruit (such as strawberries or grapes) or nutmeats to give them a brilliant sheen. Use the glaze immediately after preparation, while it is still very hot and thin so the coating will also be thin and delicate after the glaze hardens. Have all items to be glazed ready prior to preparing the glaze.

1 BATCH COOKED SUGAR SYRUP (PAGE 21)

Cooking. Prepare Cooked Sugar Syrup up to inserting the candy thermometer.

After inserting the candy thermometer, cook the syrup to 320°F. Dip the bottom of the pan in at least 2 inches of cold water for 30 seconds to arrest the cooking.

Finishing. Immediately dip the completed pastries or other items to be glazed in the syrup. For pastries, glaze only the tops, and stand them on a rack, glaze-side up, to cool and set the glaze. Sometimes pastries finished in this way are sprinkled with a decoration, such as chopped nuts; this should be done immediately after dipping, before the glaze sets, so that the decoration will set in the glaze.

Items dipped *into* the glaze and therefore substantially covered should be placed on a lightly buttered pan or marble slab to cool. To prevent the glaze from accumulating and forming a base or "foot" under the item being glazed, carefully allow the excess glaze to drip off before placing it down to set.

If the glaze hardens before all the glazing is completed, reheat it gently over very low heat, just enough to liquefy it. *Do not allow the glaze to return to a boil* or it may continue cooking beyond the original temperature.

Special care must be taken to prevent crumbs or other foreign material from falling into the glaze, because they may cause the glaze to crystallize before all the glazing is finished.

To prevent crumbs from entering the glaze, make sure articles to be glazed are completely free of loose crumbs. Use a soft pastry brush gently to remove the crumbs.

If any crumbs or foreign material—such as a bit of pastry cream from *choux* to be glazed— *do* fall into the glaze, remove immediately with a small spoon.

Holding. It is best to avoid refrigerating pastries glazed with Hard Crack Glaze. The refrigerator's humidity will cause the glaze to rapidly break down.

Glaze on fruits like strawberries or grapes can be expected to survive no longer than 2 to 3 hours since the fruit's juices will begin to break down the glaze from the inside.

Yield. About 2 cups, about 1/2 pound

SUGAR-BASED CHOCOLATE GLAZE

This glaze will impart a thin, high sheen when poured over a cake or other pastries. Although not as fine in flavor as more perishable cream-based chocolate glazes, this sugar-based glaze has better keeping qualities at room temperature.

Since the glaze must be used *immediately* after preparation, all items to be dipped or glazed must be ready. The cakes should be placed on a rack over a clean pan to catch any drippings.

1/3 CUP WATER

1 CUP SUGAR, ABOUT 7 1/2 OUNCES

1/3 CUP LIGHT CORN SYRUP

8 OUNCES BITTERSWEET OR SEMISWEET CHOCOLATE, FINELY CUT

Mixing. Combine the water, sugar and corn syrup in a 2-quart saucepan. Stir to blend.

Cooking. Place the saucepan on medium heat. Cook, stirring often to dissolve the sugar. Wash the sides of the pan with a clean brush dipped in cold water to eliminate any sugar crystals. Bring to a full rolling boil. Remove the pan from the heat, add the chocolate all at once, and allow to stand for about 2 minutes to melt the chocolate. Whisk just until smooth. Avoid overmixing or the glaze will be full of bubbles.

Finishing. Immediately dip items to be glazed, or pour the glaze over cakes or pastries set on a rack. The glaze will set within 5 to 10 minutes.

Holding. Items covered with this glaze keep well either at room temperature or in the refrigerator. Any leftover glaze should be stored, tightly wrapped, in the refrigerator. To reuse, cut into ½-inch pieces, place in a round-bottom bowl and add 1 tablespoon of water. Place the bowl over, not in, lightly simmering water, and stir occasionally with a rubber spatula until the glaze is melted and smooth.

Yield. About 2 cups, 1 pound

FONDANT

This shiny, opaque icing is made from Cooked Sugar Syrup taken to the soft ball stage, 238°F. After being cooled, worked with a spatula and kneaded, the syrup whitens due to the formation of fine, uniform crystals.

Although homemade fondant is easily pre- pared, excellent commercially prepared fondant is available. Most easily bought from a grocery wholesaler, it may also be found through importers of specialty products and at cake decorating and candy making supply stores. Commercially made fondant may vary in consistency from one brand to another, so that the amount of liquid needed to dilute it may also vary.

The recipe for Cooked Sugar Syrup may be increased to prepare larger quantities of fondant, but the cream of tartar or corn syrup should not be increased proportionately. For a large batch, use 5 POUNDS SUGAR, 3 CUPS WATER, 1 TEASPOON CREAM OF TARTAR OR 3 TABLESPOONS LIGHT CORN SYRUP. Bear in mind that you will need a large surface to pour the fondant to cool.

1 BATCH COOKED SUGAR SYRUP
(PAGE 21)

Cooking. Prepare Cooked Sugar Syrup up to inserting the candy thermometer.

After inserting the thermometer, cook the syrup to 238°F. Remove the pan from heat and dip the bottom of the pan in at least 2 inches of ice water for 30 seconds to stop the cooking. Immediately pour the syrup onto a marble slab or into a stainless steel or enamel roasting pan. (Reactive metals like aluminum may discolor the fondant.)

Cooling. Cool the syrup, undisturbed, to approximately 110°F. At this point, the syrup will be warm to the touch. (On the marble, a fingertip inserted in the syrup can comfortably remain there; if the syrup is in a pan, the bottom of the pan can be held comfortably on the palms of the hands.) Beginning to work the syrup before it has cooled to this temper-

ature will form coarse crystals, making the fondant dull when used.

Working. Using a stainless steel bench scraper or spatula (a pancake turner is excellent for this), work the fondant in a back and forth motion, scraping it up from the surface. Occasionally, scrape all of the fondant together in a mass to prevent neglecting any of it. During this stage, the fondant begins to whiten.

Kneading. As the fondant continues to whiten, it will ultimately set in a very firm mass, no longer flexible enough to be worked with a spatula. Break off small pieces of the hardened fondant the size of a golf ball and press and knead them with the heel of the hand, until they are smooth and semisolid.

Ripening. Place the pieces of kneaded fondant in a dry bowl and sprinkle drops of water, not to exceed ½ teaspoon in all, on the surface. Press plastic wrap directly against the fondant, then cover with a paper towel which has been wrung out in cold water. Finally, cover the top of the bowl with plastic wrap. (All these precautions prevent the fondant from dehydrating or forming a crust.) Allow the fondant to ripen about 24 hours at a cool room temperature or in the refrigerator.

Holding. After ripening, refrigerate the fondant until used. It keeps well indefinitely.

Yield. Approximately 1 pound, enough to glaze a 10-inch cake, three or four 10-inch mille feuilles, or five or six dozen small choux

FONDANT ICING

Either homemade or commercially prepared fondant can be used to make this icing.

1 POUND FONDANT

1 TABLESPOON LIGHT CORN SYRUP OR LIGHTLY BEATEN RAW EGG WHITE

1 TO 2 TEASPOONS FLAVORING SUCH AS LIQUEUR, FLAVORING EXTRACT, LEMON JUICE OR INSTANT ESPRESSO COFFEE DILUTED WITH WATER OR LIQUEUR

1 OR 2 DROPS LIQUID FOOD COLORING IF NECESSARY (YELLOW FOR LEMON, PINK FOR KIRSCH, ETC.)

Place the fondant in a round-bottomed 2- to 3-quart bowl. Using a large, heavy wooden or metal spoon, work the corn syrup or egg white into the fondant. Check the consist-

ency by withdrawing the spoon and noting the thickness of the fondant. If the fondant is about ¼-inch thick, add the flavoring and optional coloring. If less than ¼-inch thick, add no more than 1 teaspoon of flavoring or the fondant may become too thin after warming. If thicker than ¼ inch, continue adding corn syrup or egg white, 1 teaspoon at a time, until the fondant is about ¼-inch thick on the spoon.

Gently heat the fondant over simmering water to warm it slightly, rather than to melt it, which would also cause it to lose its sheen. The ideal temperature is 100°F (at this point, the fondant feels neither warm nor cold). During the heating, work the fondant with repeated sweeping strokes across the diame-

ter of the bowl using a wooden or metal spoon or flat wooden spatula. Don't stir the fondant. This might cause it to accumulate air and develop bubbles which would mar its appearance.

Arrange the items to be glazed on a rack over a pan. Pour the fondant over them and let them dry 5 to 10 minutes. Once poured, a properly treated fondant should retain its sheen for up to 24 hours.

If possible, avoid refrigerating fondant-glazed items, since this may cause condensation on the surface. If refrigeration is necessary, allow the items to stand at room temperature for about one hour before serving to evaporate the condensation.

Holding. Use immediately. Store any left-over icing, covered with plastic, a damp paper towel and more plastic, in the refrigerator, up to 3 weeks.

Yield. Enough to glaze a 10-inch cake, three or four 10-inch mille feuilles, or five or six dozen small choux

Caramel

Cooking a sugar syrup to the point where all the water has evaporated and the sugar begins to burn results in caramel. Use caramel in its molten state as a glaze for pastries such as the Gâteau Saint-Honoré. Or, add nuts to it to make Pralin or Nougatine. Dilute caramel with water or cream and use it as a flavoring or as a sauce.

The sugar begins to color when it reaches about 325°F. Take care that the sugar does not become excessively dark or it will develop a bitter taste.

COOKED SYRUP CARAMEL

This brittle glaze can be used immediately after cooking in many of the same ways as a Hard Crack Glaze—for coating completed pastries or dipping fruit or nuts to be used as a decoration for a dessert. As with the Hard Crack Glaze, have the items to be glazed ready before preparing the glaze.

1 BATCH COOKED SUGAR SYRUP (PAGE 21)

Cooking. Prepare the Cooked Sugar Syrup up to the point of inserting the thermometer.

After inserting the thermometer, cook the syrup to 325°F. At this point the caramel smokes abundantly and a foam of fine bubbles forms on the surface. Immediately dip the bottom of the pan in at least 2 inches of ice water for 30 seconds to stop the cooking.

Finishing. Use for glazing and handle in the same way as Hard Crack Glaze. It can also be used as a base for Pralin and Nougatine.

Yield. About 2 cups, about 1 pound

DRY CARAMEL

This is a fast way of preparing caramel. Since it uses no water to dissolve the sugar, it eliminates the evaporating time. Because of this shortcut, it must be watched closely to avoid having the caramel crystallize or overcook and burn.

1 CUP SUGAR, ABOUT 7½ OUNCES
1 TEASPOON LEMON JUICE

Mixing. Combine the sugar and lemon juice in a 2-quart saucepan. Stir continuously with a metal spoon until the lemon juice is evenly distributed in the sugar and the mixture looks like wet sand. Place the pan over medium heat and allow the sugar to begin melting without stirring it. The sugar will melt and caramelize simultaneously.

When the first wisp of smoke appears, stir the melting sugar so it caramelizes evenly. Stir occasionally as the sugar continues melting. Lower the heat when most of the sugar has melted so all the sugar crystals dissolve into the caramel. Cook the caramel until it is a light amber color, and it smokes abundantly. There will be a fine foam of bubbles on the surface when it is ready. Remove the pan from the heat and dip the bottom into at least 2 inches of ice water for 30 seconds to stop the cooking.

Finishing. Use like Hard Crack Glaze or as a base for Pralin or Nougatine.

Yield. About ¾ cup, 6 ounces

DILUTED CARAMEL

Once the caramel is fully cooked, a liquid may be added to it to retain a fluid texture. It may then be used easily as a flavoring without reheating. Water and cream are the liquids most commonly used. Water makes the caramel into a thick syrup used to flavor items like Praline Paste and buttercreams. Cream enriches the caramel and makes it into a sauce.

    1 CUP SUGAR, ABOUT 7½ OUNCES
    1 TEASPOON LEMON JUICE
    ½ CUP WATER OR ¾ CUP HEAVY WHIPPING
       CREAM

Cooking. Prepare a Dry Caramel from the sugar and lemon juice as in the preceding recipe. While the sugar is cooking, bring the water or cream to a boil in a small saucepan. When the caramel is ready, pour in the liquid all at once, at arm's length, averting the face. The caramel will splatter when the liquid is added.

Allow the caramel to come to a full, rolling boil, then remove from the heat and pour into a heatproof container to cool. Stir the caramel occasionally to cool and prevent it from separating.

Holding. Keep the Diluted Caramel covered with plastic wrap at a cool room temperature up to several weeks. To keep longer, refrigerate, then bring to room temperature before using.

Yield. About 1 cup when made with water, about 1¼ cups when made with cream

FLOURS, OTHER STARCHES AND THICKENERS

Wheat and the flour made from it are classified as hard or soft depending on the variety of wheat, and to a lesser extent, the season and the location in which it is grown. Each wheat berry is composed of three parts: the starchy endosperm, from which white flour is made; the outer covering or bran; and the oily germ. To produce flour, the berries are milled and sifted to remove the bran and germ. After milling, flour is sometimes bleached with benzol peroxide to lighten its color. It also may be treated with chlorine gas to alter the flour's acidity, somewhat changing its liquid absorption capabilities.

Protein content determines whether a flour is hard (strong) or soft (weak). When flour is moistened and mixed, the proteins change shape and form a substance called gluten, a web of elastic strands in the dough or batter. The degree of mixing and the protein content of the flour determine whether a weak or strong gluten is formed. The development of a strong gluten is desirable in bread doughs, where gluten helps to preserve shape, provide a good crumb and prevent leavening gases from escaping during fermentation. It is undesirable in pastry doughs and cake batters, where it would toughen them. For these reasons, specific flours are used for some purposes.

The strongest flours, usually used for commercial bread making, may have a protein content of as much as 15 percent.

Unbleached all-purpose flour is used for all recipes in this book unless otherwise specified. It has a protein content of approximately 10½ to 11½ percent. Unfortunately, flour packaged for consumers does not state the protein content as a percentage, but in terms of grams of protein per cup of flour. The flour I use has 12 to 13 grams of protein per cup.

Cake flour, an extremely weak flour, is only 7 percent protein (about 8 grams protein per cup). It is also higher in starch. These characteristics make it ideal for cake making, where elasticity is undesirable.

Pastry flour may have a protein content of between 8½ and 9½ percent. It is ideal for preparations where some development of gluten is desired, but not so much to render the dough too elastic. Since pastry flour is not readily available to consumers, I use a combination of all-purpose and cake flours as a substitute for it.

Gluten Examples

VERY WEAK GLUTEN: CAKE BATTER. A very weak gluten structure develops during the gentle mixing of the batter, whether for a spongecake or butter cake. This gluten holds in steam while the cake rises, giving it structure. Overmixing—the development of too strong a gluten—will result in a tough, heavy cake.

WEAK GLUTEN: PASTRY DOUGH. Gently mixing liquid into dough after fat has been incorporated forms sufficient gluten to hold the dough together and trap steam in the dough as it bakes. This creates a flaky texture. Overmixing and developing too strong a gluten will toughen the dough and render it too elastic to be rolled. After baking, such a dough will remain heavy and tough.

MODERATELY STRONG GLUTEN: PUFF PASTRY. During the rolling and folding the dough undergoes, a fairly strong gluten develops. Initially the dough, called *detrempe* at this point, is mixed very gently to prevent a strong gluten from developing too early on.

Then a moderately strong gluten, necessary for the slight retraction that helps push the layers upward and away from each other during baking, develops during the rolling and folding process. Too strong a gluten would make the dough difficult to roll and fold, difficult to roll out, and tough and distorted in shape after baking.

STRONG AND VERY STRONG GLUTEN: BREAD DOUGHS. A strong gluten is necessary to preserve shape and to ensure a good crumb after baking. The gluten traps the carbon dioxide gas formed during fermentation in the dough, rather than allowing it to escape.

Once strands of gluten form, their elasticity may loosen through resting. This is why many recipes specify resting and chilling periods after mixing, rolling and forming for pastry doughs and between turns for puff pastry. But when too strong a gluten forms initially, no amount of resting will relax it.

Measure flour, like all dry ingredients, by scooping it up with a dry measure cup and leveling it with a straight-edged implement. Never shake or tap the cup against a surface or the flour will compact and weigh too much for its volume.

Other Starches

Corn

In baking, corn is sometimes relied upon to provide body or texture and flavor to a product, usually in the form of cornstarch or cornmeal.

CORNSTARCH. An almost pure starch with negligible protein content, cornstarch is the result of a long milling and purifying process. Two properties make it ideal for use in cake batters: Its fine grain produces a feathery crumb, and its high absorption power in very liquid batters sets them more efficiently and ensures better air retention and lightness.

CORNMEAL. Dried corn kernels are ground to make cornmeal, sometimes used in doughs and fillings for its distinctive flavor and texture.

Tapioca

A starch made from the root of the cassava, or manioc plant, tapioca is usually available in pearled form: Pealike drops are dehydrated to a gelatinized state, ready for soaking, brief cooking, and use as a thickener for fruit pies and tarts. Tapioca also comes as a flour, for thickening purposes.

Crumbs

The idea of using crumbs in baking originated for economic reasons: Saving trimmings and unusable cakes and loaves is a tradition still observed today.

Dry bread and cake crumbs are often used to replace flour or other starches as a binder in batters. Rich cake crumbs, with a high proportion of butter and eggs, are sometimes used to replace ground nuts. They should be stored in the refrigerator up to 1 week, or frozen up to 1 month, to retain freshness and prevent rancidity.

Gelatin

A substance commercially derived from pig-skin, gelatin is used to set liquids. Once the gelatin is rehydrated, heated, melted and dispersed in a liquid, that liquid will become semisolid when cooled.

Gelatin is available in both granulated and leaf forms. Granulated gelatin is packaged in bulk and in the more familiar envelopes. Leaf gelatin is usually sold in bulk by weight and in smaller packages of several leaves.

Granulated Gelatin

Granulated gelatin needs to be rehydrated in a cool liquid before being dissolved over hot water. Each recipe calls for a specific amount and type of liquid in which to soak the gelatin. One envelope of granulated gelatin = ¼ ounce = about 2½ teaspoons.

Sprinkle the gelatin on the liquid in a heat-proof bowl and wait until all of the granules are moistened. (If some remain dry, stir quickly with a fork.) Allow the gelatin to soak for 5 minutes, until the granules swell. Place the bowl over a pan of gently simmering water for 2 or 3 minutes, without stirring, until the gelatin and liquid mixture melts and is clear. Do not heat for more than 3 minutes or allow the water to boil. Otherwise the gelatin may overheat and lose some of its jelling power. Or, some of the liquid in which the gelatin is dissolved may evaporate, making the gelatin mixture too thick and viscous to easily combine with other ingredients.

Gelatin's setting power varies greatly with the density of the liquid being set. One envelope of granulated gelatin will set 2 cups of water. But to set semisolid preparations, such as mousses or Bavarian creams, the same amount of gelatin will set approximately 4 cups.

Leaf or Sheet Gelatin

The most commonly used form of gelatin outside the United States, leaf gelatin is imported to this country from France and Germany. A great deal of confusion may result from trying to substitute granulated gelatin for leaf gelatin or from using recipes which measure leaf gelatin by leaves rather than by weight. In a recent test of different brands of leaf gelatin, there were leaves which weighed 1½ grams, 1⅔ grams, 2 grams, 3 grams and 5 grams.

It is safest to use leaf gelatin especially marketed for home use—these are packaged by a German concern which specializes in supplies for home baking and are 1⅔ gram sheets. Five of these sheets are equal to one envelope of granulated gelatin.

Like granulated gelatin, leaf gelatin must be softened in cold water prior to being heated: Soak the leaves in a large quantity of cold water until limp, about 15 minutes. Remove the soaked leaves from the cold water and squeeze to extract any excess water.

Place the squeezed-out gelatin in a round-bottomed bowl with additional liquid as specified in the recipe. Place the bowl over a pan of very hot water (bring the water to a simmer, then turn off the heat), until the gelatin melts.

TEMPERING THE GELATIN. Once melted, either form of gelatin must be mixed with a small amount of the liquid to be jelled before being added to the remaining liquid. This ensures uniform setting and prevents lumps: Beat about one quarter of the liquid into the dissolved gelatin. After mixing, beat the tempered gelatin into the remaining liquid.

CHEMICAL LEAVENERS

The presence of a leavener causes rising in a dough or batter, due to the production of carbon dioxide. Although some cakes, such as génoises, derive their aeration solely from the steam generated by the eggs in the batter, most leavening is produced by yeast or chemical leaveners. Both produce the necessary carbon dioxide—both before and during baking—to create a risen product. But they do so in such a different manner that their uses are very different.

Yeast, a fungal leavener, is suited to elastic, gluten-forming doughs that accommodate its slow development of carbon dioxide. Batters without this capability for slow stretching require a faster leavener: This is where chemical leaveners are needed.

Chemical leaveners, such as baking powder and baking soda, produce carbon dioxide when an acid and alkaline are combined in the presence of a liquid. This chemical reaction takes place instantly and may continue while the batter is baked in the oven.

Baking Soda

Baking soda, or sodium bicarbonate, is an alkali which requires the presence of an acid in the dough or batter to begin the leavening process. Acids which can be paired with bak-

ing soda include buttermilk, molasses, cocoa or chocolate, and cream of tartar.

Use only the amount of baking soda called for, sift it over the other dry ingredients and stir it in well to avoid an excess of alkalinity and pockets of undissolved baking soda. This eliminates the possibility of a chemical aftertaste.

Because baking soda reacts instantly when moistened, any batter made from it should be placed in the oven at once to avoid the loss of carbon dioxide.

Cream of Tartar

Derived from the acidic sediment that develops on the sides of wine casks, cream of tartar was once the most widely used acid in the manufacturing of commercial baking powder. Although it can still be combined with baking soda to form a rudimentary single-acting baking powder, cream of tartar is now more commonly used in sugar cooking because its acidity helps to prevent recrystallization.

Baking Powder

In baking powder, both the alkali and the acid are included. The alkali is almost always baking soda, combined with one or several acids.

Starch, usually cornstarch, is also mixed into baking powder, both to stabilize it and neutralize the chemical reaction, as well as to absorb the excess moisture in the air which would cause caking and lack of potency.

DOUBLE-ACTING BAKING POWDER. Most baking powder available today is double-acting. Single-acting (tartrate) and phosphate baking powders are much less commonly used since the bulk of their leavening power dissipates rapidly once a batter is mixed. In double-acting baking powder, the presence of two kinds of acid (calcium acid phosphate and sodium aluminum sulfate) creates two chemical reactions—one as soon as the baking powder is moistened, the other when the batter is exposed to heat. Even though this double process reduces the carbon dioxide dissipation that occurs when the batter is being mixed, the batter should still promptly be placed in the oven.

All recipes in this book that call for baking powder use double-acting baking powder.

Buy all chemical leaveners in small quantities, since they lose their potency quite rapidly. Replace them every 6 months or so. Keep containers in a dry spot so they do not absorb moisture which would cause caking and loss of potency.

3

BASIC FLAVORINGS, NUTS AND FRUIT

Understanding the nature of flavorings makes it possible to create delicate desserts with subtle and delicious taste. Sometimes flavorings dominate a preparation as in a Kirsch or chocolate buttercream or in a lemon mousse. In other cases, they accentuate the dominant flavor of a preparation, deepening it or adding a note of contrast. A little Kirsch can intensify strawberries, pineapple or cherries; a squeeze of lemon juice is welcome with all fruit and berries, except the most acidic. In the *Guide Culinaire,* Escoffier recommended the addition of a small amount of lemon and orange juice to all fruit Bavarian creams to heighten the flavor. Deep, dark flavors such as rum and brandy pair well with chocolate and its rich flavor. Slightly acidic flavors such as raspberry and orange extend the chocolate's own acidity into theirs. Spices can help accentuate flavor (cinnamon is widely used with apples and walnuts or pecans), but beware of too heavy a hand with spices or they will dominate other flavors and can contribute a strong medicinal taste.

Use the following guidelines to create pleasing and subtle combinations of flavors:

1. Identify the basic flavor of a preparation. If you are preparing a raspberry Bavarian cream or a lemon mousse, this is easy. Then choose flavoring that will blend or contrast well with it. Both lemon juice and a raspberry flavored *eau de vie* or liqueur would be appropriate with the Bavarian cream—the lemon accentuates the bright freshness of the berries and the Framboise or liqueur deepens its flavor, the alcohol adding a subtle perfume. White rum or even Kirsch or Framboise, the latter two in minute quantities, are great accents to the lemon flavor, rounding off its acidity and deepening the non-acidic elements of the lemon flavor.

2. In a recipe that has many elements, choose a dominant flavor and accentuate it, leaving all the other flavors subordinate. In a strawberry tart with an almond filling, emphasize the strawberries, perhaps adding a drop of Kirsch to the glaze or to the almond filling. A Mille Feuille with pastry cream, whipped cream, raspberries and fondant glaze would benefit from the addition of other raspberry flavored elements—Framboise in the pastry cream and/or whipped cream, and a reduced raspberry glaze on the layers.

3. Add strong flavorings carefully, beginning with a small amount. It is better to make a Kirsch buttercream or an addition of rum to a chocolate mousse less rather than more intense. Be especially careful with strong spirits such as Framboise and other *eaux de vie* which can contribute an incredible bitterness to a preparation when overused.

4. Avoid using too many flavors in a dessert. A banana walnut tart with cinnamon in the filling and a dash of rum doesn't need other spices, liquors or fruit flavors to help either the walnuts or the bananas.

5. Freshness is the best flavor. Whatever flavor you choose, make sure that the dominant note is a fresh, clean one—old fruit, berries, spices or chocolate will never replace the bright flavor of fresh products.

Herbs and Spices

In the days before refrigeration, herbs and spices were needed to mask the flavor of food past its prime. Today, herbs and spices are valued for the infinite flavor nuances they provide. Herbs, usually grown in the temperate parts of the world, are the leaves and sometimes the stems of nonwoody plants. Spices, from tropical areas, are the seeds, bark, nuts and roots of certain plants. Most desserts use spices rather than herbs for flavoring.

Although whole spices last longer than ground spices, most pastry making relies on the ground version. For best results, buy small quantities of ground spices and store them in tightly closed containers (glass is ideal) in a cool, dark and dry place no more than 1 year. This minimizes loss of important volatile oils.

Spice blends undoubtedly save time and money, but the user has little control over flavoring because blends vary from manufacturer to manufacturer. For this reason, all recipes in this book use measured amounts of individual spices.

Extracts

Essential oils removed from aromatic substances are distilled and blended with ethyl alcohol to make flavoring extracts. Although pure extracts may seem expensive, their flavor is so concentrated that only a small amount is needed.

Because alcohol evaporates, extracts should be bought in small, tightly capped bottles and stored in a cool, dry place.

Vanilla

One of the most valued and widely used flavorings, vanilla deserves a special section of its own. It is used as a primary flavoring or as a flavor enhancer to other ingredients like chocolate or coffee.

Although native to the Americas, notably Mexico, most of the vanilla grown today comes from Madagascar. Flowers in the orchid family produce the vanilla beans, actually pods containing a multitude of tiny seeds.

Harvested while green, the pods only develop flavor and aroma once they are cured, turning brown as a result of heating in ovens, hot water or the sun. It takes about 5 pounds of uncured beans to yield 1 pound of cured beans.

Mexican and Bourbon varieties of vanilla beans are reputedly superior to Indonesian vanilla. Richly aromatic Tahiti vanilla beans are not widely available in the United States, but specialty importers have begun distributing them.

The flavor of vanilla can be imparted to food through cured beans or vanilla extract. Cured beans, whole or split (to expose their interior seeds and therefore maximize their potency), can be buried in a container of sugar for several weeks until the sugar has absorbed the vanilla flavor and scent. More expediently, the essence can be released by steeping the bean in a hot liquid such as milk or cream for 10 to 20 minutes, or by splitting the bean and scraping out the tiny seeds directly into a preparation.

Because the processing of vanilla extract can be subject to adulteration, it is very important to select a pure extract from a reliable manufacturer.

In the extraction process, vanilla beans are chopped, mixed several times with a blend of ethyl alcohol and water, then filtered. Depending on the ratio of vanilla to total volume, and the percentage of alcohol, the vanilla is described as *pure vanilla extract* or *pure vanilla flavor.* By a Food and Drug Administration (F.D.A.) law, pure vanilla extract must be 35 percent alcohol by volume; anything less is labeled as pure vanilla flavor. Since vanilla extract is a more concentrated natural flavoring, its higher cost is worthwhile.

Vanilla/vanillin blends and imitation vanilla should be avoided. Although natural vanillin is the largest flavor component in vanilla, the kind used in flavorings is U.S.P. (the United States Pharmacoepia, a list of pure substances capable of being used in prescriptions) vanillin, an artificial by-product of the paper industry. Ethyl vanillin, another artificially derived flavoring, is three times as strong as the U.S.P. vanillin. It is only used in imitation vanilla. Another related flavoring which should be mentioned here is coumarin extract, the supposed bargain vanilla found in Mexico. This extract of the South American tonka beans is toxic and prohibited by the F.D.A. as a food or food additive.

Purchase vanilla like other extracts, in quantities that can be used in a relatively short time. Decant large quantities into small, tightly capped bottles. Always store vanilla in a cool, dark place to minimize evaporation. Store for no longer than a year to retain maximum flavor.

Beans can be stored in a canister of sugar or in an airtight jar in the refrigerator. If used for flavoring a hot liquid, whether whole or split, they can be rinsed, wiped dry and used several times.

Liqueurs, Fruit Alcohols and Wine

Liqueurs

Also called cordials, these alcoholic beverages combine a spirit such as brandy or grain alcohol, flavorings and sugar syrup. Liqueurs are sweet and sometimes almost thick on the palate as a result of their high sugar content.

Fruit liqueurs such as crème de cassis are usually made by the infusion method, soaking the fruit in brandy to give the brandy its aroma, flavor and color before sweetening.

Plant liqueurs, such as crème de menthe and anisette, are made from leaves, herbs, seeds and roots, often in combination. The brandy is pumped through the ingredients for as long as it takes to extract the flavor from them. The ingredients are then distilled to extract any remaining flavor. The two essences are blended and sweetened before being bottled or aged.

Fruit Alcohols

Intensely flavored fruit alcohols and brandies, unlike liqueurs, are not made with sugar. Thus they can be used to flavor mousses and buttercreams, for example, without adding any additional sweetness.

All of these alcohols are made from well-ripened fruit which is mashed, fermented and then distilled off at 100 proof or less to retain the most aroma and flavor. The white alcohols (eaux de vie), such as Framboise (raspberry), Kirsch (cherry) and Poire or Pear Williams, are bottled immediately after distillation, so they remain clear and colorless. Other fruit brandies, such as slivovitz (plum) and Calvados (apple) or applejack, are aged in wood, giving them a dark color.

Liqueurs and fruit alcohols may be stored in a cool, dark cupboard indefinitely. Although some evaporation may take place, they will not deteriorate.

Wines

Wines, both red and white, sweet and dry, may be used for poaching fruit, making mousses and making some syrups. A recipe will specify a particular type of wine.

Once opened, wine should be used as soon as possible. Fortified wines (with added brandy or spirit) such as sherry and Port, and aromatized wines such as vermouth, do not deteriorate as readily, due to their higher alcohol content.

CHOCOLATE

Many books have been solely devoted to chocolate, attesting to its tremendous popularity as a flavoring, beverage and confection.

Once revered as a gift of God by early Latin Americans, chocolate first made its way to Europe as a drink via the Spanish explorer Cortez. American consumption probably began as early as the time of the Dutch colonists, although chocolate was not manufactured in the United States until the mid-1700s.

Until the nineteenth century, chocolate was usually consumed as a beverage. Solid eating chocolate was invented in 1904 by Swiss manufacturer Daniel Peter. Its coarse, grainy consistency soon evolved into the smooth textured confection enjoyed today.

Cocoa beans grow in pods on the Theobroma cacao tree, within 20 degrees north and 20 degrees south of the Equator. The pods are opened and the beans fermented and dried at the growing site before being sacked for shipping.

At the chocolate factory, the beans are roasted to develop their aroma and flavor. Once cooled, the beans are crushed into nibs and their hulls are blown away. The cleaned nibs are heated and ground into a paste called chocolate liquor. Usually chocolate liquor is about 53 percent cocoa butter, although there are slight variations.

Occasionally, this pure chocolate liquor is tempered and molded as is into different sizes for both domestic and commercial use and is often sold as "unsweetened chocolate." At other times, the pure chocolate liquor is separated into cocoa butter and cocoa solid "cakes" (partially defatted cocoa solids used in the manufacturing of cocoa powder). The cakes are shipped to factories where they are further defatted and ground into cocoa powder. When the process is accompanied by the addition of alkaline chemicals, the cocoa is said to be "Dutched." The alkalines remove some of the bitterness of the unrefined cocoa, resulting in a cocoa powder that is darker than nonalkalized cocoa powder, as well as somewhat milder in flavor.

All the recipes in this book use nonalkalized cocoa powder. Measure cocoa powder like flour, scooping with a measuring spoon or dry measure cup and leveling.

There are three basic categories of chocolate: couverture, baking/eating chocolate and compound chocolate. Actually, compound chocolate, like white chocolate, is not literally a chocolate, but both will still be described below.

In the production of couverture and eating/baking chocolates, the pure chocolate liquor stage is bypassed. Instead, the various additives such as sugar and dried milk powder are mixed directly into the beans while they are being ground into a paste.

Once the paste is made, it is milled through progressively finer openings between granite rollers and then conched: Several hundred pounds or more of the chocolate mass are constantly beaten and scraped in a confined vat for a period of 24 to 144 hours. This conching process removes the characteristic bitterness and acidity of unrefined chocolate. During conching, lecithin (an emulsifier) and extra cocoa butter (for improved texture and richness) are sometimes added.

Couverture Chocolate

Literally "covering chocolate," couverture chocolate is distinguished by a high proportion of cocoa butter. This makes the chocolate more fluid in its liquid state so that dipping and molding are easily accomplished. The high proportion of cocoa butter also gives the finished chocolate articles a high sheen. Couverture is available at specialty shops and mail order source listed on pages 317–318.

Baking/Eating Chocolate

The quality of chocolate is determined by its cocoa butter content. Some European manufacturers value high levels of cocoa butter, thus producing exceptionally fine chocolate.

Solid chocolate used for baking and eating includes many categories. Their differences lie not only in their varying proportions of chocolate liquor, sugar and cocoa butter, but also added ingredients such as milk and vanilla.

Unsweetened chocolate, sometimes also known as bitter chocolate, is unadulterated chocolate liquor which has been tempered so it can be molded. By U.S. law, it must contain at least 50 percent cocoa butter.

Bittersweet chocolate, with a chocolate liquor content of at least 35 percent, also contains sugar, cocoa butter (an average of 27 percent), lecithin and flavoring.

Semisweet chocolate, similar to bittersweet chocolate in its ingredients, has a higher level of sugar and a lower percentage of chocolate liquor (by law, at least 15 percent).

Sweet chocolate, even sweeter than semisweet chocolate, has a similar fat and chocolate liquor content.

Milk chocolate has added dried milk powder, along with cocoa butter, sweeteners and flavorings, producing this popular eating chocolate. The milk is added in powdered form because milk's high water content would render the chocolate too liquid. To be designated milk chocolate, it must contain a minimum of 10 percent chocolate liquor and 12 percent milk solids.

White chocolate is not regarded as chocolate in the pure sense because it has no chocolate liquor. Rather, it is a mixture of sugar, cocoa butter, milk powder and vanilla or vanillin. To avoid buying ersatz white chocolate, look for one that contains cocoa butter and no other fats.

Compound Chocolate

Again, this is a misnomer, since compound chocolate does not contain any chocolate liquor. Rather, it is composed of hard vegetable fat mixed with sugar, lowfat cocoa powder and/or powdered milk, as well as flavorings which are usually artificial. Related summer coatings are compound chocolates artificially colored to produce a variety of pastel shades.

Compound chocolate is used for molding and dipping, and sometimes for glazing desserts. Because it does not have to be tempered, it is a convenient ingredient to use.

Although chocolate has a long shelf life, it should not be subjected to wide variations in temperature and humidity. It should be stored, double-wrapped in foil and plastic, in a cool, dark and dry place, ideally 65°F with 50 percent humidity. High temperatures, besides encouraging melting, often cause fat bloom: the surfacing of cocoa butter crystals that have melted, then rehardened, making the chocolate gray. High humidity often results in sugar bloom: the surfacing of sugar crystals, resulting in a rough texture and appearance.

Even with these precautions, white and milk chocolates will not keep long (8 months and a year, respectively), because of their milk content.

Chopping Chocolate

Most superior quality chocolate comes in blocks and must therefore be chopped for use. For easier chopping, have the chocolate at room temperature.

Place the chocolate on a clean, dry cutting board. Using a sharp chef's knife or other chopping knife, cut the chocolate into even, finely shredded pieces, so that it will melt evenly. After chopping, use the blade of the knife to sweep the chocolate from the cutting board to a clean, dry bowl.

Melting Chocolate

Since chocolate is a delicate balance of fat, sugar, cocoa solids and flavorings, it must be treated very gently when melted, or it will form lumps, exude fat or scorch. **Never melt chocolate over direct heat.**

Place finely chopped chocolate in a clean, dry metal bowl that will form a sort of double boiler when placed over a saucepan of hot water. The bowl should be large enough so steam cannot escape from the saucepan and get water into the chocolate.

To melt the chocolate, bring the water to a simmer, turn off the heat and place the bowl over the saucepan. Wait 1 or 2 minutes, then stir vigorously with a wooden spoon or rubber spatula. If the chocolate is not completely melted, remove the chocolate bowl from the water, bring the water to a simmer, remove it from the heat and replace the bowl of chocolate. Let stand a minute before stirring again.

Some preparations, such as ganaches, involve the incorporation of liquid into the melted chocolate. These preparations are best handled by heating the liquid separately until it comes to a boil, then pouring it *all at once* over the chopped chocolate in the bowl. Let stand 2 minutes, or until all the chocolate is melted, then whisk to a smooth mixture.

Some recipes call for melting chocolate with a liquid from the outset. As long as the proportion of liquid is not less than one quarter the weight of the chocolate, there is no danger. Melt the chocolate and liquid as you would chocolate alone.

Cold liquids, such as milk, cream or liqueur, should *never* be added directly to melted chocolate because the chocolate will seize up and form lumps.

Tempering Chocolate

When you melt chocolate, the crystals in the cocoa butter dissolve and become unstable. If the chocolate sets again after being melted, the cocoa butter rises to the surface and forms a gray film. To prevent this, you need to temper the chocolate so the crystals become stable and the chocolate sets with a good texture and sheen.

To make any number of chocolate decorations—cutouts or fine piping done on paper and transferred—it is important to temper the chocolate.

There are several different methods for tempering, all of which are geared toward re-stabilizing the crystals of cocoa butter so the chocolate returns to the same state it was in before melting. It is not practical to temper less than 1½ pounds of chocolate since in a small quantity, temperature changes occur so rapidly that the chocolate will go in and out of temper haphazardly during the process.

Temperature is an important part of tempering and a good instant-read thermometer makes the process a lot easier. Bear in mind the temperatures in the chart opposite when tempering chocolate.

To Temper 1½ Pounds of Chocolate

1. Very finely cut the chocolate and place two thirds of it in a heatproof bowl. Bring a pan of water to a simmer, remove from the heat and place the bowl of chocolate over the water. Be careful that the bottom of the bowl does not touch the surface of the water or the chocolate will overheat. Stir the chocolate frequently as it is melting. Take the choco-

110°F to 125°F	The chocolate should be melted to this temperature before tempering. The chocolate should be cooled by adding finely cut chocolate to begin restabilizing the crystals.
87°F to 91°F	The chocolate should be elevated to this temperature to be in temper for bittersweet and semisweet chocolates.
84°F to 88°F	The chocolate should be elevated to this temperature to be in temper for milk and white chocolates.

late's temperature occasionally, to make sure that it does not exceed 125°F.

2. Remove the bowl from the water; dry the bottom of the bowl, so that there is no risk of water falling into the melted chocolate. Add the remaining chocolate to the melted chocolate. Stir constantly to melt and incorporate the remaining chocolate. This process should take between 5 and 10 minutes.

3. To bring the chocolate into a completely tempered state, reheat it repeatedly over the same pan of hot water for no more than 2 or 3 seconds at a time, until it reaches a temperature of 87°F to 91°F for bittersweet or semisweet chocolate or 84°F to 88°F for milk or white chocolate. Check the temperature of the chocolate after every heating to prevent overheating it. If the temperature rises above 91°F, the chocolate goes out of temper and you must start the process from the beginning.

NUTS

Nuts derive most of their flavor from the oils they contain. These oils, like other fats, have a tendency to become rancid and render the nuts stale tasting.

Buying nuts in their shells usually means they will be fresh. (If they make a noise when you shake them, they are apt to be stale.) Good-quality shelled nuts, especially those in vacuum-packed containers, are also perfectly suitable for baking.

For storage of a month or less, nuts should be kept in airtight containers in a cool, dry spot away from direct light. Freezing is recommended for long-term storage, between 1 and 6 months.

Since the larger the nutmeat, the longer it will stay fresh, do not grind or finely chop nuts until just before using.

Almonds

Oval-shaped almonds come in both sweet and bitter varieties. The sweet almond is found at the retail level and used in baking and confections. The bitter almond is primarily used in making almond extract; it cannot be eaten out of hand because it has a high level of toxic prussic acid.

Virtually all the almonds in American grocery stores are from California. They are readily available all year, fresh and packaged, varying in price according to the amount of processing. They are sold in or out of the shell; blanched (skinned) or unblanched ("raw"); halved, sliced or slivered; toasted, buttered or salted. Almonds are also the principal ingredient in almond paste, and are used for making decorations, marzipan, and fillings such as frangipane. Almonds ground for light-colored batters or doughs should be blanched first.

ALMOND PASTE. Several recipes, notably those for frangipane and marzipan, call for almond paste. Available in 7-pound cans from wholesalers, almond paste can be found in 8-ounce cans in retail stores. Many supermarkets and grocers carry Blue Diamond or Solo brand almond paste. If you cannot find it, substitute 1 cup whole blanched almonds and ½ cup sugar finely ground in the food processor for 8 ounces almond paste. For recipes using less than 8 ounces, reduce the quantities of almonds and sugar proportionately. This works well in the frangipane recipes, but should not be used for marzipan, which needs a smooth paste.

If you have an opportunity to purchase a large quantity of almond paste, divide it into 8-ounce pieces, double wrap in plastic and freeze up to 1 year. I often keep almond paste in this way with excellent results.

Chestnuts

Lower in fat and higher in carbohydrates than other nuts, chestnuts are in season and available fresh from mid-September to March. Though fresh American chestnuts are available, they have a tendency to be small and mealy. If possible, choose the superior Italian chestnuts which are fairly common in American stores. The large French marrons are also available at a higher price.

When choosing fresh chestnuts, select those that have hard, shiny brown shells free from scars and soft spots.

Store chestnuts, loosely covered, in the refrigerator, up to several weeks.

Chestnuts are also available canned, sweetened or unsweetened, either whole or pureed; dried (rehydrate for several hours before using); and pulverized into a flour.

Coconut

Fresh coconuts are in season from October to December and are generally sold in the shell stripped of the fibrous protective husk. Choose coconuts that are heavy for their size. The shell should be devoid of wet "eyes" and, when gently tapped, should sound full of milk. The unshelled nut will keep several months at room temperature. Once opened, the meat should be refrigerated and used as soon as possible.

Coconut is available in processed forms all year round. Of these, the closest to the fresh product is the unsweetened meat, sold in vacuum-packed cans. The meat is also available grated or shredded in plastic bags or in cans; sweetened or unsweetened; as toasted or plain chips; and in extra-long strips intended for decorative purposes. There is also coconut milk and coconut "cream" which is actually a combination of pureed coconut meat and milk, often heavily sweetened and treated with preservatives.

Hazelnuts

Frequently used synonymously with filberts (which are the European version), hazelnuts are often toasted to bring out their pronounced flavor and aroma. They have less oil than almonds and pecans, and are therefore somewhat harder. Ground hazelnuts are mixed with caramelized sugar to form Praline Paste. Hazelnuts are a frequently used garnish because of their compact, slightly pointed round shape.

It is unnecessary to blanch hazelnuts if they will be used ground, unless a light colored dough or batter is desired. Hazelnuts for chopping should be blanched first; the skin becomes brittle and unappetizing when left in bigger pieces.

Macadamias

Most of the macadamias currently available in the United States come from Hawaii, although a small amount is produced in California. Rich in oil, macadamias come whole and in pieces. Purchase unsalted macadamia nuts. The most expensive of these are the whole, fully processed nuts. Macadamia pieces, if available, are less expensive and are usually adequate for baking.

Like other nuts macadamias should be stored in the freezer.

Pecans

Fresh pecans are in season from September to November. Of the processed forms, whole halves are the most expensive but are appropriate for decorative purposes. Pieces are also sold; they are adequate for many uses, but do not remain fresh as long as the larger halves or unshelled nuts. Pecans bought fresh or packaged in the shell should be free of cracks and scars and should be tested to see if they rattle loosely in their shells (a sign of age and staleness). In any form, the pecans will keep best if frozen for several months.

Pine Nuts (Pignoli)

The term "pine nut" refers to the edible seeds from certain pine tree cones. Pine nuts come from many parts of the world, and so are widely available, usually packaged with their shell and inner skin removed.

Pine nuts should be refrigerated or frozen, no more than 6 months, to prevent rancidity.

Pine nuts in jars are often found with other Italian ingredients in supermarkets.

Pistachios

Pistachios are commonly used in Middle Eastern pastries and desserts. In European baking, they are often used as a garnish because of their subtle green color, although their cherrylike flavor is also valued.

Most of the pistachios available in this country are imported from the Near East and are in season in late summer. The red coloring which we associate with "red" pistachios is purely decorative and has nothing to do with the taste of the nutmeat itself. So-called "natural" pistachios are less processed, better for culinary purposes and less expensive. Also available are salted "white" pistachios which are generally eaten as a snack food.

Pistachios are graded according to size; they range from the "8-Star" Colossal (350 nuts to the pound) to the "3-Star" Buds (700 nuts to a pound). Whatever size, pistachios keep best unshelled. Because all unshelled nuts can become moldy when refrigerated, the pistachios should only be stored at cool room temperature or frozen.

Walnuts

Walnuts are available in two varieties, strong-flavored black walnuts and milder, more frequently used, English walnuts.

BLACK WALNUTS. The uses of the black walnut, native to the American East Coast states, are limited by its pronounced, almost bitter flavor, which it retains even after cooking.

Black walnuts are commercially available only in bits because the compartmentalized formation of the nutmeat in the shell makes it impossible to remove the meat in any but small pieces. Because the shells are difficult to open and the strongly flavored skin is difficult to remove, it is advisable to buy shelled black walnuts.

Black walnuts do not keep well and should be used immediately after purchasing.

ENGLISH WALNUTS. In comparison to the black walnut, the English walnut is milder in flavor, easily cracked and more suitable for general culinary purposes. When shelled, it yields a large two-lobed nutmeat which does not need blanching. The English walnut with its uniform lobes is used for decorative purposes.

Whole halves of English walnuts are available and are expensive. Bits are also available; they are less expensive, have many uses, but do not keep as well as do whole halves or unshelled nuts.

The fresh unshelled nuts keep best, are usually less expensive and not too difficult to shell and process. Fresh nuts should not rattle in their shell (a sign of staleness). Once shelled, the nuts must be refrigerated or frozen, and will keep several months.

Blanching Nuts

Blanch almonds, pistachios and hazelnuts before using them whole or chopped. When grinding nuts, blanch only if the color of the skins will detract from the appearance of the recipe. I would blanch almonds for an almond cake batter, but not bother if adding them to a chocolate batter.

ALMONDS AND PISTACHIOS. To blanch almonds or pistachios, cover with cold water in a saucepan and bring to a boil. Drain the nuts and rub in a towel, to loosen the skins. For thorough results, inspect each nut to make sure the skin has been removed.

HAZELNUTS. To remove the skins from hazelnuts, place in a single layer on a baking sheet into a 350-degree oven for about 10 minutes, or until the skins crack and appear to be loosening. Rub the nuts in a towel, inspecting them one at a time. This blanching method also lightly toasts the hazelnuts, enhancing their flavor.

Shelling Fresh Chestnuts

To shell fresh chestnuts, cut an "x" on the flat side of each using a sharp paring knife. Place them in a saucepan of boiling water, return to a boil, lower the heat and simmer 10 to 15 minutes. Drain and shell while they are hot, removing the tough outer shell and the dark papery inside skin. The shelling process also cooks the chestnuts somewhat, but they will require further cooking before being used.

SWEETENED CHESTNUT PUREE

There are several brands of imported French chestnut pastes available through importers and specialty grocers. Be careful to buy *chestnut spread* which is sweetened and rather loose in consistency. *Chestnut puree* is unsweetened and produces a rather rough texture when used in Bavarian creams and buttercreams.

1 CUP WATER
1 CUP SUGAR, ABOUT 7½ OUNCES
2 TABLESPOONS LIGHT CORN SYRUP
1 POUND FRESH CHESTNUTS, BLANCHED,
  SHELLED AND SKINNED

Cooking. Combine the water, sugar and corn syrup in a 3-quart saucepan. Bring to a boil over medium heat, stirring occasionally to dissolve the sugar. Add the chestnuts, return to a boil, lower the heat and simmer about 30 minutes until the chestnuts are very soft and have absorbed most of the syrup.

Be careful that the syrup does not crystallize. The corn syrup will help to prevent this, but if it occurs, add ¼ cup water and stir to dissolve the sugar again. The chestnuts may stick toward the end of cooking when most of the syrup has been absorbed. Stir with a flat wooden or metal spatula to prevent scorching.

Remove chestnuts from the pan and spread on a plate to cool slightly. Puree in a food processor while still warm. If too thick, thin with drops of water. The puree should have the consistency of thick applesauce.

Holding. Keep refrigerated in a tightly covered container up to one week or freeze.

Yield. About 3 cups, 1½ pounds

Chopping Nuts

Chop nuts by hand or with a food processor. The former method allows for greater control and uniformity of size. It also minimizes the chance of overchopping, which is very easy to do with the processor.

For hand chopping, place the nuts, a handful at a time, on a clean, dry chopping board. Using a heavy chef's knife, cut the nuts into big pieces, then continue chopping with an up-and-down motion, anchoring the tip of the knife with one hand, until the pieces are the desired size.

To chop in a food processor, place the nuts in a clean, dry workbowl. Cover and process with *very quick* on-and-off motions, until the pieces are the desired size.

Grinding Nuts

Nut flours or finely ground nuts are an ingredient in many doughs and batters. It is always preferable to grind the nuts freshly since pre-ground nuts become rancid more quickly than whole ones. If necessary, store extra ground nuts, securely wrapped in plastic, in the freezer, for several months.

A rotary nut grinder works well but is a time-consuming alternative to the food processor. When using a processor, proceed as for chopping nuts, but continue to pulse the machine on and off until the nuts are chopped to a fine powder. Too much processing will turn nuts oily and lumpy, especially high-fat walnuts and hazelnuts.

If possible, add part of the sugar called for in a recipe to the nuts before processing them;

this prevents them from being overprocessed and pasty.

Toasting Nuts

Toast nuts, whether whole, chopped or ground, on a jelly-roll pan or in a roasting pan. Bake the nuts in a 350-degree oven and stir often with a flat, wide spatula or pancake turner until they are evenly golden colored. Toasting the nuts too much may result in a bitter taste. If the nuts are to be chopped or ground after toasting, cool and chill them first so that the oils will not exude and make the nuts pasty.

Pralin

A classic hard caramel-and-nut combination (almonds, hazelnuts or a blend), pralin is made by combining nuts with molten caramel and cooling the mixture until it hardens.

Pralin powder is made by pulverizing the hard pralin in the food processor. It imparts flavor and texture to buttercreams and other fillings, and can also be used to decorate pastries.

Sometimes the same caramel-nut mixture is used to prepare Nougatine. In this form it is poured onto oiled marble and rolled out thinly like a pastry dough with a rolling pin. While the Nougatine is still pliable it is cut into decorative shapes.

The last form is Praline Paste, where the caramel-nut mixture is ground to a paste. I prefer to prepare this with a Diluted Caramel, since the hard caramel can make the finished paste somewhat grainy. Commercially prepared paste is available from grocery wholesalers in 7-pound cans (it keeps indefinitely when repackaged in plastic containers and stored in the refrigerator). Imported French praline paste is available from importers of specialty products.

PRALIN POWDER

1 CUP SUGAR, ABOUT 7½ OUNCES
1 TEASPOON LEMON JUICE
1¼ CUPS TOASTED, SLICED ALMONDS, OR
   BLANCHED, CRUSHED HAZELNUTS, OR A
   COMBINATION, ABOUT 4 TO 5 OUNCES
BUTTER FOR THE PAN

Preparing the Caramel. Combine the sugar and lemon juice in a 2-quart saucepan and mix well with a metal spoon. Place over medium heat to begin melting the sugar. Stir occasionally so the sugar melts and caramelizes evenly. Cook to a light amber color.

Mixing. Remove the caramel from the heat, add the nuts all at once, stir well and pour on a buttered pan. Use a spoon to scrape all the pralin from the saucepan and spread it about ¼-inch thick on the pan. Cool at room temperature about 5 minutes. Using a spatula, loosen and turn over the pralin and allow to cool until hard. (If the pralin is not loosened, it may stick despite the butter on the pan.)

Pulverizing. Break the hard pralin into 1½-inch pieces. Place in bowl of a food processor and quickly pulse. Coarsely grind the pralin for use as a decoration, more finely grind if adding to a buttercream.

Holding. Store the pralin in a tightly covered container in a cool, dry place. If the pralin stays dry it will keep for a month.

Yield. 1½ cups, about 12 ounces

NOUGATINE

Use caution when handling Nougatine: Although the caramel has cooled by the time it is rolled out, it still retains quite a bit of heat. Protect your hands with oiled rubber gloves to avoid burns. If you don't have marble, use a cookie sheet instead.

1¼ CUPS BLANCHED SLICED ALMONDS,
   ABOUT 4 OUNCES, OR ⅞ CUP WHOLE
   HAZELNUTS, ABOUT 4 OUNCES
1 CUP SUGAR, ABOUT 7½ OUNCES
1 TEASPOON LEMON JUICE
OIL OR BUTTER FOR THE MARBLE AND
   TOOLS

Preparing the Almonds: Toast the almonds at 350°F for about 10 minutes, stirring often until they are a light golden color. Remove from the oven and cover loosely with another pan to keep the almonds warm.

Preparing the Hazelnuts. Toast the hazelnuts as for the almonds. Remove from the oven and rub in a towel to loosen the skins. Rub off as much of the skins as possible. Coarsely crush the hazelnuts.

Reheat if necessary and keep warm as for the almonds.

Preparing the Caramel. Combine the sugar and lemon juice in a 2-quart saucepan and mix well with a metal spoon. Place over medium heat to begin melting the sugar. Stir occasionally so the sugar melts and caramelizes evenly. Cook to a light amber color.

Mixing. Remove the caramel from the heat, add the warm almonds or hazelnuts all at once, stir well and pour onto a buttered marble or a cookie sheet.

Cooling. After the Nougatine is on the marble, some of the caramel may begin to run from it. Using a buttered spatula or bench scraper, fold the edges of the Nougatine back in toward the center. While doing this, move it to a cooler place on the marble. Turn the Nougatine over once or twice, then flatten it with the spatula.

Rolling. Using a buttered rolling pin roll the Nougatine ⅛- to ¼-inch thick. Roll slowly and gently; too much pressure can make the Nougatine stick to the rolling pin. Stop rolling occasionally and slide a long buttered spatula under the Nougatine to make sure that it has not stuck to the marble.

Cutting. Butter a chef's knife (not your best) and cut the Nougatine into shapes. An easy shape is a diamond: Cut the Nougatine into 1-inch strips, then cut the strips diagonally to form diamonds. If the Nougatine hardens and begins to shatter during cutting, warm it on a pan lined with parchment paper for a minute or two in a 275-degree oven just until flexible again, then finish cutting.

Reserve any scraps for pralin powder.

Holding. Use the shapes within the day, placing them on a pan lined with parchment paper or buttered wax paper as they are cut. To keep longer, place the shapes between sheets of parchment paper in an airtight tin and store in a cool, dry place up to 2 weeks. The Nougatine softens and should be used quickly because it absorbs humidity.

Yield. About 12 ounces of decorations, enough for 1 large or 2 smaller desserts, about 2 dozen 1½-inch pieces

PRALINE PASTE

One of the richest flavorings that can be used for a dessert, Praline Paste imparts a subtle, delicate, unmatched flavor. Excellent in combination with chocolate, it also makes wonderful buttercreams and Bavarian creams. The quantity given here is large. It keeps well in the refrigerator and is good to have in reserve, rather than prepare it every time it is needed.

2 CUPS + 3 TABLESPOONS SUGAR, ABOUT 1 POUND
2 TEASPOONS LEMON JUICE
¾ CUP WATER
1 POUND TOASTED, BLANCHED HAZELNUTS

Preparing the Caramel. Combine the sugar and lemon juice in a 2-quart saucepan and mix well. Place over medium heat to begin melting the sugar. Stir occasionally so the sugar melts and caramelizes evenly. Meanwhile, bring the water to a boil, then remove from the heat. When the caramel is a light amber color, pour in the water at arm's length, averting your face. Let the diluted caramel boil up once, then remove it from the heat. Pour the caramel into another pan, preferably one with a pouring lip, and cool 10 minutes.

Grinding. Place the hazelnuts in the bowl of a food processor. Start the processor and allow the hazelnuts to begin grinding. While the machine is running, pour the caramel in a slow stream through the opening in the cover. After all the caramel has been added, stop the machine and scrape down the sides of the

bowl. Continue processing until the nuts and caramel are reduced to a soft paste.

Holding. Scrape the Praline Paste into a bowl or plastic container, cover with plastic wrap and store in the refrigerator. The Praline Paste will keep indefinitely.

Yield. About 2 pounds

FRUIT

The range of different fruit used for dessert-making is almost limitless. This bounty is made possible by an increased production of American fruit and by a widened availability of imported fruit, including many exotic tropical fruits seldom seen before.

Apples

Fall and winter apple varieties are in season from September to March, peaking in October.

Fresh apples of any variety should be firm, crisp and well colored, with no sign of rot, infestation or dehydration. They should not yield to gentle pressure.

Keep apples loosely covered at a cool room temperature. If basic room temperature is warm, it is better to store apples in plastic bags in the refrigerator. Sort the apples regularly and discard any that show signs of decay. Wash apples just before using them.

Raw apples do not freeze well, but cooked preparations may be frozen for short-term storage.

Apples are commonly categorized as eating, cooking or all-purpose. This list only includes those that can be cooked with good results.

Baldwin and Cortland

Available from November to April and from September to April, respectively, these less common varieties are also good for baking. Baldwins are known for their moderate acidity and aroma. Cortlands, though not as tangy as McIntoshes, discolor more slowly and keep longer.

Golden Delicious

Though they lack the tart flavor of other cooking varieties, Golden Delicious apples are readily available and have good keeping and cooking qualities.

Grown all over the United States, they vary in skin color from yellow/green to bright yellow. Their season is long, from September to June. Slow to discolor when peeled, Golden Delicious hold their shape when cooked. Do not substitute the Red Delicious, an excellent eating apple, since it does not survive cooking well.

Granny Smith

Vivid green, with a tangy, almost sour, taste and extra-crisp texture, Granny Smith apples originally grew almost exclusively in New Zealand and Australia. Now also grown in California, they are in season throughout most of the year. They are best for purees and in thin slices on a tart.

McIntosh

Second in production to Red Delicious apples in this country, McIntosh apples have a fine tart flavor. Since they disintegrate rapidly when cooked, they make excellent purees. I leave the red skin on the McIntosh when cooking so that the resulting puree is tinted a pale pink. Strain the puree through a food mill to remove the skins. In season from mid-fall through spring, McIntosh apples do not keep well and should be used soon after purchase.

Rhode Island Greening

With a peak season from mid-autumn through late winter, this firm, tart green-skinned apple is well suited for pies because its flavor is enhanced by cooking and it holds its shape well. It also makes an excellent puree.

Techniques and Recipes

Paring and Coring

Always wash and dry apples before paring them, to remove any chemicals and wax coat-

ing that may remain on the skin. Using a stainless steel paring knife, cut away the stem and blossom ends with a circular motion, holding the knife handle against the inside of the curved fingers with the thumb close to the tip of the blade, and turning the apple against the knife. Then pare away the skin in a spiral, from stem to blossom end. Halve the apple from stem to blossom end and remove the core with a melon ball scoop or a sharp measuring spoon.

Slicing for Filling

Cut each pared apple half from stem to blossom end into four or five 1-inch-thick wedges, making sure the wedges are uniform for even cooking.

Slicing for Tarts

Cut each pared apple half across the core into ¼-inch-thick slices.

Dicing

Use halved, pared and cored apples. With cut-side down, cut each apple half into four even strips from stem to blossom end, then cut across the strips to form uniform cubes. For purees, cut across the strips in no more than ¼-inch slices, so that they cook through quickly.

Do not dip cut apples into acidulated water if they will be baked or cooked soon after cutting. Since the apples have porous flesh, they easily become waterlogged.

COOKED APPLE FILLING

This mixture of apples cooked with butter and sugar and flavored with lemon juice and cinnamon is used in pies, tarts and turnovers.

The method of cooking allows the apple juices to evaporate before the filling comes in contact with any pastry dough and prevents soggy bottoms. Since the filling will be further cooked in the pastry, it is important not to overcook the apples so they remain firm. Chilling the filling well before using it also minimizes mushiness.

> 2½ POUNDS GOLDEN DELICIOUS APPLES, 5 OR 6 MEDIUM
> ½ STICK BUTTER, 2 OUNCES
> ½ CUP SUGAR, ABOUT 3¾ OUNCES
> ¼ TEASPOON CINNAMON
> 1 TABLESPOON LEMON JUICE

Preparing. Peel, halve, core and slice the apples as for a filling, cutting each half into five or six slices from stem to blossom end.

Cooking. Melt the butter in a wide, shallow pan with a cover, large enough to hold the apples in approximately one layer, and add the sugar, cinnamon and lemon juice and stir well to combine. Cook over medium heat until the apples begin to sizzle. Lower the heat and cover the pan. Let the apples steam about 5 minutes, until the juices begin to exude from them.

Continue cooking, covered, about 5 minutes longer or until the apples have exuded a large quantity of juice. Uncover and continue cooking at a low heat to evaporate the juices, about 10 minutes longer. The apples should remain in firm, distinct pieces.

Cooling. Pour the filling into a glass or stainless steel pan in one layer. Cool to room temperature.

Holding. Refrigerate the filling, covered with plastic wrap, until needed, up to 5 days.

Yield. About 4 cups

SWEETENED, COOKED APPLE PUREE

Used for Apple Bavarian Cream and some tart fillings, this mixture of apples, sugar and water is cooked until thick and slightly reduced. Once cooked, the mixture is pureed and cooled.

2 POUNDS GOLDEN DELICIOUS APPLES, 4 OR
   5 MEDIUM
½ CUP SUGAR, ABOUT 3¾ OUNCES
⅓ CUP WATER

Preparing. Peel, halve, core and dice the apples, cutting them in four lengthwise strips from stem to blossom end, then cutting across the strips in ¼-inch slices.

Cooking. Combine the apples, sugar and water in a saucepan and cover the pan. Cook the apples over low heat until the juices exude, about 10 minutes. Uncover the pan and continue cooking very slowly until the juices evaporate and the apples have become very soft and translucent, about 10-15 minutes. Stir frequently while the juices are evaporating, so that the apples do not stick and scorch. Puree the apples in a food processor, then cool to room temperature.

Holding. Refrigerate the puree, covered with plastic wrap, until needed, up to 5 days, or freeze.

Yield. About 2 cups

Pears

Pears for desserts are in season throughout the fall, winter and spring, with lesser availability during the summer.

Ranging in size from the tiny *Seckel* to the pudgy *Comice,* pears are an exquisite fruit whose delicate perfume and silky texture when cooked make them ideal for poaching and pureeing.

More delicate in flavor and texture than apples, pears must be handled with a gentle touch, from paring to poaching. They are usually poached before being used in tarts, unlike apples which are sometimes baked raw.

Pears *should be purchased when not fully ripe* and allowed to mature at room temperature. Those which completely ripen on the tree do not develop as full a flavor or as fine a texture. Slightly underripe specimens are preferable for poaching and other cooked preparations where it is important for the pear to hold its shape. Avoid pears with breaks in the skin or bruises or blemishes.

Ripen pears at home by storing them at room temperature. The pears are ripe when they are soft at the stem end only; softness at the bottom end may indicate spoilage at the core. Skin color is not a good gauge of ripeness, because of the wide range of characteristic colors.

Once ripe, pears should be refrigerated for 1 or 2 days, and only washed immediately prior to use.

Although many varieties of pears exist, the following are available nationwide and suitable for dessert-making. Most American pears are grown in California and the Pacific Northwest.

Anjou

Of all the fresh pears, the Anjou, in season from October to April, is the best variety for most desserts. It is large and plump, with a thin yellow/green skin, short neck and winy flavor.

Bartlett

Suitable for cooked preparations, these are the variety of pear known as Poire Williams in Europe, used for making pear alcohol. In season from July to mid-October, the Bartlett is red or yellow with a green blush.

Bosc

In season from October to February, this slightly tart pear is an excellent choice for baking and cooking. It is large, with a long neck and russet skin.

Comice

The fragrant and buttery Comice has a smooth flesh making it perfect for poaching. In season from October through March, these are a good choice when Bartletts are out of season.

Seckel

Tiny Seckel pears have a piquant, almost spicy, flavor. Discovered in Pennsylvania, they are now marketed from late August to December. Although a bit more work to pare and core than larger varieties, Seckel pears are excellent because of their rich flavor.

Techniques and Recipes

Paring/Acidulating

Because pears have a low acid level and a softer flesh than apples, they must be treated differently. Gently pull off the stem. Pare with a swivel-bladed peeler, using gentle up and down strokes. Once peeled, the pears should be halved and cored, then immediately dropped into acidulated ice water (3 cups water to 3 tablespoons lemon juice). It is better to poach pear halves first before slicing or dicing them.

POACHED PEARS

Cooking pears before using them in a dessert guarantees that they will be uniformly cooked, retain their color without darkening and not exude excess liquid into the preparation.

3 CUPS WATER

2 CUPS ICE CUBES

3 TABLESPOONS LEMON JUICE

1½ POUNDS FIRM, RIPE PEARS, ABOUT 5

1 CUP SUGAR, ABOUT 7½ OUNCES

½ VANILLA BEAN, OR 2 TEASPOONS
VANILLA EXTRACT

Preparing. Combine the water, ice cubes and lemon juice in a large saucepan. Peel, halve and core the pears and immediately plunge into the acidulated ice water. When all the pears are in the water, remove the ice and enough water to leave the pears covered by 1 inch.

Add the sugar and vanilla bean or extract and position the pears so that the cut sides are up, if possible (if any oxidization occurs, it will occur on the flat side which will eventually be positioned downward in a dessert).

Cut a round of parchment or wax paper to fit inside the saucepan and make a 1½-inch hole in the center. Cover the pears with the paper, pressing it down so that the paper is below the surface of the liquid. (This will keep the pears submerged in the syrup so they do not develop dark spots.)

Cooking. Bring the pears to a boil over medium heat and simmer them 1 to 2 minutes. Turn off the heat and allow the pears to cool in the syrup. If the pears are ripe, the heat remaining in the cooling syrup will be enough to cook them until they are tender.

For pears that are more firm, or underripe, begin the cooking as above, bringing them to a simmer in the syrup. Simmer until the pears are fully tender and can be easily pierced with the dull point of a table knife, about 15 minutes.

Remove the pears from the syrup with a slotted spoon immediately after they are tender and cool them, cut-side down, on a pan lined with paper towel.

Holding. If the pears are to be kept more than a few hours before use, cool the syrup and refrigerate the pears in it, covered, until needed, up to 3 or 4 days.

Yield. About 10 halves

Pears Poached in Wine

Poaching in a syrup made with white wine, red wine or Port adds flavor and sometimes color to the pears.

Preparing and Cooking the Pears. Pour the acidulated ice water off the peeled and cored pears and immediately add 2 CUPS OF RED WINE, WHITE WINE OR PORT, then enough water so that the pears are covered by about 1 inch of liquid. Add the sugar and the vanilla bean and cook as for poached pears, above. For pears cooked in red wine or Port, the STRIPPED ZEST OF AN ORANGE, 3 OR 4 CLOVES AND 2 CINNAMON STICKS (tied together in a square of cheesecloth) may be added for extra flavor.

Holding. If the pears are to be kept more

than a few hours before use, cool the syrup and refrigerate the pears in the syrup, covered, until needed.

Yield. About 10 halves

Sweetened, Cooked Pear Puree

Like sweetened cooked apple puree, this is made for incorporating into Bavarian creams. Because of the different water and acid contents of pears and apples, however, the cooking methods differ. Poach the pears in syrup as above, continuing to cook them until they are very soft but not disintegrating. Remove the pears from the syrup and puree them in a food processor; cool the puree.

Holding. Refrigerate the puree, covered with plastic wrap, until needed, about 5 days, or freeze.

Yield. About 3 cups

Berries

Berries are generally available from late spring to the beginning of fall; hothouse and imported berries are also available out of season. Fruit of different botanical types fall under the general name of berries: small, thin-skinned fruit with fairly small seeds.

Since all berries are soft and perishable, they should be handled gently and used quickly—ideally on the day of purchase. Look for berries that are firm, with radiant color and sheen.

Excess liquid staining on the bottom of a container indicates crushed berries that may be decayed. Once berries are purchased, they should be tipped out of their containers and culled, so that any bruised, moldy or fermented fruit will be discarded. To minimize molding do not wash or hull berries until just before using. Avoid heating berries (even sunlight will warm them up) and then refrigerating them; this combination of warmth and moisture quickly promotes rotting.

Strawberries

Choose strawberries with a rich, bright color and shine, and fresh-looking hulls. Very dark, dull or soft berries should be rejected, as should those with white or green coloring, indicating premature picking.

The flavor of strawberries depends more on variety than on size, although smaller berries often have better flavor than oversized ones. Large cultivated strawberries are very eye-catching but usually lack the flavor of smaller berries.

Keep strawberries unwashed and unhulled in a humid area of the refrigerator until ready to use. Never leave berries soaking in water, since they will become waterlogged and soggy.

Always rinse strawberries before hulling them, so they do not absorb excessive amounts of water. Use the tip of a paring knife to carefully dislodge the hull from the top of the berry.

To slice, use a small, stainless steel paring knife and cut through each hulled berry from hull to point, to make four or five slices.

FRAISES DES BOIS. Although these tiny, wild strawberries are becoming more popular in this country, they are still not easy to find. Do not substitute for regular cultivated strawberries in recipes (they have a different texture and water content). They are a splendid addition, though, to pastries and tarts because of their special flavor and fragrance, as well as their size.

FROZEN STRAWBERRIES. Available either in block form or individually quick frozen (I.Q.F.), they may be substituted for fresh in cooked preparations. Since block frozen berries are usually sweetened before being frozen, use only three fourths of the sugar called for in a recipe.

Raspberries

Primarily a summer fruit, raspberries are available throughout the year due to the popularity of imported varieties. A composite fruit made of many seeded cells, raspberries are fragrant and tangy with an exquisite color and shape. Unlike strawberries, they should not have their stem caps attached (this would be a sign of underripeness). Their color should be bright and they should have an obvious sheen.

Do not wash raspberries. Keep them covered in the refrigerator and plan on using them promptly since they are highly perishable.

Besides basic red raspberries, there are also black and golden ones. Black raspberries should not be confused with blackberries. Golden raspberries have a bright yellow/orange color and a flavor identical to red raspberries.

FROZEN RASPBERRIES. Like strawberries, these are available frozen in block form or individually quick frozen (I.Q.F.). The block form is almost always sweetened. Take the added sugar into account by reducing the sugar in the recipe. As with block-frozen strawberries, use only three fourths of the sugar called for.

Blackberries

Blackberries' peak season is from June to August with some exceptions from region to region. Firmer and less sweet than raspberries, blackberries are closely related to a number of varieties, such as *boysenberry, loganberry, marionberry and olallieberry.* Use these like raspberries.

As with other berries, blackberries should be bright and well-colored, with a gleam on their surface (even more pronounced than for raspberries). Like raspberries, they should not have hulls attached (this is a sign of underripeness and the berries will be sour and tasteless).

Blueberries

At their peak during June and July, blueberries can be bought fresh through September. These native North American berries thrive on even the most depleted soils.

Blueberries should not be confused with *huckleberries.* Huckleberries are smaller, sourer, tougher skinned and usually wild rather than cultivated.

Optimally, blueberries should be uniformly sized and colored with a bluish, almost powdery finish. They should be plump and free of mold, many leaves and stems, and shriveled or green berries.

Like other berries, blueberries should be

sorted at home, left unwashed and refrigerated until used. Unlike strawberries, however, blueberries benefit from dry, cold storage, rather than a moist humid environment.

FROZEN BLUEBERRIES. Available I.Q.F., they may be substituted for fresh in cooked preparations. Since frozen blueberries bleed, they should be used while still frozen.

Currants

Not to be confused with Zante currants, a type of dried grape similar to the raisin, currants are small tart berries that grow on stalks. Fresh currants are seldom available in this country because they harbor white pine blight and their cultivation is restricted by law.

Red and *white* currants are used in the preparation of jelly and the exclusive French preserve, *Bar-le-Duc. Ribes nigrum—black* currants—are used to produce Crème de Cassis, a liqueur, especially in the Dijon region of France.

If domestic red currants are available fresh, they will be found at the market during the summer months. Imported red and black currants from New Zealand can sometimes be found during the winter months. Look for firm, brightly colored berries.

Currants should be refrigerated on their stalks and removed just before use to maximize flavor, moisture and freshness.

Gooseberries

Seldom seen fresh in this country because, like currants, they harbor white pine blight,

disease-resistant gooseberries are now being developed.

In Europe, gooseberries are divided into dessert and cooking varieties. Both need to be washed just prior to use, then "topped and tailed" with scissors, removing the stem and blossom ends.

Cranberries

Associated with the Thanksgiving and Christmas holiday meals, cranberries are available fresh from September through December, as well as year round in processed forms. Cranberries sold raw in packages are harvested by hand.

When purchasing whole berries, look for those which are plump and hard, with no sign of leakage or sogginess.

Cranberries can be frozen in their unopened package and used in the same way as other individually quick frozen berries.

SWEETENED, COOKED BERRY PUREE

Used as a base for Bavarian creams and glazes and as a flavoring for buttercreams, this is a simple and straightforward technique. Be careful that the fruit has sufficiently reduced and concentrated before pureeing it, or the puree will lack body and flavor.

1½ POUNDS BERRIES
¾ TO 1 CUP SUGAR, DEPENDING ON
  SWEETNESS OF BERRIES, ABOUT 5¾ TO
  7½ OUNCES

Preparing. Rinse the berries, hull if necessary and slice if the berries are large. Combine with the sugar in a 3- to 4-quart saucepan. Mash the berries and sugar with a wooden spoon.

Cooking. Place over low heat, stirring occasionally. The sugar will draw juice from the berries and the mixture will begin to simmer. Allow to simmer 10 to 15 minutes, until slightly thickened. Do not overcook or the berries will lose their fresh taste and take on a caramelized flavor.

Pureeing. Cool the cooked berries, then puree in a food processor, blender or food mill. With the finest blade of the food mill, it is usually unnecessary to strain the seeds after pureeing.

Straining. The easiest way to strain berry purees, especially those with many seeds, like raspberries, is to pass the mixture through two progressively finer strainers. The first should be just small enough to easily remove most of the seeds.

Holding. Cover and refrigerate until needed, up to 5 days, or freeze.

Yield. About 3 cups

Kiwi

Native to New Zealand where it was dubbed the Chinese gooseberry, the kiwi is now also cultivated in California, making it available almost year round.

This egg-shaped fruit holds a delicately flavored and vividly colored flesh under its fuzzy skin. Kiwis can be bought slightly firm, then allowed to ripen at room temperature. Once ripe, the unpeeled fruit keeps in the refrigerator for up to several weeks. Note that firmer fruit is easier to peel and slice.

Kiwis should not be peeled and sliced too far in advance of usage, or they will dry out and lose some of their color. Firm kiwis should be cut at both ends to remove tough skin and stem and blossom remnants. With a sharp paring knife, carefully remove the peel in a spiral from end to end, so the kiwi retains its round shape and is ready for slicing. For perfect rounds, slice an unpeeled kiwi and stamp out circles with a round cookie cutter.

Stone Fruit

The category stone (or drupe) fruit includes a wide selection of seemingly different species, from peaches and apricots to cherries. All share a similar structure with a hard central pit. Store ripe stone fruit in plastic bags in the refrigerator. Because they are highly perishable, they should be used soon after ripening, usually within 2 or 3 days.

To Pit Stone Fruit

Plunge the tip of a paring knife into the blossom end of the fruit until it hits the pit, then work the knife around the fruit, from stem to blossom end, and then back up to the stem end. Twist gently to separate halves of fruit, then carefully pry out the pit with the knife.

Cherries may be pitted with a paring knife carefully inserted into the stem end to expose and extricate the pit, with a chopstick (push the pit through the cherry by inserting the chopstick in one end) or with a pitter specifically designed for this purpose. Once pitted, the cherries may be halved, if desired.

Peaches

Abundantly in season from mid-May through mid-October, peaches reach their peak flavor in the late summer. Once characterized by soft fuzz, peaches are now mechanically de-fuzzed; some are bred for smoother skin.

Look for peaches that have a pronounced fragrance. Smell is the best indication of ripeness. The peach should be neither rock-hard nor mushy; rather, it should yield to gentle pressure. It should have no hint of green on its skin and should be vibrant and fresh-looking. Avoid peaches that are bruised, blemished or shriveled, or that have sticky surfaces indicating loss of juice due to infestation or mishandling. Shape and size are also good indicators. Plump, round peaches are preferable to flattened ones. Medium peaches are better choices than large or small ones of the same variety.

Since peaches are highly perishable, they should only be bought for quick use within a day or two.

Yellow peaches, the most common type, are either *cling* or *freestone,* categories which are virtually self-explanatory. Freestone peaches can be easily pitted, while cling peaches have flesh that adheres to the pit. Most processed peaches are of the cling variety, with firmer flesh and greater uniformity. Most fresh peaches available on the retail level are freestone.

White peaches have a greenish white flesh as opposed to the subtle orange color of regular peaches.

Nectarines

Today's nectarine is probably more similar to a peach than in days past, although it still has a smooth, rather than fuzzy, skin, firmer flesh and less juice. Nectarines are also divided between freestone or cling varieties, marketed from mid-June through late September, with a peak period during July and August.

Buying tips for nectarines are similar to those for peaches, with fragrance and lack of green tint the best signs of ripeness. Nectarines range in color from pale white to warm red. Handle nectarines the same way as peaches.

Peeling Peaches and Nectarines

Peaches and nectarines that are perfectly ripe can be quickly and easily blanched to remove their skins. (To check for ripeness, try to peel off a little skin with a paring knife; if it does not come off easily, the fruit cannot be blanched and must be totally peeled with a knife.) Immerse the fruit in rapidly boiling water for 30 seconds, then immediately plunge into ice water. The skin

3 CUPS WATER
1 CUP SUGAR, ABOUT 7½ OUNCES
1 TABLESPOON LEMON JUICE
½ VANILLA BEAN

Preparing. Blanch, peel and stone the peaches or nectarines.

Cooking. Combine the water, sugar, lemon juice and vanilla bean in a large saucepan. Add the prepared fruit and additional water, if necessary, to cover the fruit by about 1 inch. Cut a piece of parchment paper to fit inside the saucepan, and make a hole in the center. Cover the fruit with the paper, pressing it down so that the paper is below the surface of the liquid. (This will keep the fruit submerged in the syrup so it does not develop dark spots.)

Bring the peaches or nectarines to a boil over medium heat; lower the heat and simmer very gently, less than 5 minutes, or until barely tender. Check the fruit for doneness by piercing with the dull point of a table knife. The fruit is done when it may be easily pierced. Immediately remove from the syrup with a slotted spoon and cool, cut-side down, on a pan lined with paper towels.

If the fruit is to be kept more than a few hours, cool the syrup and refrigerate the fruit in it, covered, until needed.

Yield. About 12 halves

should peel off easily with the help of the paring knife.

POACHED PEACHES OR NECTARINES

Peaches or nectarines are usually peeled before poaching. Since the peeling may heat them slightly, the poaching must proceed very carefully to avoid overcooking these very delicate fruits.

2 POUNDS RIPE PEACHES OR NECTARINES,
ABOUT 5 OR 6

Apricots

Available from May to August in the West and June and July in the East, fresh apricots are usually shipped unripe because they are otherwise far too delicate to survive shipping.

Mostly grown in California, fresh American apricots are a much rarer commodity across the country than plums or peaches because small harvests and delicate flesh make apricots poor shippers. Consequently, most fresh apricots are consumed in the Western states, leaving the dried version for more widespread use.

Apricots should be firm and plump with no bruises or dark spots. If they need additional ripening at home, place in a paper bag containing holes and keep in a draft-free spot away from direct sunlight. Once ripe, the fruit will be characteristically golden in color and highly fragrant. Refrigerate unwashed and unpeeled ripe apricots for no more than 4 or 5 days. The skin of the apricot is tender and need not be removed for most preparations unless specified.

Plums

Plums are marketed from late May to September. Prune plums, smaller and oval, are available from July to October. Look for ripe plums that are firm but yield to slight pressure, with smooth, evenly colored skin and no soft spots, cracks or shriveled areas. Brown skin indicates too much exposure to the sun. Refrigerate ripe plums and use them within several days.

Plums are grown in varieties ranging from the green, slightly pointed *Greengage* to the round, darkly colored *Santa Rosa,* with many subvarieties. Small black plums are referred to as *Italian prune* plums, though they are neither Italian nor dried. They are the best for tarts and pastries. Another variety of plum, the small black *sloe,* is fermented and distilled to make sloe gin. *Beach* plums are best for jam- and jelly-making, not baking.

Cherries

Sweet cherries are available from May through August, at a peak from mid-June through July. *Sour* cherries come into season several weeks later. Cherries are divided into sweet, sour and sweet-sour categories, the latter being a hybrid of the other two varieties.

Since cherries do not ripen off the tree, they should be bought as ripe as possible. They should be firm but not rock-hard (sour cherries are softer than sweet ones), with a deep color and glossy skin. Avoid cherries that are dull, shriveled or mushy, as well as those exuding juice or a fermented smell.

Although cherries with their stems still attached have more waste, they keep longer than those without stems, probably because the stems prevent drying out. The stems should be supple, not dried out. Refrigerate unwashed cherries for up to a few days, periodically checking to remove any that have spoiled.

Sweet cherries include *Bing, Lambert* and *Tartarian* cherries; all are eaten fresh but can be cooked, too. The pale *Royal Ann* cherry is also processed into maraschino cherries.

Sour cherries, rounder and softer than the sweet variety, are usually too tangy to be eaten raw, but they make superb pies and preserves. The three most common sour cherry varieties are *Early Richmond, Montmorency* and *English Morello.* The Montmorency is the best choice for general baking and is widely available when in season, usually from late June to mid-July.

POACHED APRICOTS

The method for poaching apricots differs from that used for other fruit, since ripe apricots have an extremely fragile texture and can become overcooked very easily. This technique employs the heat from a boiled syrup to cook the fruit without putting the fruit over direct heat.

2 POUNDS RIPE APRICOTS, ABOUT 16
3 CUPS WATER
1 CUP SUGAR, ABOUT 7½ OUNCES
1 TABLESPOON LEMON JUICE
½ VANILLA BEAN

Preparing the Fruit. Halve and pit the apricots. Place the apricot halves in a large heatproof glass or stainless steel bowl.

Preparing the Syrup. Combine the water, sugar, lemon juice and vanilla bean in a large saucepan. Bring the ingredients to a boil over medium heat.

Cooking. When the syrup has reached a full rolling boil, remove from the heat and immediately pour over the apricot halves. Allow the fruit to cool in the syrup. The heat in the syrup will be just enough to tenderize the apricots without overcooking them. If the fruit is very ripe, check it after 5 minutes of cooling, to make sure it has not overcooked. If it is already tender, add ice cubes to arrest further cooking.

Holding. Refrigerate the apricots in their syrup, covered with plastic wrap, for up to 5 days.

Yield. About 32 halves

Poached Plums or Cherries

Use the same method as for Poached Apricots, decreasing the sugar to ½ cup for sweet cherries.

Purees of Stone Fruit

Drain the fruit well, reserving the syrup for another use, such as moistening syrup for a cake using the same flavor puree in the filling, or to poach more of the same fruit. Puree the fruit in the food processor. Refrigerate the puree, covered, for 5 days or freeze. The reserved syrup also freezes well.

Citrus Fruits

Citrus fruits are used to enhance other flavors as well as to impart their own flavor to desserts. Citrus zest, which contains a large quantity of citrus oil, is added to liquids for infusions or grated directly into batters or other mixtures. Freshly squeezed juice is used as a flavoring as well as to prevent low-acid fruit from darkening.

Look for fruit that is heavy for its size (this indicates a high juice content), with a vibrant-looking skin that is neither dried out nor moldy and with no mushy spots.

For short-term storage, citrus fruit may be kept at room temperature. Otherwise, especially in hot weather, they should be kept in a plastic bag in the refrigerator, removed as needed and, for maximum juice yield, brought to room temperature before being juiced. Citrus fruit keeps for at least a week when refrigerated. Always tightly cover cut surfaces of fruit with plastic wrap and refrigerate the halves or wedges promptly.

Since it is easier to remove zest from a whole piece of citrus fruit than from a cut or juiced one, always grate or strip the required amount of zest before juicing the fruit.

Once cut, peeled or juiced, all citrus products should be tightly covered with plastic wrap and refrigerated.

Lemons

Most of the lemons grown in this country come from California, so this once-tropical fruit is available year round, with particular abundance during the summer months.

The flavor of lemon comes from both its juice and its zest, which contains a larger proportion of the essential oil. Lemon is used as a flavor on its own as well as to enhance other flavors—the flavor of most fruit is intensified when a small quantity of lemon juice or zest is added. The juice is often used to prevent other fruit from darkening. For example, just-peeled pears are always placed in water acidulated with lemon juice.

Look for brightly colored lemons, with no dark or mushy areas. Fresh lemons should give off a pleasing citrus aroma.

Nationwide, the *Eureka* lemon is the most common variety. The increasingly popular *Meyer* lemon is more limited in availability, although its flavor is regarded by many to be more complex and interesting.

An average lemon yields between 1 to 2 ounces of juice, and 1 to 2 teaspoons of grated zest.

Limes

Limes are available year round, but they peak in production and quality during the summer. Unlike lemons, a bit of brown speckling on a lime is acceptable, although limes with soft spots and bruises should still be avoided. *Key* limes are yellow, although most limes at their peak are a vibrant green. Like lemons, limes should smell fresh.

Limes usually yield less juice than lemons because they are often smaller and somewhat woodier. Plan on getting about an ounce of juice and 1/2 to 1 teaspoon of grated zest from an average lime, less of each from key limes.

Oranges

Oranges are available year round, with the greatest variety in winter and early spring. When buying oranges, look for those that are heavy for their size, with a decisive firmness. Although loose-skinned oranges such as the *tangerine* will yield when lightly pressed, they should not be mushy. As with other citrus fruits, oranges should have a bright, glowing skin with no mold, blemishes or holes.

Since almost all varieties are picked when mature, a light green tinge is not a sign of underripe fruit. In fact, some varieties turn green in areas after the fruit has ripened (a process called regreening). Some oranges are dyed to cover normal russeting of the skin for cosmetic reasons, and this does not harm the taste.

Because an entire batch of oranges, like apples, can be ruined due to one bad piece of fruit, it is preferable to buy the fruit by the piece from open boxes.

An average orange yields about 1/3 cup

juice and 2 tablespoons grated zest.

Store oranges in a cool, dry place for several days. Like other citrus fruits, their storage life increases if they are kept refrigerated in plastic bags: This retains moisture and keeps other refrigerator tastes and odors from affecting the fruit.

Once cut, peeled or juiced, orange products should be tightly wrapped in plastic, refrigerated and used promptly.

The type of orange selected should depend on its ultimate use. Juice oranges, as their name indicates, are best used for juicing. Because they have ample juice in them, they are less apt to be woody. They can usually be cut into neat slices (although their seeds may interfere). On the other hand, their rind is thin and unyielding. If zest is needed, a good eating orange such as the *Navel,* with a thick, oil-rich peel, is preferable. Eating oranges are also good choices for sectioning and slicing.

Most juice oranges come from Florida. They are sweeter and less acidic than eating oranges, and they usually contain more seeds. Examples include the popular *Valencia* and *Hamlin* varieties.

Primarily cultivated in California, eating oranges have a thick, easily removed peel and a pleasing tart flavor. Varieties as diverse as the navel, tangerine and *Temple* all fall under this general category. Navel oranges, thick-skinned with a navel-like mark on the blossom end, are large and usually seedless.

Tangerines belong to the mandarin group of orange varieties, with rough, loose skin that is easily peeled and flesh that neatly divides into segments. Although not very acidic, they have a pleasing flavor that is distinct from other oranges.

Temple oranges are thought to be a cross between the tangerine and the orange. They are also easy to peel and thick skinned.

Other Fruits

Pineapples

Truly ripe fresh pineapples are hard to come by. Because pineapples are very perishable when ripe, they are usually picked before reaching maturity, so they can survive shipping. Unfortunately, pineapple does not appreciably ripen once picked.

Since air-shipped pineapples reach the market in a shorter period of time, they can be allowed to ripen before they are harvested; although their price reflects this extra care, they are worth seeking.

Contrary to popular belief, pulling out a leaf from a pineapple's crown does not necessarily indicate ripeness. As with many other fruits, a pleasant pineapple smell, free of acrid or rotting undertones, is one's best indication of ripeness. Other qualities to look for include a fresh green crown of leaves, a base free of mold and stickiness, plump eyes that protrude from the skin, heaviness for size, and flesh that yields gently when squeezed.

Although a pineapple should be bought with the above ripeness indicators, if it seems a bit underripe, it can be left for a day or two at room temperature, loosely wrapped in a perforated paper bag so the ethylene gases can accumulate and hasten ripening. Once the pineapple is ripe, store in the refrigerator and use promptly. Tightly wrap peeled, sliced pineapple in plastic before refrigerating.

The tropical fruit pineapple that reaches the United States is grown in Hawaii, Puerto Rico, Central America, the West Indies and Mexico. Although Hawaii is the world's biggest pineapple producer, most Hawaiian pineapple is processed immediately after harvesting. Fresh pineapple from Puerto Rico, however, is widely available.

Pineapples vary in size, shape and color, depending on variety. The less commonly available smooth *Cayenne* variety from Hawaii is yellow when ripe, and sports a single-tufted crown on its tall shape. Puerto Rican *Red Spanish* pineapples are more abundantly available, with a pale red skin and multi-tufted crown. The *Sugar Loaf,* which remains green even when ripe, has long, broad leaves.

Techniques and Recipes

Peeling and Coring

Peel the whole pineapple with a sharp knife, once the crown has been cut off. Always remove the eyes, too, since they are both unattractive and sharp when bitten into.

To remove the core, you may use a special pineapple corer designed for this purpose.

Treat pineapple to be cut into half slices or fans differently: Remove the crown, then cut the fruit lengthwise into halves or quarters. Loosen the whole halves or quarters from the skin with a thin, flexible-bladed serrated knife (some are made just for this purpose), being sure to cut away enough skin so that the eyes are removed, too.

Quarters of pineapple can be cored by cutting away the core in one long strip, across the top.

POACHED PINEAPPLE

If a fresh pineapple is perfectly ripe, it only needs to be peeled, cored and sliced before being used in a dessert such as a fruit tart or in a cake filling containing fresh fruit. More often, pineapples in the market are underripe and benefit from poaching before use.

1 FRESH PINEAPPLE, ABOUT 2 TO 2½
   POUNDS
3 CUPS WATER
1 TABLESPOON LEMON JUICE
1 CUP SUGAR, ABOUT 7½ OUNCES
½ VANILLA BEAN OR 2 TEASPOONS VANILLA
   EXTRACT

Paring. Peel and quarter the pineapple, then core and slice about ¼-inch thick. Place in a 2-quart saucepan and add the remaining ingredients. Add more water if necessary to cover the pineapple by 1 inch. Cut a round of parchment or wax paper to fit inside the saucepan and make a 1½-inch hole in the center. Cover the pineapple with the paper, pressing it down so that the paper is below the surface of the liquid. This will keep the fruit submerged in the syrup while it is cooking so that it cooks evenly.

Cooking. Bring the pineapple to a boil over medium heat and simmer 5 to 10 minutes. Turn off the heat and allow the pineapple to cool in the syrup. The heat in the syrup will finish cooking the pineapple.

Holding. If the pineapple is to be kept more than a few hours before use, hold the pineapple in the syrup, covered, in the refrigerator.

Yield. About 1½ to 2 pounds

Figs

The market for fresh figs extends from mid-summer to early autumn.

One of the most fragrant and delicate of all fruit, figs are extremely perishable when ripe. Dried figs are commonly available in the fall and winter. They are used mostly alone, as a confection, rather than as a dessert ingredient.

Many varieties of fresh figs exist, a good percentage grown in California, but some from the South and others imported. Varieties run the gamut in color and size from light green to prune plum black skin; from flattened round to teardrop shape; from light pink to purple interior.

All fresh figs should yield to gentle pressure but not be mushy. They should be well filled out, rather than puckered, with smooth skin free of cracks, leaks and decay. Never buy sour-smelling figs; they are overripe and starting to ferment.

Once ripe, figs are highly perishable. Keep them for only a day or two in plastic bags in the refrigerator.

Leading varieties of fresh figs include the yellow-green *Smyrna* fig, known as the *Calimyrna* when grown in California; the purple *Mission* fig and thick-skinned *Kadota,* also from California.

Techniques and Recipes

Peeling

Always wash figs well before using them. Although they can be consumed with their skins on, figs are more delicate with them removed. To peel, remove the stem with a small, sharp paring knife. Then cut a shallow cross in the blossom end. Pull away the skin with the point of the knife in the same way as peeling a blanched peach.

Since the fresh, peeled figs have such a fragile texture, they are usually left whole, or halved at most.

POACHED FRESH FIGS

Poached figs are excellent as a dessert served with a raspberry puree and garnished with some fresh mint.

2 POUNDS RIPE, FRESH FIGS, PEELED AND
   LEFT WHOLE, ABOUT 12–18 FIGS
3 CUPS WATER
1 CUP SUGAR, ABOUT 7½ OUNCES

Combine the sugar and water in a 3- to 4-quart saucepan and bring to a boil. Drop the figs in one at a time, taking care not to crowd them in the syrup. Turn off the heat and allow the figs to cool in the syrup.

Holding. If the figs are to be kept more than a few hours before use, hold them in the syrup, covered, in the refrigerator.

Yield. 12–18 poached figs

Mangoes

Mangoes are plentiful almost year round.

The vibrant color, suave texture and peach-and-lemon flavor of a ripe mango compensate for its leathery skin, fibrous flesh and large, hard-to-extract pit.

If the mango is still unripe when purchased, it can be held at room temperature until it softens. Store ripe mangoes in the refrigerator and plan on using them within a day or two.

Although mangoes are cultivated in the United States, over 75 percent of the fruit available fresh comes from Haiti and Mexico. Although some varieties are less fibrous and more flavorful than others, the two most common varieties are the large *Keitt,* which remains green when ripe, and the yellow-orange *Tommy Atkins.* The Keitt in particular is worth looking for, since it combines piquant sweetness with a delightful texture relatively free of fiber.

Mangoes should be well-colored, with the exception of the aforementioned green Keitt. No matter what the variety, the fruit should be aromatic, although not sour-smelling; its skin should be filled out and its flesh should yield gently to pressure, with no mushy areas.

Techniques and Recipes

Paring

The best way to peel and cube a mango is to isolate it from its fibrous pit first. Holding the mango stem-end up, cut it about ½ inch from the stem on either side, yielding two rounded pieces and the flesh-covered pit. Pare the skin from the middle section, then cut the flesh from the pit into cubes. For each remaining rounded piece, score the flesh with a table knife, down to, but not through, the skin. Push the piece inside out, so the cubes spring up and the skin is concave, then cut away the cubes at their base.

Slices can be obtained by cutting the flesh from its center pit area as above, then loosening each entire rounded piece of mango from the skin, as close to the skin as possible. Once pared, the flesh can be sliced into crescents.

MANGO PUREE

Mango puree may be used as a sauce or as the base of a Bavarian cream.

½ CUP WATER
½ CUP SUGAR, ABOUT 3¾ OUNCES
3 TO 4 LARGE MANGOES, ABOUT 2 TO 2½ POUNDS
1 TABLESPOON LEMON OR LIME JUICE
1 TO 2 TABLESPOONS WHITE RUM

Cooking the Syrup. Combine the sugar and water in a small saucepan. Stir well and place over low heat, stirring frequently so that all the sugar dissolves. Bring to a boil, and remove from the heat and cool.

Paring the Mangoes. Cut the flesh from the mangoes close to the pit, then score the flesh against the skin and cut away the cubes.

Preparing the Puree. Puree the mango cubes in the bowl of a food processor until very fine. Gradually add the cooled syrup. Remove from the processor and pass the puree through a fine strainer or sieve if it seems very fibrous. Stir in the lemon or lime juice and the rum.

Holding. Refrigerate the puree, covered, up to 5 days.

Yield. About 2½ to 3 cups

Grapes

Table grapes are available year round in white (actually green), red and black varieties, both seedless and seeded, although they are most plentiful from late summer through late autumn.

Grapes are usually classified as table, raisin, wine, juice, jam or jelly variety. For the most part, pastry making relies on table varieties, sweet and ready to use after rinsing and removing from the stem.

Whatever variety is being selected, grapes should be firmly attached to their stems, which should be green and resilient rather than hard and dried out. The grape's color should be robust, with a minimum of white discoloration under the skin. Avoid grapes that are shriveled, show signs of mold or are excessively sticky (the latter indicating loss of juice and mishandling).

Keep grapes on their stems and unrinsed until just ready to use; loosely wrap in paper towels to absorb excess moisture, then place in a plastic bag and refrigerate. Rinse and drain on paper towels, then stem them.

Most table grapes come from California— *Thompson seedless* are pale green and firm, the largest selling fresh grape in the United States. They are at their sweetest when they are yellow-green in color.

Red Flame seedless and other red varieties are at their best when all the grapes are predominantly red.

Champagne grapes are less widely available than other types of grape. Their appeal is in their sweetness, as well as in their diminutive size, which makes them a delicate garnish in tiny clusters for individual pastries and cakes.

Rhubarb

Rhubarb is primarily a spring fruit, although it is often found from late winter on.

Tangy rhubarb is often paired with strawberries in desserts, so the sweetness of the berries offsets the tartness of the rhubarb. It is always cooked and sweetened before being eaten.

Resembling celery in structure, rhubarb is available in both a pink hothouse variety and a crimson field variety. The field variety is more flavorful and is therefore worth seeking out.

Choose rhubarb as you would celery: Look for colorful stalks with fresh looking leaves and a crisp texture. Avoid stalks that are limp or oversized; limp ones have lost moisture and flavor, while very large, mature stalks will be tough and stringy.

Keep rhubarb refrigerated before use. Although the leaves can be kept on during storage, they *must* be removed before the rhubarb is cooked. The leaves contain *toxic* oxalic acid.

Like celery, rhubarb often has stringy fibers along its sides. If the rhubarb is young and thin, make two crosswise cuts on opposite ends of each stalk; pull these end pieces away, along with their attached strings. If the stalks are tough, mature and large, this destringing will have to be repeated on the other two crosswise ends of each stalk. After stringing, slice each stalk into 2½-inch lengths.

POACHED RHUBARB

2 POUNDS RHUBARB, SLICED INTO $2\frac{1}{2}$-INCH
    LENGTHS
3 CUPS WATER
1 CUP SUGAR, ABOUT $7\frac{1}{2}$ OUNCES

Combine the sugar and water in a 3- to 4-quart saucepan and bring to a full, rolling boil. Turn off the heat, add the rhubarb, cover the pan and allow to cool. If the rhubarb is young and thin, the heat in the syrup will be enough to cook it until it is tender.

If the rhubarb is old and tough, it may be necessary to bring it to a simmer after adding it to the syrup. Be especially careful that the syrup does not start to move at all; if a boil is approached, even tough rhubarb will begin to disintegrate.

Yield. About 2 pounds

Bananas

The familiar yellow banana is available fresh all year long, whereas the more exotic varieties such as the richer flavored red banana and the related cooking plantain are sometimes available in U.S. markets.

Size is not a factor in the richness of the banana's flavor. The firmness and color of the skin are more reliable indicators. Bananas ripen best off the tree, so it is safe to buy them slightly underripe, though not of a deep green. Fruit should be chosen with the stems still on, and the fruit should not be peeled until ready for use. Bananas deteriorate rapidly when exposed to light and air. They may be stored at room temperature until ripe, then will keep in the refrigerator for up to three days. A harmless darkening of the skin occurs in refrigeration.

Dried Fruits

Sometimes dried fruits are added to fresh fruit preparations, such as raisins to a cooked apple filling, to add a touch of sweetness and a different texture. Others, such as prunes and apricots, are also used in cooked fruit compotes and purees.

Store dried fruit, once out of the package, in closed plastic bags or glass jars. For long periods of time, especially in warm weather, store in the refrigerator.

Raisins

Raisins are high-sugar grapes dried by artificial means or sunlight.

The most common raisins in American markets are the *dark seedless raisins* made from Thompson seedless or Sultana grapes and dried in the sun. These are also the best all-purpose raisins.

Golden seedless are also dried Thompson seedless grapes, but they are treated with sulphur dioxide to retain their original color, and dried in artificial heat. They are similar in flavor to the dark variety of raisin, with a bit more tang, but they are more expensive and more processed.

Muscat raisins are made from muscat grapes. They are large and sweet but they are harder to find than the two other varieties, and are more expensive. When available, muscat raisins come with or without seeds.

Currants

Zante currants, or as they are sometimes known, Zante raisins, are made from tiny Zante Corinth grapes. They have a stronger flavor and harder texture than other raisins and should not be used unless specified in a recipe.

Prunes

Prunes are dried plums, packed whole or pitted. The plums used are specifically selected for their high sweetness and ability to remain firm when dried. Most prunes available in this country come from California.

The French *pruneaux d'Agen,* from southwestern France, are particularly good and are available through importers and in specialty stores. These prunes have a vivid fruit flavor and a tender, moist flesh.

As with other dried fruit, prunes should be purchased in a store with a quick turnover of fruit because, even though they are dehydrated, they should still retain some moisture and pliancy. High-quality prunes have a pleasant aroma, shiny skin and vibrant deep blue-black color.

Apricots

Often dried apricots are used instead of fresh in dessert preparations; their intense flavor is achieved by harvesting the apricots at the peak of ripeness. Dried apricots from California have a firm texture and tangy flavor. Imported varieties tend to have a sweeter flavor and a more tender texture.

Techniques and Recipes

Plumped Raisins and Currants

Fast rehydration of raisins and currants is achieved by plumping. Cover the fruit with cold water in a saucepan. Bring to a boil, then drain well. Use immediately, or prepare a quantity in advance and store in a covered jar or plastic container in the refrigerator. The plumped fruit may be flavored with dark rum or brandy: Pack the fruit into a jar or plastic container and add dark rum or brandy to cover. Rehydrating the fruit in water first prevents the use of too great a quantity of liquor, which would give the fruit too strong a taste.

DRIED PRUNES PLUMPED IN TEA

If dried prunes are moist and tender, they need only to be rehydrated in water before they are used in a dessert. If they are more firm and dry, follow the directions for poaching them, below.

1 POUND PITTED, DRIED PRUNES

2 OR 3 CLOVES

1 CINNAMON STICK

1 TEASPOON BLACK TEA TIED IN A SMALL SQUARE OF CHEESECLOTH, *OR* 1 TEABAG (DO NOT USE GREEN OR ANY TYPE OF

FLAVORED TEA, WHICH WOULD NOT BLEND
WELL WITH THE TASTE OF THE PRUNES.)
1 QUART WATER

Place the prunes, with the spices tied in a
small square of cheesecloth, and the tea in a
large bowl. Bring the water to a boil and pour
over the prunes to cover. Allow to stand 10
minutes. Remove the tea, cover the bowl with
plastic wrap and allow to stand until the
prunes are cool. Refrigerate the cooled prunes
and drain well before using. The prunes may
be placed in a covered jar or plastic container
after being drained, then covered with
brandy or Armagnac and kept at a cool room
temperature or refrigerated.

Yield. About 2 pounds

DRIED PRUNES POACHED IN RED WINE

These prunes make an excellent dessert on
their own, sprinkled with a handful of
toasted, sliced almonds or sugared almonds.

1 POUND PITTED, DRIED PRUNES
3 CUPS RED WINE (JUG WINE WILL DO)
3 CUPS WATER
1 CUP SUGAR, ABOUT 7½ OUNCES
2 OR 3 CLOVES
1 CINNAMON STICK
3 OR 4 STRIPS LEMON ZEST

Combine all the ingredients in a 3- to 4-
quart saucepan. (Tie the spices in a square of
cheesecloth for easier removal later on.)

Bring to a boil over medium heat, lower
heat and simmer until the prunes are tender,
about 30 minutes. Cool in the syrup. Drain
and use in desserts.

Yield. About 2 pounds

PLUMPED DRIED APRICOTS

Depending on the type used, the apricots may
be ready to use in a dessert or puree after
plumping. If the apricots are still too firm
after plumping, they should be poached.

1 POUND DRIED APRICOTS
2 OR 3 STRIPS LEMON ZEST
1 QUART WATER

Place the apricots and lemon zest in a large
bowl. Bring the water to a boil and pour it
over the fruit to cover. Cover the bowl with
plastic wrap and allow the apricots to cool in
the water, then refrigerate. Drain well before
using them. If desired, drain and place the
apricots in a covered jar or plastic container,
cover with dark rum or a sweet white wine
and refrigerate.

Yield. About 2 pounds

POACHED DRIED APRICOTS

1 POUND DRIED APRICOTS

3 CUPS DRY, WHITE WINE

3 CUPS WATER

1 CUP SUGAR, ABOUT 7½ OUNCES

2 OR 3 STRIPS LEMON ZEST

Combine all the ingredients in a 3- or 4-quart saucepan. Bring to a boil over medium heat, lower heat and simmer until the apricots are tender, 30 minutes. Cool in the syrup and use for a dessert, or puree after draining. Store in the syrup, in a covered jar or plastic container, in the refrigerator if not to be used immediately.

Yield. About 2 pounds

4

CREAMS, CUSTARDS, MOUSSES AND MERINGUES

All the preparations in this chapter are linked because of their use of cream and/or eggs for structure and richness. Many of them are creams of different types—Ganache, buttercream, mousses, Bavarian creams—meant to be used as desserts in themselves or as fillings and coverings for composite desserts. Others, the meringues in particular, are made into layers and containers which are then filled. Meringues are also used as bases for buttercreams and mousses.

WHIPPED CREAM

When whipping heavy cream, the fat globules consolidate, enabling the cream to thicken and absorb air. The volume of the cream doubles due to the air absorption.

What the cream will be used for determines how stiffly you should whip it.

Lightly whipped cream or Crème Chantilly is an ingredient in such dessert preparations as mousses and Bavarian creams. For this use, only whip the cream until it begins to hold its shape and the whip leaves light traces on the surface of the cream. Sweetened Crème Chantilly is used as an accompaniment to desserts.

Firmly whipped cream, usually sweetened, is used for spreading, filling and covering desserts, as well as for piping. For this use, whip the cream until it holds its shape when the whip is withdrawn. Although the cream should be firm, do not whip it until it separates and is grainy.

Always be sure to have the bowl, cream and whip as cold as possible—warm cream will separate during the whipping. Once the cream is whipped, cover and refrigerate it if not used immediately. Even after a short time in the refrigerator, the cream may thin down due to loss of air and seepage of water. Before using it, rewhip the cream by hand to restore its density.

When the kitchen is very warm, place the bowl, cream and whip in the freezer for about

10 to 15 minutes before whipping. This works equally well for hand- or machine-whipping. If the cream freezes slightly and there are small ice crystals around the edge of the cream where it meets the bowl, they will melt into the cream as you are whipping it and keep it cold.

Whisking Cream by Hand

Pour the cream into a chilled bowl. If the cream is to be sweetened, add 2 TABLESPOONS SUGAR and 1 TEASPOON VANILLA EXTRACT to each cup of cream. Tilt the bowl in one hand, holding it at a 45-degree angle to the work surface, touching the surface closest to you. Holding a balloon whisk or any hand whisk with flexible wires, make a circle through the cream perpendicular to the work surface.

Or place the bowl flat on the surface and move the whisk through it in a figure-eight motion, holding the whisk like a pencil perpendicular to the bottom of the bowl.

For Crème Chantilly, whisk only until the cream begins to hold its shape and the whisk leaves traces on the surface of the cream. For firmly whipped cream, continue whisking

until the cream holds its shape when the whisk is withdrawn.

Always keep the cream smooth-textured. If the cream is whisked to the point that it is grainy, it will separate and spread or pipe poorly.

Whipping Cream by Machine

With a hand mixer, use medium speed and proceed as for hand whisking. Keep the bowl flat on the surface and move the mixer in a circular pattern around the bottom of the bowl. If you hold the mixer too long in one place, the cream will become over-whipped in that area while the rest of the cream will remain liquid.

With a table-model mixer, use the balloon whip on medium speed. Stop the mixer occasionally to check the consistency. Never increase the speed to hurry the cream. This is the easiest way to overwhip it.

Holding. Whipped cream keeps, covered, in the refrigerator for several hours. Rewhip it slightly before using.

Flavored Whipped Cream

Liqueurs are the most practical flavorings to add to the cream before it is whipped: 1 TABLESPOON LIQUEUR is usually sufficient for 1 CUP OF HEAVY CREAM.

For coffee-flavored whipped cream, dissolve 1 TABLESPOON OF INSTANT ESPRESSO COFFEE in 2 TEASPOONS OF HOT WATER; cool completely before adding to the cream.

CHOCOLATE CHANTILLY

This chocolate whipped cream, similar in flavor to Ganache, is more delicate in texture. It is an ideal filling for *choux,* tarts and some molded cakes, where a firm consistency is not needed for support.

  1 POUND BITTERSWEET OR SEMISWEET
    CHOCOLATE, FINELY CUT
  1½ CUPS HEAVY WHIPPING CREAM

Melting the Chocolate. Place the chocolate in a 1-quart bowl and set aside. Bring ½ cup cream to a simmer in a small saucepan over medium heat. Remove from the heat and pour over the chocolate, shaking the bowl once or twice to ensure that the chocolate is covered by the cream. Allow to stand 2 minutes to melt the chocolate. Whisk the chocolate and cream briefly, until smooth. If the chocolate is not completely melted, stir briefly over hot water. Cool to room temperature.

Mixing in the Whipped Cream. Whip the remaining cream lightly, as for Crème Chantilly. Quickly fold the whipped cream into the chocolate mixture. Avoid overmixing or the Chocolate Chantilly will separate.

Holding. Use immediately as a filling, before it sets.

Yield. About 2½ to 3 cups

GANACHE

A rich chocolate preparation, Ganache has a variety of uses, both as a glaze and, whipped, as a buttercreamlike filling and spreading mixture. Since the only ingredients are chocolate and cream, the chocolate must be of the highest quality.

There are a variety of different methods for combining the chocolate and cream, the most practical and successful of which follow.

ORDINARY GANACHE FOR GLAZING

This is a generous quantity for glazing a cake. It is better to have some extra rather than to have not enough to completely cover the cake.

  12 OUNCES BITTERSWEET OR SEMISWEET
    CHOCOLATE, FINELY CUT
  1½ CUPS HEAVY WHIPPING CREAM

Heating the Cream. Place the cream over medium heat in a 2- or 3-quart saucepan. Bring to a full rolling boil.

Melting the Chocolate. Meanwhile, place the chocolate in a 2-quart bowl. Pour the boiled cream over the chocolate and shake the bowl to submerge the chocolate in the cream.

Allow the mixture to stand 2 minutes to melt the chocolate.

Smoothing. Whisk the Ganache gently until smooth. Avoid whisking too much or the Ganache will be full of air bubbles.

Cooling and Glazing. Cool at room temperature. Place the cake or other items to be glazed on a rack over a baking pan to catch the drippings. Pour the Ganache over them.

Yield. About 1½ pounds, enough to glaze two 9- or 10-inch cakes

RICH GANACHE

The increased proportion of chocolate in this Ganache gives it a dense and rich texture. After mixing the chocolate and cream, the Rich Ganache is cooled, then whipped until light, before use as a filling or spreading cream.

1 POUND BITTERSWEET OR SEMISWEET
    CHOCOLATE, FINELY CUT
1⅓ CUPS HEAVY WHIPPING CREAM

Heating the Cream. Place the cream over medium heat in a 2- or 3-quart saucepan. Bring to a full rolling boil.

Melting the Chocolate. Meanwhile, place the chocolate in a 2-quart bowl. Pour the boiled cream over the chocolate and shake the bowl to submerge the chocolate in the cream. Allow the mixture to stand 2 minutes to melt the chocolate.

Smoothing. Whisk gently until smooth. Avoid whisking too much or the Ganache will be full of air bubbles.

Cooling. Use one of the following methods:

1. Leave the Ganache at room temperature until it sets. This may take from 2 to 12 hours, depending on the temperature of the room.

2. Stir the Ganache with a rubber spatula over a bowl of ice water until cool. The Gan-

ache closest to the sides of the bowl will cool very quickly—as the cooled Ganache is stirred into the rest, it will begin to cool it. Scrape the bottom of the bowl often to avoid lumps. Remove the Ganache from the water when cool to the touch but not entirely set.

3. Refrigerate the Ganache, stirring every 5 minutes until it is cool as in Method 2.

Using. Scrape the Ganache into the bowl of an electric mixer and beat with the paddle on medium speed or with a hand mixer, about 1 minute. It will lighten both in color and texture. Avoid overbeating or the Ganache will separate.

Yield. About 1 1/2 pounds, enough to fill or frost a 9- or 10-inch cake

Corrective Measures

1. *The Ganache hardens over ice or in the refrigerator.* Heat the bowl of Ganache slightly over hot water to unmold. Cut into 8 to 10 pieces and place in the bowl of an electric mixer. Heat the bowl over hot water for about 10 seconds—about one fifth of the Ganache should melt. Then beat with the paddle on medium speed until smooth.

2. *The Ganache sets and hardens before the cake has been finished.* Set the bowl containing the Ganache over a bowl of hot water and allow about one fifth of it to melt. Then beat again with the paddle on medium speed until smooth.

3. *The Ganache separates during whipping.* Beat in butter to equal 20 percent of the weight of the Ganache. For this recipe, beat 1 stick of butter until soft and light with the paddle on medium speed. Stop the mixer and scrape down the sides of the bowl. Add the separated Ganache all at once. Beat on medium speed until smooth and light, about 1 minute.

Flavored Ganaches

Liqueur Ganache

Add 2 TO 3 TABLESPOONS LIQUEUR slowly to the Rich Ganache during the whipping after the Ganache has begun to lighten.

Buttered Ganache

This is similar to the method for restoring separated Ganache.

Beat 1 STICK BUTTER in the mixer on medium speed with the paddle until soft and light. Scrape down the sides of the bowl and add all the cooled and unwhipped Rich Ganache. Beat until smooth and light on medium speed, about 2 minutes.

Ganache Praline

Beat together 6 TABLESPOONS BUTTER and 1/2 CUP PRALINE PASTE with the paddle on medium speed. Scrape down the sides of the bowl and add all the cooled and unwhipped Rich Ganache. Beat until smooth and light on medium speed, about 2 minutes.

CRÈME ANGLAISE

Crème Anglaise, one of the most widely used preparations in dessert making, is a rich, delicate custard cream. Composed of milk, cream, sugar and egg yolks, it has a suave and delicate texture. Crème Anglaise may be combined with butter to prepare a rich and elegant buttercream. With the addition of flavoring, it may be used as a sauce for dessert. Or it may be flavored, bound with gelatin and enriched with whipped cream, to make a *Bavarois* or Bavarian cream.

Simple to prepare, Crème Anglaise illustrates one of the most basic foundation techniques of all dessert making, that of liaison or tempering—the process of combining two elements of disparate temperature or consistency so that they blend smoothly, without lumping or separating.

In cooking Crème Anglaise, be careful not to boil it. If the temperature comes close to a boil, the yolks will coagulate and the Crème Anglaise will separate.

VANILLA CRÈME ANGLAISE

¾ CUP MILK

¾ CUP HEAVY WHIPPING CREAM

⅓ CUP SUGAR, ABOUT 2½ OUNCES

½ VANILLA BEAN, SPLIT, *OR* 2 TEASPOONS VANILLA EXTRACT

4 EGG YOLKS

Mixing. Combine the milk, cream, sugar and vanilla bean in a 2-quart saucepan. (Extract, if used, is added later.) Stir to begin dissolving the sugar.

Place the yolks in a 1-quart bowl and whisk, just enough to break them.

Cooking. Bring the milk mixture over medium heat to a full rolling boil. Remove the pan from the heat.

Tempering. Whisk about one third of the boiling liquid into the yolks. Remember to begin whisking before pouring in the hot liquid.

Return the saucepan to medium heat and return the remaining liquid to a full boil.

Whisk the yolk mixture into the boiling liquid. Continue whisking until the cream thickens slightly, about 30 seconds.

There are several signs that the Crème Anglaise has thickened:

1. The increased density can be felt against the whisk.

2. The foam that formed on the surface when the yolk mixture was first added has subsided.

3. A large quantity of steam will emerge from the cream.

Without ceasing to whisk, remove the saucepan from the heat. Immediately pour the Crème Anglaise through a fine strainer into a 1-quart bowl. Rinse and reserve the vanilla bean for another use.

Cooling. Cool the Crème Anglaise quickly over a bowl of ice water, stirring occasionally.

Stir in the vanilla extract, if used.

Holding. Cover the surface directly with plastic wrap. Refrigerate up to 2 days.

Yield. About 2 cups

Other Crème Anglaise Flavorings

Use one of these flavorings instead of the vanilla bean or extract.

Solid Flavorings

⅓ CUP PRALINE PASTE, ABOUT 3 OUNCES
(REDUCE SUGAR IN RECIPE TO ¼ CUP),
OR
ZEST FROM 2 LEMONS REMOVED WITH A
VEGETABLE PEELER OR
ZEST FROM 2 ORANGES REMOVED WITH A
VEGETABLE PEELER OR
¾ CUP FRESHLY SHREDDED COCONUT,
ABOUT 2 OUNCES

Add the solid flavoring to the cold milk, cream and sugar. Bring to a boil over medium heat. Remove from heat; allow to steep 30 minutes, if possible. Strain the liquid, return to a full rolling boil and proceed with the basic recipe.

Chocolate

4 OUNCES BITTERSWEET OR SEMISWEET
CHOCOLATE, FINELY CUT
⅓ CUP WATER

Place the chocolate in a bowl. Bring the water to a boil, pour over the chocolate.

Allow to stand 2 to 3 minutes, then whisk smooth. Whisk the chocolate mixture into the hot Crème Anglaise before straining.

Liquid Flavorings

2 TEASPOONS VANILLA EXTRACT *OR*

3 TABLESPOONS LIQUEUR *OR*

2 TABLESPOONS INSTANT ESPRESSO COFFEE, DISSOLVED IN 1 TABLESPOON OF WATER, BRANDY OR DARK RUM

Beat the liquid into the strained and cooled Crème Anglaise.

Corrective Measures

1. *The milk boils over.* Measure what is left in the saucepan and add milk, cream and sugar proportionately to the amount of liquid missing. For example, if the liquid left is 1 cup, add ½ cup each milk and cream plus about 2 tablespoons of sugar.

2. *The Crème Anglaise curdles.* Immediately pour the Crème Anglaise into a blender or food processor. Process on high speed. Since the eggs have been scrambled, they are harder than they would be otherwise. The cream will therefore be thicker after emulsification and should be treated as cream that is too thick (see *6.* below).

3. *The Crème Anglaise curdles upon standing after cooking.* Proceed as for curdled Crème Anglaise, above.

4. *The solid flavoring is weak.* Compensate by adding liquid flavorings at the end.

5. *The cold Crème Anglaise separates after standing.* Whisk smooth.

6. *The Crème Anglaise is too thick.* Whisk in liquid cream. Bear in mind that the sweetness and flavorings will be diminished. If necessary, add superfine sugar.

7. *The Crème Anglaise is too thin.* This is still usable for Bavarian creams or buttercream.

CRÈME ANGLAISE BUTTERCREAM

This is the smoothest and most delicate of all buttercreams, and also the most perishable. It is made from equal parts of Crème Anglaise and butter.

4 STICKS BUTTER, (1 POUND), SOFTENED

1 BATCH CRÈME ANGLAISE, FLAVORED AND COOLED, 2 CUPS

Mixing. Beat the butter until soft with the paddle on medium speed. Gradually beat in the Crème Anglaise. Continue beating until the buttercream is shiny and smooth.

Holding. Transfer the buttercream to a container. Cover and refrigerate for up to 3 days.

Yield. About 2 pounds

Corrective Measures

1. *The buttercream separates.* Heat it briefly over simmering water—just for 4 or 5 seconds—then continue whipping it.

2. *The buttercream is too thin.* Stir it briefly over ice water. It will probably separate at this point. Proceed as for separated buttercream.

BAVARIAN CREAMS

In his *Guide Culinaire,* Escoffier describes the preparation known as *Bavarois* as a shortened version of *Fromage Bavarois,* Bavarian cheese. The name implies a certain density and firmness. Because it is used for molded preparations—either as a filling for a molded cake or on its own—a Bavarian cream has a denser texture than a mousse, deriving its only aeration from whipped cream, while a mousse is also lightened by whipped eggs.

Bavarian creams are of two types, cream-based and fruit-based. The cream-based is made of a flavored Crème Anglaise bound with gelatin and lightened and enriched with whipped cream. The fruit-based substitutes cooked fruit puree for Crème Anglaise.

Observe these precautions in preparing Bavarian creams:

If the Crème Anglaise, fruit puree base or dissolved gelatin is too cold, the gelatin may lump when the cream is mixed in. To avoid this, make sure that the Crème Anglaise or fruit puree is at room temperature and the gelatin is lukewarm to the touch (100°F to 110°F).

If the mixture with the gelatin is too warm when the whipped cream is incorporated, the cream will melt and separate.

BAVARIAN CREAM —VANILLA OR STRAWBERRY

This recipe serves as a model for all the cream-based Bavarian creams, as well as the fruit-based ones. Other recipes based on both techniques follow. In the variations the flavorings will change, but the gelatin, whipped cream and mixing techniques will remain the same.

Vanilla Crème Anglaise
¾ CUP MILK
¾ CUP HEAVY WHIPPING CREAM
⅓ CUP SUGAR, ABOUT 2½ OUNCES
½ VANILLA BEAN, SPLIT, *OR* 1 TABLESPOON VANILLA EXTRACT
4 EGG YOLKS

Strawberry Puree
2 PINTS FRESH STRAWBERRIES, ABOUT 1¼ POUNDS
¾ CUP SUGAR, ABOUT 5 OUNCES
2 TABLESPOONS KIRSCH
1 TABLESPOON LEMON JUICE

1½ ENVELOPES UNFLAVORED GELATIN, ABOUT 1 TABLESPOON PLUS 1 TEASPOON
¼ CUP COLD WATER
2 CUPS HEAVY WHIPPING CREAM

Preparing the Crème Anglaise. Combine the milk, ¾ cup cream, sugar and vanilla bean, if used, in a 2-quart saucepan. Bring the mixture to a boil over medium heat. Meanwhile, whisk yolks until liquid in a 1-quart bowl. Beat about one third of the milk into the yolks. Return the remaining milk and cream to a boil; begin whisking with a hand whip. Pour in yolk mixture; continue whisking until cream thickens slightly. Strain into a 2-quart bowl and cool to room temperature. Incorporate vanilla extract, if used.

Preparing the Puree. Rinse, hull and thinly slice the berries to help them cook quickly. Place in a 3-quart saucepan with the sugar and stir with a wooden spoon to combine. Place the pan on medium heat and bring to a boil. Lower the heat and simmer until the mixture thickens slightly, about 5 to 10 minutes. Puree the mixture in a blender or food processor. Measure 2 cups of the puree and pour into a 2-quart bowl and cool to room temperature. Stir in the Kirsch and lemon juice.

Melting the Gelatin. Sprinkle the gelatin on the surface of the water in a 1-quart bowl. Allow the gelatin to soften for 5 minutes. Place the bowl over a pan of gently simmering water to melt the gelatin, about 5 minutes. Remove the bowl from the water.

Whipping. Whip the 2 cups cream by machine or hand until it just begins to hold its shape and the whip leaves traces on the surface of the cream.

Assembling. Whisk ½ cup of the Crème Anglaise or fruit puree into the warm, dissolved gelatin. Quickly whisk the tempered gelatin mixture into the remaining Crème Anglaise or puree. Test the temperature to ensure that the mixture has not become warm. If it has, allow it to cool to room temperature. Fold in the whipped cream.

Molding. Immediately use the Bavarian cream as a filling for a charlotte or molded cake. Or pour it into a 1½-quart mold previously rinsed with cold water. Cover with plastic wrap. Refrigerate until set, about 8 hours. (May be refrigerated a day or two at this point.)

Unmolding. Run a small, sharp knife only around the top edge of the mold between the mold and the Bavarian cream. Quickly dip the mold into a large bowl of warm water (about 110°F). Invert a slightly moistened platter over the mold. Invert and shake with a sharp downward movement. Carefully remove the mold.

Holding. Cover loosely with plastic wrap and keep refrigerated until serving time, no more than 5 or 6 hours.

Finishing. Serve the Vanilla Bavarian Cream with a fruit puree, whipped cream or a chocolate sauce. Serve the Strawberry Bavarian Cream with a fruit puree, whipped cream or Crème Anglaise.

Other Cream-Based Bavarian Creams

These are prepared according to the same method as the Vanilla Bavarian Cream. To extract the flavor from solids, bring them to a boil with the milk, cream and sugar; remove from heat and allow them to steep in the milk mixture for about 30 minutes. Return to a boil and proceed with the recipe.

Liquid flavorings are added after the Crème Anglaise has cooled, to prevent loss of flavor due to evaporation.

Chestnut. Halve MILK, HEAVY CREAM, SUGAR, and EGG YOLK in the basic Crème Anglaise. Combine cooled Crème Anglaise with 1 CUP SWEETENED CHESTNUT SPREAD and 2 TABLESPOONS RUM OR KIRSCH.

Coffee. Dissolve ¼ CUP INSTANT ESPRESSO in 2 TABLESPOONS WATER OR LIQUOR, such as dark rum or brandy. Stir into the cooled Crème Anglaise.

Lemon. Add the stripped ZESTS OF 4 LARGE LEMONS to the milk and cream when preparing the Crème Anglaise. Add 2 TABLESPOONS WHITE RUM to the cooled Crème Anglaise.

Liqueur. Stir ¼ CUP LIQUEUR into the cooled Crème Anglaise.

Orange. Add the stripped ZEST OF 3 LARGE ORANGES to the milk and cream while preparing the Crème Anglaise. Add 2 TABLESPOONS ORANGE LIQUEUR to the cooled Crème Anglaise.

Praliné. REDUCE THE SUGAR in the Crème Anglaise TO ¼ CUP. Beat ⅔ CUP PRALINE PASTE into the milk and cream when preparing the Crème Anglaise.

Other Fruit-Based Bavarian Creams

The quantities below are for the fruit, followed by the flavorings added after the fruit puree is cool. Sugar remains the same, except where noted.

Apple. 2 POUNDS GOLDEN DELICIOUS or MCINTOSH APPLES (about 4 or 5); ½ cup sugar; 2 TABLESPOONS APPLEJACK or CALVADOS, 1 TABLESPOON lemon juice, ½ TEASPOON CINNAMON.

Blueberry. 1½ PINTS; 2 TABLESPOONS WHITE RUM, 1 TABLESPOON LEMON JUICE.

Cranberry. 1½ POUNDS; 1 CUP SUGAR; 2 TABLESPOONS ORANGE LIQUEUR or ORANGE JUICE.

Peach or Apricot. 1½ POUNDS (about 6 peaches or 12 apricots); 2 TABLESPOONS DARK OR WHITE RUM.

Pear. 1½ POUNDS (about 3 or 4); 2 TABLESPOONS PEAR WILLIAMS, 1 TABLESPOON LEMON JUICE.

Pineapple. 1½ POUNDS (about ½ pineapple); 2 TABLESPOONS KIRSCH.

Raspberry. 2 PINTS or 2 10-OUNCE PACKAGES FROZEN; 2 TABLESPOONS FRAMBOISE, 1 TABLESPOON LEMON JUICE.

Rhubarb. 1½ POUNDS; 1 CUP SUGAR; 2 TABLESPOONS ORANGE LIQUEUR or ORANGE JUICE.

Corrective Measures

1. *The Bavarian cream does not set.* Chill several hours longer. If this does not help, pour the Bavarian cream into glasses, or layer it with fresh or cooked fruit in glasses. Or, make a fruit salad and use the unset Bavarian cream as a sauce, passing it in a bowl.

2. *The Bavarian cream is too firm.* After unmolding, leave the dessert at room temperature for an hour. The warmer temperature should soften it somewhat.

3. *The Bavarian cream has lumps of gelatin in it.* If the flavor of the Bavarian cream makes it appropriate to do so, serve the dessert with some toasted chopped nuts as a garnish. The gritty texture of the nuts will make the softer lumps of gelatin less obvious.

SABAYON

Sabayon is a foamy preparation of egg yolks, liquid and sugar, cooked together over water until thickened, then beaten until cool. Like Crème Anglaise, Sabayon is used alone as a sauce and also as a base for other preparations, such as mousses and buttercreams.

Sabayon has three preparation stages: mixing, heating and cooling/aerating. Complete each step carefully to avoid losing the smooth, aerated consistency of the Sabayon.

During the mixing and heating stages of this cooking process, the Sabayon is very thin and forms a large amount of foam as it is whisked. As the foam begins to subside, the Sabayon starts to thicken. At this point, it is beneficial to move the bowl from the pan of simmering water from time to time while still continuing to whisk the Sabayon constantly. This will prevent the Sabayon from thickening abruptly and unevenly.

Sometimes used in this warm state as a sauce, the Sabayon has a fresher flavor and a more appealing consistency after it has been whipped until cool. After whipping and aerating, the Sabayon is ready to use as a sauce or as a base for a mousse or buttercream. Whatever the purpose, use the Sabayon immediately or the air will dissipate.

6 EGG YOLKS
½ CUP SUGAR, ABOUT 3¾ OUNCES
½ CUP LIQUID, AS SPECIFIED BELOW

Mixing. Using a hand whip, whisk the yolks until liquid, just enough to break them up in the bowl of an electric mixer. Whisk in the sugar in a slow stream to avoid graining or "burning" the yolks. Then whisk in the liquid, also in a stream.

Heating. Place the bowl over a pan of simmering water and whisk the Sabayon continuously for about 4 minutes until it begins to thicken, leaving a slowly dissolving trail on its surface when the whisk is withdrawn. (Test the consistency of the Sabayon off the heat, to avoid overcooking.) At this point, the Sabayon is lightly thickened.

To use the Sabayon for mousses and buttercreams, cook it longer until it is very thick, about 6 minutes in all, so that the bottom of the bowl can be seen when the whip is drawn through the Sabayon.

Cooling and Aerating. Place the Sabayon in the bowl of an electric mixer fitted with the whip. Whip on medium speed until the Sabayon is cool and increased in volume.

Holding. Use the Sabayon at once.

Yield. About 2 cups

Liquid Flavorings for the Sabayon

Use ½ cup of any of the following:

MARSALA OR OTHER FORTIFIED WINE
DARK RUM OR OTHER DARK SPIRITS
KIRSCH OR OTHER FRUIT ALCOHOL
CHARTREUSE OR OTHER HERB LIQUEUR
ORANGE LIQUEUR OR OTHER FRUIT LIQUEUR
ORANGE JUICE
LEMON JUICE (INCREASE SUGAR IN RECIPE TO ¾ CUP)
DOUBLE-STRENGTH COFFEE OR 3 TABLESPOONS INSTANT ESPRESSO DISSOLVED IN ½ CUP WATER

Corrective Measures

1. *The Sabayon starts to curdle over the heat.* Move the bowl from the heat and whisk very hard. This should produce a fairly smooth consistency. The Sabayon may become *too* thick, but this should not affect the final outcome of the preparation.

2. *The Sabayon is undercooked.* The preparation will be more liquid because the yolks have not thickened completely. It may easily deflate with the addition of other ingredients. This should not affect the Sabayon's performance as a base so adversely as to render it unusable. If time permits, reheat the Sabayon and beat it cool again.

SABAYON BUTTERCREAM

Since a Sabayon is already flavored, buttercream made from it only requires the addition of butter.

1 BATCH SABAYON
3 STICKS BUTTER, ³/₄ POUND, SOFTENED

Mixing. Prepare the Sabayon as above and whip it until cool. Add the butter, divided into 6 or 8 pieces. Continue to whip until the buttercream is thick and smooth.

Holding. Use the buttercream within several hours to prevent a change in consistency. Keep it covered with plastic wrap at a cool room temperature.

Yield. About 3 ¹/₂ cups, 1 ³/₄ pounds

PÂTE À BOMBE

The name of this cream derives from bombe, a two-layered frozen dessert made in a half-sphere mold. The soft whipped paste used for the inner filling is a Pâte à Bombe. This term is used to describe egg yolks beaten with a hot sugar syrup. The heat of the syrup cooks the yolks, aiding in their absorption of a large amount of air.

This process is like that of making Sabayon, except the yolks are sweetened and aerated without the addition of flavorings. Because of this, the Pâte à Bombe is an ideal base for a large amount of basic, unflavored Egg Yolk-Based Buttercream which will have different flavorings added to it later on.

6 EGG YOLKS
¹/₂ CUP SUGAR, ABOUT 3³/₄ OUNCES
3 TABLESPOONS WATER
2 TEASPOONS LIGHT CORN SYRUP OR ¹/₈ TEASPOON CREAM OF TARTAR

Mixing. Place the egg yolks in the bowl of an electric mixer fitted with the whip.

Preparing the Sugar Syrup. Combine the sugar, water and corn syrup or cream of tartar in a 1-quart saucepan. Heat to boiling, wiping the inside of the pan with a brush dipped in cold water. Insert a candy thermometer. After about 3 minutes of boiling, the syrup will thicken somewhat—a sign that it is at the "soft ball" stage. Cook the syrup to the soft ball stage (238°F).

For such a small quantity of syrup, it may be difficult to ascertain the temperature on a candy thermometer. About 3 minutes of boiling over medium heat should bring this quantity of syrup to the proper temperature.

Beating the Pâte à Bombe. When the syrup begins to boil, begin whipping the yolks on medium speed. Continue beating the yolks until the syrup reaches the desired temperature, then pour the syrup in a stream down the side of the bowl, avoiding the whip.

If the syrup touches the whip as it is turning, most of the syrup will be thrown against the sides of the bowl instead of being incorporated into the yolks.

Allow the mixture to continue beating on medium speed until cool, about 5 minutes.

Yield. About 2 cups

EGG YOLK–BASED BUTTERCREAM

This is a base buttercream to which other flavorings can be added, a practical choice if several different flavors of buttercream are needed for different uses.

1 BATCH PÂTE À BOMBE
3 STICKS BUTTER, ¾ POUND, SOFTENED
⅓ CUP FLAVORING, AS SPECIFIED BELOW

Mixing. When the egg yolk mixture is completely cool, beat in the butter, divided into six or eight pieces. Continue beating until the buttercream is thick and smooth. Beat in the flavorings drop by drop.

Holding. Use the buttercream immediately or pack it into a bowl and cover its surface directly with plastic wrap. Refrigerate for 2 to 3 days.

Yield. About 1 pound

Flavoring the Egg Yolk–Based Buttercream

This buttercream is most suitable for citrus or liqueur flavors. Other fruit flavors are best prepared with Egg White–Based Buttercream.

Using approximately *⅓ cup strained citrus juice* or *liqueur,* add the flavoring to the buttercream a very little at a time, beating after each addition. This is crucial because too much liquid added at once will cause the buttercream to separate. Unfortunately, if this happens, heating the buttercream (which often corrects the problem) usually will not work after liquid has been added.

Taste the buttercream to see if the flavor is sufficiently strong. If necessary, add more flavoring, drop by drop, to taste.

Corrective Measures

1. *The Pâte à Bombe is too thin after beating cold.* Use the Pâte à Bombe anyway; or whisk over simmering water, like a Sabayon, until thickened, then beat until cooled.

2. *The Egg Yolk–Based Buttercream separates while adding the flavoring.* Continue adding the remaining flavoring and then remove the separated buttercream from the bowl. Take ½ stick (2 ounces) of butter and beat until soft and light. While continuing to beat, add the separated buttercream, little by little. The buttercream should become firm and smooth again.

MOUSSE WITH SABAYON BASE

This is a versatile method for preparing a mousse from a Sabayon base. The technique for assembly is very similar to that for a Bavarian cream, substituting Sabayon for the Crème Anglaise or fruit puree. Its texture is much lighter than that of a Bavarian cream because the air beaten into the egg base augments that in the whipped cream.

The Mousse derives its flavoring from the liquid used to make the base Sabayon.

Sabayon

½ CUP SUGAR, ABOUT 3¾ OUNCES

6 EGG YOLKS

½ CUP LIQUID, SUCH AS COFFEE *OR* FORTIFIED WINE (SEE PAGE 84)

1½ ENVELOPES UNFLAVORED GELATIN, 1 TABLESPOON AND 1 TEASPOON

¼ CUP WATER

2 CUPS HEAVY WHIPPING CREAM, LIGHTLY WHIPPED

Preparing the Sabayon. Slowly whisk the sugar into the yolks in a stream to prevent burning. Whisk in the liquid and place the bowl over a pan of simmering water, whisking constantly until very thick. Whip by machine until cool.

Mixing. Whisk ½ cup Sabayon into the gelatin. Quickly whisk the mixture into the remaining Sabayon. Test the temperature to ensure that the Sabayon has not become warm. If it has, allow it to cool to room temperature. Fold in the whipped cream.

Molding. Immediately use the Mousse as a filling or pour it into a bowl or individual bowls or glasses. Refrigerate until set, about 3 to 4 hours, loosely covered with plastic wrap.

Holding. Keep the Mousse refrigerated until time to serve it. Plan to use it within 24 hours.

Yield. About 1½ quarts

Corrective Measures

See Bavarian Cream (page 83).

CHOCOLATE MOUSSES

Chocolate mousses, in general, fall into two categories: rich and light. Rich Chocolate Mousse contains butter, which contributes stability and a richer flavor. Light Chocolate Mousse is bound with gelatin and lightened with whipped cream.

They both can be prepared with a Sabayon or Pâte à Bombe base. The Sabayon base is used when extra flavor—such as liqueur or coffee—is desired. Either mousse can be used to fill a charlotte or molded cake, although the Light Chocolate Mousse's consistency will be more delicate and less rich.

Substitute Pâte à Bombe for the Sabayon in the Rich Chocolate Mousse when the extra flavor that the liquid in the Sabayon would impart is not desired.

RICH CHOCOLATE MOUSSE

12 OUNCES BITTERSWEET OR SEMISWEET CHOCOLATE, FINELY CUT

6 TABLESPOONS BUTTER, 3 OUNCES, SOFTENED

½ CUP SUGAR, ABOUT 3¾ OUNCES

6 EGG YOLKS

½ CUP LIQUID (ORANGE JUICE, COFFEE, LIQUEUR)

1 CUP HEAVY WHIPPING CREAM

Melting the Chocolate. Place the chocolate in a round-bottomed 2-quart bowl and place over a pan of water which has been brought to a simmer and removed from the heat. After the chocolate begins to melt, stir with a rubber spatula. Continue stirring until the chocolate is three quarters melted. Remove the bowl from over the water; stir continuously to complete the melting. If some chocolate remains unmelted, return the bowl briefly to the pan of hot water, stirring to complete the melting.

Whisk in the butter, divided into six or eight pieces, until the butter is absorbed smoothly. Set the chocolate mixture aside to cool to room temperature.

Preparing the Sabayon. Slowly whisk the sugar into the yolks in a stream to prevent burning. Whisk in the liquid and place the bowl over a pan of simmering water, whisking constantly until very thick. Whip by machine until cool.

Mixing. When the Sabayon is cold, fold it into the chocolate/butter mixture. Whip the cream by hand or by machine until it is just beginning to hold its shape; fold it into the chocolate mixture.

Holding. Use immediately as a filling for a Chocolate Charlotte or other molded cake. Refrigerate, covered with plastic wrap, until set.

The mousse can also be served on its own in very small portions, accompanied by Crème Chantilly or a liqueur-flavored Crème Anglaise.

Yield. About 1 1/2 quarts

LIGHT CHOCOLATE MOUSSE

12 OUNCES BITTERSWEET OR SEMISWEET CHOCOLATE, FINELY CUT
1/2 CUP BOILING WATER OR HOT COFFEE
1 ENVELOPE UNFLAVORED GELATIN, ABOUT 2 1/2 TEASPOONS
1/4 CUP WATER

6 EGG YOLKS
1/2 CUP SUGAR, ABOUT 3 3/4 OUNCES
3 TABLESPOONS WATER
2 TEASPOONS LIGHT CORN SYRUP OR 1/8 TEASPOON CREAM OF TARTAR
3 TABLESPOONS LIQUEUR (OPTIONAL)
2 CUPS HEAVY WHIPPING CREAM

Melting the Chocolate. Place the chocolate in a round-bottomed bowl. Pour the boiling water over the chocolate and stir it to melt. If the chocolate retains any lumps, place over a pan of water brought to a simmer and then removed from the heat. Stir to melt. Set aside to cool.

Melting the Gelatin. Sprinkle the gelatin over the 1/4 cup of water in a small bowl; allow to stand 5 minutes to soften. Place the bowl over a pan of gently simmering water to clear and melt the gelatin, about 5 minutes. Remove from water and cool slightly till lukewarm.

Preparing the Pâte à Bombe. Place the egg yolks in the bowl of a mixer fitted with a whip. Prepare a Cooked Sugar Syrup, heated to 238°F. Whip the yolks while the syrup boils, then whip the syrup into the yolks. Whip until cold.

Whip the cream until it just begins to hold its shape.

Assembly. Fold the Pâte à Bombe into the chocolate. Fold in the optional liqueur. Whisk about one quarter of the chocolate mixture into the melted gelatin. Then whisk the gelatin mixture into the remaining chocolate. If it feels at all warm to the touch, cool it to room temperature, stirring occasionally. Fold in the whipped cream.

Holding. Use the Light Chocolate Mousse immediately to fill charlottes or molded cakes, or pour the mousse into bowls or glasses. Cover loosely with plastic wrap. Refrigerate until set.

Yield. About 1 1/2 quarts

Corrective Measures

See Bavarian Cream (page 83).

PASTRY CREAM

Pastry cream is one of the great foundation fillings of desserts and pastries. Sometimes used on its own, it is also used as the base for other types of fillings.

All the techniques used in the preparation of Pastry Cream are geared toward having the cream thicken smoothly while preventing it from scorching. In fact, scorching is the greatest potential difficulty in preparing Pastry Cream.

Choosing the proper pan for preparing the Pastry Cream is very important. Select a heavy pan of nonreactive metal. Tin-lined copper, stainless steel-lined aluminum, or heavy enameled iron are the best choices. An all–stainless steel pan is not suitable because it heats unevenly.

To accelerate the process of thickening, the milk is heated with some sugar in advance. This also prevents the milk from scorching.

A liaison is then made between the hot milk and the egg/starch mixture. Here the liaison is used to prevent the starch granules from thickening unevenly.

Unlike some other preparations where the eggs must be handled delicately, eggs in Pastry Cream are a secondary consideration. Eggs combined with starch of any kind will not curdle as easily as eggs on their own.

Either flour or cornstarch can be used as a thickener. I prefer cornstarch because it provides a stable thickening, which permits the pastry cream to be whipped until light without liquefying. Flour-thickened Pastry Cream works well in preparations that add a binder (gelatin) or an enrichment (butter); on its own, it can liquefy if beaten after cooling.

Because Pastry Cream is not a delicate preparation and can be starchy, whipped cream or butter is often added to enrich it. The Pastry Cream is either lightened with whipped cream and bound with gelatin to create a Bavarian cream–like texture, or enriched with butter to make a filling halfway between Pastry Cream and buttercream in texture and richness.

PASTRY CREAM

2 CUPS MILK

⅔ CUP SUGAR, ABOUT 5 OUNCES

¼ CUP CORNSTARCH, ABOUT 1 OUNCE

6 EGG YOLKS

2 TABLESPOONS BUTTER, 1 OUNCE, SOFTENED

2 TEASPOONS VANILLA EXTRACT

FLAVORINGS AS SPECIFIED, SEE BELOW

Mixing. Combine 1½ cups of the milk and all the sugar in a 1½-quart saucepan. Stir once or twice to dissolve the sugar, then place the saucepan over medium heat and bring to a boil.

Pour the remaining milk into a 1-quart bowl and whisk in the cornstarch, then the egg yolks.

Tempering. Whisk about ⅓ cup of the boiling milk into the yolk mixture. If there are any apparent lumps, strain the yolk mixture into another bowl. Return the remaining milk to medium heat and bring to a boil. Begin whisking the milk with a hand whip, then pour the yolk mixture into the milk in a steady stream. The Pastry Cream will begin to thicken immediately.

Cooking. Whisk until the Pastry Cream comes to a boil, taking care that the whip reaches all corners of the pan, to prevent the cream from scorching. Continue cooking while whisking constantly, about 1 minute. Immediately remove the pan from the heat. Add the butter and vanilla; whisk smooth.

Holding. Pour the Pastry Cream into a 1-quart glass or stainless steel bowl. Cover the surface of the Pastry Cream directly with plastic wrap and chill it immediately until cold. Use within 48 hours.

Yield. About 3 cups

If you wish to flavor a whole batch of Pastry Cream, add the appropriate flavoring to the hot Pastry Cream. If you have prepared a large batch, to make several different flavors, flavor the cold Pastry Cream before using it.

Chocolate Flavoring

¼ CUP MILK OR WATER

4 OUNCES BITTERSWEET OR SEMISWEET CHOCOLATE, FINELY CUT

Bring the milk or water to a boil in a 1-quart saucepan over medium heat. Remove from the heat; add the chocolate and stir with a wooden spoon or small hand whip until melted. Beat the chocolate into the hot Pastry Cream after adding the butter and vanilla.

If flavoring the Pastry Cream after it has been cooled, first beat it smooth by hand, then beat in the chocolate mixture.

Coffee Flavoring

1 TABLESPOON INSTANT ESPRESSO COFFEE
1 TABLESPOON WATER OR LIQUEUR, DARK
   RUM OR COGNAC

Combine the coffee and water or liqueur in a 1-cup measure, stirring to dissolve. Add to the hot or cold Pastry Cream as above.

Pralin Flavoring

½ CUP PRALIN POWDER, ABOUT 2 OUNCES
   (SEE PAGE 47)

Beat the pralin powder into the Pastry Cream as above.

Liqueur Flavoring

2 TABLESPOONS LIQUEUR

Beat liqueur into cooled Pastry Cream. (If liqueur is beaten into hot Pastry Cream, the flavor will easily dissipate.)

Corrective Measures

1. *The Pastry Cream is lumpy.* Press it through a sieve.

2. *The Pastry Cream is too thin after cooking.* Treat it as a Bavarian cream base and add gelatin and whipped cream.

PASTRY CREAM LIGHTENED WITH WHIPPED CREAM

1 ENVELOPE UNFLAVORED GELATIN, ABOUT
   2½ TEASPOONS
¼ CUP WATER
1 BATCH CHILLED PASTRY CREAM,
   FLAVORED OR UNFLAVORED, ABOUT 2
   CUPS
¾ CUP HEAVY WHIPPING CREAM

Mixing. Soften gelatin in the water for about 5 minutes. Place over simmering water until the gelatin melts. Place the Pastry Cream in a 1½-quart bowl and stir gently with a rubber spatula until smooth. Whisk one fourth of the Pastry Cream into the melted gelatin and whisk the tempered gelatin back into the Pastry Cream. Quickly fold in the whipped cream.

Use as a filling for pastries made of Pâte à Choux, as the Pastry Cream in the base of a tart, or in puff pastries.

Holding. Use immediately as a filling. Or scrape the Lightened Pastry Cream into a bowl, cover the surface with plastic wrap and refrigerate.

Yield. 3 to 3½ cups, about 1½ pounds

CRÈME MOUSSELINE

2 STICKS BUTTER, ½ POUND, SOFTENED

FLAVORING, SELECT ONE:
½ CUP PRALIN POWDER, 2 OUNCES
½ CUP PRALINE PASTE, 4½ OUNCES
¼ CUP LIQUEUR
3 TABLESPOONS INSTANT ESPRESSO COFFEE
  DISSOLVED IN 1 TABLESPOON WATER OR
  LIQUEUR

1 BATCH CHILLED PASTRY CREAM,
  UNFLAVORED, ABOUT 2 CUPS

Mixing. Beat the butter and flavoring with the paddle on medium speed until it is soft and light. Add the chilled Pastry Cream and continue beating about 5 minutes until very light. Scrape down the sides of the bowl several times to prevent lumps.

Holding. Use the Crème Mousseline immediately as a filling. If it is refrigerated before use, it will become too firm to pipe or spread easily.

Yield. About 3 cups

Corrective Measures

1. *The Crème Mousseline has lumps of butter in it.* Continue beating on medium speed until the Crème Mousseline is smooth.

2. *The Crème Mousseline seems grainy and separated.* Continue beating about 4 to 5 minutes at medium speed and the cream should beat smooth.

3. *The Crème Mousseline remains separated.* Warm the bottom of the bowl briefly (4 or 5 seconds) and continue beating on medium

speed. Repeat if the Crème Mousseline is not smooth. Or, begin with ½ stick (2 ounces) more butter and beat until soft and light, then gradually beat in the separated Crème Mousseline.

MERINGUES

The term meringue is said to be derived from the name Meiringen, a town in Switzerland, where the preparation supposedly originated in the eighteenth century.

True meringues are combinations of egg whites and sugar, usually in the proportion of two parts sugar to one part egg whites (about ¼ cup sugar per egg white). There are several systems for categorizing meringues—according to the degree of cooking or to the manner of mixing the ingredients. I prefer the latter, since it makes the preparation of the different types of meringue easier to understand.

Ordinary Meringue

Sometimes called *French meringue,* this is the most elementary meringue. To prepare, whip the egg whites until they hold a soft peak, then whip in half the sugar. Fold in the remaining sugar by hand, to retain more air in the meringue. Use to make layers or containers that are dried in the oven until they are crisp, then fill them with mousses, buttercreams or combinations of whipped cream and fruit.

In a *nut meringue* and *chocolate meringue* ground nuts and a little cornstarch or cocoa powder are added to the whipped egg whites and sugar along with the second half of the sugar. Use these meringues to make crisp, fragile layers that combine well with buttercreams, either on their own or in combination with sponge cake layers.

Although ordinary meringue variations are good on their own, they are best when used in combination with other types of cake layers which help to tone down their intense sweetness.

Swiss Meringue

In a Swiss Meringue, the egg whites and sugar are whisked gently over simmering water to heat the mixture to about 130°F. The sugar dissolves during the heating, rendering the finished meringue more stable. After heating, the meringue is whipped until cool and increased in volume.

Use this meringue as a base for buttercreams or as a sweetener and stabilizer in fruit mousses. By reducing the sugar slightly, I use this same technique to make meringue for covering such desserts as a Lemon Meringue Pie or the outside of a layer cake. As opposed to buttercream, meringue gives cakes a tailored, finished appearance without adding extra richness.

Italian Meringue

Italian Meringue is made by whipping egg whites with a small quantity of the sugar until they hold a firm peak. Hot syrup is poured over the whipped egg whites and the meringue is whipped until it has cooled.

Although the resulting meringue is similar to that made by using Swiss technique, the Italian Meringue is more "cooked" because of the higher syrup temperature, making it more stable. It is more practical and less time-consuming to use the Italian Meringue technique when making large quantities.

Suggestions for Successful Meringues

1. Separate the eggs carefully so the yolks do not break and enter the whites. The yolks contain fat which is the enemy of whipped egg whites. Little specks of yolk can prevent the egg whites from whipping to the volume necessary for a successful meringue.

2. For the same reason, keep all containers for separating eggs plus the bowl and whip for whipping the egg whites scrupulously clean, dry and free of fat of any kind.

3. Use room-temperature egg whites. Although cold eggs are easier to separate, room temperature or warm egg whites whip more quickly. If you do not have time to let the egg whites come to room temperature, warm the bowl of egg whites, gently whisking over some hot tap water, before beginning to whip them.

4. Use the bowl of a table-model electric mixer or a stainless-steel bowl if using a hand mixer. If you have a copper bowl, use it, although I still recommend using at least the hand mixer, rather than whipping by hand.

ORDINARY MERINGUE

In following particular recipes for meringue desserts, you may find that there is some meringue left. Use the extra to make mushrooms, small meringue shells for serving ices or fruit, or just a few stars or rosettes which make a good addition to a cookie assortment. It is much better to have a little too much meringue—especially if you are working with this type of preparation for the first time—than to have just enough, or worse, not enough.

Remember to have all the pans and any other equipment (pastry bags and tubes) ready before beginning to mix the meringue. This helps avoid loss of air and poor texture in the baked meringue.

6 EGG WHITES, ¾ CUP
PINCH SALT
1½ CUPS SUGAR, ABOUT 11¼ OUNCES

Mixing. Pour the egg whites into a clean, dry bowl. Begin by whipping the egg whites with a mixer set on medium speed. Add the salt and allow the egg whites to whip until

they are white, opaque and begin to hold a soft peak—2 or 3 minutes.

Increase the speed to high and pour in half the sugar (¾ cup) in a very slow stream. This should take about 2 minutes.

The egg whites should retain a dull appearance. If they become shiny, you are adding the sugar too quickly, it is melting too fast and the meringue is losing air. By the time you have added this first part of the sugar, the egg whites should be very stiff, but not dry and separated. Stop whipping.

Incorporating the Remaining Sugar. With a rubber spatula, fold in the remaining sugar, scattering it over the egg whites in three or four additions. Fold quickly but gently to retain as much air as possible.

Holding. Proceed immediately to the piping or shaping of the meringue before it has a chance to lose air from standing.

Yield. Enough to make 2 or 3 9- to 10-inch layers or a large shell and cover

Nut Meringues

Prepared since the early nineteenth century, nut meringues are popular because the flavor of the nuts neutralizes the sweetness of the meringue.

Nut meringues are known by various names—*Succès, Progrès, Japonais, Grillage, Broyage, Dacquoise*—but there is a great deal of disagreement about what distinguishes each type from the others. Rather than use these ambiguous terms, the main recipe and its variations are named according to the kind of nut used.

Nut meringues have a more fragile texture after baking than ordinary meringues, because of the nut's high fat content. This fat can also make mixing the meringue a problem because it has a tendency to break down the structure of the egg whites. For this reason, I like to mix a little cornstarch into the ground nuts and the second half of the sugar. The

starch coats the surfaces of the ground nuts so that the fat is not directly in contact with the whipped egg whites.

ALMOND MERINGUE

Make sure to grind the almonds and have them ready before beginning to whip the egg whites. If the whipped egg whites have to wait for the nut mixture to be ready, they may fall and liquefy and ruin the texture of the baked Almond Meringue.

> 1 CUP WHOLE BLANCHED ALMONDS, ABOUT
> 5½ OUNCES
> 1½ CUPS SUGAR, ABOUT 11¼ OUNCES
> 3 TABLESPOONS CORNSTARCH, ABOUT ¾
> OUNCE
> 6 EGG WHITES, ¾ CUP
> PINCH SALT

Grinding the Almonds. Combine the almonds and half the sugar in a food processor fitted with a metal blade. Finely grind them.

If the mixture processes too long, it will accumulate in a heavy mass in the bottom of the bowl. To prevent this, stop the processor several times during the grinding and scrape the bottom of the bowl, so that the nuts are evenly ground to a fine powder. Pour into a bowl and stir in the cornstarch.

Whipping the Egg Whites. Pour the egg whites into a clean, dry bowl. Begin by whipping the egg whites with a mixer set on medium speed. Add the salt and allow the egg whites to whip until they are white, opaque and begin to hold a soft peak, 2 or 3 minutes.

Increase the speed to high and pour in the remaining half of the sugar (¾ cup) in a very slow stream. This should take about 2 minutes.

The egg whites should retain a dull appearance. If they become shiny, you are adding the sugar too quickly, it is melting too fast and the meringue is losing air. By the time you have added this first part of the sugar, the egg whites should be very stiff, but not dry and separated. Stop whipping.

Incorporating the Almond Mixture. With a rubber spatula, fold in the almond mixture, scattering it over the egg whites in three or four additions. Fold quickly but gently to retain as much air as possible.

Holding. Proceed immediately to the piping or shaping of the meringue before it has a chance to lose air from standing.

Yield. Enough to make 2 or 3 9- or 10-inch layers or a large shell and cover.

Variations

Hazelnut meringue. Substitute 1 CUP (ABOUT 6 OUNCES) BLANCHED OR UNBLANCHED HAZELNUTS for the almonds in the above recipe.

For a Dacquoise, I usually use equal parts of almonds and hazelnuts.

Pecan meringue. Substitute 1¼ CUPS (ABOUT 5 OUNCES) PECAN PIECES and ¼ TEASPOON GROUND CINNAMON for the almonds in the above recipe.

Pistachio meringue. Substitute 1¼ CUPS (ABOUT 5½ OUNCES) BLANCHED PISTACHIOS for the almonds in the above recipe.

Chocolate nut meringue. Substitute 3 TABLESPOONS COCOA POWDER (ABOUT ½ OUNCE) for the cornstarch in any nut meringue.

CHOCOLATE MERINGUE

There are several ways to prepare a chocolate meringue. Some pastry chefs favor the use of a cooked Swiss or Italian meringue, as a base. I have had the best results using an Ordinary Meringue. The slightly reduced amount of sugar here makes the Chocolate Meringue somewhat lighter and compensates for the heavy quality of the added cocoa powder.

Any leftover chocolate meringue makes excellent cookies, either on their own or sandwiched together with some ganache or melted chocolate.

¼ CUP COCOA POWDER, ABOUT ¾ OUNCES
1¼ CUPS SUGAR, ABOUT 9¼ OUNCES, DIVIDED
6 EGG WHITES, ¾ CUP
PINCH SALT

Preliminary Mixing. Sift the cocoa powder through the finest strainer you have, to eliminate any little lumps. Thoroughly combine it with ½ cup of the sugar.

Whipping the Egg Whites. Pour the egg whites into a clean, dry bowl. Begin by whipping the egg whites with a mixer set on medium speed. Add the salt and allow the egg whites to whip until they are white, opaque and begin to hold a soft peak, 2 or 3 minutes. Increase the speed to high and pour in the remaining sugar (¾ cup) in a very slow stream. This should take about 2 minutes.

The egg whites should retain a dull appearance. If they become shiny, you are adding the sugar too quickly, it is too melting fast and the meringue is losing air. By the time you have added this first part of the sugar, the egg whites should be very stiff, but not dry and separated. Stop whipping.

Incorporating the Sugar and Cocoa Mixture. With a rubber spatula, fold in the sugar and cocoa mixture, scattering it over the egg whites in three or four additions. Fold quickly but gently to retain as much air as possible.

Holding. Proceed immediately to the piping or shaping of the meringue before it has a chance to lose air from standing.

Yield. Enough to make 2 or 3 9- or 10-inch layers or a large shell and cover

Piping and Shaping Ordinary Meringue

Large Meringue Disks or Layers
(FOR ORDINARY, NUT OR CHOCOLATE MERINGUE)

Use these as cake layers, either on their own with a filling or in combination with other types of layers, such as Génoise.

Line three 10 × 15-inch pans or cookie sheets with parchment paper. Trace a 9-inch circle on each one, then invert the paper.

Using a pastry bag fitted with a ½-inch plain tube, pipe the meringue in a continuous spiral, starting from the center of the circle. During the piping, hold the pastry bag perpendicular to the pan an inch or two from the surface.

Yield. 3 9- or 10-inch disks

Small Meringue Disks
(FOR ORDINARY, NUT OR CHOCOLATE MERINGUE)

Line two 10 × 15-inch pans or cookie sheets with parchment paper. Trace 3-inch circles on the paper and invert the paper. Pipe out small disks using the same technique as for large disks.

Yield. 12 to 18 small disks

Large Meringue Shell and Cover
(FOR ORDINARY MERINGUE)

Line two 10 × 15-inch pans or cookie sheets with parchment paper. Trace a 9-inch circle on each paper and invert the paper.

Divide the meringue between two pastry bags, placing two thirds of the meringue in one bag fitted with a ½-inch plain tube, and one third of the meringue in the second bag fitted with a ½-inch star tube.

On the first circle, pipe out a disk with the pastry bag fitted with the plain tube, making a continuous spiral starting from the center of the circle. During the piping, hold the pastry bag perpendicular to the pan an inch or two from the surface.

Using the pastry bag fitted with the star tube, pipe out a series of rosettes around the

perimeter of the disk, to form a straight-sided container about 1 inch deep.

On the second circle, pipe out a lattice of diagonally crossed lines, five in each direction, with the plain tube. Use the remaining meringue in the bag fitted with the star tube to pipe out a border of rosettes around the lattice. This will form the container's cover.

To give a chocolate or nut flavor to the meringue, heavily dust the outside with cocoa powder or finely ground nuts before baking.

Yield. 1 9-inch shell and cover

To substitute a nut or chocolate meringue, omit the border of rosettes on the base since it will collapse during baking. The fat in the nuts and cocoa prevents tall shapes from setting.

Meringue Shells
(FOR ORDINARY MERINGUE)

Line two 10 × 15-inch pans or cookie sheets with parchment paper. Trace 3-inch circles on each paper, then invert the paper. Pipe out small disks, using the same technique as for large disks.

Pipe a continuous coil or a series of rosettes

of meringue around the perimeter of each disk, forming containers.

For chocolate or nut flavor. As with the large meringue shell and cover, dust the meringue with cocoa or ground nuts before baking.

Yield. 12 to 15

Meringue Fingers
(FOR ORDINARY, NUT OR CHOCOLATE MERINGUE)

Line two 10 × 15-inch pans or cookie sheets with parchment paper. With a pastry bag fitted with a ½-inch plain or star tube, pipe out 4-inch-long fingers.

Yield. 36 to 48

Meringue Stars and Rosettes
(FOR ORDINARY MERINGUE)

Use these as petits fours, or to decorate other desserts.

Line two 10 × 15-inch pans or cookie sheets with parchment paper. With a pastry bag fitted with a ½-inch star tube, pipe out rosettes.

Yield. About 75

Tiny Meringue Kisses
(FOR ORDINARY, NUT OR CHOCOLATE MERINGUE)

Use these as as petits fours or to decorate other desserts.

Line three 10 × 15-inch pans or cookie sheets with parchment paper. With a pastry bag fitted with a ½-inch plain tube, pipe out small half-spheres or ovals.

Yield. 100 to 150

Mushrooms
(FOR ORDINARY OR CHOCOLATE MERINGUE)

Line two 10 × 15-inch pans or cookie sheets with parchment paper. Fill a pastry bag fitted with a ½-inch plain tube. Holding the bag perpendicular to the pan, about 1½ inches from the surface, pipe out ½-inch half-spheres on one sheet. Release pressure after piping out each half-sphere, twisting the bag away from the "cap" so as not to leave a point.

Holding the bag in the same position, pipe out "stems" onto a second sheet. From a 1- or 1½-inch height, squeeze the bag, then lift it from the pan.

After baking the caps and stems, join them together with some buttercream or Ganache.

Yield. 25 to 30

Baking Ordinary Meringue

Baking ordinary meringue can present a problem because most ovens do not have a setting low enough to prevent the meringue from taking on color. The best meringue is pure white, crisp and light, with a fragile texture that makes it easy to cut or bite into after baking.

One method is to set the oven at the absolute lowest setting and allow the meringue to dry for 1½ to 2 hours, checking to see that it does not take on any color. Move the pans around at 20 minute intervals, changing shelves and revolving them back to front for even baking.

Or, preheat the oven to 250°F. Place meringue in the oven. Bake for 15 minutes, then turn off heat without opening the door. Let dry for 6 to 8 hours. Be careful when using an oven with a pilot light; it may continue to heat enough to color the meringue even after the oven is off.

Baking Nut and Chocolate Meringues

These are baked at a higher temperature, 300°F, and will take on some color during baking. The higher temperature sets the meringue more quickly, before the fatty elements in the nuts or cocoa have enough time to break down the air cell structure, making the meringue fall. This might result in a meringue with a dense, heavy texture.

Bake Nut and Chocolate Meringues at 300°F about 30 minutes. Be sure to change the positions of the pans once or twice so the meringues bake evenly.

Cooling Baked Meringues

Slide the meringues, still on the paper, from the pans to wire racks. Cool at room temperature.

Holding. Leave the meringues on paper for holding. Wrap them loosely in plastic wrap or pile the sheets of cooled meringues gently on each other on a pan and slide into a plastic bag; store at room temperature. Leaving the meringues on paper allows them to be easily slid onto a pan and into the oven for crisping about 15 minutes at the lowest temperature, if necessary.

Meringues which do not release from the paper are underdone and should be returned to the oven, for at least 30 minutes, set at the lowest temperature.

Swiss Meringue

This method of heating the whites and sugar together, then beating them, makes a very stiff meringue. Used mainly as a base for buttercream, Swiss Meringue can also be used for covering a cake or tart.

As a base for buttercream, the weight of the sugar in the meringue is equal to two times the weight of the egg whites (about ¼ cup sugar per egg white).

When used for a covering, the quantity of sugar is reduced to produce a meringue that is less sweet, as well as less stiff.

SWISS MERINGUE BUTTERCREAM

4 EGG WHITES, ½ CUP
1 CUP SUGAR, 7½ OUNCES
3 TO 4 STICKS BUTTER, ¾ TO 1 POUND, SOFTENED

Mixing. Place the egg whites and sugar in the bowl of an electric mixer. Whisk to combine. Place the bowl over a pan of simmering water. Whisk gently until the sugar dissolves completely (there should be no gritty feeling when you rub some of the mixture between your thumb and index finger), and the egg

whites are uniformly hot (about 130°F).

Whipping. Remove the bowl from the pan to the electric mixer fitted with the whip, or use a hand mixer. Whip on medium speed until the meringue is cool and increased in volume. Swiss Meringue should be stiff, but not dry and clotted.

Adding the Butter. When the Swiss Meringue is completely cold, add the butter, divided into 2-tablespoon pieces, one piece at a time. The amount will depend on the flavoring used (see below). If you are using a table-model mixer, switch to the paddle. If you are using a hand mixer, use the lowest speed. Continue beating until smooth.

The buttercream may separate during the mixing. Continue mixing until the butter is fully absorbed and the buttercream appears thick and shiny. Scrape down the sides of the bowl thoroughly. Then continue beating 1 or 2 minutes longer, to ensure smoothness. Add any flavorings at this point, or flavor the buttercream just before using it.

Holding. Meringue buttercream can be held for several hours at a cool temperature or refrigerated up to 1 week. If the buttercream is prepared in advance, add flavorings only at the time of use.

Yield. 1 1/2 to 1 3/4 pounds, depending on the quantity of butter used

Flavoring Swiss Meringue Buttercream

The quantity of butter added to a meringue to prepare a buttercream varies according to the way the buttercream will eventually be flavored. (See the chart on page 102.) In general, the more butter added, the less sweet the buttercream will be.

To prevent the buttercream from separating or becoming too thin due to the addition of liquid, use the larger amount of butter for liquid flavorings such as brandies and liqueurs.

Use the smaller amount of butter for sharp liquid flavorings such as acidic lemon juice or bitter coffee, so the buttercream is sweeter and able to offset the strong character of the flavorings. Because these sharp flavorings are more intense than other liquid flavorings, less is added to the buttercream, minimizing the risk of its thinning or separating.

For very sweet flavorings such as Praline Paste, use the larger amount of butter.

FLAVORING MERINGUE BUTTERCREAMS

	3 Sticks Butter (¾ Pound)	4 Sticks Butter (1 Pound)
Chocolate		4 ounces bittersweet or semisweet chocolate melted with ¼ cup water
Coffee	2 tablespoons instant espresso dissolved in 2 tablespoons liqueur	
Lemon	⅓ cup juice	
Liqueur		3 tablespoons
Orange		⅓ cup juice +1 teaspoon finely grated zest
Praline Paste		⅓ cup
Raspberry		½ cup cooked sweetened puree
Vanilla extract		1½ tablespoons

Swiss Meringue for Covering

Heating the egg whites and sugar makes a stable covering meringue—one that is less likely to separate and leak moisture on the pie, tart or cake on which it is spread than a meringue where sugar is whipped into raw egg whites.

4 EGG WHITES, ½ CUP
¾ CUP SUGAR, ABOUT 5¾ OUNCES
CONFECTIONERS' SUGAR FOR DUSTING

Follow the *mixing* and *whipping* instructions for Swiss Meringue Buttercream, reducing the sugar to ¾ cup.

Use this meringue to spread or pipe over items to be covered, being sure the items are cool, if possible.

Dust the meringue thoroughly with confectioners' sugar. Place on a baking pan and into a hot oven (400°F) just until the meringue colors, about 5 minutes.

Yield. Enough to cover a 9- or 10-inch pie or tart, or a 9-inch layer cake

ITALIAN MERINGUE

Italian Meringue is a stable covering. It is also the only type of meringue which can be prepared in advance, covered and refrigerated for up to one week, to be used as needed.

When Italian Meringue is prepared, egg whites are beaten with a small amount of sugar. The remaining sugar is incorporated into the egg whites in the form of a hot syrup. The key to success with Italian Meringue is to coordinate the steps in a logical time sequence so that the egg whites are beaten to the necessary degree of stiffness at the same time the syrup is ready.

Cooked Sugar Syrup

¾ CUP SUGAR, ABOUT 5¾ OUNCES

⅓ CUP WATER

⅛ TEASPOON CREAM OF TARTAR

4 EGG WHITES, ½ CUP

¼ CUP SUGAR, ABOUT 1¾ OUNCES

Preparing the Syrup. Combine the sugar, water and cream of tartar in a 1-quart heavy saucepan. Bring to a boil over low heat, wiping the inside of the pan with a brush dipped in cold water. Skim any foam from the surface.

Beating the Egg Whites. When the syrup begins to boil, begin whipping the egg whites. Place them in the bowl of an electric mixer fitted with the whip. Whip on medium speed until they are white and opaque. Increase speed to maximum. Whip in the ¼ cup sugar in a steady stream. Reduce speed to medium and continue whipping until the syrup reaches the soft ball stage, about 238°F. Pour the syrup in a steady stream down the side of the bowl. Avoid having the syrup hit the whip, which would splatter it on the side of the bowl and not into the egg whites. Continue whipping the meringue on medium speed until it is cool.

Holding. Use the Italian Meringue immediately as a base for a buttercream like Swiss Meringue as on pages 100-101 or as a covering, page 102. Or, scrape the meringue into a clean bowl, cover the surface with plastic wrap and refrigerate it for up to 1 week.

Yield. About 4 to 5 cups

MERINGUE DESSERTS

LEMON RASPBERRY MERINGUE

The sharpness of the Lemon Sabayon Buttercream acts as a perfect foil to the sweetness of the meringue. The freshness of the raspberries also complements the other two flavors.

Ordinary Meringue Layers

4 EGG WHITES, ½ CUP

PINCH SALT

1 CUP SUGAR, ABOUT 7½ OUNCES

Lemon Sabayon Buttercream

4 EGG YOLKS

⅓ CUP LEMON JUICE

½ CUP SUGAR, ABOUT 3¾ OUNCES

2 STICKS BUTTER, ½ POUND, SOFTENED

2 HALF PINTS FRESH RASPBERRIES

Preparing the Meringue Layers. Whip the egg whites with the salt until white and opaque, incorporating half of the sugar. Fold in the remaining sugar and pipe into two 9-inch disks on paper-lined 10 × 15-inch pans. Bake the disks at the lowest possible temperature until dry. Cool on paper on a wire rack.

Preparing the Buttercream. Combine the yolks, lemon juice and sugar, and whisk over simmering water until thickened. Whip by machine until cold and increased in volume. Whip in the butter, 2 tablespoons at a time.

Assembling the Dessert. Cut a piece of cardboard to a 9-inch diameter. Trim each of the meringue disks to an even 9-inch diameter, with the point of a sharp paring knife, using the cardboard as a guide. Place a dab of buttercream on the cardboard disk. Affix one of the meringue disks to it, flat-side down. Spread ½ cup of the buttercream evenly on the meringue disk, spreading it to the edge. Scatter less than half the raspberries on the buttercream and press them gently. Top with the other meringue disk, flat-side up. Press to adhere. Spread the top and sides evenly with buttercream, reserving ½ cup of the buttercream for decorating the dessert.

Finishing the Dessert. Place the reserved buttercream in a pastry bag fitted with a star tube; pipe out a border around the top edge of the dessert. Fill in the remaining area on top of the dessert with the raspberries. Crush any scraps from trimming the disks for decorating the sides of the dessert, pressing them to adhere.

Chill the dessert until the buttercream is firm, about 1 hour.

Holding. Keep the dessert refrigerated, loosely covered with plastic wrap, up to 8 hours.

Yield. About 10 portions

CHOCOLATE RASPBERRY MERINGUE

Covering the outside of a chocolate meringue dessert with small meringue pieces is remotely based on Gaston Le Notre's *Concorde,* although techniques, shape and flavors used here differ widely from the standard *Concorde.*

Chocolate Meringue Disks and Decoration
2 CUPS SUGAR, ABOUT 1 POUND
¼ CUP COCOA POWDER, ABOUT ¾ OUNCE
8 EGG WHITES, 1 CUP
PINCH SALT

Raspberry Swiss Meringue Buttercream
½ PINT FRESH RASPBERRIES OR 1 10-OUNCE
   PACKAGE FROZEN RASPBERRIES IN SYRUP
¼ CUP SUGAR, ABOUT 1¾ OUNCES
¼ CUP WATER

1 CUP SUGAR, ABOUT 7½ OUNCES
4 EGG WHITES, ½ CUP
2 STICKS BUTTER, ½ POUND, SOFTENED

3 TABLESPOONS FRAMBOISE OR RASPBERRY
   LIQUEUR

CONFECTIONERS' SUGAR

Preparing the Meringue Disks. Sift half of the sugar with the cocoa powder. Whip the egg whites with the salt, incorporating the remaining sugar. Fold in the cocoa mixture. Pipe out the meringue into two 9-inch disks on two paper-lined 10 × 15-inch pans or cookie sheets. Use the remaining meringue to pipe out tiny meringue kisses. Bake at 300°F for about 30 minutes or until dry. Cool on paper on racks.

Preparing the Puree. Combine the raspberries, ¼ cup sugar and water in a 1-quart saucepan. Bring to a boil over medium heat. Cook until slightly thickened, about 5 minutes. Puree the raspberries, then strain to eliminate the seeds. Cool the puree.

Preparing the Buttercream. Combine the 1 cup sugar with the egg whites in the bowl of an electric mixer and whisk over simmering water until the sugar dissolves and the egg whites are hot. Whip the meringue cool by machine. Incorporate the butter, 2 tablespoons at a time.

Whip the puree gradually into the buttercream, scraping down the sides of the bowl several times; continue beating until the buttercream is smooth, then beat in the liqueur.

Assembling the Dessert. Cut a 10-inch disk from cardboard. Trim each chocolate meringue disk to a 9-inch diameter with the tip of a sharp paring knife.

Place a dab of buttercream on the cardboard disk and affix one of the chocolate meringue disks to it, flat-side down. Spread the meringue disk evenly with 1 cup of the buttercream, spreading it to the edge. Top with the second meringue disk, flat-side up. Press to adhere. Spread the top and sides of the dessert evenly with the remaining buttercream. Adhere the tiny meringue kisses to the buttercream all over the top and sides. Dust the top and sides lightly with the confectioners' sugar.

Holding. Refrigerate until the buttercream sets, about 1 hour.

Yield. About 10 to 12 portions

VIENNESE MERINGUE TORTE

The combination of strawberries and cream with meringue echoes a classic Viennese dessert, the *Spanische Windtorte.* The filling can be varied with other fruit, alone or in a combination like peaches and blueberries.

Meringue Shell and Cover

6 EGG WHITES, ¾ CUP
PINCH SALT
1½ CUPS SUGAR, ABOUT 11¼ OUNCES

1½ CUPS HEAVY WHIPPING CREAM
¼ CUP SUGAR, ABOUT 1¾ OUNCES
2 TEASPOONS VANILLA EXTRACT

2 PINTS STRAWBERRIES

Preparing the Meringue Shell and Cover. Whip the egg whites with the salt until white and opaque, incorporating half the sugar. Fold in the remaining sugar and pipe out one container and one lattice cover on two paper-lined 10 × 15-inch pans. Bake at the lowest possible temperature until dry. Cool on paper on a rack.

Preparing the Filling. Combine the cream with the sugar and vanilla and whip until it holds a firm peak.

Preparing the Fruit. Reserve 8 strawberries for a decoration. Rinse, hull and slice the remaining berries.

Assembling the Dessert. Place the meringue container on a piece of cardboard or a serving plate. Spread half of the whipped cream in the bottom of the container. Top with the sliced berries, spreading them flat and even.

Top with the remaining whipped cream, spreading it flat and even. Place the meringue cover on the top.

Finishing the Dessert. Slice the reserved berries in half through the hulls. Arrange, cut-side up, in the interstices of the lattice.

Holding. Chill the dessert several hours to mellow it. Serve within 3 or 4 hours.

Yield. 10 to 12 portions

Viennese Chocolate Meringue Torte

After piping the base and cover, dust them very lightly with cocoa powder, using no more than a teaspoon of cocoa in all. Cocoa should appear like droplets on the surface. Fill the baked and cooled meringue shell with Rich Chocolate Mousse (see page 87). Place meringue cover on top. Refrigerate. May be prepared a day ahead. Wrap well in plastic and chill.

DACQUOISE

Although no one seems to agree on what constitutes the standard Dacquoise, it remains one of the great classic meringue desserts.

Usually composed of nut meringue disks sandwiched with buttercream, there are many variations for finishing the outside of the Dacquoise. I like this version which leaves the top meringue disk uncovered to show the spiral pattern of the piping.

This recipe calls for a coffee buttercream, but you can substitute one flavored with praline paste or dark rum.

Meringue Layers

⅓ CUP WHOLE BLANCHED ALMONDS, ABOUT 1¾ OUNCES

⅓ CUP WHOLE UNBLANCHED HAZELNUTS, ABOUT 1¾ OUNCES

1 CUP SUGAR, DIVIDED, ABOUT 7½ OUNCES

2 TABLESPOONS CORNSTARCH, ABOUT ½ OUNCE

4 EGG WHITES, ½ CUP

PINCH SALT

Coffee Buttercream

3 EGG WHITES, 6 TABLESPOONS

⅔ CUP SUGAR, 5 OUNCES

2½ STICKS UNSALTED BUTTER, SOFT, 10 OUNCES

2 TABLESPOONS INSTANT ESPRESSO COFFEE

2 TABLESPOONS RUM OR BRANDY

CONFECTIONERS' SUGAR FOR FINISHING

½ CUP TOASTED SLICED ALMONDS *OR* TOASTED HAZELNUTS, SKINS RUBBED OFF AND CHOPPED, FOR FINISHING

Preparing the Meringue Layers. Combine the almonds, hazelnuts and half of the sugar in the food processor and pulse repeatedly until the mixture is a fine powder. Pour the ground mixture into a 1-quart bowl and stir in the cornstarch.

Whip the egg whites with salt until white and opaque, incorporating the remaining half of the sugar. Whip until the whites hold a firm peak. Remove from the mixer and fold in the nut and sugar mixture by hand. Pipe out two 9- or 10-inch disks and bake at 300°F about 30 minutes, until crisp and golden. Cool on a rack.

Preparing the Buttercream. Combine the egg whites and sugar in the bowl of an electric mixer and whisk over a pan of simmering water until the egg whites are hot and the sugar is dissolved. Whip the meringue cool. Incorporate the butter 2 tablespoons at a time. Combine the instant coffee and liquor until dissolved and slowly whip into the buttercream.

Assembling the Dacquoise. Trim each meringue layer to an even 9- or 10-inch diameter. Place a dab of the buttercream on a 9- or 10-inch cardboard round and place one of the meringue disks on it, flat-side down. Spread with ¾ of the buttercream. Place the other meringue disk on the buttercream and press down so the layers adhere.

Use the remaining buttercream to cover the side of the Dacquoise. Be careful not to spread any of the buttercream on top of the dessert.

Dust the top lightly with the confectioners' sugar and press the almonds or hazelnuts against the side.

More Ideas for Meringue Variations

Assemble two meringue disks together using any sharp-tasting buttercream, such as raspberry, cassis or lemon.

A variety of miniature versions of the meringue disks with lemon buttercream and fresh raspberries, the chocolate meringue and raspberry buttercream, and the Dacquoise can be made, using the techniques for the larger meringue disks.

Meringue shells make elegant containers for sherbets or mousses. A decoration made from the fruit used in the sherbet or the mousse is appropriate, as is a fruit puree or dark chocolate sauce placed under the meringue shell on the plate.

Meringue disks or layers are used to great advantage in combination with other kinds of cake layers, where they offer interesting contrast of texture and appearance. Some meringue layers will be used later on in the construction of different kinds of cakes.

5

PÂTE À CHOUX

Cream puff pastry, known as Pâte à Choux (the name derives from the old French meaning "to cherish"; *petit chou* is often a term of endearment), is among the most classic of pastries. In use since the sixteenth century, it is still popular today.

The only pastry dough that is cooked before being baked, Pâte à Choux starts with a *panade*—a cooked mixture of water, butter and flour. Eggs are then beaten into the *panade,* thinning it out and contributing leavening power. During baking, the Pâte à Choux rises due to steam expansion: the paste crusts on the outside, trapping steam inside, causing the pastry to expand until the starches in the flour and proteins in the egg coagulate. The pastry retains its puffed shape, with a hollow interior.

Used to fashion crisp, light shells which are then filled with a variety of creams, the texture of the baked Pâte à Choux is a perfect contrast to the creamy fillings.

Cream puff pastries are often finished with a glaze which enhances their appearance as well as their flavor.

Pâte à Choux is one of the simplest pastries to prepare. Because of this, it is often the first kind of pastry that an apprentice makes alone. Despite its simplicity, adherence to a few fine points is important.

1. Cook the *panade* carefully so that it becomes smooth and just begins to stick to the pan. Undercooking may result in an uneven mixing of the ingredients, while overcooking will cause it to separate and the fat to ooze out.

2. Be careful in adding the eggs. Too many liquefy a Pâte à Choux, making it difficult to pipe and unable to hold its shape when baked.

3. Pipe and bake the just-cooked dough as quickly as possible. Placing the dough in the oven while still warm ensures the greatest expansion and lightness.

4. Bake the paste until it is crisp and fairly dry. Underbaking can result in *choux* that will collapse when removed from the oven.

Pâte à Choux offers an excellent opportunity to practice piping with a pastry bag. Since the piped shapes expand, almost doubling in size during baking, little shape irregularities are hardly visible.

Used for both sweet and savory pastries, the following recipes and variations illustrate the versatility of the Pâte à Choux.

PÂTE À CHOUX

This is a general recipe for Pâte à Choux. The quantities given here will be used in most of the recipes in this chapter; some recipes call for less, depending on the nature of the finished product. Do not be alarmed if a particular recipe calls for different quantities of the ingredients for the Pâte à Choux; the proportions of the ingredients' weight are the same.

¾ CUP COLD WATER

6 TABLESPOONS BUTTER, 3 OUNCES

PINCH SALT

1 CUP UNBLEACHED ALL-PURPOSE FLOUR, ABOUT 5 OUNCES

4 LARGE EGGS

Mixing and Cooking the Pâte à Choux. Combine water, butter and salt in a 2-quart saucepan and place it over medium heat. Cook, stirring occasionally with a wooden spoon, until the butter melts and the liquid comes to a full rolling boil.

Mixing the Flour into the Paste. Remove the saucepan from the heat and sift in the flour all at once. Beat with a wooden spoon until smooth.

Cooking the Paste. Return the saucepan to the heat and cook, beating constantly with a spoon, until the mixture holds together and begins to leave the side of the pan. The bottom of the pan will be lightly filmed with the paste. To avoid overcooking the paste and letting the fat separate out, beat over heat only 1 to 2 minutes, then remove from heat.

Slightly Cooling the Paste. Transfer the paste to a 2- to 3-quart bowl or the bowl of an electric mixer. Beat the paste either by hand with a

Using the Pâte à Choux. Proceed as quickly as possible to piping the Pâte à Choux, so it is still warm when it enters the oven. This will ensure the greatest expansion and lightness.

Yield. About 3 cups

CHOUX À LA CRÈME

Large puffs filled with whipped cream or a combination of whipped cream and fruit are the simplest *choux* pastries. Despite their simplicity, the Choux à la Crème are extremely delicate—the sweetness of the cream emphasizes the light, buttery flavor of the pastry.

Pâte à Choux
> ¾ CUP WATER
> 6 TABLESPOONS BUTTER, 3 OUNCES
> PINCH SALT
> 1 CUP UNBLEACHED ALL-PURPOSE FLOUR,
>   ABOUT 5 OUNCES
> 4 EGGS

Egg Wash
> 1 EGG
> PINCH SALT

Whipped Cream
> 1½ CUPS HEAVY WHIPPING CREAM, VERY
>   COLD
> 3 TABLESPOONS SUGAR, ABOUT 1½ OUNCES
> 1½ TEASPOONS VANILLA EXTRACT

CONFECTIONERS' SUGAR FOR DUSTING

Making the Pâte à Choux. Over medium heat, bring the water, butter and salt to a boil in a

wooden spoon or by machine with the paddle on lowest speed, 1 minute, or until slightly cooled.

Incorporating the Eggs. Beat in the eggs, one at a time. To prevent the paste from separating, be sure to incorporate each egg completely before adding the next.

saucepan. Remove from the heat and stir in the flour all at once. Return to the heat and cook the paste, beating with a wooden spoon, 1 to 2 minutes. Remove the paste to a bowl, beat to cool slightly, then beat in the eggs one at a time.

Piping. Using a ½-inch plain tube, pipe the Pâte à Choux on paper-lined baking pans. Hold the bag perpendicular to, about 1 inch above, the pan and pipe 1½-inch-round *choux,* then release the pressure and gently pull the tube away. Pipe the *choux* 2 inches apart, making 18 to 20 in all.

Making the Egg Wash. Beat the egg and salt together, then gently brush the tops of the *choux* with the egg wash, smoothing over any points left from the piping.

Baking. Bake the *choux* at 425°F until well-risen and beginning to color, about 10 minutes. Lower the temperature to 350°F and continue baking until well-colored and dry, about 20 minutes. Test a *chou* by breaking one open to be sure the inside is dry.

Whipping the Cream. Whip the cream with the sugar and vanilla until it holds a firm peak.

Assembling. Cut off the top third of each *chou* with a sharp, serrated knife. Line up the bottoms on a pan and, using a star tube with a ½-inch opening, pipe in the whipped cream. Allow the cream to extend about 1 inch over the top of the pastry. Dust the tops with confectioners' sugar and place them on the whipped cream.

Holding. Fill the *choux* as close as possible to serving time, no longer than 1 hour.

Yield. 18 to 20

Choux aux Fruits

Fill the bottom of each *chou* with raspberries or sliced strawberries before piping in the whipped cream. Do not dust the tops with sugar before replacing them. After replacing the tops, pipe a small rosette of whipped cream on top and decorate with a raspberry or small strawberry.

TRUFFLES

A chocolate-filled *chou* rolled in chocolate shavings is a rich little morsel that I learned to prepare at the Réserve de Beaulieu, a lovely resort hotel between Nice and Monaco on the Côte d'Azur, where I worked in 1974.

Pâte à Choux

¾ CUP WATER

6 TABLESPOONS BUTTER, 3 OUNCES

PINCH SALT

1 CUP UNBLEACHED ALL-PURPOSE FLOUR, 5 OUNCES

4 EGGS

Egg Wash
1 EGG
PINCH SALT

Ganache
½ CUP HEAVY WHIPPING CREAM
4 OUNCES BITTERSWEET OR SEMISWEET
    CHOCOLATE, FINELY CUT

Chocolate Chantilly
¾ CUP HEAVY WHIPPING CREAM
8 OUNCES BITTERSWEET OR SEMISWEET
    CHOCOLATE, FINELY CUT

2 CUPS BITTERSWEET OR SEMISWEET
    CHOCOLATE SHAVINGS
CONFECTIONERS' SUGAR FOR DUSTING

Making the Pâte à Choux. Over medium heat bring the water, butter and salt to a boil in a saucepan. Remove from the heat and stir in the flour all at once. Return to the heat and cook the paste, beating with a wooden spoon, 1 to 2 minutes. Remove the paste to a bowl, beat to cool slightly, then beat in the eggs one at a time.

Piping. Using a ½-inch plain tube, pipe the Pâte à Choux on paper-lined baking pans. Hold the bag perpendicular to, and about 1 inch above, the pan and pipe 1½ inch *choux,* then release the pressure and gently pull the tube away. Pipe the *choux* 2 inches apart, making 18 to 20 *choux* in all.

Making the Egg Wash. Beat the egg and salt together and gently brush the tops of the *choux* with the egg wash, smoothing over any points left from the piping.

Baking. Bake the *choux* at 425°F until well-risen and beginning to color, about 10 minutes. Lower the temperature to 350°F and continue baking until the *choux* are well-colored and dry, about 20 minutes. Remove to a rack to cool.

Preparing the Ganache. Bring the cream to a boil in a small saucepan and pour it over the chocolate in a bowl. Allow to stand 2 minutes or so and whisk smooth. Strain and cool.

Preparing the Chocolate Chantilly. Heat ¼ cup of the cream to a simmer. Pour over the chocolate in a bowl. Allow to stand 2 minutes, then whisk smooth. Cool to room temperature. Whip the remaining cream lightly. Fold it into the chocolate mixture.

Assembling. Using a plain tube with a ¼-inch opening, pierce the bottom of each *chou.* Fit a pastry bag with the same tube, fill with the Chocolate Chantilly, then fill the *choux.* Using one hand, dip the palm into the cooled Ganache. Smear the Ganache all over the outside of each truffle, then set on a rack.

Place the chocolate shavings on a paper-lined baking pan and, using two forks, pick up the truffles and roll them in the chocolate shavings, one at a time, so that the shavings adhere to the Ganache.

Remove the truffles to another pan and dust them very lightly with confectioners' sugar.

Holding. Refrigerate 4 to 5 hours, loosely covered with plastic wrap.

Yield. About 18

White Truffles

Roll the truffles in 2 CUPS WHITE CHOCOLATE SHAVINGS. Dust them lightly with COCOA POWDER.

PETITS CHOUX AU CAFÉ

Tiny *choux* such as these often form a part of an assortment of rich petits fours or after-dinner pastries. At the Sporting Club in Monte Carlo, we would prepare one third of the *choux* filled with a vanilla pastry cream and glazed with vanilla-flavored fondant; then we would add instant espresso dissolved in rum to both the vanilla pastry cream and fondant, then fill and glaze another third of the *choux* with that. Finally, we would add chocolate melted with water to the remaining pastry cream and fondant, and make chocolate *choux*. To prepare the *choux* this way requires a little organization, but the array of the three different flavors makes an elegant presentation. Instructions and quantities for this variation, *Choux Tricolores,* are given at the end of the recipe.

Pâte à Choux
- ¾ cup water
- 6 tablespoons butter, 3 ounces
- Pinch salt
- 1 cup unbleached all-purpose flour, 5 ounces
- 4 eggs

Egg Wash
- 1 egg
- Pinch salt

Coffee Pastry Cream
- 2 cups milk
- ⅔ cup sugar, about 5 ounces
- ¼ cup cornstarch, about 1 ounce
- 6 egg yolks
- 2 tablespoons butter, 1 ounce
- 1 tablespoon instant espresso coffee
- 1 tablespoon dark rum or water

Coffee Fondant Icing
- ½ batch fondant *or* ½ pound commercial fondant
- 1 tablespoon light corn syrup
- 1 tablespoon instant espresso coffee
- 1 teaspoon dark rum or water

Making the Pâte à Choux. Bring the water, butter and salt to a boil in a saucepan. Remove from the heat and stir in the flour all at once. Return to the heat and cook the paste, beating with a wooden spoon, 1 to 2 minutes. Remove the paste to a bowl, beat to cool slightly, then beat in the eggs one at a time.

Piping. Using a ½-inch plain tube, pipe the Pâte à Choux on paper-lined baking pans. Hold the bag at a 45-degree angle to the pan with the tube touching the pan. Without changing the position of the bag or tube, pipe ¾-inch *choux* about 1 inch apart. Release the pressure and lift the bag toward the *choux* to avoid leaving a tail. This makes about 36 *choux*.

Making the Egg Wash. Beat the egg and salt together, then gently brush the tops of the *choux* with the egg wash, smoothing over any points left from the piping.

Baking. Bake the *choux* at 425°F until well-risen and beginning to color, about 10 minutes. Lower the temperature to 350°F and continue baking until well-colored and dry, about 20 minutes. Remove to a rack to cool.

Preparing the Pastry Cream. Bring 1½ cups of the milk and the sugar to a boil in a 2-quart saucepan. Meanwhile whisk together the remaining milk and cornstarch in a 2-quart bowl until smooth. Whisk in the yolks. Whisk one third of the boiling milk into the yolk mixture. Return the remaining milk to a boil and beat in the tempered yolk mixture. Whisk constantly until the pastry cream thickens and returns to a boil. Pour into a bowl and whisk in the butter. Press plastic wrap against the surface of the cream and refrigerate until cold. Dissolve the instant espresso in the rum or water and gently stir into the cold pastry cream with a rubber spatula.

Assembling. Using a plain ¼-inch tube pierce the bottom of each *chou.* Insert the tube in a pastry bag, fill with the pastry cream, then fill the *choux.* Place the filled *choux* on paper to avoid contact between the exposed pastry cream and anything metallic.

Preparing the Fondant. Make fondant as described in Basic Techniques chapter. Place in a 2-quart bowl and work in the corn syrup and coffee/rum mixture, making repeated sweeping strokes with a wooden or metal spoon or flat wooden spatula. Set the bowl over a pan of simmering water and work the fondant with the spoon or spatula until it softens slightly and is neither warm nor cold to the touch—100°F maximum. Remove from the pan of water and use immediately.

Glaze the *choux* with the fondant. Dip the top third of each *chou* in the fondant and allow the excess to drip back into the bowl. With an index finger, gently wipe away the excess fondant from each *chou* to leave a thin coating and to prevent it from dripping. Turn the *choux* right-side up on a paper-lined pan. Allow the fondant to set, about 5 minutes.

Reheat the fondant if necessary during the glazing.

Holding. Refrigerate about 4 or 5 hours. Prolonged refrigeration will soften the fondant.

Yield. About 36

Choux Tricolores

To prepare the assortment of vanilla, coffee and chocolate *choux* described above, proceed in this way: Divide the pastry cream into three parts. Flavor one part with 1 TEASPOON VANILLA; the second with 1 TEASPOON INSTANT ESPRESSO COFFEE dissolved in 1 TEASPOON DARK RUM OR WATER; and the third with 4 OUNCES FINELY CUT BITTERSWEET OR SEMISWEET CHOCOLATE melted in 2 TABLESPOONS HOT MILK OR WATER. Fill one third of the *choux* with each flavor cream.

Soften the fondant with the corn syrup and heat it. Stir in 1 TEASPOON VANILLA and ice the vanilla-filled *choux.* Stir in 1 TEASPOON INSTANT ESPRESSO dissolved in 1 TEASPOON DARK RUM OR WATER into the remaining vanilla fondant and ice the coffee-filled *choux* with it. (If the fondant cools and thickens it may be necessary to reheat it slightly.) Finally, stir 1 OUNCE BITTERSWEET OR SEMISWEET CHOCOLATE melted in 1½ TABLESPOONS HOT WATER into the remaining coffee fondant. The chocolate may cause the fondant to thicken and it may be necessary to add 1 TO 2 TEASPOONS CORN SYRUP and reheat it. Finally, ice the chocolate-filled *choux.*

CHOCOLATE ECLAIRS

The literal meaning of eclair is "lightning bolt." Always one of the most popular pastries made from Pâte à Choux, this version uses both a chocolate filling and glaze.

Pâte à Choux
¾ CUP WATER
6 TABLESPOONS BUTTER, 3 OUNCES
PINCH SALT
1 CUP UNBLEACHED ALL-PURPOSE FLOUR, 5 OUNCES
4 EGGS

Egg Wash
1 EGG
PINCH SALT

Chocolate Pastry Cream Lightened with Whipped Cream
1½ CUPS MILK
½ CUP SUGAR, ABOUT 3¾ OUNCES
4 EGG YOLKS
3 TABLESPOONS CORNSTARCH, ABOUT ¾ OUNCE
4 TABLESPOONS BUTTER, 2 OUNCES, SOFTENED
2 TEASPOONS VANILLA EXTRACT
4 OUNCES BITTERSWEET OR SEMISWEET CHOCOLATE, FINELY CUT

¼ CUP HOT MILK OR WATER
1 ENVELOPE UNFLAVORED GELATIN, 2½ TEASPOONS
¼ CUP COLD WATER
¾ CUP HEAVY WHIPPING CREAM

Chocolate Glaze
⅓ CUP WATER
⅓ CUP LIGHT CORN SYRUP
1 CUP SUGAR, ABOUT 7½ OUNCES
8 OUNCES BITTERSWEET OR SEMISWEET CHOCOLATE, FINELY CUT

Making the Pâte à Choux. Bring the water, butter and salt to a boil in a saucepan. Remove from the heat and stir in the flour all at once. Return to the heat and cook the paste, beating with a wooden spoon, 1 to 2 minutes. Remove the paste to a bowl, beat to cool slightly, then beat in the eggs one at a time.

Piping. Using a ½-inch plain tube, pipe the eclairs on a paper-lined pan. Holding the bag at a 45-degree angle to the pan, drag the tip slowly on the paper toward you. Pipe 4-inch diagonal lengths, about ¾ inch wide and 2 inches apart. It is important to maintain an even pressure during the piping. At the end of each eclair, release the pressure and lift the bag toward the eclair to avoid leaving a tail.

Making the Egg Wash. Whisk the egg and salt together, then gently brush the tops of the eclairs with the egg wash. Lightly streak the eclairs lengthwise with the back of a fork.

Baking. Bake the eclairs at 425°F until well-risen and beginning to color, about 10 minutes. Lower the temperature to 350°F and continue baking until well-colored and dry, about 20 minutes. Remove to a rack to cool.

Preparing the Chocolate Pastry Cream. Bring 1 cup of the milk and the sugar to a boil in a 2-quart saucepan. Meanwhile, whisk together the remaining milk and the cornstarch in a small bowl until smooth. Whisk in the yolks. Whisk one third of the boiling milk into the yolk mixture. Return the remaining milk to a boil and whisk in the tempered yolk mixture. Beat constantly until the pastry cream thickens and returns to a boil. Pour into a bowl and whisk in the butter and vanilla. Melt the chocolate in ¼ cup hot milk or water and beat into the pastry cream. Press plastic wrap against the surface of the cream and refrigerate until cold.

Sprinkle the gelatin on the surface of ¼ cup water in a small bowl. Allow the gelatin to soften about 5 minutes, then place the bowl over a pan of gently simmering water about 5 minutes to melt the gelatin.

Whisk about ½ cup of the cold Chocolate Pastry Cream into the dissolved gelatin, then whisk the dissolved gelatin into the remaining pastry cream. Whip the heavy cream lightly until it just begins to hold its shape and fold it into the pastry cream mixture. Cover the filling and refrigerate it until needed.

Filling the Eclairs. Using a ¼-inch plain tube, pierce the bottoms of the eclairs at either end. Insert the tube in a pastry bag, fill with the Chocolate Pastry Cream, then fill the eclairs.

Preparing the Chocolate Glaze. Prepare the glaze only after the eclairs have been filled. If it is prepared in advance it will set and be too firm to apply. Combine the water, corn syrup and sugar in a 1-quart saucepan. Stir with a wooden spoon to combine. Place the pan on medium heat and bring to a full rolling boil, stirring occasionally. Remove from the heat and add the chocolate. Allow the glaze to stand 1 minute without stirring to melt the chocolate. Whisk the glaze smooth.

Glazing the Eclairs. Dip the top third of each eclair into the glaze, allowing the excess to drip back into the pan. Turn the eclairs right-side up on a paper-lined pan.

Holding. Refrigerate up to 4 or 5 hours. The glaze holds well under refrigeration, but the Pâte à Choux will soften somewhat if left longer.

Yield. About 18

GOUGÈRE

Gougère is a traditional mid-morning Burgundian pastry. This variation adds walnuts, a perfect complement to the cheese. Although it is presented as a wreath, it may also be piped as a series of small *choux,* which are excellent as cocktail pastries.

Pâte à Choux
6 TABLESPOONS WATER

3 TABLESPOONS BUTTER, 1½ OUNCES

½ CUP UNBLEACHED ALL-PURPOSE FLOUR, ABOUT 2½ OUNCES

2 EGGS

½ TEASPOON SALT

½ TEASPOON FRESHLY GROUND PEPPER

⅛ teaspoon nutmeg

4 ounces Swiss Gruyère cheese, grated,
1 cup

½ cup walnuts, coarsely chopped,
about 1½ ounces

Egg Wash
1 egg

Pinch salt

1 ounce Swiss Gruyère cheese, grated,
¼ cup

¼ cup walnuts, coarsely chopped,
about 1 ounce

Mixing the Pâte à Choux. Bring the water, butter and salt to a boil in a saucepan. Remove from the heat and stir in the flour all at once. Return to the heat and cook the paste, beating with a wooden spoon, 1 to 2 minutes. Remove the paste to a bowl, beat to cool slightly, then beat in the eggs one at a time.

Stir in the salt, pepper, nutmeg, 1 cup of the grated cheese and ½ cup of the walnuts.

Piping. Trace a 9-inch circle on parchment paper and invert it on a baking pan. Using a pastry bag, with a 1-inch opening without a tube, pipe the paste in 1½-inch spheres touching each other on the circle, or pipe 24 separate 1-inch spheres.

Making the Egg Wash. Whisk the egg and salt together, gently brush the top of the wreath or small *gougères* with the egg wash and strew with the remaining cheese and walnuts.

Baking. Bake the *gougère* at 425°F until well puffed, about 10 minutes. Lower the temperature to 350°F and continue baking about 20 minutes longer until well colored. The gougère should remain slightly moist within. Serve warm.

Yield. One 9-inch wreath or about 24 small puffs

PARIS-BREST

Named to commemorate a bicycle race between the two cities, the shape of the *Paris-Brest* resembles a bicycle tire.

The filling for this *Paris-Brest* is a rich pastry cream flavored with Praline Paste. It may also be filled simply with whipped cream and fruit or berries, with the lightened Chocolate Pastry Cream used in the eclairs above, or with Rich Ganache.

Pâte à Choux
½ cup water

4 tablespoons butter, 2 ounces

Pinch salt

⅔ cup unbleached all-purpose flour,
about 3½ ounces

3 eggs

Egg Wash
1 egg

Pinch salt

½ cup sliced almonds, about 2 ounces

Hazelnut Crème Mousseline
1½ cups milk

½ cup sugar, about 3¾ ounces

4 egg yolks

3 tablespoons cornstarch, about ¾ ounce

2 teaspoons vanilla extract

2 sticks butter, 8 ounces

½ cup Praline Paste, about 4½ ounces

2 tablespoons Cognac, optional

Confectioners' sugar for dusting

Making the Pâte à Choux. Bring the water, butter and salt to a boil in a saucepan. Remove from the heat and stir in the flour all at once. Return to the heat and cook the paste, beating with a wooden spoon, 1 to 2 minutes. Remove the paste to a bowl, beat to cool slightly, then beat in the eggs one at a time.

Piping. Draw a 9- or 10-inch circle on parchment paper; invert onto a baking pan. Using a ½-inch plain tube held 1 inch over the pan at a 90-degree angle, pipe a ½-inch ring of Pâte à Choux on the line. Pipe a concentric ring inside the first, touching it, then pipe one more ring on top, in between the first two.

Making the Egg Wash. Whisk the egg and salt together, then gently brush the top of the *Paris-Brest* with the egg wash. Sprinkle the *Paris-Brest* with the sliced almonds and press gently with your fingertips to adhere them.

Baking. Bake the *Paris-Brest* at 425°F until well-risen and beginning to color, about 10 minutes. Lower the temperature to 350°F and continue baking until well-colored and dry, about 20 minutes. Remove to a rack to cool.

Preparing the Crème Mousseline. Bring 1 cup of the milk and the sugar to a boil in a 1½-quart saucepan. Meanwhile, whisk together the re-

maining milk and cornstarch in a 1½-quart bowl until smooth. Whisk in the yolks. Beat one third of the boiling milk into the yolk mixture. Return the remaining milk to a boil and whisk in the tempered yolk mixture. Whisk constantly until the pastry cream thickens and returns to a boil. Cook, whisking, about 1 minute. Whisk in the vanilla. Pour the pastry cream into a bowl, cover with plastic wrap and refrigerate until cold.

Beat the butter until soft and light. Beat in the Praline Paste and the optional Cognac until smooth. Add the cold pastry cream all at once and beat on medium speed until smooth and light, about 3 to 4 minutes.

Assembling. Slice off the top third of the ring with a sharp serrated knife. Place the bottom on a cardboard or serving platter. Using a pastry bag fitted with a ½-inch star tube, pipe

the Crème Mousseline in sixteen 2-inch rosettes into the bottom so it is completely filled.

Cut the top of the ring into 16 pieces; reassemble over the rosettes. Dust with the confectioners' sugar.

Holding. Refrigerate the *Paris-Brest* 4 to 5 hours. Bring to room temperature before serving or the *Crème Mousseline* will be too firm.

Yield. About 16 portions

Chocolate Paris-Brest

Fill with whipped Rich Ganache, pages 76–77.

Paris-Brest aux Fruits

Lighten Vanilla Pastry Cream with some WHIPPED CREAM and spread on the ring. Top with A LAYER OF FRUIT OR BERRIES. Pipe rosettes of sweetened whipped cream over the fruit, cover with the top cut in pieces, as above.

Bande

Follow the recipe for *Paris-Brest* but shaping the Pâte à Choux in the following manner: Pipe out two 12-inch strips, each about 1 inch wide, next to each other on a paper-lined baking pan. Pipe a third strip between and on top of the first two strips. Brush with EGG WASH and strew with SLICED ALMONDS before baking. Bake, cut and fill as for *Paris-Brest.*

CROQUEMBOUCHE

The traditional French wedding and christening cake, the *Croquembouche* is a conical tower of caramelized *choux.* Although many systems for building it call for the use of a mold, this system of free-hand assembly works well. After the *choux* are filled and glazed with caramel, more caramel is prepared to adhere the *choux* together in building the *Croquembouche.* A first layer of *choux* is adhered around a base of baked pastry dough, then each subsequent layer is adhered to the top of the previous one, making each layer one *chou* less than the previous one, so that eventually one *chou* and an *aigrette,* or trellis, of spun caramel crowns the top of the *Croquembouche.*

Refer to the decorating chapter for more ideas on garnishing the *Croquembouche.* Off-white marzipan flowers or leaves stand out dramatically against the caramel.

Pastry Dough for Base
  1 CUP UNBLEACHED ALL-PURPOSE FLOUR,
    ABOUT 5 OUNCES
  2 TABLESPOONS CAKE FLOUR, ABOUT 1/2
    OUNCE
  1/4 TEASPOON SALT
  1/8 TEASPOON BAKING POWDER
  1 STICK BUTTER, 4 OUNCES, COOL
  3 TO 4 TABLESPOONS ICE WATER

Pâte à Choux
  3/4 CUP WATER
  6 TABLESPOONS BUTTER, 3 OUNCES
  PINCH SALT
  1 CUP UNBLEACHED ALL-PURPOSE FLOUR,
    ABOUT 5 OUNCES
  4 EGGS

Egg Wash

    1 EGG
    PINCH SALT

Vanilla Crème Mousseline

    3 CUPS MILK
    1 CUP SUGAR, ABOUT 7½ OUNCES
    9 EGG YOLKS
    6 TABLESPOONS CORNSTARCH, ABOUT 1½
        OUNCES
    1 TABLESPOON VANILLA EXTRACT
    4 STICKS BUTTER, 1 POUND, SOFTENED

Caramel Glaze

    3 CUPS SUGAR, 22½ OUNCES
    1 TABLESPOON LEMON JUICE

Mixing the Flaky Pastry Dough. Stir together the flour, cake flour and salt in a bowl. Cut up the butter, add and toss gently to coat. Rub in the butter until the mixture looks sandy. Sprinkle over 3 tablespoons of ice water; toss with a fork. Add another tablespoon of water if necessary. Press the dough together. Wrap and chill several hours.

Rolling. Place the dough on a lightly floured surface, lightly flour the dough and roll it to about an 8-inch diameter about ¼-inch thick. Place the dough on a paper-lined pan and cut it into an 8-inch disk using a pattern. Dock the dough well with a fork at ½-inch intervals and chill the dough several hours.

Baking. Bake the disk at 350°F until a deep, golden color, about 15 to 20 minutes. Cool the disk on the baking pan.

Making the Pâte à Choux. Bring the water, butter and salt to a boil in a saucepan. Remove from the heat and stir in the flour all at once. Return to the heat and cook the paste, beating with a wooden spoon, 1 to 2 minutes.

Remove the paste to a bowl, beat to cool slightly, then beat in the eggs one at a time.

Using a ½-inch plain tube, pipe 80 to 90 *choux* on two paper-lined baking pans. Holding the bag at a 45-degree angle to the pan, with the tube touching the pan, pipe ¾-inch *choux*, 1 inch apart. At the end of each *chou,* release the pressure and lift the bag toward the *chou* to avoid leaving a tail.

Making the Egg Wash. Whisk the egg and salt together, then gently brush the tops of the *choux* with the egg wash, smoothing over any points left from the piping.

Baking the Choux. Bake at 425°F until well-risen and beginning to color, about 10 minutes. Lower the temperature to 350°F and continue baking until well-colored and dry, about 10 to 15 minutes. Remove to a rack to cool.

Preparing the Crème Mousseline. Bring 2½ cups of the milk and the sugar to a boil. Combine the remaining milk and cornstarch in a 2-quart bowl and whisk smooth. Beat in the yolks. When the milk boils, whisk one third of the boiling milk into the yolk mixture, return the remaining milk to a boil and whisk in the yolk mixture, whisking constantly, until the pastry cream thickens and returns to a boil. Whisk in the vanilla. Pour the pastry cream into a bowl, cover with plastic wrap and refrigerate until cold.

Beat the butter until soft and light. Add the cold pastry cream all at once and beat on medium speed until smooth and light, about 3 to 4 minutes.

Filling the Choux. Using a plain ¼-inch tube, pierce the bottom of each *choux.* Insert the tube in a pastry bag, fill with the Crème Mousseline, then fill the *choux.* Place the filled *choux* on paper to avoid contact between the exposed pastry cream and anything metallic.

Preparing the Caramel. Divide the ingredients in half to prepare two separate batches, one to glaze the *choux* and another to adhere them together. If the caramel thickens too much during the glazing or the assembly, reheat it briefly over very low heat.

Prepare the first batch of caramel for glazing the *choux.* Combine the sugar and lemon juice in a saucepan with a wooden spoon. Place on medium heat; cook without stirring until the sugar starts to melt around the sides of the pan and the center begins to smoke. Start to stir the sugar. Continue heating, stirring occasionally, until the glaze turns amber in color and is clear and free of sugar crystals. Remove from the heat at once. Dip the bottom of the pan in at least 2 inches of cold water for 30 seconds to stop the cooking.

Glazing the Choux. Glaze the top of each *chou* with caramel, working quickly. Place the *choux,* glazed-side up, on paper-lined pans. Allow the caramel to set.

Assembling. Prepare the second batch of caramel. Place the pastry base on cardboard or a serving platter. Adhere a ring of twelve *choux* around the edge of the base on their sides, glazed-side out, using additional caramel. Top with a ring of eleven *choux.* Continue layering, decreasing the number of puffs in each layer by one.

Finishing. Decorate the *Croquembouche* with marzipan leaves and flowers, pages 303–307. Dip the flowers' bottoms into the caramel and adhere them around the sides of the *Croquembouche.* Accent the flowers with some leaves. Dip the bases of the leaves into the caramel and position two or three leaves around each flower.

For simpler presentation, spin threads of caramel over the *Croquembouche* so it is covered with a golden veil: Reheat any leftover caramel just to the point where it is thick and syrupy. Cover the work surface with newspaper or sheets of parchment or wax paper. Place the *Croquembouche* on the paper-covered surface and place the pan of caramel close by. Dip a pointed-bowled soup spoon into the caramel, holding the spoon perpendicular to caramel in the pan and immersing only one third of the bowl of the spoon in the caramel. Grasping the spoon by the end of the handle, lift it straight out of the pan to a height of two or three feet, keeping the spoon above the pan. Wait a few seconds until the caramel is falling off the spoon in a very thin stream. Holding the spoon parallel to the *Croquembouche,* and about three or four inches away from it, spin the thread of caramel in a circular motion, around and around the *Croquembouche.* Repeat the process eight or ten times, until the *Croquembouche* is covered with a haze of caramel. Reheat the caramel, if necessary, during the process.

To make an *Aigrette* or trellis to decorate the very top of the *Croquembouche,* use the leftover caramel or prepare a fresh batch. Use the caramel at a thick consistency, as in spinning the threads, above.

Place a piece of parchment paper, about 12 × 18 inches, on the work surface and very lightly grease it with a teaspoon or so of soft butter. Use the palm of your hand to spread the butter very thinly and evenly. Using a teaspoon, drop four dabs of caramel 2 inches apart on the paper. The caramel should spread out to form small disks about ¾ inch in diameter. These will be the bases for the *Aigrettes.*

To form the branches of the *Aigrettes,* use a

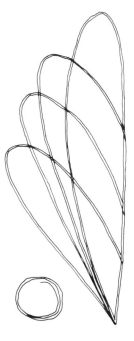

pointed-bowled spoon to spin threads as above. From a distance of three or four inches above the paper, make a series of loops, as in the illustration above. Make the first loop five inches tall and about an inch wide, the second, an inch shorter and half an inch wider, the third, an inch shorter and half an inch wider, and the fourth, an inch shorter and half an inch wider. Make at least twelve to sixteen sets of loops since they shatter easily on assembly. Let the disks and loops harden for five minutes.

To assemble an *Aigrette,* place one of the caramel disks on a piece of lightly buttered paper. With a hot knife-blade, trim the bases of three or four of the loop sets. Loosen them from the paper with a thin metal spatula. Place a drop of hot caramel on the disk, then quickly drizzle a thin thread of hot caramel on the outer edge of the tall loop in one set of loops, lift it from the paper and embed the base into the drop of hot caramel on the disk. Quickly lift the other two or three sets of loops and assemble them, straight sides in, against the first one, making sure that their bases are in the drop of hot caramel on the disk, and their outer edges are well pressed against each other in the center. If using three sets of loops, they should make 120-degree angles to each other; with four, 90-degree angles. Assemble several more in the same way in case of breakage.

Reheat the caramel again and pour a large drop on the top of the *Croquembouche.* Lift one of the *Aigrettes* by its disk base and press it into the hot caramel on the *Croquembouche.* Hold it in place for a minute to make sure it has adhered firmly.

Holding. Place the *Croquembouche* in a cool room and serve within 4 to 5 hours.

Yield. About 40 portions

6

PASTRY DOUGHS

Simple doughs such as those used to fashion pies and tarts have many features in common. Flour, fat and a liquid combine in various proportions using many techniques to make doughs that have a delicate texture after baking. Some doughs are made into empty shells, filled after they are baked; others have fillings baked directly in them.

Whatever the final use of the dough determines the type of dough chosen for a specific purpose. The following recipes are for three different simple doughs: a flaky dough, similar to the French Pâte Brisée, for pie and tart shells to be filled after baking and occasionally for double-crust American pies; a sweet dough that contains some baking powder, like a French Pâte Sucrée, to be filled before baking so that both the dough and filling bake through at the same time; and a cookie dough, like the French Pâte Sablée, to fashion delicate, fragile, sweet shells filled after baking. Some of the doughs have variations in flavoring, but the techniques for mixing and handling remain substantially the same as the base recipes.

MIXING AND HANDLING SIMPLE PASTRY DOUGHS

Simple pastry doughs are combinations of flour, butter and a liquid with other ingredients added for flavor (salt, sugar, cocoa powder), richness (eggs in place of water), or performance (baking powder).

Flour

Use unbleached all-purpose flour unless specified. In hot weather, refrigerate the flour before making the dough to prevent the butter from melting.

Butter

Use butter that is slightly softened by pounding it with a rolling pin so it is malleable and plastic but still cool. It mixes more readily into the dough. Do not soften the butter to room temperature.

123

Liquid

Whether you use water, eggs or a combination, make sure that the liquid used to moisten the dough is as cold as possible. After working the butter into the dry ingredients, the slight chill of the moistening ingredient helps to keep the butter as firm as possible through the final mixing stage. If you use a warm liquid to moisten a dough, even butter which was incorporated successfully will melt and ruin the texture of the dough.

Mixing

Quick, careful handling makes the difference between a fragile-textured and a leaden dough. Rub the butter into the dry ingredients quickly and deftly to prevent it from melting and "burning" the dough, thus rendering it heavy and sodden after baking. Using butter for the doughs presents a small difficulty in that butter contains water. While rubbing in the butter, the water reacts with and develops some gluten in the flour. Another type of fat would present less of a problem, but not contribute as delicate a flavor.

Be careful not to overmix when moistening the dough. Overmixing causes the liquid to react with the proteins and develop a strong gluten. I prefer to mix the liquid into the dough using a fork, then gently press the dough together, keeping the gluten development to a minimum. These precautions mostly concern the flaky dough, with less importance to the sweet dough because of its high sugar content and no application to the cookie dough because cake flour is used in the recipe.

Resting/Chilling

After mixing the dough, wrap and chill it. This accomplishes two things: It allows the butter to reharden so that the dough is firm when rolled; and it allows the gluten developed during mixing to relax (some *always* develops, no matter how careful you are). For most doughs, an hour or two in the refrigerator will suffice. When I make doughs in large quantities, I prefer to let them rest overnight.

Practice

Everyone's ability to handle doughs, both the mixing and the rolling, increases with experience. If your first efforts at pastry doughs are not successful, refer to the corrective measures described on pages 130–131. Above all keep practicing. The rewards will be beautiful tarts and pies, appealing to the palate as well as the eye.

FLAKY DOUGH

Crisp and flaky after baking, this dough is best used to make prebaked tart or pie shells which are filled after cooling.

The technique for incorporating the butter with the dry ingredients (whether done by hand or by machine) produces a sandy mixture of tiny flour-coated butter particles. When the mixture is moistened, the liquid binds with the flour, leaving the butter particles trapped in the dough. When the dough is rolled, these become irregular strata throughout it. During baking, the butter strata melt and are reabsorbed by the dough. The spaces previously occupied by the butter are inflated by the steam generated by the evaporation of the liquid, causing the dough to have its characteristic flaky texture.

1 CUP UNBLEACHED ALL-PURPOSE FLOUR,
  ABOUT 5 OUNCES
2 TABLESPOONS CAKE FLOUR, ABOUT 1/2
  OUNCE
1/4 TEASPOON SALT
1/8 TEASPOON BAKING POWDER
1 STICK BUTTER, 4 OUNCES, COOL
3 TO 4 TABLESPOONS ICE WATER

Yield. Enough for 1 9- or 10-inch tart or 9-inch single-crust pie, 11 ounces of dough

2 CUPS UNBLEACHED ALL-PURPOSE FLOUR,
  ABOUT 10 OUNCES
1/4 CUP CAKE FLOUR, ABOUT 1 OUNCE
1/2 TEASPOON SALT
1/4 TEASPOON BAKING POWDER
2 STICKS BUTTER, 8 OUNCES, COOL
5 TO 6 TABLESPOONS ICE WATER

Yield. Enough for 1 9-inch, lattice-top or double-crust pie, about 22 ounces of dough

Mixing the Dough by Hand

Stir together the unbleached all-purpose flour, cake flour, salt and baking powder in a 2-quart bowl. Cut the butter into eight to ten pieces, add it to the flour, and gently toss together to coat the butter.

Using your fingertips, break the pieces of butter into smaller pieces, gently squeezing to rub it into the flour, while continually tossing up the flour from the bottom of the bowl. Continue rubbing in the butter just until the mixture has a sandy appearance—there should still be some visible pieces of the butter, no larger than 1/4 inch across. At no time should the mixture become pasty nor should it begin to feel warm. If the butter shows signs of melting, refrigerate the butter/flour mixture for 30 minutes, then proceed.

Sprinkle the smaller amount of the ice water over the butter/flour mixture and toss it in with a fork—work the fork upwards from the bottom of the bowl through the dough, without exerting pressure on the dough.

bowl of an electric mixer with the paddle attachment. Mix the dry ingredients on the lowest speed until combined, about 30 seconds. Turn off the mixer.

Cut the butter into eight to ten pieces and add to the dry ingredients. Mix on the lowest speed about 30 seconds, stop the mixer and scrape the bowl and paddle with a rubber spatula. Mix 30 seconds more and repeat this operation. Continue mixing until the mixture is sandy in appearance and only ¼-inch particles of butter remain. Stop the mixer.

With the mixer running on the lowest speed, pour in the water in a thin stream. Continue mixing until the dough masses around the paddle, about 10 to 15 seconds. Stop the mixer, scrape the dough off the paddle with a rubber spatula and press it into a flat disk about ½ inch thick. Wrap and chill the dough.

Mixing the Dough in the Food Processor

Combine the dry ingredients in the work bowl of a food processor fitted with the steel blade. Pulse several times for a second at a time to mix the dry ingredients. Remove the cover and add the butter, cold from the refrigerator and cut into eight or ten pieces. Evenly distribute the butter over the dry ingredients.

Cover the work bowl again and pulse five or six times to cut the butter into the dry ingredients. The mixture should appear mealy, with some pieces of butter, no larger than ¼ inch, still visible. Pulse several more times if necessary to reduce the pieces of butter to the right size.

Remove the flour and butter mixture to a

To see if the dough is sufficiently moistened, pick up a handful and gently squeeze it. If the dough holds together without appearing crumbly, it is sufficiently moistened. If the dough does not hold, continue adding water, a tablespoon at a time, and toss it until the dough is sufficiently moistened. Press it together against the side of the bowl with the fork. Press once or twice with your hand and remove the dough from the bowl. Tightly wrap it in plastic wrap or aluminum foil and refrigerate it several hours or overnight.

Mixing the Dough by Machine

Combine the unbleached all-purpose flour, cake flour, salt and baking powder in the

2-quart bowl. Add the water by hand, tossing it in with a fork, as in the hand-mixing method, above. Adding the water to the food processor can be risky—it is an easy way to over-mix the dough, developing an excessive amount of gluten.

SWEET DOUGH

Tender and crumbly after baking, this dough is used to prepare tarts and other pastries where a raw filling and raw dough are baked together. It is composed of flour, sugar, salt, baking powder, butter and egg. The action of the baking powder causes the dough to expand slightly. Because of this expansion, the dough is in constant contact with the bottom of the pan, ensuring a dry, baked-through crust.

Sweet Dough is especially suitable for liquid fillings which would render other types of dough sodden and wet. For savory pastries with liquid fillings, it can also be made without sugar. Although the dough is not flaky, the guarantee of a good bottom crust is more than adequate compensation.

The butter is rubbed into the dry ingredients after they are combined. Although the same precautions apply to prevent the butter from melting, there is less butter in the Sweet Dough, so there is less risk of this occurring. Even though the butter is worked into the flour more finely, it must remain sandy in appearance. If the butter melts, burning will result.

Since the dough is moistened with egg, it coheres more firmly than a dough moistened with water. The sugar interferes somewhat with the development of a strong gluten, because it dilutes the protein content of the flour, so it may be handled less gently, without fear of toughening it.

The Chocolate Dough which follows the Sweet Dough cannot always be used interchangeably with it, but is an interesting variation that contrasts well with certain fruit and nut fillings.

1 CUP UNBLEACHED ALL-PURPOSE FLOUR, ABOUT 5 OUNCES
1/4 CUP SUGAR, ABOUT 1 3/4 OUNCES
PINCH SALT
1/4 TEASPOON BAKING POWDER
4 TABLESPOONS BUTTER, 2 OUNCES, COOL
1 LARGE EGG

Yield. Enough for 1 9- or 10-inch tart or 1 9-inch single-crust pie, about 11 ounces of dough

2 CUPS UNBLEACHED ALL-PURPOSE FLOUR, ABOUT 10 OUNCES
1/2 CUP SUGAR, ABOUT 3 3/4 OUNCES
1/4 TEASPOON SALT
1/2 TEASPOON BAKING POWDER
1 STICK BUTTER, 4 OUNCES, COOL
2 LARGE EGGS

Yield. Enough for 1 9-inch lattice-top or double-crust pie, about 22 ounces of dough

Mixing the Dough by Hand

Stir together the flour, sugar, salt and baking powder in a 2-quart bowl. Cut the cool butter into eight to ten pieces, add to the dry ingredients and toss together to coat the butter.

Using your fingertips, break the pieces of

Tightly wrap the dough in plastic wrap or aluminum foil and refrigerate it several hours or overnight.

Mixing the Dough by Machine

Follow the same procedure for mixing the Flaky Dough by machine, as described above, beating the egg or eggs before adding them in a thin stream to the butter/flour mixture.

Mixing the Dough in the Food Processor

Combine the dry ingredients in the work bowl of the food processor fitted with the steel blade. Pulse several times for a second at a time to mix the dry ingredients. Remove the cover and add the butter, cold from the refrigerator and cut into eight or ten pieces. Evenly distribute the butter over the dry ingredients.

Cover the work bowl again and pulse eight or ten times to cut the butter into the dry ingredients. The mixture should appear fine and mealy, with no pieces of butter visible.

Remove the mixture to a 2-quart bowl. Add the beaten egg(s) by hand, tossing in with a fork, as in the hand-mixing method, above. Adding the egg(s) to the food processor can be risky—it is an easy way to overmix the dough.

Chocolate Dough

A variation of the Sweet Dough, the Chocolate Dough has the same crumbly texture. Use it with a filling, baking both together, or

butter into smaller pieces, gently squeezing to rub it into the flour, while continually tossing up the flour from the bottom of the bowl. Continue rubbing in the butter until the mixture has a sandy appearance. No visible pieces of butter should remain.

Beat the egg or eggs in a small bowl or cup with a fork. Pour over the butter mixture and stir it in vigorously with a fork, until the dough is evenly moistened and begins to hold together. Press the dough together with a hand against the side of the bowl. Lightly flour the work surface and the dough and press the dough together, folding it over on itself once or twice. Work quickly and be careful the butter does not melt and the dough does not excessively soften. Shape the dough into a flat disk about ½ inch thick.

make a chocolate tart or pie shell, baking it empty. The baking soda in the dough reacts with the cocoa powder and slightly leavens the dough, lightening an otherwise dry and heavy dough.

3 TABLESPOONS COCOA POWDER, ABOUT ½ OUNCE

1 CUP UNBLEACHED ALL-PURPOSE FLOUR, ABOUT 5 OUNCES

¼ CUP SUGAR, 1¾ OUNCES

PINCH SALT

¼ TEASPOON BAKING SODA

4 TABLESPOONS BUTTER, 2 OUNCES, COOL

1 LARGE EGG

Force the cocoa powder through the finest strainer possible to crush any lumps. Mix together the dry ingredients in a bowl. Rub in the butter by hand or by machine and moisten with the egg as for Sweet Dough. Shape into a disk, wrap and refrigerate.

Yield. Enough for 1 9- or 10-inch tart or 9-inch single-crust pie shell, about 11 ounces of dough

COOKIE DOUGH

The texture of this dough after baking is sandy (*sablée* means sandy in French) and cookielike. An extremely fragile and delicate dough, it is mixed by creaming the ingredients together, like a cake batter.

Like the Flaky Dough, the Cookie Dough is best suited for empty shells, filled after baking. It is also suitable as a base for desserts with soft and delicate fillings, like cheesecakes, which need a flat-disk base as opposed to a shell or container like a pie or tart.

Perhaps the simplest of all pastry doughs to prepare, Cookie Dough must rest for a long time in the refrigerator after mixing. The dough is extremely soft and must be chilled to firm the butter before rolling. Gluten development is not a problem since the dough is made with low-protein cake flour.

The cookie dough prepared with almonds or hazelnuts is even more fragile and delicate than the Cookie Dough.

1 STICK BUTTER, 4 OUNCES, COOL

¼ CUP SUGAR, ABOUT 1¾ OUNCES

1 EGG

1¼ CUPS CAKE FLOUR, ABOUT 5 OUNCES

Cream the butter by hand or by machine until soft. Add the sugar in a steady stream and continue beating until the mixture is lightened in color and in texture.

Beat the egg in a small bowl and add half of it, continuing to beat until the mixture is smooth. Add the remaining egg and continue beating. The butter/egg mixture should be soft and shiny, like buttercream.

Sift the cake flour to remove any lumps and stir into the butter mixture. Mix only until the flour disappears into the dough.

Scrape the dough onto a piece of plastic wrap and refrigerate it until firm—at least 5 to 6 hours.

Yield. Enough for 1 9- or 10-inch tart, about 12 ounces of dough

Almond or Hazelnut Dough

This rich and even more fragile type of cookie dough is used for delicate tart shells.

⅓ CUP GROUND ALMONDS *OR* GROUND
  UNBLANCHED HAZELNUTS, ABOUT 1 OUNCE
6 TABLESPOONS BUTTER, 3 OUNCES, COOL

¼ CUP SUGAR, ABOUT 1¾ OUNCES
1 LARGE EGG
1¼ CUPS CAKE FLOUR, ABOUT 5 OUNCES

Proceed as for the Cookie Dough, mixing the almonds or hazelnuts in along with the sifted cake flour.

Yield. Enough for 1 10-inch tart, about 12 ounces of dough

Corrective Measures

Although these measures will help to correct inaccuracies in mixing the doughs, the texture of the baked dough will suffer as a result of the extra handling. If any of the following remedies is used, be sure to allow additional resting time to relax the gluten developed by the extra handling.

Flaky Dough

1. *The flour and butter mixture becomes pasty* (the butter is melting). Proceed as quickly as possible to moistening the dough. Since the dough is pasty, it will absorb much less liquid. Force the dough to accept at least three quarters of the liquid called for by gently stirring the liquid in with a fork. The dough will be excessively soft. Flour the outside of the dough generously (1 to 2 tablespoons flour), wrap and chill it.

2. *There are large lumps of butter left in the dough after moistening.* Flour a work surface and turn the dough out on it. Without flouring the dough, press it into a rectangle about ⅜ inch thick. This will flatten the lumps of butter somewhat. Fold the dough over on itself once, gently mold it into a disk, wrap and chill.

3. *The dough is still very dry after moistening and being pressed together.* Return the dry dough to the bowl and gently tear it into particles using two forks. Scatter drops of water on it and toss them in with a fork until the dough coheres better. Wrap and chill the dough.

Sweet Dough

Because of the sugar in the Sweet Dough, the dough will have a different appearance during the mixing. Since the dough is less likely to develop gluten if handled too much, the problems that may arise during mixing are not as serious.

1. *The dough is still dry after moistening.* Leave the dough in the bowl and scatter 1 tablespoon of water over it. Toss the water in with a fork and press the dough together. It should cohere well at this point.

2. *The dough seems uneven in texture after being pressed together* (there are rough dry spots in the dough). Turn the dough out on a lightly floured surface and fold the dough over on itself three or four times. This should be enough extra mixing to render the dough smooth and even in texture. The extra gluten formed will not adversely affect the baked dough.

3. *The dough is excessively soft after mixing.* Flour the surface and turn the dough out on it. Scatter 1 tablespoon flour on the dough and fold the dough over on itself three or four times so that it absorbs the extra flour. Wrap and chill the dough.

Cookie Dough and Nut Dough

1. *The butter and sugar mixture separates after the addition of the egg.* This will occur if the egg is cold when added to the soft butter and sugar mixture. Heat the mixing bowl for 2 or 3 seconds over direct heat or very hot water and continue mixing. The butter should absorb the egg easily after heating. If the mixture still appears scrambled, repeat the process and continue mixing.

2. *The dough seems excessively soft after mixing.* Chill the dough.

ROLLING AND FORMING FLAKY DOUGH INTO TARTS AND PIES

Use Flaky Dough to prepare crusts for pies and tarts that are baked and cooled before being filled and occasionally for double-crust American pies. The technique for making an empty baked crust is referred to as baking "blind," that is, without a filling. The dough has a tendency to puff irregularly during baking because of the steam expansion. For this reason the dough is docked (the surface is punctured at regular intervals with a fork to allow some of the steam to escape) and weighted to ensure a flat surface. The dough should be lined with paper and weighted with some type of dried bean—Navy beans, lentils, or lima beans. Rice is not a good choice because, if the paper shifts, some of the grains may adhere to the dough. The dried beans are large enough to be visible and removed, but rice can easily be missed.

Rolling

Preparation. Prepare the pan, equipment and surface before removing the dough from the refrigerator, to avoid having the dough soften and become difficult to roll.

Butter the pan with melted butter, using a brush, or smear soft butter on it with your fingertips. Although the melted butter is not necessary to prevent the baked dough from sticking (the dough's high proportion of butter achieves this), it does help the raw dough adhere to the pan.

Use a nonporous surface such as marble (marble is always about 10 degrees cooler than room temperature and keeps the dough cooler during rolling), formica or even wood. The surface should be large enough to roll the dough: To fit the dough into a 10-inch tart or 9-inch pie pan, it should be rolled to about a 14-inch disk. A straight boxwood rolling pin is the most convenient to use for rolling crusts, but a large ball-bearing rolling pin is also useful.

Have a bowl of flour and a long flexible spatula on hand. Both are useful in preventing the dough from sticking to the surface and loosening it if it does stick.

Lightly flour the surface. Dust the surface repeatedly with small pinches of flour, rather than place a large amount of flour on the surface at one time. Since the dough will absorb any amount of flour and excessive absorption will toughen the dough, it is better to flour less and more often than to use generous quantities of flour less frequently.

Pounding the Dough. Unwrap the dough and place the disk of dough on the floured surface. Lightly flour the surface of the dough and pound the dough gently with the rolling

pin, using regular even strokes about 1 inch apart. The pounding helps to slightly soften the dough so that it can be rolled without cracking. While pounding the dough, move the dough clockwise, revolving it about 30 degrees at a time. This helps the dough remain round. Renew pinches of flour under and on the dough as needed to prevent the dough from sticking to the surface, or the rolling pin from sticking to the dough.

Rolling the Dough. Roll the dough when it feels malleable and flexible. The size of the dough should have increased during the pounding so that a great deal of rolling is not necessary. Position the rolling pin at end of the disk of dough closest to you. Roll back and forth once, taking care not to roll over the ends of the dough in the same direction—this

would produce an uneven thickness and cause the ends to stick to the surface. Move the dough, reflour the surface and reposition the dough, revolving it as before. Roll back and forth again. Although the shape of the dough distorts somewhat, after the dough is rolled and revolved three or four times, it will be round.

Lining a Straight-Sided Tart Pan

When the dough has been rolled to a ⅛-inch thickness, it should be about 14 inches in diameter and large enough to fit the pan. Fold the dough in half and slip both hands under the dough to support it. Lift the dough into the pan and position the fold at the center of the pan. Unfold the dough, covering the pán's surface.

At this point the dough is resting at a slant along the side. Carefully lift the edge and ease the dough into the pan along the side so it fits well. Press the dough into the bottom of the pan using the palm of your hand. With your fingertips, gently press the dough against the side of the pan.

Using a small knife or scissors, trim off all but ¼ inch of the excess dough around the rim of the pan. If the dough was correctly rolled, there should be very little scrap trimmed away. Fold the edge of the dough into the pan so the top edge of the dough is even. With your thumb on the inside of the pan, gently press the dough against the side of the pan.

Slip the dough-lined pan into a plastic bag or cover with plastic wrap and refrigerate at least 2 hours, to firm the dough and relax the gluten. The longer this crust rests, the better the texture after baking will be. Allowing the gluten to relax over a long period of time (up to 24 hours) will ensure a more tender result.

Lining a Sloping-Sided Pie Pan

Roll the dough as above and fold it in half. Place the dough into a pie pan and unfold it. Press the dough gently into the bottom and side of the pan using your fingertips.

Trim off all but ¼ inch of the excess dough and fold under to make a clean, even rim. Using your fingertips, flute the edge of the dough: Pinch the outer rim of the dough with the thumb and forefinger of one hand while pushing against the inner rim of the dough with the forefinger of the other hand. Wrap and refrigerate the dough-lined pan.

Preparing the Empty Tart Shell for Baking

Remove from the refrigerator and unwrap. Dock the dough: Pierce only the bottom of the dough with the tines of a fork at ½-inch intervals. Cut a disk of parchment paper or wax paper large enough to reach up the sides of the pan and press it into the pan following the outline of the dough (aluminum foil is not suitable for this purpose since folds in the foil may cut through the dough when molding the foil to the sides of the pan). Fill the paper-covered raw tart shell with dried beans.

Preparing the Empty Pie Shell for Baking

Use the same procedure as for preparing the empty tart shell, but dock the dough on the bottom *and* the side.

Baking Empty Tart and Pie Shells

Bake at 350°F for about 20 minutes, then check to see whether the dough is dull and dry looking—a sign the dough has set and will no longer bubble up. If not, continue baking another 5 minutes and check again. Once the dough is no longer shiny, remove the paper and beans and return the tart shell to the oven to color, about 5 to 10 minutes more, until the dough is an even golden color. Watch the tart shell carefully after removing the paper and beans. The rise in temperature of the dough will accelerate very rapidly, which may cause the dough to burn easily.

Remove the baked tart shell from the oven and cool on a rack.

NOTE: Cool the beans and store them in a loosely covered container at a cool room temperature. Use the beans several times over a period of a month or so. The beans do not last indefinitely since they will develop a strong odor.

EMPTY TART SHELLS FROM OTHER DOUGHS

Empty tart shells may also be prepared using Chocolate Dough, Cookie Dough and Nut Dough. This Sweet Dough is never baked without a filling.

The procedure is the same as for Flaky Dough, with the following exceptions: After fitting the dough into the tart pan, trim away the excess dough at the edge by rolling over the top of the pan with a rolling pin. A doubled-pastry edge is not desirable since these doughs expand during baking. Be careful not to burn these specialty doughs after the paper and weights are removed. Because of the high sugar content, the doughs quickly can color too deeply. Chocolate Dough is baked when

it looks dull and feels firm, but resilient, when lightly pressed with a fingertip. If the Chocolate Dough bakes too long it will be very hard.

FILLED TARTS AND SINGLE-CRUST PIES FROM RAW SWEET DOUGH

The procedure for rolling the dough and fitting it into the pans remains the same as above. In preparing the crusts for baking, the dough is not docked since the filling is placed on the raw dough and docking would cause the filling to seep into the crust. Bake the tarts and single-crust pies according to individual recipes.

DOUBLE-CRUST PIES WITH FLAKY DOUGH OR SWEET DOUGH

Divide the dough into two equal pieces, cutting through the center of the disk of dough to make two disks.

crust with water or egg wash and place the top crust on the pie. Trim the edges of the top crust to an even ½-inch overhang. Evenly fold the exposed edges of the top crust under the bottom crust. Flute the edge of the pie and make several vent holes in the center of the top crust. Carefully brush the top crust with egg wash. Bake the pie according to the individual recipe.

LATTICE-TOPPED PIE OR TART WITH FLAKY DOUGH OR SWEET DOUGH

Divide the dough into two pieces as above, roll one of the pieces and fit into a pie or tart pan. Trim the edge of the dough even with the edge of the pan, without folding over to finish the edge. Roll the second piece of dough into a 10- to 12-inch square and cut the dough into ten 1-inch-wide strips. Egg wash the edge of the bottom crust or moisten with water and pour in the filling. Egg wash the strips, then apply the strips of dough, five

Roll one disk, fit it into the 9-inch pie pan, and using a small knife, trim the edges even with the rim of the pan. Place the filling on the bottom crust, according to individual recipes. Roll the second disk of dough into a 10-inch disk. Moisten the rim of the bottom

in each direction, making a diagonal lattice. Trim the ends of the strips even with the edge of the bottom crust. Flute the edge of the crust on a pie, flouring your fingers to prevent sticking. Leave the edge of a tart straight, without attempting to flute. Bake according to individual recipes.

Corrective Measures

1. *The dough sticks to the surface or the rolling pin.* Carefully pry the dough from the surface, using a long spatula or the edge of a thin cookie sheet, or pry the dough from the rolling pin by scraping it with a small spatula. Sticking is avoided by continuously flouring the surface and the dough with small amounts of flour during the rolling and moving of it.

2. *The dough tears during rolling.* With Flaky Dough, *very* slightly moisten the edge of the tear with water and overlap the torn dough to repair it. Carefully roll over this area to prevent sticking on account of the moisture. For other doughs, merely press together and continue rolling. If one of the other doughs sticks or tears irreparably, lightly flour the dough, squeeze it back into a disk and reroll. Or, if the dough is too soft, reform the disk and allow it to chill before rerolling.

3. *The dough cracks during rolling.* This usually occurs when the dough has not been sufficiently softened by pounding before being rolled. Press the cracked areas together, moistening them slightly if rolling flaky pastry dough, and continue rolling, using a more gentle pressure than before.

4. *The dough tears while being moved to or fitted into the pan.* Depending on how extensive the tearing is, merely press the dough back together in the pan with your fingertips. If using Flaky Dough, moisten the torn edges and adhere them together. If using other doughs, merely press together to adhere.

7

TARTS, PIES AND OTHER PASTRY DOUGH DESSERTS

Pastries, such as these with fillings in a pastry container, are ancient in origin. The Romans made savory pies—sometimes with bizarre fillings. The nursery rhyme which speaks of "four and twenty blackbirds baked in a pie" probably refers to the Roman practice of making enormous pies with removable covers. Live birds were placed on the filling under the cover after the pie was baked; to the delight of the banquet guests, the birds would fly out of the pie after the first portion was removed.

The pastries considered here fall into several categories. Tarts are open-faced pastries baked in fluted straight-sided pans; sometimes, though, a tart may have a lattice-crust top. Pies are pastries baked in sloping-sided pie pans and are often covered with a top crust either of lattice strips or an entire piece of dough. Some other specialty pastries, made with the pastry doughs from the previous chapter as well as a few made from unique doughs, are also included here.

Techniques for tart and pie making overlap in many instances. Until you are comfortable with them, you may want to refer back to the previous chapter for detailed directions on handling and forming the doughs for the recipes that follow.

ARC EN CIEL

A typical fruit tart in the French manner, the *Arc en Ciel* is so called because of the rows of fruit in alternating colors creating a rainbow effect. It derives its delicacy from the combination of fresh fruit, pastry cream, and a crisp, flaky pastry shell.

The fruit should be arranged in concentric circles, starting at the outside of the tart. Good combinations are: strawberry, kiwi and orange; seedless green grapes, raspberry and kiwi; alternating colors of seedless grapes; or narrow rows, one berry wide, of all the berries possible—raspberries, blueberries, strawberries and blackberries.

The recipes that follow use the same principles for a pear and an apple tart; the fruit is cooked then placed on the pastry cream and pastry. These presentations can be varied by adding accents of another fruit—raspberries would be excellent with the pears.

Flaky Pastry Dough

- 1 CUP UNBLEACHED ALL-PURPOSE FLOUR, ABOUT 5 OUNCES
- 2 TABLESPOONS CAKE FLOUR, ABOUT ½ OUNCE
- ¼ TEASPOON SALT
- ⅛ TEASPOON BAKING POWDER
- 1 STICK BUTTER, 4 OUNCES, COOL
- 3 TO 4 TABLESPOONS ICE WATER

Pastry Cream

- 1 CUP MILK
- ⅓ CUP SUGAR, ABOUT 2½ OUNCES
- 2 TABLESPOONS CORNSTARCH, ABOUT ½ OUNCE
- 3 EGG YOLKS
- 1 TABLESPOON BUTTER, ½ OUNCE, SOFTENED
- 1 TEASPOON VANILLA EXTRACT
- 1 TABLESPOON LIQUEUR, OPTIONAL

Neutral Glaze

- ⅔ CUP APPLE JELLY

HULLED, HALVED STRAWBERRIES; RASPBERRIES; PEELED AND SLICED ORANGES OR KIWI; OR SEEDLESS GRAPES

Mixing the Flaky Pastry Dough. Combine the all-purpose flour, cake flour, salt and baking powder; cut up the butter, add and gently toss to coat. Rub in the butter until the mixture looks sandy. Sprinkle over 3 tablespoons of ice water; toss with a fork. Add another tablespoon of water if necessary. Press the dough together. Wrap and chill.

Rolling the Dough: Lightly flour the work surface and the dough, then roll the dough into a 14-inch disk and line a 10-inch tart pan with it. Chill for several hours or overnight.

Baking the Tart Shell. Dock the base of the tart well; cover with a disk of parchment paper and weigh with dried beans. Bake at 350°F until set, about 25 minutes. Remove paper and beans and continue baking until very lightly colored. Cool on a rack.

Preparing the Pastry Cream. Bring ¾ cup milk and all the sugar to a boil in a saucepan. Whisk cornstarch into remaining milk; whisk in egg yolks. Whisk about one third of the boiling milk into the yolk mixture. Return the remaining milk to a boil and whisk in the yolk mixture, whisking constantly until the Pastry Cream thickens and returns to a boil; immediately remove from heat. Whisk in the butter and vanilla. Chill with plastic wrap against the surface. Gently stir the liqueur into the cold Pastry Cream.

Preparing the Neutral Glaze. Reduce the apple jelly in a small saucepan over medium heat until it coats the back of a spoon.

Assembling. Spread the Pastry Cream evenly in the tart shell. Arrange the fruit in concentric circles over the cream, then brush with the glaze.

Holding. Store at a cool room temperature for no more than three or four hours.

Yield. About 8 to 10 portions

PEAR WILLIAMS TART

This delightful pear tart is simple in its presentation and idea, but has a delicate elusive flavor. The pear alcohol, *Eau de Vie de Poire* or Pear Williams as it is sometimes called, has a strong pear flavor which perfumes the tart.

Flaky Pastry Dough
- 1 CUP UNBLEACHED ALL-PURPOSE FLOUR, ABOUT 5 OUNCES
- 2 TABLESPOONS CAKE FLOUR, ABOUT ½ OUNCE
- ¼ TEASPOON SALT
- ⅛ TEASPOON BAKING POWDER
- 1 STICK BUTTER, 4 OUNCES, COOL
- 3 TO 4 TABLESPOONS ICE WATER

Pear Pastry Cream
- 1 CUP MILK
- ⅓ CUP SUGAR, ABOUT 2½ OUNCES
- 2 TABLESPOONS CORNSTARCH, ABOUT ½ OUNCE
- 3 EGG YOLKS
- 1 TABLESPOON BUTTER, ½ OUNCE, SOFTENED
- 1 TABLESPOON PEAR ALCOHOL

Poached Pears
- 2 TABLESPOONS LEMON JUICE
- 5 BARTLETT OR ANJOU PEARS, ABOUT 2½ POUNDS
- 1 CUP SUGAR, ABOUT 7½ OUNCES
- 1 VANILLA BEAN

Apricot Glaze
- ¾ CUP APRICOT PRESERVES
- 2 TABLESPOONS POACHING SYRUP

TOASTED SLICED ALMONDS

Mixing the Flaky Pastry Dough. Combine the all-purpose flour, cake flour, salt and baking powder; cut up the butter, add and gently toss to coat. Rub in the butter until the mixture looks sandy. Sprinkle over 3 tablespoons of ice water; toss with a fork. Add another tablespoon of water if necessary. Press the dough together. Wrap and chill.

Rolling the Dough. Lightly flour the work surface and dough then roll the dough into a 14-inch disk and line a 10-inch tart pan with it. Chill for several hours or overnight.

Baking the Tart Shell. Dock the base of the tart well; cover with a disk of parchment paper and fill with dried beans. Bake at 350°F until set, about 25 minutes. Remove paper and beans and continue baking until very lightly colored. Cool on a rack.

Preparing the Pastry Cream. Bring ¾ cup milk and all the sugar to a boil in a saucepan. Whisk the cornstarch into remaining milk; whisk in yolks. Whisk about one third of the boiling milk into the yolk mixture. Return the remaining milk to a boil and whisk in the yolk mixture. Whisk constantly until the Pastry Cream thickens and returns to a boil; immediately remove from heat. Whisk in the butter and vanilla. Chill with plastic wrap against the surface. Stir the Eau de Vie into cold Pastry Cream.

Preparing the Poached Pears. Fill a large saucepan with ice water and add the lemon juice. Peel, core and halve the pears and place immediately in the ice water. Drain away all but enough water to cover the pears; add sugar and vanilla bean. Cover pears with a round of parchment or wax paper with a hole in the center. Simmer over medium heat until the pears are tender. Lift the pears from the syrup with a slotted spoon and place on a paper-towel lined pan. Cool and refrigerate.

Preparing the Apricot Glaze. Bring the apricot preserves and poaching syrup to a boil, strain into another saucepan and reduce, simmering, until the glaze coats the back of a spoon.

Assembling. Spread the Pastry Cream evenly in the tart shell. Slice through eight of the cooked pear halves from blossom to stem end. Fan out the halves toward the stem-end, like the spokes of a wheel, over the Pastry Cream. Use remaining halves, sliced thinly, to fill in any gaps around the edge. Reheat apricot glaze if necessary. Brush fruit with glaze. Sprinkle almonds around edge of tart and some in the center.

Holding. Store loosely covered at a cool room temperature for no more than three hours.

Yield. About 8 to 10 portions

Apple and Calvados Tart

Prepare as for Pear Williams Tart, substituting Calvados for the pear alcohol and wine-poached apples for the poached pears.

Wine-Poached Apples
    4 GOLDEN DELICIOUS APPLES, ABOUT 2
        POUNDS
    2/3 CUP SUGAR, ABOUT 5 OUNCES
    2 1/2 CUPS WHITE WINE, APPROXIMATELY
    1 STRIP LEMON ZEST

Cooking the Apples. Peel, halve, core and slice the apples as for a tart, across the core into 1/4-inch slices, keeping the halves intact. Place in a pan that will just hold them and sprinkle with the sugar. Add white wine to cover and lemon zest. Cover with a piece of parchment or wax paper with a small hole cut in the center. Cook over medium heat until the wine begins to simmer. Simmer very gently 5 minutes. Lift the apples out of the syrup with a slotted spoon and drain on a paper-towel-lined pan. Cool and refrigerate.

When assembling the tart, overlap the apple slices in concentric rows, rather than in a spoke pattern like the pear tart. Glaze and garnish with toasted sliced almonds.

RASPBERRY TART

Here only the fruit and pastry are combined together with no other flavors to detract. Especially good with freshly picked, very sweet berries.

Flaky Pastry Dough
    1 CUP UNBLEACHED ALL PURPOSE FLOUR,
        ABOUT 5 OUNCES
    2 TABLESPOONS CAKE FLOUR, ABOUT 1/2
        OUNCE
    1/4 TEASPOON SALT
    1/8 TEASPOON BAKING POWDER
    1 STICK BUTTER, 4 OUNCES, COOL
    3 TO 4 TABLESPOONS ICE WATER

Raspberries and Glaze
    2 PINTS FRESH RASPBERRIES, ABOUT 1 1/2
        POUNDS
    2/3 CUP APPLE JELLY

Mixing the Flaky Pastry Dough. Combine the all-purpose flour, cake flour, salt and baking powder; cut up the butter, add and gently toss to coat. Rub in the butter until the mixture looks sandy. Sprinkle over 3 tablespoons of ice water; toss with a fork. Add another table-spoon of water if necessary. Press the dough together. Wrap and chill.

Rolling the Dough. Lightly flour the work sur-face and the dough, then roll the dough into a 14-inch disk and line a 10-inch tart pan with it. Chill for several hours or overnight.

Baking the Tart Shell. Dock the base of the tart well; cover with a disk of parchment paper and weight with dried beans. Bake at 350°F until set, about 25 minutes. Remove paper and beans and continue baking until very lightly colored. Cool on a rack.

Making the Glaze. Place about 1 cup (one quarter) of the berries in a small saucepan. Bring to a boil with the apple jelly; simmer 5 to 10 minutes, or until reduced and slightly thickened. Strain.

Assembling. Arrange the remaining berries in the baked shell. Brush with glaze.

Holding. Store at a cool room temperature for no more than three hours.

Yield. About 8 to 10 portions

Blueberry or Blackberry Tart

Follow recipe for raspberry tart, substituting 2 PINTS BLUEBERRIES or BLACKBERRIES for the raspberries.

GOLDEN LEMON TART

One of the signature desserts created by Al-bert Kumin at the opening of Windows on the World in March 1976.

Flaky Pastry Dough
- 1 CUP UNBLEACHED ALL-PURPOSE FLOUR, ABOUT 5 OUNCES
- 2 TABLESPOONS CAKE FLOUR, ABOUT ½ OUNCE
- ¼ TEASPOON SALT
- ⅛ TEASPOON BAKING POWDER
- 1 STICK BUTTER, 4 OUNCES, COOL
- 3 TO 4 TABLESPOONS ICE WATER

Lemon Filling
- 1 CUP WATER
- ⅔ CUP SUGAR, ABOUT 5 OUNCES
- 3 TO 4 LEMONS
- ¼ CUP CORNSTARCH, ABOUT 1 OUNCE
- 5 EGG YOLKS
- 4 TABLESPOONS BUTTER, 2 OUNCES, SOFTENED
- 1 TEASPOON VANILLA EXTRACT
- 1 ENVELOPE UNFLAVORED GELATIN, ABOUT 2½ TEASPOONS
- 1 CUP HEAVY WHIPPING CREAM

Apricot Glaze
- 1 CUP APRICOT PRESERVES
- ¼ CUP WATER

2 TO 3 LEMONS FOR FINISHING

Mixing the Flaky Pastry Dough. Combine the all-purpose flour, cake flour, salt and baking powder; cut up the butter, add and gently toss to coat. Rub in the butter until the mixture looks sandy. Sprinkle over 3 tablespoons of ice water; toss with a fork. Add another table-spoon of water if necessary. Press the dough together. Wrap and chill.

Rolling the Dough. Lightly flour the work sur-face and dough, then roll the dough into a 14-inch disk and line a 10-inch tart pan with it. Chill for several hours or overnight.

Baking the Tart Shell. Dock the base of the tart well; cover with a disk of parchment paper and weight with dried beans. Bake at 350°F until set, about 25 minutes. Remove paper and beans and continue baking until very lightly colored. Cool on a rack.

Preparing the Lemon Filling. Combine the water and sugar in a saucepan. Strip the zests from the lemons with a vegetable peeler; add to the pan. Bring to a simmer, remove from heat, and steep 15 to 20 minutes. Squeeze and strain juice from lemons to yield ½ cup. Place in a bowl; whisk in cornstarch then yolks. Strain the syrup into another saucepan. Bring to a boil. Whisk about one fourth of the syrup into the egg mixture. Return the remaining syrup to a boil and whisk in the egg mixture. Whisk constantly over medium heat until the lemon cream thickens and returns to a boil. Boil, whisking, 1 to 2 minutes. Immediately remove from heat. Whisk in the butter and vanilla; whisk until smooth. Chill with plastic wrap against surface.

Soften gelatin in ¼ cup water for about 5 minutes. Place over simmering water until gelatin melts. Whisk lemon mixture until smooth. Whisk about one quarter of it into the gelatin. Whisk gelatin into remaining lemon mixture. Whip the cream until it holds its shape; fold into lemon mixture, being sure that the lemon mixture is cool before folding in the cream.

Assembling. Fill the baked shell with the lemon cream, doming the top. Chill to set the filling.

Preparing the Apricot Glaze. Bring the preserves and water to a boil, strain into another saucepan and reduce, simmering, until the glaze coats the back of a spoon. Cool.

Finishing. Slice lemons paper-thin with a slicing machine or very sharp knife. Arrange lemon slices overlapping on surface of cream. Brush very lightly with the Apricot Glaze.

Holding. Refrigerate the tart to set the glaze. Bring the tart to room temperature for several hours before serving to improve the texture of the pastry. Be careful that the tart does not become too warm or the filling will liquefy.

Yield. About 8 to 10 portions

PEAR AND CURRANT PIE

Pear pies are traditionally made in pear growing areas. Use firm pears so that the filling retains good texture.

Flaky Pastry Dough
>   2 CUPS UNBLEACHED ALL-PURPOSE FLOUR, ABOUT 10 OUNCES
>   ¼ CUP CAKE FLOUR, ABOUT 1 OUNCE
>   ½ TEASPOON SALT
>   ¼ TEASPOON BAKING POWDER
>   2 STICKS BUTTER, 8 OUNCES, COOL
>   5 TO 6 TABLESPOONS ICE WATER

Cooked Pear Filling
>   3 POUNDS FIRM, RIPE PEARS, BARTLETT, ANJOU OR COMICE
>   6 TABLESPOONS BUTTER, 3 OUNCES
>   ¾ CUP SUGAR, ABOUT 5¾ OUNCES
>   3 TABLESPOONS LEMON JUICE
>   ⅔ CUP CURRANTS, ABOUT 3 OUNCES

Egg Wash
>   1 EGG
>   PINCH SALT

Mixing the Flaky Pastry Dough. Combine the all-purpose flour, cake flour, salt and baking powder; cut up the butter, add and gently toss to coat. Rub in the butter until the mixture looks sandy. Sprinkle over 3 tablespoons of ice water; toss it with a fork. Add another tablespoon of water if necessary. Press the dough together. Wrap and chill.

Preparing the Cooked Pear Filling. Peel, halve, and core the pears; slice each half into ½-inch-thick pieces. Melt the butter in a sauté pan over high heat. Add pears and toss to coat. Add sugar, then lemon juice. Cook over high heat, tossing often, until pears are just tender. Pour the filling onto a large platter and refrigerate or cool it at room temperature. Combine the currants and 2 cups of cold water in a 1½-quart saucepan. Bring to a boil, drain and rinse. Gently fold into the cooled filling.

Mixing the Egg Wash. Whisk the egg and salt in a small bowl until very liquid.

Assembling. Lightly flour the work surface and dough, then roll half the dough to a 14-inch disk, ⅛-inch thick. Fit the dough into a 9-inch pie pan and trim the edges of the dough even with the rim of the pan. Pour in the cooled filling, smoothing the top. Roll the remaining dough to a disk ⅛ inch thick. Moisten the edge of the bottom crust with water or egg wash. Place dough on the filling. Turn the edge of the top crust under the edge of the bottom crust. Flute the edge. Cut vent holes in the center of the pie. Brush with the egg wash.

Baking. Bake at 425°F for 15 minutes on the lowest rack in the oven. Lower temperature to 350°F and bake until the juices just start to bubble up and the crust is baked through, about 30 minutes longer.

Holding. Store the pie at room temperature up to 1 day.

Yield. About 10 to 12 portions

ULTIMATE APPLE PIE

The use of the cooked filling here ensures a bottom crust that is dry and baked through. Since most of the water in the filling is evaporated before baking, less water exudes from the apples as the pie bakes.

Flaky Pastry Dough
   2 CUPS UNBLEACHED ALL-PURPOSE FLOUR, ABOUT 10 OUNCES
   ¼ CUP CAKE FLOUR, ABOUT 1 OUNCE
   ½ TEASPOON SALT
   ¼ TEASPOON BAKING POWDER
   2 STICKS UNSALTED BUTTER, 8 OUNCES, COOL
   5 TO 6 TABLESPOONS ICE WATER

Cooked Apple Filling
   3 POUNDS GOLDEN DELICIOUS APPLES, ABOUT 6 OR 7
   ⅔ CUP SUGAR, ABOUT 5 OUNCES
   4 TABLESPOONS BUTTER, 2 OUNCES
   1 TEASPOON FINELY GRATED LEMON ZEST
   1 TABLESPOON STRAINED LEMON JUICE
   ½ TEASPOON CINNAMON

Egg Wash
   1 EGG
   PINCH SALT

Mixing the Flaky Pastry Dough. Combine the all-purpose flour, cake flour, salt and baking powder; cut up and add the butter, and gently toss to coat. Rub in the butter until the mixture looks sandy. Sprinkle over 3 tablespoons of ice water; toss with a fork. Add another tablespoon of water if necessary. Press the dough together. Wrap and chill.

Cooking the Filling. Melt the butter in a wide,

shallow pan with a cover, large enough to hold the apples in approximately one layer. Peel, halve, core, then slice each apple half into four or five wedges. Add the apple slices. Add the remaining filling ingredients and stir well to combine. Cook over medium heat until the apples begin to sizzle, then lower the heat and cover. Let steam about 5 minutes, until the apples begin to exude their juices. Continue cooking, covered, about 5 minutes longer, or until the apples have exuded a large quantity of juice. Uncover and continue cooking at a low heat to evaporate the juices, about 10 minutes longer. The apples should remain in firm, distinct pieces. Cool.

Mixing the Egg Wash. Whisk the egg and salt in a small bowl until very liquid.

Assembling. Lightly flour the work surface and dough, then roll half the dough into a 14-inch disk, ⅛ inch thick. Fit the dough into a 9-inch pie pan and trim the edges of the dough even with the rim of the pan. Pour in the cooled filling, filling to the top. Roll the remaining dough to a disk ⅛ inch thick. Moisten the edge of the bottom crust with water or egg wash. Place dough on the filling. Turn the edge of the top crust under the edge of the bottom crust. Flute the edge. Cut vent holes in the center of the pie. Brush with the egg wash.

Baking. Bake at 425°F for 15 minutes on the lowest rack of the oven. Lower temperature to 350°F and bake until the juices just start to bubble up and the bottom crust is baked through, about 30 minutes longer.

Holding. Store the pie at room temperature up to 1 day.

Yield. About 10 to 12 portions

MEATLESS MINCE PIE

Not traditional, but a light, fast version of mincemeat. For variety, substitute pears for the apples or use a combination.

Flaky Pastry Dough
>   2 CUPS UNBLEACHED ALL-PURPOSE FLOUR, ABOUT 10 OUNCES
>   ¼ CUP CAKE FLOUR, ABOUT 1 OUNCE
>   ½ TEASPOON SALT
>   ¼ TEASPOON BAKING POWDER
>   2 STICKS BUTTER, 8 OUNCES, COOL
>   5 TO 6 TABLESPOONS ICE WATER

Meatless Mincemeat Filling
>   3 GOLDEN DELICIOUS APPLES, ABOUT 1½ POUNDS
>   ¾ CUP YELLOW RAISINS, ABOUT 3 OUNCES
>   ¾ CUP CURRANTS, ABOUT 3 OUNCES
>   ½ STICK BUTTER, 2 OUNCES
>   1 TEASPOON GRATED ORANGE ZEST
>   1 TEASPOON GRATED LEMON ZEST
>   ⅓ CUP BRANDY OR DARK RUM
>   ½ CUP FIRMLY PACKED LIGHT BROWN SUGAR, ABOUT 4 OUNCES
>   1 CUP WALNUT PIECES, COARSELY CHOPPED, ABOUT 4 OUNCES
>   ½ TEASPOON CINNAMON
>   ¼ TEASPOON ALLSPICE
>   ½ TEASPOON GINGER

Egg Wash
>   1 EGG
>   PINCH SALT

Mixing the Flaky Pastry Dough. Combine the all-purpose flour, cake flour, salt and baking powder; cut up the butter, add and gently toss to coat. Rub in the butter until the mixture looks sandy. Sprinkle over 3 tablespoons of ice water; toss with a fork. Add another tablespoon of water if necessary. Press the dough together. Wrap and chill.

Preparing the Mincemeat Filling. Peel, halve, core, and grate the apples by hand or in a food processor. Combine with the remaining filling ingredients in a large saucepan and cook, covered, over medium heat, until the mixture is very liquid, about 15 minutes. Uncover, lower the heat and simmer, stirring frequently, until most of the liquid has evaporated, about 20 minutes. Cool.

Mixing the Egg Wash. Whisk the egg and salt in a small bowl until very liquid.

Assembling. Lightly flour the work surface and dough, then roll half the dough into a 14-inch disk, ⅛ inch thick. Fit the dough into a 9-inch pan and trim the edges of the dough even with the rim of the pan. Roll the remaining dough to a 10 × 14-inch rectangle. Cut into at least ten 1-inch strips and egg wash the strips and the edge of the bottom crust. Pour in the filling, smoothing the top. Apply the strips of dough, five in each direction, making a diagonal lattice. Trim the ends of the strips even with the edge of the bottom crust. With floured fingers, flute the edges of the crust.

Baking. Bake at 425°F for 15 minutes on the lowest rack of the oven. Lower the temperature to 350°F and bake until the juices just start to bubble up and the bottom crust is baked through, about 30 minutes longer.

Holding. Store the pie at room temperature up to 1 day.

Yield. About 10 to 12 portions

GÂTEAU SAINT-HONORÉ

Named for one of the patron saints of pastry cooks, this dessert combines diverse elements for a striking presentation.

The Saint-Honoré is composed of an empty pastry dough shell that has a rim of Pâte à Choux piped around it. The remaining Pâte à Choux is used to make twenty or so small *choux.* After baking, both the shell and small *choux* are filled with a lightened and flavored pastry cream. The caramel in the recipe functions both as a glaze for the small *choux* and as an adhesive to hold them to the rim of the shell. Finally, the caramel is used to spin decorative threads over the small *choux.*

Be careful to keep the caramel free of any foreign matter when glazing the *choux:* Any crumbs or bits of pastry cream that fall into the caramel will encourage it to crystallize, making it useless for adhering the *choux* to the rim of the dessert and for spinning the decorative caramel threads.

Flaky Pastry Dough Base
1 CUP UNBLEACHED ALL-PURPOSE FLOUR, ABOUT 5 OUNCES
2 TABLESPOONS CAKE FLOUR, ABOUT ½ OUNCE
¼ TEASPOON SALT
⅛ TEASPOON BAKING POWDER
1 STICK BUTTER, 4 OUNCES, COOL
3 TO 4 TABLESPOONS ICE WATER

Pâte à Choux
¾ CUP WATER
6 TABLESPOONS BUTTER, 3 OUNCES
PINCH SALT

1 CUP UNBLEACHED ALL-PURPOSE FLOUR,
ABOUT 5 OUNCES

4 EGGS

Egg Wash

1 EGG

PINCH SALT

Pastry Cream

2 CUPS MILK

2/3 CUP SUGAR, ABOUT 5 OUNCES

1/4 CUP CORNSTARCH, ABOUT 1 OUNCE

6 EGG YOLKS

2 TABLESPOONS BUTTER, 1 OUNCE, SOFTENED

1 TABLESPOON LIQUEUR

2 TEASPOONS VANILLA EXTRACT

Whipped Cream

1 CUP HEAVY WHIPPING CREAM

2 TABLESPOONS SUGAR, ABOUT 1 OUNCE

1 TEASPOON VANILLA EXTRACT

Caramel

1 CUP SUGAR, ABOUT 7 1/2 OUNCES

1 TEASPOON LEMON JUICE

Mixing the Flaky Pastry Dough Base. Stir together the flour, cake flour, salt and baking powder in a bowl. Cut up the butter, add and toss gently to coat. Rub in the butter until the mixture looks sandy. Sprinkle over 3 tablespoons of ice water; toss with a fork. Add another tablespoon of water if necessary. Press the dough together. Wrap and chill several hours.

Lightly flour the work surface and dough. Roll the dough into a 9-inch circle about 3/16 inch thick. Place the dough on a paper-lined baking pan and cut it into an 9-inch disk,

using a pattern. Dock the dough well with a fork. Chill while preparing the Pâte à Choux.

Mixing the Pâte à Choux. Bring the water, butter and salt to a boil in a saucepan. Remove from the heat and stir in the flour all at once. Return to the heat and cook the paste, stirring with a wooden spoon, 1 to 2 minutes. Remove the paste to a bowl, beat to cool slightly, then beat in the eggs one at a time.

Mixing the Egg Wash. Beat the egg and salt together. Brush on the chilled disk of dough.

Piping the Rim of the Shell. Using a 1/2-inch plain tube, pipe a ring of Pâte à Choux on the perimeter of the dough, then pipe a spiral starting in the center of the dough (this acts as a support for the filling later on).

Piping the small Choux. With the remaining Pâte à Choux, pipe about twenty small *choux*, 1-inch in diameter, on a separate paper-lined pan.

Baking. Bake the base and the *choux* at 375°F about 20 to 30 minutes. (The low temperature is to prevent the Pâte Brisée from burning before the Pâte á Choux is baked.) Cool the base on the pan and the *choux* on a rack.

Preparing the Pastry Cream. Bring 1 1/2 cups of

the milk and the sugar to a boil in a 3-quart saucepan. Whisk cornstarch into the remaining milk. Whisk in the yolks. Whisk one third of the boiling milk into the yolk mixture. Return the remaining milk to a boil and beat in the yolk mixture, whisking constantly until the Pastry Cream thickens and returns to a boil. Pour into a bowl and whisk in the butter, liqueur and vanilla. Chill with plastic wrap against the surface.

Making the Whipped Cream. Combine the heavy cream with the sugar and vanilla and whip until it holds a firm peak.

Finishing the Filling. Fold about one third of the whipped cream into the cold Pastry Cream, to lighten it. Refrigerate the remaining whipped cream for finishing the dessert.

Filling. Using a ¼-inch plain tube, pierce

the bottoms of the *choux.* Insert the tube in a pastry bag and fill with about 1 cup of the lightened pastry cream. Fill the *choux.* Set aside on a paper-lined pan. Pour the remaining lightened Pastry Cream into the cooled shell and spread evenly with a spatula.

Preparing the Caramel. Combine the sugar and lemon juice in a saucepan with a wooden spoon. Place on medium heat; cook without stirring until the sugar starts to melt around the sides of the pan and the center begins to smoke. Start to stir the sugar. Continue heating, stirring occasionally, until the glaze turns amber in color and is clear and free of sugar crystals. Remove from heat at once. Dip the bottom of the pan in at least 2 inches of cold water for 30 seconds to arrest the cooking. If the caramel is prepared too far in advance, it will harden. Reheat gently over low heat to liquefy it.

Glazing. Dip the top of each *chou* into the caramel to glaze it. Drip the excess caramel on the rim of the shell. Adhere the *choux* next to each other to cover the border, reserving one for the center.

Finishing. Using a ½-inch star or Saint-Honore tube, pipe the reserved whipped cream over the filling in a decorative pattern. Place the reserved *chou* in the center.

Dip a teaspoon into the remaining caramel. (It will probably be necessary to reheat the caramel at this point: Place the pan over the lowest heat possible and heat the caramel until it has a thick, honeylike consistency.) Spin threads of caramel over the border *choux*, allowing the caramel to drop from a height of several inches.

Holding. Refrigerate 4 to 5 hours. Prolonged refrigeration may cause the caramel to melt.

Yield. About 10 to 12 portions

BANANA WALNUT TART

Baking bananas under a walnut filling in this tart gives them a jamlike consistency. Sprinkling rum on the hot tart gives a rum flavor while most of the alcohol dissipates as the tart cools.

Try this tart with poached, dried prunes or apricots.

Sweet Pastry Dough

1 CUP UNBLEACHED ALL-PURPOSE FLOUR, ABOUT 5 OUNCES

¼ CUP SUGAR, ABOUT 1¾ OUNCES
PINCH SALT
¼ TEASPOON BAKING POWDER
4 TABLESPOONS UNSALTED BUTTER, 2 OUNCES, COOL
1 LARGE EGG

Walnut Filling

½ CUP WALNUT PIECES, ABOUT 2 OUNCES
½ CUP FIRMLY PACKED LIGHT BROWN SUGAR, ABOUT 4 OUNCES
6 TABLESPOONS BUTTER, 3 OUNCES
1 EGG
¼ TEASPOON CINNAMON
½ TEASPOON VANILLA EXTRACT
¼ CUP UNBLEACHED ALL-PURPOSE FLOUR, ABOUT 1¾ OUNCES
¼ TEASPOON BAKING POWDER
2 LARGE BANANAS, ABOUT ¾ TO 1 POUND

½ CUP WALNUT PIECES, COARSELY CHOPPED, ABOUT 2 OUNCES
1 TABLESPOON DARK RUM

Mixing the Dough. Stir together the dry ingredients in a bowl. Cut up and add the butter; toss gently to coat. Rub in the butter until the mixture looks sandy. Beat the egg and toss into the flour/butter mixture with a fork. Press the dough together, wrap and chill it.

Mixing the Walnut Filling. Finely grind the walnut pieces and brown sugar in a food processor. Cream the butter and beat in the walnut mixture. Beat in the egg, then the cinnamon and vanilla. Sift the flour with the baking powder, add and mix in only until it disappears.

Assembling. Lightly flour the work surface and the dough. Roll the dough to a 14-inch disk ⅛ inch thick. Line a 10-inch tart pan with the dough, trimming away the excess.

Slice the bananas ¼ inch thick and arrange them overlapping on the crust. Spoon or pipe the walnut filling in six or eight places on the surface of the fruit and spread smooth with a metal spatula to cover the bananas entirely. Strew with the chopped walnuts.

Baking. Bake at 350°F until the walnut filling is set and golden and the crust is baked through, about 40 minutes. Remove from the oven and sprinkle with the rum. Cool on a rack, then unmold.

Holding. Store the tart at room temperature up to 1 day.

Yield. About 8 to 10 portions

DOUBLE APPLE TART

Usually referred to as a *Tarte aux Pommes à la Parisienne,* this tart combines two forms of apples. A cooked apple filling with currants is spread on a sweet pastry dough, then covered with overlapping apple slices. The two different apple preparations contrast in flavor and texture.

Sweet Pastry Dough
    1 CUP UNBLEACHED ALL-PURPOSE FLOUR,
        ABOUT 5 OUNCES
    ¼ CUP SUGAR, ABOUT 1¾ OUNCES
    PINCH SALT
    ¼ TEASPOON BAKING POWDER
    4 TABLESPOONS BUTTER, 2 OUNCES, COOL
    1 LARGE EGG

Cooked Apple Filling
    2½ POUNDS GOLDEN DELICIOUS APPLES,
        ABOUT 5 TO 6 MEDIUM

    ½ CUP SUGAR, ABOUT 3¾ OUNCES
    4 TABLESPOONS BUTTER, 2 OUNCES
    1 LEMON, GRATED ZEST AND JUICE
    ¼ TEASPOON CINNAMON
    ½ CUP CURRANTS, ABOUT 2 OUNCES

Apple Topping
    1½ POUNDS GOLDEN DELICIOUS APPLES,
        ABOUT 3 TO 4 MEDIUM
    2 TABLESPOONS BUTTER, 1 OUNCE

Apricot Glaze
    ¾ CUP APRICOT PRESERVES
    2 TABLESPOONS WATER

Mixing the Dough. Stir together the dry ingredients in a bowl. Cut up and add the butter; toss gently to coat. Rub in the butter until the mixture looks sandy. Beat the egg and toss into the flour/butter mixture with a fork. Press the dough together, wrap and chill it.

Cooking the Apple Filling. Melt the butter in a wide, shallow pan with a cover, large enough to hold the apples in approximately one layer. Peel, halve, core, then slice each apple half into four or five wedges. Add the apple slices to the pan. Add the remaining filling ingredients and stir well to combine. Cook over medium heat until the apples begin to sizzle, then lower the heat and cover. Let steam about 5 minutes, until the apples begin to exude their juices. Continue cooking, covered, about 5 minutes longer, or until the apples have exuded a large quantity of juice. Uncover and continue cooking at a low heat to evaporate the juices, about 10 minutes longer. The apples should remain in firm, distinct pieces. Cool.

Combine the currants and 2 cups of cold water in a 1½-quart saucepan. Bring to a boil and drain. Gently fold into the cooled filling.

Preparing the Apricot Glaze. Bring the preserves and water to a boil, strain into another saucepan and reduce, simmering, until the glaze coats the back of a spoon.

Assembling. Lightly flour the work surface and the dough. Roll the dough to a 14-inch disk, ⅛ inch thick. Line a 10-inch tart pan with the dough, trimming away the excess. Spread the cooled filling on the dough. Peel, core, slice, and arrange the apples on the apple filling. Melt the butter and brush on the apples.

Baking. Bake at 350°F until the apples are tender and the crust is baked through, about 45 minutes. Cool on a rack. Reheat the apricot glaze and brush on the apples. Unmold the tart.

Holding. Store at room temperature up to 1 day.

Yield. About 8 to 10 portions

MAPLE WALNUT TART

This classic combination of flavors makes a rich, custardy pie appropriate for the winter months. I often flavor the filling with 1 or 2 tablespoons of Canadian whiskey.

Sweet Pastry Dough

1 CUP UNBLEACHED ALL-PURPOSE FLOUR, ABOUT 5 OUNCES
¼ CUP SUGAR, ABOUT 1¾ OUNCES
PINCH SALT
¼ TEASPOON BAKING POWDER
4 TABLESPOONS BUTTER, 2 OUNCES, COOL
1 LARGE EGG

Maple Walnut Filling

¾ CUP SUGAR, ABOUT 5¾ OUNCES
¾ CUP PURE MAPLE SYRUP
6 TABLESPOONS BUTTER, 3 OUNCES
3 EGGS
PINCH SALT
1 TO 2 TABLESPOONS WHISKEY, OPTIONAL

2 CUPS WALNUT PIECES, ABOUT 8 OUNCES

Mixing the Dough. Stir together the dry ingredients in a bowl. Cut up and add the butter; toss gently to coat. Rub in the butter until the mixture looks sandy. Beat the egg and toss into the flour/butter mixture with a fork. Press the dough together, wrap and chill it.

Cooking the Filling. Bring the sugar and maple syrup to a full rolling boil in a small saucepan over medium heat. Remove from the heat. Cut the butter into several pieces and add to the syrup/sugar mixture. Allow to stand until the butter melts. Beat the eggs with the salt (and the optional whiskey) and beat in the syrup/butter mixture taking care not to overbeat.

Assembling. Lightly flour the work surface and the dough. Roll the dough to a 14-inch disk ⅛ inch thick. Line a 10-inch tart pan with the dough, trimming away the excess. Scatter the walnuts on the dough then pour over the filling. Press the walnuts into the filling with the back of a fork as they float to the surface to make sure they are submerged.

Baking. Bake at 350°F until the filling is set and the dough is baked through, about 40 minutes. Cool on a rack.

Holding. Store at room temperature up to 2 days.

Yield. About 8 to 10 portions

HONEY AND ALMOND TART

Another rich nut tart. The flavor of the toasted almonds and honey is reminiscent of *Torrone,* the Italian nougat candy.

Sweet Pastry Dough

1 CUP UNBLEACHED ALL-PURPOSE FLOUR, ABOUT 5 OUNCES

¼ CUP SUGAR, ABOUT 1¾ OUNCES

PINCH SALT

¼ TEASPOON BAKING POWDER

4 TABLESPOONS BUTTER, 2 OUNCES, COOL

1 LARGE EGG

Honey and Almond Filling

¾ CUP HONEY

½ CUP SUGAR, ABOUT 3¾ OUNCES

6 TABLESPOONS BUTTER, 3 OUNCES

3 EGGS

PINCH SALT

1 TEASPOON GRATED LEMON ZEST

2 CUPS SLICED ALMONDS, LIGHTLY TOASTED, ABOUT 6 OUNCES

Mixing the Dough. Stir together the dry ingredients in a bowl. Cut up and add the butter; toss gently to coat. Rub in the butter until the mixture looks sandy. Beat the egg and toss into the flour/butter mixture with a fork. Press the dough together, wrap and chill it.

Cooking the Honey-Almond Filling. Bring the honey and sugar to a full rolling boil in a small saucepan over medium heat. Remove from heat and stir in the butter. Beat the eggs with the salt and lemon zest. Beat in the honey mixture, taking care not to overbeat.

Assembling. Lightly flour the work surface and the dough. Roll the dough to a 14-inch disk, ⅛ inch thick. Line the 10-inch tart pan with the dough, trimming away the excess. Scatter the almonds on the dough and pour over the filling. Press the almonds into the filling with the back of a fork as they float to the surface to make sure that all the almonds are submerged.

Baking. Bake the tart at 350°F until the filling is set and the bottom crust is baked through, about 40 minutes. Cool on a rack.

Holding. Keep the tart loosely covered at room temperature, up to 2 days.

Yield. About 8 to 10 portions

RHUBARB ALMOND TART

The tangy flavor of the rhubarb is a good contrast to the sweetness of the frangipane filling. Poaching the rhubarb in advance eliminates a lot of excess water and sweetens it slightly. Feel free to substitute frozen rhubarb, but do not defrost it before poaching. Poached dried apricots make an interesting variation on this tart.

Sweet Pastry Dough

1 CUP UNBLEACHED ALL-PURPOSE FLOUR, ABOUT 5 OUNCES

¼ CUP SUGAR, ABOUT 1¾ OUNCES

PINCH SALT

¼ TEASPOON BAKING POWDER

4 TABLESPOONS UNSALTED BUTTER, 2 OUNCES, COOL

1 EGG

Poached Rhubarb

  2 POUNDS FRESH RHUBARB

  3 CUPS WATER

  1 CUP SUGAR, ABOUT 7½ OUNCES

  ½ VANILLA BEAN *OR* 2 TEASPOONS VANILLA
  EXTRACT

Almond Frangipane Filling

  ¼ POUND ALMOND PASTE

  ¼ CUP SUGAR, ABOUT 1¾ OUNCES

  1 TEASPOON GRATED ORANGE ZEST

  1 EGG YOLK

  4 TABLESPOONS BUTTER, 2 OUNCES, SOFT

  1 EGG

  3 TABLESPOONS UNBLEACHED ALL-PURPOSE
  FLOUR, ABOUT 1 OUNCE

⅓ CUP SLICED ALMONDS, ABOUT 1 OUNCE
CONFECTIONERS' SUGAR

Mixing the Dough. Stir together the dry ingredients in a bowl. Cut up and add the butter; toss gently to coat. Rub in the butter until the mixture looks sandy. Beat the egg and toss into the flour/butter mixture with a fork. Press the dough together, wrap and chill it.

Poaching the Rhubarb. String and cut the rhubarb into 2½-inch lengths. Bring the water, sugar, and vanilla bean or extract to a boil in a 3- to 4-quart saucepan and remove from the heat. Add the rhubarb, cover the pan and allow to cool. Remove the rhubarb and drain on paper towels for a few minutes before assembling the tart.

Mixing the Frangipane. Break the almond paste into 1-inch pieces and place in the bowl of an electric mixer with the sugar, egg yolk and orange zest. Beat with the paddle on medium speed until smooth. With a rubber spatula, scrape the sides of the bowl and the beaters. Add the butter and continue beating until

smooth and light. Scrape down again and beat in the egg until it is absorbed. Scrape down again and beat until smooth. Beat in the flour just until it disappears.

Assembling. Lightly flour the work surface and the dough. Roll the dough to a 14-inch diameter disk ⅛ inch thick and line a 10-inch tart pan with it. Trim away the excess dough. Distribute the rhubarb evenly in the bottom crust. Spoon or pipe the frangipane in six or eight places on the rhubarb and spread it evenly. Strew with the sliced almonds.

Baking. Bake at 350°F until the filling is set and the bottom crust is baked through, about 40 minutes. Cool on a rack. Dust lightly with confectioners' sugar.

Holding. Keep the tart at room temperature up to 1 day.

Yield. About 8 to 10 portions

APPLE CUSTARD TART

This tart is traditionally known as a *Tarte à la Normande,* because the combination of apples, Calvados and cream is a classic Norman one. I first learned this recipe from Mme. Raymonde Pinelli, the mother of a Monégasque family who kept a small *pension* where I lived for several months in 1974, before working at the opening of the new Sporting Club in Monte Carlo. The *pension,* grandly named the Hôtel de l'Etoile (which was still standing on my last visit in 1986), was on the Rue des Oliviers, an old back alley in the Portier section, now mostly taken over by luxury high rises. Since Mme. Pinelli was from Normandy, she had a collection of old Calvados in beautiful apple-shaped earthenware de-canters. She frequently prepared this tart for special family occasions.

Sweet Pastry Dough

1 CUP UNBLEACHED ALL-PURPOSE FLOUR, ABOUT 5 OUNCES

¼ CUP SUGAR, ABOUT 1¾ OUNCES

PINCH SALT

¼ TEASPOON BAKING POWDER

4 TABLESPOONS BUTTER, 2 OUNCES, COOL

1 LARGE EGG

Custard Mixture

¾ CUP HEAVY WHIPPING CREAM

2 TABLESPOONS SUGAR, ABOUT 1 OUNCE

3 EGG YOLKS

2 TABLESPOONS CALVADOS OR APPLE JACK

3 TO 4 GOLDEN DELICIOUS APPLES, ABOUT 1½ POUNDS

Mixing the Pastry Dough. Stir together the dry ingredients in a bowl. Cut up and add the butter; toss gently to coat. Rub in the butter until the mixture looks sandy. Beat the egg and water and toss into the flour/butter mixture. Press the dough together, wrap and chill it.

Preparing the Custard Mixture. Whisk together all the custard ingredients in a small bowl. Strain.

Assembling. Lightly flour the work surface and the dough, then roll the dough to a 14-inch diameter disk ⅛ inch thick and line a 10-inch tart pan with it. Peel, core, halve, and slice the apples. Arrange overlapping on the dough.

Baking. Bake at 350°F about 30 minutes. Pour the custard mixture into the tart while

it is still in the oven and bake until the custard is just set, about 10 minutes longer.

Holding. Keep the tart at room temperature up to 1 day.

Yield. About 8 to 10 portions

Other Custard Tarts

In the following variations, the custard mixture is poured over *raw* fruit on raw dough. In the case of the blueberry, cherry and cranberry custard tarts, if baked before adding the custard the fruit would produce so much juice that there would be little room for the custard mixture. Since the poached pears are already cooked baking them without the custard mixture would make them mushy.

Cherry Custard Tart

Follow the recipe for Apple Custard Tart, substituting ½ POUNDS SWEET or SOUR CHERRIES, PITTED, for the apples and 2 TABLESPOONS KIRSCH for the Calvados in the custard mixture. Pour the custard mixture over the raw fruit on the raw dough. Increase the oven temperature to 375°F and bake the tart for about 30 minutes.

Blueberry Custard Tart

Follow the recipe for Apple Custard Tart, substituting 3 CUPS BLUEBERRIES (ABOUT 1½ 1-PINT BASKETS) for the apples and 2 TABLESPOONS DARK RUM OR 1 TEASPOON VANILLA for the Calvados in the custard mixture. Pour the custard mixture over raw fruit on the raw dough. Increase the oven temperature to 375°F and bake the tart about 30 minutes.

Cranberry Custard Tart

Because of the cranberries, this tart has a more piquant flavor than those made with other fruit. Follow the recipe for Apple Custard Tart, substituting 3 CUPS CRANBERRIES (1 12-OUNCE BAG) for the apples. Increase the amount of sugar in the custard mixture to ¼ cup and substitute 2 TABLESPOONS ORANGE LIQUEUR for the Calvados in the custard mixture. Pour the custard mixture over the raw fruit on the raw dough. Increase the oven temperature to 375°F and bake the tart about 30 minutes.

Pear Custard Tart

Follow the recipe for Apple Custard Tart, substituting poached pears for the apples and 2 TABLESPOONS PEAR ALCOHOL for the Calvados in the custard mixture. Pour the custard mixture over the raw fruit on the raw dough. Increase the oven temperature to 375°F and bake the tart about 30 minutes.

APRICOT AND ALMOND TART

Feel free to substitute Cookie or Almond Dough, pages 129–130, for the Sweet Pastry Dough in this recipe. Sometimes I like to scatter a handful of toasted, sliced almonds over the glaze, especially if the apricots have shriveled a little during baking.

Sweet Pastry Dough

1 CUP UNBLEACHED ALL PURPOSE FLOUR, ABOUT 5 OUNCES
¼ CUP SUGAR, ABOUT 1¾ OUNCES
PINCH SALT
¼ TEASPOON BAKING POWDER
4 TABLESPOONS BUTTER, 2 OUNCES, COOL
1 LARGE EGG

Almond Frangipane

¼ POUND ALMOND PASTE
¼ CUP SUGAR, ABOUT 1¾ OUNCES
1 EGG YOLK
1 TEASPOON GRATED LEMON ZEST
4 TABLESPOONS BUTTER, 2 OUNCES, SOFTENED
1 EGG
3 TABLESPOONS UNBLEACHED ALL-PURPOSE FLOUR, ABOUT 1 OUNCE

2 POUNDS FRESH APRICOTS, ABOUT 12

Apricot Glaze

¾ CUP APRICOT PRESERVES
2 TABLESPOONS WATER

Mixing the Pastry Dough. Stir together the dry ingredients in a bowl. Cut up and add the butter; toss gently to coat. Rub in the butter until the mixture looks sandy. Beat the egg and water and toss into the flour/butter mixture. Press the dough together, wrap and chill it.

Mixing the Frangipane. Break the almond paste into 1-inch pieces and place in the bowl of an electric mixer with the sugar, egg yolk and lemon zest. Beat with the paddle on medium speed until smooth. With a rubber spatula, scrape the sides of the bowl and the beaters. Add the butter and continue beating until smooth and light. Scrape down again and beat in the egg until it is absorbed. Scrape down again and beat until smooth. Beat in the flour just until it disappears.

Assembling. Lightly flour the work surface and the dough. Roll the dough to a 14-inch diameter, ⅛-inch-thick disk and line a 10-inch tart pan with it. Trim away the excess dough. Spread the almond filling evenly over the dough. Rinse, halve, and stone the apricots. Slash each apricot half several times from blossom end to center. Arrange apricot halves at an angle, skin-side down and slashes out, in concentric circles over the almond filling. (Only the uncut portion of each half should be embedded in the filling.)

Baking. Bake at 350°F about 45 minutes until the filling is set and the pastry is golden. Cool on a rack.

Preparing the Apricot Glaze. Bring the preserves and water to a boil, strain into another saucepan and reduce, simmering, until the glaze coats the back of a spoon.

Finishing. Reheat the glaze, if necessary, and brush evenly over the surface of the tart.

Holding. Keep the tart at room temperature up to 1 day.

Yield. About 8 to 10 portions

Other Fruit and Almond Tarts

In the following variations, all the fruits are brushed with apricot glaze. Although dark fruits are traditionally brushed with a red glaze of currant jelly or raspberry preserves, this type of glaze would discolor the almond filling.

Peach and Almond Tart

Follow the recipe for Apricot and Almond Tart, substituting 2 POUNDS (4 OR 5 MEDIUM) FIRM RIPE PEACHES for the apricots. Slit, blanch, and peel the peaches; halve, stone, and halve again. Arrange the peaches on the frangipane, rounded-side up, perpendicular to the edge, all around the tart. Fill in the center with more pieces radiating out from the center.

Pear and Almond Tart

Follow the recipe for Apricot and Almond Tart, substituting 2 POUNDS (3 OR 4 MEDIUM) PEARS, POACHED, for the apricots. Slice through the cooked pear halves from blossom to stem end. Fan out halves toward stem end and arrange in a pattern like the spokes of a wheel over the almond filling. Use any remaining halves, sliced thinly, to fill any gaps in the center.

Blueberry and Almond Tart

Follow the recipe for Apricot and Almond Tart, substituting 1½ PINTS BLUEBERRIES, about 3 cups, for the apricots. Rinse the blueberries; dry on paper towels. Arrange in an even layer over the almond filling; press in lightly. Do not overbake the tart or the blueberries will burst.

Prune Plum and Almond Tart

Follow the recipe for Apricot and Almond Tart, substituting 2 POUNDS PRUNE PLUMS for the apricots, cutting and arranging them on top of the almond filling in the same manner.

Apple and Almond Tart

Follow the recipe for Apricot and Almond Tart, substituting 1½ POUNDS (3 OR 4 MEDIUM) GOLDEN DELICIOUS APPLES for the apricots. For a further variation, strew the Frangipane with ¼ CUP PLUMPED CURRANTS before arranging the apples on the surface. Arrange the apple slices overlapping, in concentric circles, over the almond filling. Brush with 2 TABLESPOONS MELTED BUTTER before baking.

Cherry and Almond Tart

Follow the recipe for Apricot and Almond Tart, substituting 2 POUNDS PITTED SWEET OR SOUR CHERRIES for the apricots. Arrange in an even layer over the almond filling; press in lightly. Do not overbake or the cherries will burst.

Raspberry and Almond Tart

Follow the recipe for Apricot and Almond Tart, substituting TWO ½-PINTS, ABOUT 2 CUPS, OF RASPBERRIES for the apricots. Arrange in an even layer over the almond filling; press in lightly. Do not overbake or the raspberries will blacken and burst.

TARTE TATIN

Created at the turn of the century by the Demoiselles Tatin, proprietresses of a hotel in the town of Lamotte-Beuvron in the Orleanais, this tart remains one of the great apple desserts in the French repertoire.

Sweet Pastry Dough

    1 CUP UNBLEACHED ALL-PURPOSE FLOUR, ABOUT 5 OUNCES

    ¼ CUP SUGAR, ABOUT 1¾ OUNCES

    PINCH SALT

    ¼ TEASPOON BAKING POWDER

    4 TABLESPOONS BUTTER, 2 OUNCES, COOL

    1 LARGE EGG

Apple Filling

    8 GOLDEN DELICIOUS APPLES, ABOUT 4 POUNDS

    ¾ CUP SUGAR, ABOUT 5¾ OUNCES

    ¼ CUP WATER

    1 TEASPOON LEMON JUICE

    4 TABLESPOONS BUTTER, 2 OUNCES

Mixing the Pastry Dough. Stir together the dry ingredients in a bowl. Cut up and add the butter; toss gently to coat. Rub in the butter until the mixture looks sandy. Beat the egg and toss into the flour/butter mixture. Press the dough together, wrap and chill it.

Cooking the Filling. Peel, core and halve the apples. Slice each half into ¼-inch slices, slicing all the way through, but not separating the slices. In a sloping-sided, nonstick, ovenproof sauté pan which has a 10-inch diameter at the top, combine the sugar, water and lemon juice; bring to a boil, stirring to dissolve the sugar. Cease stirring at the boil and allow the syrup to cook to a pale amber caramel. Remove from heat, add the butter and swirl to combine.

Place the apple halves, rounded-side down, on the caramel, fanning the apple halves slightly. Pack the apples closely together, making a second layer with any remaining apples. Place the pan over medium heat and allow the apples to cook, covered, until they have exuded their juices. Uncover and continue cooking until the juices reduce to a thick glaze. Remove from heat and cool.

Assembling. Lightly flour the work surface and the dough. Roll the Sweet Dough to a 12-inch disk and slide it onto a tart pan bottom or cookie sheet. Dock the dough well and slide it over the apples in the sauté pan. Trim away the excess dough and bake the tart at 375°F about 20 minutes. Cool slightly, invert on a platter and remove the pan.

Holding. Store the tart at room temperature up to 1 day.

Yield. 1 10-inch tart, 8 to 10 portions

Pineapple Tarte Tatin

Peel, quarter and core TWO 2-POUND PINEAPPLES, then cut into ¼-inch slices. Prepare caramel as for the Tarte Tatin and arrange pineapple slices overlapping in the pan, curved edges under. Make a second layer of pineapple with any leftover slices. Cook and bake as for Tarte Tatin.

Pear Tarte Tatin

Peel, halve, core and slice 6 FIRM but RIPE PEARS across the core. Prepare caramel as for Tarte Tatin and arrange pear halves in caramel, rounded-sides down, like the spokes of a wheel, stem ends meeting in the center. Make a second layer with any leftover slices. Cook and bake as for Tarte Tatin.

PEAR AND PORT TART

A variation of the Tarte Tatin in which the pears cook in their own glaze. The glaze reduces as the pears cook and absorb it, giving the pears a gleaming surface when the tart is unmolded.

Sweet Pastry Dough
> 1 CUP UNBLEACHED ALL-PURPOSE FLOUR, ABOUT 5 OUNCES
> ¼ CUP SUGAR, ABOUT 1¾ OUNCES
> PINCH SALT
> ¼ TEASPOON BAKING POWDER
> 4 TABLESPOONS BUTTER, 2 OUNCES, COOL
> 1 LARGE EGG

Pear and Port Filling
> 1 CUP PORT WINE
> ¾ CUP CURRANT JELLY
> 6 FIRM, RIPE PEARS, ABOUT 3 POUNDS

Mixing the Pastry Dough. Stir together the dry ingredients in a bowl. Cut up and add the butter; toss gently to coat. Rub in the butter until the mixture looks sandy. Beat the egg and water and toss into the flour/butter mixture. Press the dough together, wrap and chill it.

Cooking the Filling. In a sloping-sided, nonstick, ovenproof sauté pan which has a 10-inch diameter at the top, combine the Port and currant jelly; bring to a boil over medium heat, making sure that all the jelly has melted. Continue simmering until slightly thickened. Remove from the heat and allow to cool slightly.

Peel, halve and core the pears; slice through them, keeping the halves intact, and arrange them, rounded-side down, in pan. Crowd the pears together. If there are leftover halves, separate the slices and form a layer over the halves in the pan. Bring to a boil over medium heat; lower heat and cover. Simmer, covered, 20 minutes. Uncover and cook until the liquid is absorbed. Cool.

Assembling. Lightly flour the work surface and the dough. Roll the sweet pastry dough out into a 12-inch disk; fit over pears in pan as in Tarte Tatin, page 158. Bake at 375°F for 20 minutes. Cool slightly and invert onto serving plate.

Holding. Store the tart at room temperature up to 1 day.

Yield. About 8 to 10 portions

PEAR AND SOUR CREAM PIE

The buttery texture of the ripe pears blends nicely with the slightly sharp sour cream filling.

Sweet Pastry Dough
1 CUP UNBLEACHED ALL-PURPOSE FLOUR, ABOUT 5 OUNCES
1/4 CUP SUGAR, ABOUT 1 3/4 OUNCES
PINCH SALT
1/4 TEASPOON BAKING POWDER
4 TABLESPOONS BUTTER, 2 OUNCES, COOL
1 LARGE EGG

Pear and Sour Cream Filling
1/3 CUP SUGAR, ABOUT 2 1/2 OUNCES
2 TABLESPOONS UNBLEACHED ALL-PURPOSE FLOUR, ABOUT 1 OUNCE
1/4 TEASPOON NUTMEG
4 EGGS
1 CUP SOUR CREAM

3 RIPE PEARS, ABOUT 1 1/2 POUNDS

Mixing the Pastry Dough. Stir together the dry ingredients in a bowl. Cut up and add the butter; toss gently to coat. Rub in the butter until the mixture looks sandy. Beat the egg and toss into the flour/butter mixture. Press the dough together, wrap and chill it.

Forming the Pie Shell. Lightly flour the work surface and the dough. Roll the dough to a 14-inch diameter disk 1/8 inch thick. Fit the dough into a 9-inch glass pie pan and trim away all but 1/4 inch of the excess dough. Turn the excess dough under and flute the edge of the pie.

Mixing the Filling. Mix together the sugar, flour and nutmeg in a small bowl. Break the eggs into a 2-quart bowl and beat them until liquid. Beat in the sugar mixture in a stream, then the sour cream.

Assembling. Peel, halve, core and slice the pears across the core in 1/4-inch slices. Scatter them over the dough in the pan. Pour over the filling and shake the pan gently to make sure the pears are evenly distributed in the filling.

Baking. Bake at 350°F until the filling is set and the dough is baked through, about 40 minutes. Cool on a rack.

Holding. Store the pie at room temperature up to 1 day.

Yield. About 8 to 10 portions

CHERRY AND ALMOND PIE

Although sweet cherries make an excellent pie, they are no match for the sour. It is worth hunting for the sour cherries during their short season.

Sometimes I omit the almonds on the filling and finish the pie with a lattice crust.

Sweet Pastry Dough
1 CUP UNBLEACHED ALL-PURPOSE FLOUR, ABOUT 5 OUNCES
1/4 CUP SUGAR, ABOUT 1 3/4 OUNCES
PINCH SALT
1/4 TEASPOON BAKING POWDER
4 TABLESPOONS BUTTER, 2 OUNCES, COOL
1 LARGE EGG

Cherry and Almond Filling
2 1/2 POUNDS SOUR OR SWEET CHERRIES
2/3 TO 1 CUP SUGAR, DEPENDING ON THE SWEETNESS OF THE CHERRIES, ABOUT 5 TO 7 1/2 OUNCES
1/4 TEASPOON CINNAMON
2 TABLESPOONS KIRSCH OR CHERRY LIQUEUR
1 TABLESPOON LEMON JUICE
3 TABLESPOONS CORNSTARCH, ABOUT 3/4 OUNCE
3/4 CUP SLICED ALMONDS, ABOUT 2 1/4 OUNCES

1/2 CUP SLICED ALMONDS, ABOUT 1 1/2 OUNCES

Mixing the Pastry Dough. Stir together the dry ingredients in a bowl. Cut up and add the butter; toss gently to coat. Rub in the butter until the mixture looks sandy. Beat the egg and toss into the flour/butter mixture. Press the dough together, wrap and chill it.

Forming the Pie Shell. Lightly flour the work surface and the dough. Roll the dough to a 14-inch diameter disk, 1/8 inch thick. Fit the dough into a 9-inch glass pie pan and trim away all but 1/4 inch of the excess dough. Turn the excess dough under and flute the edge of the pie.

Cooking the Filling. Stem, rinse and stone the cherries. Combine them with the sugar and cinnamon in a saucepan and bring to a simmer over medium heat. Simmer the cherries in the juices that accumulate 2 or 3 minutes. Remove from the heat, then remove the cherries from the liquid with a slotted spoon to a bowl.

Pour the Kirsch and lemon juice into a small bowl and stir in the cornstarch to dissolve it. Return the cherry syrup to a boil and beat one quarter of it into the cornstarch mixture. Return the remaining syrup to a boil and beat the cornstarch mixture into it. Beat the syrup until it thickens and returns to a boil, and cook, beating constantly, about 1 to 2 minutes. Remove from heat, stir in the cherries and cool the filling.

Toast the 3/4 cup almonds at 350°F about 5 to 10 minutes, stirring frequently. Cool, then gently stir into the cooled filling.

Assembling. Pour the cooled filling into the lined pan and smooth the top. Scatter the untoasted almonds on the filling.

Baking. Bake at 350°F until the filling is set and the crust is baked through, about 40 minutes.

Holding. Store the pie at room temperature up to one day.

Yield. About 8 to 10 portions

BLUEBERRY AND WALNUT PIE

The blueberries melt to the texture of preserves as the filling bakes in the pie. The walnuts and crumbs provide textural contrast to the just-set consistency of the berries.

Sweet Pastry Dough

1 CUP UNBLEACHED ALL-PURPOSE FLOUR, ABOUT 5 OUNCES

¼ CUP SUGAR, ABOUT 1¾ OUNCES

PINCH SALT

¼ TEASPOON BAKING POWDER

4 TABLESPOONS BUTTER, 2 OUNCES, COOL

1 LARGE EGG

Blueberry Filling

2 PINTS BLUEBERRIES, ABOUT 4 CUPS

¾ CUP SUGAR, ABOUT 5¾ OUNCES

3 TABLESPOONS CORNSTARCH, ABOUT ¾ OUNCE

3 TABLESPOONS WATER

1 TABLESPOON GRATED LEMON ZEST

¾ CUP WALNUT PIECES TOASTED AND COARSELY CHOPPED, ABOUT 3 OUNCES

Walnut Crumb Topping

4 TABLESPOONS BUTTER, 2 OUNCES

¼ CUP SUGAR, ABOUT 1¾ OUNCES

½ TEASPOON CINNAMON

¾ CUP UNBLEACHED ALL-PURPOSE FLOUR, ABOUT 3¾ OUNCES

½ CUP WALNUTS, COARSELY CHOPPED, ABOUT 2 OUNCES

Mixing the Pastry Dough. Stir together the dry ingredients in a bowl. Cut up and add the butter; toss gently to coat. Rub in the butter until the mixture looks sandy. Beat the egg and toss into the flour/butter mixture. Press the dough together, wrap and chill it.

Forming the Pie Shell. Lightly flour the work surface and dough. Roll the dough to a 14-inch diameter disk, ⅛ inch thick. Fit the dough into a 9-inch glass pie pan and trim away all but ¼ inch of the excess dough. Turn the excess dough under and flute the edge of the pie. Chill while preparing the filling.

Mixing the Filling. Rinse and pick over the blueberries and drain them on a paper-towelled-lined pan. Combine one third of the berries and the sugar in a saucepan and bring to a simmer over medium heat, stirring occasionally. Simmer the berries in the juices that accumulate about 5 minutes. Strain the juices into another pan.

Pour the water into a small bowl and stir in the cornstarch to dissolve it. Return the blueberry juices to a boil and beat about one quarter of it into the dissolved cornstarch. Return the remaining juices to a boil and beat the cornstarch mixture into it. Return the juices to a boil, beating constantly, and allow to boil about 1 to 2 minutes, beating constantly. Stir in the remaining blueberries, the cooked berries, lemon zest and walnuts, and cool.

Mixing the Crumb Topping. Cream the butter until soft, add the sugar and cream until soft and light. Beat in the cinnamon. Mix in the flour, then the walnuts. The mixture should fall into large, soft crumbs.

Assembling. Pour the filling into the prepared pan and smooth. Scatter over the crumbs and bake at 350°F until the filling is set, the crumbs have colored and the crust is baked through, about 40 minutes. Cool on a rack.

Holding. Store the pie at room temperature up to 1 day.

Yield. About 8 to 10 portions

CRANBERRY PECAN PIE

A good holiday pie—the pungent filling's texture is well set off by the pecans. Walnuts can be successfully substituted for the pecans.

This is loosely adapted from a recipe given to me by Joseph Viggiani.

Sweet Pastry Dough
- 1 CUP UNBLEACHED ALL-PURPOSE FLOUR, ABOUT 5 OUNCES
- ¼ CUP SUGAR, ABOUT 1¾ OUNCES
- PINCH SALT
- ¼ TEASPOON BAKING POWDER
- 4 TABLESPOONS BUTTER, 2 OUNCES, COOL
- 1 LARGE EGG

Cranberry Pecan Filling
- 1 POUND CRANBERRIES, ABOUT 4 CUPS
- 1 CUP FIRMLY PACKED LIGHT BROWN SUGAR, ABOUT 8 OUNCES
- ½ CUP ORANGE JUICE
- 1 TABLESPOON GRATED ORANGE ZEST
- 4 TABLESPOONS BUTTER, 2 OUNCES
- ¼ TEASPOON CINNAMON
- ¼ TEASPOON GINGER
- ¾ CUP PECAN PIECES, ABOUT 3 OUNCES

Mixing the Pastry Dough. Stir together the dry ingredients in a bowl. Cut up and add the butter; toss gently to coat. Rub in the butter until the mixture looks sandy. Beat the egg and toss into the flour/butter mixture. Press the dough together, wrap and chill it.

Forming the Pie Shell. Lightly flour the work surface and dough. Roll the dough to a 14-inch diameter disk, ⅛ inch thick. Fit the dough into a 9-inch glass pie pan and trim away all but ¼ inch of the excess dough. Turn the excess dough under and flute the edge of the pie.

Cooking the Cranberry Pecan Filling. Rinse, drain and pick over the cranberries and combine in a large saucepan with the brown sugar, orange juice and orange zest. Simmer over medium heat about 5 minutes, stirring occasionally, until thick. Stir in the butter and spices and cool. When cool, stir in the pecans.

Baking. Pour the cooled filling into the pastry crust and smooth the top. Bake at 350°F until the filling is set and the bottom crust is baked through, about 40 minutes. Cool on a rack.

Holding. Store the pie at room temperature up to 1 day.

Yield. About 8 to 10 portions

CRANBERRY APPLE PIE

The apples temper the acidity of the cranberries for a sweeter and less pungent filling. Try this with the crumb topping—with or without the walnuts—from the Blueberry Walnut Pie, using only half the quantity of the dough and omitting the lattice top and egg wash.

Sweet Pastry Dough
- 2 CUPS UNBLEACHED ALL-PURPOSE FLOUR, ABOUT 10 OUNCES
- ½ CUP SUGAR, ABOUT 3¾ OUNCES
- PINCH SALT

½ TEASPOON BAKING POWDER

1 STICK BUTTER, 4 OUNCES, COOL

2 LARGE EGGS

Cranberry Apple Filling

2½ POUNDS GOLDEN DELICIOUS APPLES, 4 LARGE

4 TABLESPOONS BUTTER, 2 OUNCES

¾ CUP SUGAR, ABOUT 5¾ OUNCES

½ POUND CRANBERRIES, ABOUT 2 CUPS

¼ TEASPOON CINNAMON

Egg Wash

1 EGG BEATEN WITH 1 PINCH SALT

Mixing the Pastry Dough. Stir together the dry ingredients in a bowl. Cut up and add the butter; toss gently to coat. Rub in the butter until the mixture looks sandy. Beat the eggs and toss into the flour/butter mixture. Press the dough together, wrap and chill it.

Forming the Pie Shell. Divide the dough in half. Lightly flour the work surface and half the dough. Roll the dough into a 14-inch diameter disk, ⅛ inch thick. Fit the dough into a 9-inch glass pie pan and trim flush with the edge. Chill the pie shell and remaining dough while preparing the filling.

Cooking the Cranberry Apple Filling. Peel, core and halve the apples. Slice each half into five or six wedges. Combine the apples, butter and sugar in a large saucepan. Place, covered, over medium heat until the apples exude their juices, about 10 minutes. Uncover, lower the heat and continue cooking until the juices have evaporated. Stir in the cranberries and cook 1 minute longer. Cool the filling.

Finishing the Pie. Pour the cooled filling into the pastry crust and smooth the top. Roll the remaining dough to a 10-inch square and cut into ten 1-inch strips. Egg wash the strips and place them on the pie, five in each direction to make a diagonal lattice. Trim away the excess dough of the strips and flute the edges of the pie.

Baking. Bake at 350°F until the filling is set and the bottom crust is baked through, about 40 minutes. Cool on a rack.

Holding. Store the pie at room temperature, up to 1 day.

Yield. About 8 to 10 portions

LEMON CHEESE TART WITH STRAWBERRIES

Lighter than a traditional cheesecake, this tart can be used as a base for other fruit as well.

Sweet Pastry Dough

1 CUP UNBLEACHED ALL-PURPOSE FLOUR, ABOUT 5 OUNCES

¼ CUP SUGAR, ABOUT 1¾ OUNCES

PINCH SALT

¼ TEASPOON BAKING POWDER

4 TABLESPOONS BUTTER, 2 OUNCES, COOL

1 LARGE EGG

Cheese Filling

1 POUND CREAM CHEESE WITHOUT VEGETABLE GUM, AT ROOM TEMPERATURE

¼ CUP SUGAR, ABOUT 1¾ OUNCES

½ TEASPOON VANILLA EXTRACT

2 EGGS

2 EGG YOLKS

½ CUP HEAVY WHIPPING CREAM

1 TEASPOON GRATED LEMON ZEST

1 PINT STRAWBERRIES

Mixing the Dough. Stir together the dry ingredients in a bowl. Cut up and add the butter; toss gently to coat. Rub in the butter until the mixture looks sandy. Beat the egg and toss into the flour/butter mixture. Press the dough together, wrap and chill it.

Preparing the Cheese Filling. Beat the cream cheese with the paddle on low speed. Beat in the sugar in a stream, then the vanilla. With a rubber spatula, scrape down the sides of the bowl and the beater. Beat in one egg and scrape again. Repeat with the second egg. Beat in the yolks and scrape again. Beat in the cream and strain the filling into a bowl. Stir in the lemon zest. Avoid overbeating the filling or the surface will crack during baking.

Assembling. Lightly flour the work surface and dough. Roll the dough to a 14-inch diameter disk, ⅛ inch thick. Fit the dough into a 10-inch tart pan and trim away the excess. Pour in the filling and bake the tart at 350°F until the filling is set and the crust baked through, about 30 minutes. Cool on a rack.

Finishing. Rinse and drain the strawberries and halve them, leaving the hulls intact and cutting through them. Make a row of berries, cut-side up, at the edge of the tart.

Holding. Refrigerate the tart, loosely covered with plastic wrap, up to 1 day.

Yield. About 8 to 10 portions

TARTE AU FROMAGE BLANC

The French answer to a cheesecake, this tart is usually made with lowfat cheese. Cream cheese or ricotta can be substituted for the farmer cheese.

Sweet Pastry Dough

1 CUP UNBLEACHED ALL-PURPOSE FLOUR, ABOUT 5 OUNCES
¼ CUP SUGAR, ABOUT 1¾ OUNCES
PINCH SALT
¼ TEASPOON BAKING POWDER
4 TABLESPOONS BUTTER, 2 OUNCES, COOL
1 LARGE EGG

Cheese Filling

½ CUP YELLOW RAISINS, ABOUT 2 OUNCES
2 POUNDS FARMER CHEESE
⅓ CUP SUGAR, ABOUT 2½ OUNCES
3 EGGS
2 EGG YOLKS
1 TEASPOON VANILLA EXTRACT

Mixing the Dough. Stir together the dry ingredients in a bowl. Cut up and add the butter; toss gently to coat. Rub in the butter until the mixture looks sandy. Beat the egg and toss into the flour/butter mixture. Press the dough together, wrap and chill it.

Mixing the Filling. Combine the raisins and 2 cups water in a small saucepan. Bring to a boil; drain. Rub the farmer cheese through a fine sieve or pulse until smooth in a food processor. Place the cheese in a 3-quart mixing bowl and stir in the sugar, the eggs and yolks one at a time, then the vanilla. Stir in the raisins.

Assembling. Lightly flour the work surface and dough. Roll the dough to a 15-inch disk, ⅛ inch thick. Butter a 9 × 2-inch-deep straight-sided cake pan, line the bottom with wax paper and fit the dough into it. Allow the excess dough to hang over the sides of the pan until the tart is filled. Pour in the filling and smooth the top. Trim away the excess dough on the top edge even with the top of the pan.

Baking. Bake the tart at 350°F until the filling is set and the crust is baked through, about 45 minutes. Cool on a rack.

Unmolding the Tart. Invert a plate on the tart and invert the tart onto it. Carefully lift off the pan and peel off the paper. Invert another plate on the tart (at this point the tart is upside down between the two plates), reinvert the tart and remove the top plate.

Holding. Refrigerate the tart, loosely covered with plastic wrap, up to 1 day.

Yield. About 10 to 12 portions

TORTA DI RICOTTA

This classic Italian Easter pastry is one of the first things I learned to bake. Flavors vary according to region—sometimes grated lemon and orange zest are added, sometimes toasted sliced almonds and chopped bitter chocolate.

Sweet Pastry Dough
2 CUPS UNBLEACHED ALL-PURPOSE FLOUR,
    ABOUT 10 OUNCES
½ CUP SUGAR, ABOUT 3¾ OUNCES
¼ TEASPOON SALT
½ TEASPOON BAKING POWDER

1 STICK BUTTER, 4 OUNCES, COOL
2 LARGE EGGS

Ricotta Filling
1½ POUNDS WHOLE MILK RICOTTA
⅓ CUP SUGAR, ABOUT 2½ OUNCES
4 EGGS
1 TEASPOON VANILLA EXTRACT
1 TABLESPOON ANISETTE
3 TABLESPOONS CITRON OR MIXED CANDIED
    FRUIT, RINSED AND CHOPPED, ABOUT 1
    OUNCE
¼ TEASPOON CINNAMON, PLUS ADDITIONAL
    FOR SPRINKLING ON THE FILLING

Egg Wash
1 EGG
1 PINCH SALT

Mixing the Dough. Stir together the dry ingredients in a bowl. Cut up and add the butter; toss gently to coat. Rub in the butter until the mixture looks sandy. Beat the eggs and toss into the flour/butter mixture. Press the dough together, wrap and chill it.

Mixing the Ricotta Filling. Rub the ricotta through a sieve or pulse until smooth in a food processor. Place the ricotta in a 3-quart bowl and stir in the sugar, then eggs, one at a time. Stir in the vanilla extract, anisette, citron or candied fruit and cinnamon.

Assembling. Cut off one half of the dough and reserve it. Lightly flour the work surface and the dough. Roll one half of the dough into a 15-inch disk ⅛ inch thick and line a buttered and paper-lined 9 × 2-inch-deep straight-sided cake pan with it. Allow the excess dough to hang over the edge of the pan. Pour in the filling and sprinkle with additional cinnamon. Roll the remaining one half of the dough into a 10-inch square and cut it into ten 1-inch-wide strips. Beat the egg and salt until liquid, then paint the strips with the egg wash. Moisten the edge of the dough on the pan with egg wash and adhere five strips to it in each direction, forming a diagonal lattice. Trim away any excess dough even with the top rim of the pan so that it is completely within the pan.

Baking. Bake at 350°F until the filling is set and the crust is baked through, about 45 minutes. Cool before unmolding.

Unmolding the Torta. Invert a plate on the Torta and invert the Torta onto it. Carefully lift off the pan and peel off the paper. Invert another plate on the Torta (at this point the Torta is upside down between the two plates), reinvert the Torta and remove the top plate.

Holding. Refrigerate the Torta, loosely covered with plastic wrap, up to 2 days.

Yield. About 12 portions

CHOCOLATE HAZELNUT TART

The already buttery flavor of the hazelnuts pairs them naturally with the chocolate filling. Walnuts or pecans make good variations.

Chocolate Dough
  1 CUP UNBLEACHED ALL-PURPOSE FLOUR, ABOUT 5 OUNCES
  3 TABLESPOONS COCOA POWDER, ABOUT ½ OUNCE
  ¼ CUP SUGAR, ABOUT 1¾ OUNCES

PINCH SALT
¼ TEASPOON BAKING SODA
4 TABLESPOONS BUTTER, 2 OUNCES, COOL
1 LARGE EGG

Chocolate-Hazelnut Filling
  2 CUPS WHOLE HAZELNUTS, ABOUT 11 OUNCES
  4 OUNCES BITTERSWEET OR SEMISWEET CHOCOLATE, FINELY CUT
  4 TABLESPOONS BUTTER, 2 OUNCES
  1 CUP DARK CORN SYRUP
  ½ CUP SUGAR, ABOUT 3¾ OUNCES
  3 EGGS
  PINCH SALT
  2 TABLESPOONS DARK RUM (OPTIONAL)

Mixing the Dough. Sift the dry ingredients together three times. Rub in the butter and moisten with the egg as for Sweet Pastry Dough. Shape into a disk, wrap, and refrigerate.

Cooking the Chocolate-Hazelnut Filling. Place the hazelnuts on a baking pan and toast at 350°F until the skins are loose and come off easily, about 10 minutes. Rub the hazelnuts in a towel to remove the skins. Chop the hazelnuts coarsely, by hand or with a food processor.

Combine the chocolate with the butter in a small bowl. Bring a small pan of water to a simmer and turn off the heat. Place the bowl of chocolate and butter over the hot water and stir to melt. Combine the corn syrup and sugar in a small saucepan. Bring to a full rolling boil over medium heat. Remove from heat and stir in the chocolate mixture.

Beat the eggs and salt with the optional rum. Beat in the chocolate mixture, taking care not to overbeat.

Assembling. Lightly flour the work surface and dough. Roll the dough to a 14-inch diameter disk, ⅛ inch thick. Line a 10-inch tart pan with the dough, trimming away the excess. Stir the chopped hazelnuts into the filling and pour the filling into the pan.

Baking. Bake at 350°F until the filling is set and the crust is baked through, about 40 minutes.

Holding. Store the tart at room temperature up to 2 days.

Yield. 1 10-inch tart, about 8 to 10 portions

CHOCOLATE RASPBERRY TART

The tartness of the raspberries in this dessert offsets the rich sweetness of the chocolate filling.

Chocolate Dough

1 CUP UNBLEACHED ALL-PURPOSE FLOUR, ABOUT 5 OUNCES

3 TABLESPOONS COCOA POWDER, ABOUT ½ OUNCE

¼ CUP SUGAR, 1¾ OUNCES

PINCH SALT

¼ TEASPOON BAKING SODA

4 TABLESPOONS BUTTER, 2 OUNCES, COOL

1 LARGE EGG

Rich Chocolate Mousse Filling

6 OUNCES BITTERSWEET OR SEMISWEET CHOCOLATE, FINELY CUT

3 TABLESPOONS BUTTER, 1½ OUNCES, SOFTENED

3 EGG YOLKS

¼ CUP SUGAR, ABOUT 1¾ OUNCES

2 TABLESPOONS FRAMBOISE

½ CUP HEAVY WHIPPING CREAM

TWO ½-PINTS RASPBERRIES

CONFECTIONERS' SUGAR

CHOCOLATE SHAVINGS

Mixing the Chocolate Dough. Sift the dry ingredients together three times. Rub in the butter and moisten with the egg as for Sweet Pastry Dough. Shape into a disk, wrap and refrigerate.

Rolling the Dough. Lightly flour the work surface and dough, then roll to a 14-inch diameter disk, ⅛ inch thick. Line a 10-inch tart pan with the dough, trimming away the excess. Chill for several hours or overnight. Dock the base of the tart well; cover with a disk of parchment paper and weight with dried beans.

Baking. Bake at 350°F until set, about 20 minutes. Remove paper and beans and continue baking until the shell looks dull and dry, and feels firm but slightly resilient, 5 to 10 minutes. Be careful not to overbake. Cool on a rack.

Preparing the Rich Chocolate Mousse. Heat chocolate in a 1-quart bowl over hot, but not simmering, water until it is three-quarters melted. To finish the melting, remove the bowl from the water and stir with a rubber spatula. Whisk in the butter, a tablespoon at a time.

Prepare a Sabayon by whisking the yolks, adding the sugar in a slow stream and whisking in the Framboise. Whisk constantly over simmering water until very thick. Whip the Sabayon in the mixer with the whip on medium speed until cool. Fold the cool Sabayon into the chocolate/butter mixture.

Whip the cream until it holds its shape but

is not stiff. Fold the cream gently into the chocolate mixture. Immediately pour filling into the cooled pastry shell. Refrigerate to set the filling.

Finishing. Arrange raspberries on the chilled filling. Dust with confectioners' sugar. Sprinkle chocolate shavings around the edge of the tart.

Holding. Refrigerate up to 1 day. Remove from refrigerator 1 hour before serving.

Yield. About 8 to 10 portions

Chocolate Orange Tart

Follow recipe for Chocolate Raspberry Tart, substituting orange liqueur for the Framboise and topping the tart with 4 LARGE ORANGES, PEELED, HALVED AND SLICED. Don't dust the tart with confectioners' sugar.

WHITE CHOCOLATE AND PRALIN TART

Really more a confection than a pastry. The caramel flavor of the pralin balances the sweetness of the white chocolate. Serve very small wedges.

Chocolate Dough

1 CUP UNBLEACHED ALL-PURPOSE FLOUR, ABOUT 5 OUNCES
3 TABLESPOONS COCOA POWDER, ABOUT 1/2 OUNCE
1/4 CUP SUGAR, ABOUT 1 3/4 OUNCES
PINCH SALT
1/4 TEASPOON BAKING SODA
4 TABLESPOONS BUTTER, 2 OUNCES
1 LARGE EGG

White Chocolate Mousse Filling

1/3 CUP HEAVY WHIPPING CREAM
6 OUNCES WHITE CHOCOLATE, FINELY CUT
1/2 CUP PRALIN POWDER (PAGE 47)
4 EGG WHITES
1/4 CUP SUGAR, ABOUT 1 3/4 OUNCES

1/4 CUP PRALIN POWDER

Mixing the Dough. Sift the dry ingredients together three times. Rub in the butter and moisten with the egg as for Sweet Pastry Dough. Shape into a disk, wrap, and refrigerate.

Rolling the Dough. Lightly flour the work surface and the dough, then roll to a 14-inch diameter disk, 1/8 inch thick. Line a 10-inch tart pan with the dough, trimming away the excess. Chill for several hours or overnight. Dock the base of the tart well; cover with a disk of parchment paper and weight with dried beans.

Baking. Bake at 350°F until set, about 20 minutes. Remove paper and beans and continue baking until the shell looks dull and dry, and feels firm but slightly resilient, 5 to 10 minutes. Be careful not to overbake. Cool on a rack.

Preparing the White Chocolate Mousse Filling. Heat the cream until hot to the touch, remove from the heat and stir in the white chocolate. Stir until smooth, strain into a bowl and cool to room temperature. Stir in 1/2 cup of the pralin powder.

Whisk the egg whites and sugar over simmering water until the sugar is dissolved and the whites are hot. Whip on medium speed until cool and very soft peaks form. Fold beaten whites into the white chocolate mixture. Immediately pour filling into the cooled pastry shell and smooth the top with a metal spatula. Refrigerate to set the filling.

Finishing. Sprinkle the remaining ¼ cup pralin powder over the chilled filling.

Holding. Refrigerate, loosely covered with plastic wrap, up to 2 days. Remove from refrigerator 1 hour before serving.

Yield. About 12 to 14 portions

GRAPE TART WITH WINE CREAM

The slightly tart flavor of the wine cream brings out the sweetness in the grapes. Use a sweet wine such as a California late-harvest Riesling or an inexpensive French Sauternes. A drier wine such as a Chardonnay also works well in the recipe, but makes a more tart filling. This filling pairs well with either the cookie or nut dough. Other berries can be substituted for the grapes.

Cookie Dough
    1 STICK BUTTER, 4 OUNCES, COOL
    ¼ CUP SUGAR, ABOUT 1¾ OUNCES
    1 EGG
    1¼ CUPS CAKE FLOUR, ABOUT 5 OUNCES

Almond Dough
    6 TABLESPOONS BUTTER, 3 OUNCES, COOL
    ¼ CUP SUGAR, ABOUT 1¾ OUNCES
    1 EGG
    ⅓ CUP GROUND ALMONDS, ABOUT 1 OUNCE
    1¼ CUPS CAKE FLOUR, ABOUT 5 OUNCES

Wine Cream
    ¾ CUP WHITE WINE
    ⅓ CUP SUGAR, ABOUT 2½ OUNCES
    2 TABLESPOONS LEMON JUICE
    2 TABLESPOONS CORNSTARCH, ABOUT ½ OUNCE
    3 EGG YOLKS
    2 TABLESPOONS BUTTER, 1 OUNCE, SOFTENED
    1 TEASPOON VANILLA EXTRACT

    1½ POUNDS SEEDLESS GRAPES, BOTH RED AND GREEN IF POSSIBLE

Apricot Glaze
    ¾ CUP APRICOT PRESERVES
    2 TABLESPOONS WATER

Mixing the Cookie Dough. Cream the butter by hand or machine until soft. Beat in the sugar in a steady stream and continue beating until the mixture is lightened in color and in texture. Beat the egg in a small bowl and add half of it, continuing to beat until the mixture is smooth. Add the remaining egg and continue beating. The butter/egg mixture should be shiny like buttercream. Sift the cake flour and add to the bowl. Pulse the mixer on and off to incorporate it. Scrape from the bowl, wrap in plastic wrap and chill until firm.

Mixing the Almond Dough. Proceed as for the cookie dough, mixing the almonds in along with the sifted cake flour.

Rolling the Dough. Lightly flour the work surface and dough. Roll the dough into a 14-inch diameter disk, ⅛ inch thick, and line a 10-inch tart pan with it. Chill for several hours or overnight. Dock the base of the tart well; cover with a disk of parchment paper and weight with dried beans.

Baking. Bake at 350°F until set, about 20 minutes. Remove paper and beans and continue baking until very lightly colored, 5 to 10 minutes longer. Cool on a rack.

Cooking the Wine Cream. Bring the wine and sugar to a boil in a nonaluminum saucepan. Combine the lemon juice and cornstarch in a small bowl and whisk smooth; whisk in the yolks. Whisk a third of the boiling wine into the yolk mixture and return the remainder to a boil. Beginning to whisk first, whisk the yolk mixture into the boiling wine. Continue cooking, whisking constantly, until the cream thickens and returns to a boil. Cook, whisking constantly about 1 minute. Remove from heat and whisk in butter and vanilla. Pour into a bowl, press plastic wrap against the surface and refrigerate until cold.

Assembling. Spread the wine cream evenly in the pastry shell and arrange the grapes on the cream in even, concentric circles. Bring preserves and water to a boil, strain into another saucepan and reduce, simmering, until the glaze coats the back of a spoon. Brush the tart with the glaze.

Holding. Store the tart refrigerated. Serve on the day it is assembled.

Yield. About 8 to 10 portions

Grape Meringue Tart

Omit the glaze. Cover the tart with a Swiss Meringue made from 4 EGG WHITES and ¾ CUP SUGAR. Spread the meringue on the filling being sure it touches the edges of the crust. Dust with confectioners' sugar and color it in a 400°F oven for about 5 minutes.

LEMON CURD TART

The piquant flavor of the lemon curd is well paired with the brittle sweetness of either the cookie or nut dough. The filling is not extremely dense—keep the tart chilled to avoid liquefying the filling.

Cookie Dough
    1 STICK BUTTER, 4 OUNCES, COOL
    ¼ CUP SUGAR, ABOUT 1¾ OUNCES
    1 EGG
    1¼ CUPS CAKE FLOUR, ABOUT 5 OUNCES

Almond Dough
    6 TABLESPOONS BUTTER, 3 OUNCES, COOL
    ¼ CUP SUGAR, ABOUT 1¾ OUNCES
    1 EGG
    ⅓ CUP GROUND ALMONDS, ABOUT 1 OUNCE
    1¼ CUPS CAKE FLOUR, ABOUT 5 OUNCES

Lemon Curd
    ¾ CUP SUGAR, ABOUT 5¾ OUNCES
    2 TABLESPOONS GRATED LEMON ZEST
    ¾ CUP STRAINED LEMON JUICE
    1 STICK BUTTER, 4 OUNCES
    8 EGG YOLKS

    TOASTED SLICED ALMONDS
    CONFECTIONERS' SUGAR

Mixing the Cookie Dough. Cream the butter by hand or machine until soft. Beat in the sugar in a steady stream and continue beating until the mixture is lightened in color and in texture. Beat the egg in a small bowl and add half of it, continuing to beat until the mixture is smooth. Add the remaining egg and continue beating. The butter/egg mixture should be shiny like buttercream. Sift the cake flour and add it to the bowl. Pulse the mixer on and off to incorporate it. Scrape from the bowl and wrap in plastic wrap. Chill until firm.

Mixing the Almond Dough. Proceed as for the cookie dough, mixing the almonds in along with the sifted cake flour.

Rolling the Dough. Lightly flour the work surface and dough. Roll the dough into a 14-inch diameter disk, ⅛ inch thick, and line a 10-inch tart pan with it. Chill for several hours or overnight. Dock the base of the tart well; cover with a disk of parchment paper and weight with dried beans.

Baking. Bake at 350°F until set, about 20 minutes. Remove paper and beans and continue baking until very lightly colored, 5 to 10 minutes longer. Cool on a rack.

Cooking the Lemon Curd. Combine the sugar, lemon juice, zest and butter in a nonaluminum saucepan and bring to a boil, stirring occasionally. Whisk the yolks until liquid in a small bowl. Whisk one quarter of the boiling lemon mixture into the yolks. Return the remaining lemon mixture to a boil and whisk the yolk mixture into it. Whisk the lemon curd constantly until it thickens and approaches a boil. Pour the lemon curd into a clean bowl and press plastic wrap against the surface. Chill.

Assembling. Spread the lemon curd evenly in the cooled shell. Scatter some almonds on the border of the filling and dust the almonds and the edge of the crust with confectioners' sugar.

Holding. Store the tart in the refrigerator. Serve the tart on the day it is assembled.

Yield. About 8 to 10 portions

Lemon Meringue Tart

Cover the tart with a Swiss Meringue made from 4 EGG WHITES and ¾ CUP SUGAR. Spread the meringue on the filling. Make sure it touches the edges of the crust. Dust the meringue with confectioners' sugar and color it in a 400°F oven for about 5 minutes.

Lime Curd Tart

Substitute ¾ CUP LIME JUICE and 3 TABLESPOONS GRATED ZEST for the lemon juice and zest.

Orange Curd Tart

Substitute ½ CUP ORANGE JUICE and ¼ CUP LEMON JUICE for the ¾ cup lemon juice in the lemon curd. Use 2 TABLESPOONS GRATED ORANGE ZEST and reduce the SUGAR to ½ CUP.

STRAWBERRY ALMOND TART

This tart demonstrates the use of baked frangipane as a base for juicy fruit. The frangipane absorbs the juice from the fruit and prevents the bottom crust from becoming soggy.

Cookie Dough

1 STICK BUTTER, 4 OUNCES, COOL
¼ CUP SUGAR, ABOUT 1¾ OUNCES
1 EGG
1¼ CUPS CAKE FLOUR, ABOUT 5 OUNCES

Almond Dough

6 TABLESPOONS BUTTER, 3 OUNCES, COOL

¼ CUP SUGAR, ABOUT 1¾ OUNCES

1 EGG

⅓ CUP GROUND ALMONDS, ABOUT 1 OUNCE

1¼ CUPS CAKE FLOUR, ABOUT 5 OUNCES

Almond Frangipane Filling

¼ POUND ALMOND PASTE

¼ CUP SUGAR, ABOUT 1¾ OUNCES

1 EGG YOLK

1 TEASPOON GRATED LEMON ZEST

4 TABLESPOONS BUTTER, 2 OUNCES, SOFTENED

1 EGG

3 TABLESPOONS FLOUR, ABOUT 1 OUNCE

Currant Jelly Glaze

⅔ CUP CURRANT JELLY

2 PINTS STRAWBERRIES

¼ CUP TOASTED SLICED ALMONDS, ABOUT ¾ OUNCE

Mixing the Cookie Dough. Cream the butter by hand or machine until soft. Beat in the sugar in a steady stream and continue beating until the mixture is lightened in color and in texture. Beat the egg in a small bowl and add half of it, continuing to beat until the mixture is smooth. Add the remaining egg and continue beating. The butter/egg mixture should be shiny like buttercream. Sift the cake flour and add to the bowl. Pulse the mixer on and off to incorporate it. Scrape from the bowl, wrap in plastic wrap and chill until firm.

Mixing the Almond Dough. Proceed as for the cookie dough, mixing the almonds in along with the sifted cake flour.

Mixing the Frangipane. Break the almond paste into 1-inch pieces and place in the bowl of an electric mixer with the sugar, egg yolk and lemon zest. Beat with the paddle on medium speed until smooth. With a rubber spatula, scrape the sides of the bowl and the beaters. Add the butter and continue beating until smooth and light. Scrape down again and beat in the egg until it is absorbed. Scrape down again and beat until smooth. Beat in the flour just until it disappears.

Rolling the Dough. Lightly flour the work surface and dough. Roll the dough into a 14-inch disk, ⅛ inch thick, and line a 10-inch tart pan with it. Chill for several hours or overnight. Dock the base of the tart well and spread with the frangipane.

Baking. Bake at 350°F until the dough is lightly colored and the frangipane is set, about 25 minutes. Cool on a rack.

Finishing. Bring the jelly to a boil in a saucepan and reduce, simmering, until the glaze coats the back of a spoon. Rinse, hull, and halve the strawberries and arrange them on the almond filling overlapping in concentric circles. Reheat the glaze if necessary and evenly brush over the strawberries. Strew the almonds around the edge of the tart.

Holding. Store the tart at room temperature. Serve the tart on the day it is assembled.

Yield. About 8 to 10 portions

BORDEAUX FRUIT TART

This is an updated version of a nineteenth century pastry called *Infante de Bordeaux.* The original was made from sweet dough and the almond filling was covered with a sugar glaze.

The fruit finish makes a more appealing and less sweet presentation.

Cookie Dough

1 STICK UNSALTED BUTTER, 4 OUNCES, COOL
¼ CUP SUGAR, ABOUT 1¾ OUNCES
1 EGG
1¼ CUPS CAKE FLOUR, ABOUT 5 OUNCES

Almond Dough

6 TABLESPOONS BUTTER, 3 OUNCES, COOL
¼ CUP SUGAR, ABOUT 1¾ OUNCES
1 EGG
⅓ CUP GROUND ALMONDS, ABOUT 1 OUNCE
1¼ CUPS CAKE FLOUR, ABOUT 5 OUNCES

Almond Filling

⅔ CUP WHOLE BLANCHED ALMONDS, ABOUT 2 OUNCES
¼ CUP UNBLEACHED ALL-PURPOSE FLOUR, ABOUT 1¼ OUNCES
½ CUP SUGAR, ABOUT 3¾ OUNCES
4 EGGS, SEPARATED
3 TABLESPOONS BUTTER, 1½ OUNCES, MELTED

Neutral Glaze

⅔ CUP APPLE JELLY

HULLED, HALVED STRAWBERRIES; RASPBERRIES; PEELED AND SLICED ORANGES OR KIWI; OR SEEDLESS GRAPES

Mixing the Cookie Dough. Cream the butter by hand or machine until soft. Beat in the sugar in a steady stream and continue beating until the mixture is lightened in color and in texture. Beat the egg in a small bowl and add half of it, continuing to beat until the mixture is smooth. Add the remaining egg and continue beating. The butter/egg mixture should be shiny like buttercream. Sift the cake flour and add to the bowl. Pulse the mixer on and off to incorporate the flour. Scrape from the bowl, wrap in plastic wrap and chill until firm.

Mixing the Almond Dough. Proceed as for the cookie dough, mixing the almonds in along with the sifted cake flour.

Preparing the Almond Filling. Grind together the almonds, flour and sugar in the food processor. Place the mixture in a 1½-quart bowl. Make a well in the center and add the yolks. Gradually incorporate the dry ingredients and beat the mixture for a minute. Stir in the butter. Whip the whites to a firm peak and stir one fourth of them into the batter. Fold in the remaining whites.

Assembling. Lightly flour the work surface and the dough. Roll the dough to a 14-inch diameter disk, ⅛ inch thick. Line a 10-inch tart pan with the dough, trimming away the excess. Pour in the filling.

Baking. Bake at 350°F about 30 minutes. Cool on a rack.

Preparing the Neutral Glaze. Reduce the apple jelly in a small saucepan over medium heat until it coats the back of a spoon.

Finishing. Arrange the fruit in concentric rows over the cooled almond filling. Brush with the neutral glaze.

Holding. Store the tart at room temperature. Serve the tart on the day it is assembled.

Yield. About 8 to 10 portions

PINEAPPLE MACADAMIA TART

Poaching the pineapple improves both the flavor and texture of this typically underripe fruit. If only salted macadamia nuts are available, rinse them in hot water, then dry in a 350°F oven for 5 minutes. The macadamia nuts can be replaced by almonds if necessary.

Cookie Dough

1 STICK UNSALTED BUTTER, 4 OUNCES, COOL
¼ CUP SUGAR, ABOUT 1¾ OUNCES
1 EGG
1¼ CUPS CAKE FLOUR, ABOUT 5 OUNCES

Macadamia Nut Filling

⅔ CUP UNSALTED MACADAMIA NUTS, ABOUT 4 OUNCES
¼ CUP FLOUR, ABOUT 1¼ OUNCES
½ CUP SUGAR, ABOUT 3¾ OUNCES
4 EGGS, SEPARATED
3 TABLESPOONS BUTTER, 1½ OUNCES, MELTED

Poached Pineapple

1 RIPE PINEAPPLE, ABOUT 3 POUNDS
1 CUP SUGAR, ABOUT 7½ OUNCES
3 CUPS WATER
½ VANILLA BEAN OR 2 TEASPOONS VANILLA EXTRACT

Kirsch Glaze

⅔ CUP APPLE JELLY
2 TABLESPOONS KIRSCH

¼ CUP CHOPPED MACADAMIA NUTS, ABOUT 1 OUNCE

Mixing the Cookie Dough. Cream the butter by hand or machine until soft. Beat in the sugar in a steady stream and continue beating until the mixture is lightened in color and in texture. Beat the egg in a small bowl and add half of it, continuing to beat until the mixture is smooth. Add the remaining egg and continue beating. The butter/egg mixture should be shiny like buttercream. Sift the cake flour and add to the bowl. Pulse the mixer on and off to incorporate it. Scrape from the bowl, wrap in plastic wrap and chill until firm.

Preparing the Macadamia Nut Filling. Grind together the macadamias, flour and sugar in the food processor. Pour the mixture into a bowl. Make a well in the center and add the yolks. Gradually incorporate the dry ingredients and beat the mixture for a minute. Stir in the butter. Whip the whites to a firm peak and stir one quarter of them into the batter. Fold in the remaining whites.

Assembling. Lightly flour the work surface and the dough. Roll the dough to a 14-inch diameter disk, ⅛ inch thick. Line a 10-inch tart pan with it, trimming away the excess. Pour in the filling.

Baking. Bake at 350°F about 30 minutes, until the filling is set and golden and the crust is baked through. Cool on a rack.

Preparing the Poached Pineapple. Halve, quarter and core the pineapple. Slice quarters ¼ inch thick. Combine the sugar, water and vanilla bean or extract in a 2-quart saucepan. Cook over medium heat, stirring occasionally, until mixture comes to a full rolling boil. Add pineapple slices. Simmer 2 or 3 minutes. Cool pineapple in syrup.

Preparing the Kirsch Glaze. Reduce the apple jelly and Kirsch in a small saucepan over medium heat until it coats the back of a spoon.

Finishing. Drain the pineapple slices on paper towels. Arrange on the cooled filling. Brush with glaze. Sprinkle chopped macadamias around edge of tart.

Holding. Store the tart at room temperature. Serve the tart on the day it is assembled.

Yield. About 8 to 10 portions

BRETON AUX POMMES

The typical Gâteau Breton is dense with a texture between pastry and pound cake. The versions that follow add a layer of filling to lighten and add flavor to the dessert.

Breton Dough

2 STICKS BUTTER, 8 OUNCES

1 CUP SUGAR, ABOUT 7½ OUNCES

1 TEASPOON VANILLA EXTRACT

1 TABLESPOON DARK RUM

4 EGG YOLKS

2¾ CUPS UNBLEACHED ALL-PURPOSE FLOUR, ABOUT 14 OUNCES

Apple Filling

3 TABLESPOONS BUTTER, 1½ OUNCES

1½ POUNDS GOLDEN DELICIOUS APPLES, ABOUT 3 TO 4 MEDIUM

⅓ CUP SUGAR, ABOUT 2½ OUNCES

1 TABLESPOON LEMON JUICE

1 TABLESPOON DARK RUM

Egg Wash

1 EGG

1 PINCH SALT

Mixing the Breton Dough. Cream the butter by hand or machine until soft, then beat in the sugar in a steady stream. Continue creaming until the mixture lightens. Beat in the vanilla and rum, then the yolks, one at a time, creaming until the mixture is very smooth and light. Beat in the flour until absorbed, without overmixing. Set the paste aside, covered.

Preparing the Apple Filling. Melt the butter in a wide, shallow pan with a cover, large enough to hold the apples in approximately one layer. Peel, halve, core, then slice each apple half into four to five wedges. Add the apple slices to the pan. Add the remaining filling ingredients and stir well to combine. Cook over medium heat until the apples begin to sizzle, then lower the heat and cover. Let steam about 5 minutes, until the apples begin to exude their juices. Continue cooking, covered, about 5 minutes longer, or until the apples have exuded a large quantity of juice. Uncover and continue cooking at a low heat to evaporate the juices, about 10 minutes longer. The apples should remain in firm, distinct pieces. Cool.

Assembling. Place half the dough in the bottom of a buttered and paper-lined 10 × 2-inch-deep cake pan. Flour your hand and evenly press the dough with your fingertips over the bottom of the pan and about 1 inch up the side of the pan. Spread the cooled filling on the dough.

Flour a 10-inch cardboard round or a tart pan bottom. Flour the remaining dough and evenly press it against the cardboard or pan bottom. Slide a thin, sharp knife or spatula between the dough and the cardboard or pan bottom to loosen it. Slide the disk of dough over the apple filling and press it into place, making sure that the edge of the top crust meets the side of the bottom crust. Smooth the top crust with the back of a spoon so that there are no indentations, especially around the edge. Whisk the egg and salt together and brush the top of the Breton with the egg wash.

Trace a lattice pattern on the top crust with the tines of a fork: Using the back of the fork with the tines facing away from you, draw the fork toward you along the diameter of the crust. Make two more markings in the same fashion on either side of the center marking, so there are five parallel markings on the top crust. Make five more markings in the same fashion: This time for the center one, connect the top of the leftmost marking and the bottom of the rightmost one. Then make two more markings on either side of it. Brush again with the egg wash.

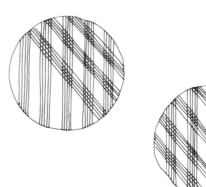

Baking. Bake at 350°F for 45 to 50 minutes on the lowest rack in the oven until well colored. Cool on a rack.

Unmolding. Invert a plate on the Breton and invert the Breton onto it. Carefully lift off the pan and peel off the paper. Invert another plate on the Breton (at this point the Breton is upside down between the two plates), reinvert the Breton and remove the top plate.

Holding. Store, loosely covered, at room temperature up to 2 days.

Yield. About 10 to 12 portions

Breton aux Poires

Follow the recipe for Breton aux Pommes, substituting pear filling for the apple filling.

Pear Filling

    3 TO 4 RIPE PEARS, SUCH AS BARTLETT OR
      ANJOU, ABOUT 1½ POUNDS
    3 TABLESPOONS BUTTER, 1½ OUNCES
    ⅓ CUP SUGAR, ABOUT 2½ OUNCES
    1 TABLESPOON LEMON JUICE
    1 TABLESPOON PEAR ALCOHOL, SUCH AS
      PEAR WILLIAMS

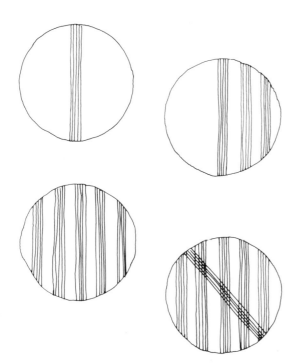

Preparing the Pear Filling. Peel, halve and core the pears; dice each half into ½-inch pieces. Melt the butter in a sauté pan over high heat, add pears and toss to coat. Add sugar, then lemon juice and pear alcohol. Cook over high heat until pears are just tender, about 8 to 10 minutes, then cool.

Breton aux Noix

Follow the recipe for Breton aux Pommes, substituting walnut filling for the apple filling.

Walnut Filling

    1 CUP FIRMLY PACKED LIGHT BROWN SUGAR,
        ABOUT 8 OUNCES
    1 STICK BUTTER, 4 OUNCES
    ½ CUP HONEY
    2 CUPS COARSELY CHOPPED WALNUTS, ABOUT
        8 OUNCES

Preparing the Walnut Filling. Bring brown sugar, butter and honey to a boil in a heavy saucepan over medium heat; boil 2 minutes. Remove from heat. Stir in walnuts. Cool.

BRAUNE LINZERTORTE

This classic Viennese pastry is seldom seen in its authentic form. Most adaptations have a crisp texture like pastry dough, but a real *Linzertorte* has a more cakelike texture. The preserves are only used to brighten the center— they are not abundantly used or they would boil over during baking.

Dark Linzer Dough

    1½ CUPS UNBLEACHED ALL-PURPOSE FLOUR,
        ABOUT 7½ OUNCES
    1 CUP GROUND HAZELNUTS, ABOUT 3
        OUNCES
    ¾ CUP SUGAR, ABOUT 5¾ OUNCES
    1 TEASPOON CINNAMON
    ¼ TEASPOON GROUND CLOVES
    1 TEASPOON BAKING POWDER
    1½ STICKS BUTTER, 6 OUNCES, COOL
    1 EGG
    1 EGG YOLK
    ⅔ CUP RASPBERRY PRESERVES
    1 EGG, BEATEN
    ¼ CUP SLICED ALMONDS, ABOUT ¾ OUNCE

    CONFECTIONERS' SUGAR

Mixing the Dark Linzer Dough. Mix all the dry ingredients together in a bowl. Rub in the butter finely by hand until the mixture looks sandy. Beat the egg and the yolk together and stir into the dough with a fork. Stir only until the dough is smooth. It will be very soft.

Assembling. Spread half the dough in the bottom of a buttered 9-inch springform pan. Spread the dough with the raspberry preserves, leaving a 1-inch margin around the outside. With the remaining dough, pipe a diagonal lattice over the preserves using a pastry bag fitted with a ⅜-inch plain tube. Pipe a border of large dots around the outside edge. Gently paint the lattice and border with beaten egg and strew with sliced almonds.

Baking. Bake at 350°F about 40 minutes. Cool the *Linzertorte* in the pan on a rack. Remove the side of the pan and loosen the bottom of the *Linzertorte* with the point of a small, sharp knife. Slide onto a platter. Dust with confectioners' sugar.

Holding. Store the *Linzertorte,* loosely covered, at room temperature up to 2 days.

Yield. About 12 portions

Weisse Linzertorte

Follow the recipe for *Braune Linzertorte,* substituting GROUND BLANCHED ALMONDS for the hazelnuts, omitting the cinnamon and adding the GRATED ZEST OF 1 LEMON and 1 TEASPOON VANILLA to the eggs before stirring them into the dough.

8

PUFF PASTRY

Puff pastry, the lightest and most delicate of pastry doughs, is prepared in a unique manner. During the mixing of most pastry doughs, all the butter is rubbed into the flour. In preparing puff pastry, only a small portion of the butter is directly incorporated into the flour. The dough is wrapped around the majority of the butter to form a layered package of dough and butter, then repeatedly rolled and folded to increase the number of layers.

The layered construction causes the dough to rise dramatically during baking. The dough develops fairly strong gluten during the rolling and folding process, causing the dough to retract slightly during baking. At the same time the dough layers retract, the butter layers melt and are absorbed by the dough. The spaces left by the butter fill with steam generated by the evaporation of the water. The dough rises due to the steam expansion and the retraction gives the dough an extra push to expand upward. As the starches and proteins in the dough coagulate, the pastry retains its puffed and risen texture.

Mixing the Dough

First an inelastic dough is prepared from most of the flour, a small portion of the butter, the water and salt. The addition of some cake flour inhibits the formation of excessively strong gluten. The small amount of butter acts as "shortening," controlling the length of the gluten strands. Finally, the dough is mixed very gently after the water is added, again preventing the formation of too strong a gluten.

These three factors—the cake flour, the butter and the gentle mixing—all help the dough to have a loose, inelastic texture after mixing. This is critical to good puff pastry preparation since the rolling and folding process which follows creates an elastic dough.

If the dough were to become elastic at the primary stage, after the rolling and folding the puff pastry would be *so* elastic it would distort badly during baking and be tough and chewy.

Forming the Square of Butter

After the dough is prepared, the remaining butter is softened along with a small amount of flour and is formed into a square. The flour helps the butter to soften without melting and also absorbs some of the water in the butter. The consistency of the butter is important; ideally, it should be exactly the same as the dough, so that there is neither resistance nor absorption between them. If the butter is too hard, it will break through the dough, preventing the formation of even layers. If it is too soft, the dough will absorb it and toughen.

Forming the Package of Dough and Butter

Before being wrapped around the butter, the dough is flattened into a square and the four corners of the square rolled out to about a quarter of their original thickness. This ensures an even thickness of dough both under and over the butter.

When wrapped around the butter, the dough is not stretched, assuring that it retains its rather inelastic texture. A controlled amount of elasticity is needed to form even layers in puff pastry; this resilience is developed during the rolling and folding process itself. The initial dough must never become elastic or it will be impossible to complete the turns and even more difficult to roll out the finished dough before baking.

Turning the Dough

After the dough is wrapped around the butter, the dough is repeatedly rolled and folded, a system known as "turning" the dough. Turning and turns (as each of the individual processes of rolling and folding the dough are called) refer to the change in position of the dough after each time it is rolled and folded. The dough is rolled in the direction opposite the previous turn. The process of changing the direction evenly develops the dough's elasticity. There are several different types of turns.

Double Turn

The widely used double turn folds the dough into four layers. Both ends are folded in toward the center and then the dough is folded over again from the center, yielding a piece of dough shaped like a book. With double turns, the dough is given four double turns with a rest between the second and third turns.

Single Turn

A single turn, the classic French method of turning puff pastry, folds the dough into three layers. The top third is folded down over the center third and the bottom third is folded up over those two, yielding a piece of dough shaped like a folded business letter. With single turns, the dough is given six single turns with rests between the second and third, and the fourth and fifth turns.

Half Turn

A half turn is not a turn used in constructing the layers in puff pastry, it is a remedy for a dough that has become slack and limp through too much resting. To give the dough a half turn, it is rolled out to twice its original length, then folded back to its original size and allowed to rest for an hour in the refrigerator. This small amount of rolling redevelops some of the gluten so that the dough has enough elasticity to retract slightly during baking and give the layers the push that they need to rise.

Resting the Dough

Since puff pastry dough develops gluten during the rolling and folding process, it is necessary to let it rest in the refrigerator. Fortunately, the elasticity in the dough, if not excessive, will dissipate somewhat after a rest. The dough will be easier to roll, whether to complete the turns or to prepare a dessert.

Normally puff pastry must rest between each two turns. However, if it seems excessively elastic, or if the butter is melting, the puff pastry should be refrigerated between each turn. Resting the dough in the refrigerator also helps firm up the butter, making the puff pastry easier to handle. The final rest is given after all the turns are completed—several hours or overnight (best) is recommended.

Further resting is needed after the puff pastry has been rolled to prepare a dessert. Since this rolling develops some gluten, resting after the rolling will ensure that the puff pastry does not distort during baking.

Storing the Completed Puff Pastry

After completing the turns, wrap the puff pastry in plastic and refrigerate it at least several hours. It may remain in the refrigerator 2 or 3 days without any loss of quality. Or double wrap and freeze the puff pastry. It may remain frozen for a month or so. If the puff pastry has been frozen, it should be defrosted in the refrigerator overnight before it is used.

Handling "Old" Dough

If the puff pastry has been stored in the refrigerator for more than 3 days, or if it has been defrosted, it should be given a half turn before preparing a dessert from it.

Preparing Prerolled Sheets of Puff Pastry

An excellent system for storing puff pastry, so that it is always available in a rested form, entails rolling sheets and stacking them on a pan with a sheet of plastic wrap between each sheet. The pan is then covered with plastic and refrigerated, or frozen after several hours rest in the refrigerator. Thus, a sheet of puff pastry need only be removed from the refrigerator and formed. Freezing is also convenient, since a thin sheet will defrost quickly at room temperature. The only disadvantage occurs when the puff pastry must be handled in a special way during rolling as in the case of Palmiers.

To prepare sheets of puff pastry to have on hand in the refrigerator or freezer, lightly flour the work surface and the puff pastry; pound, then roll it into a rectangle, as if about to give it a turn. Cut the puff pastry width-wise, into four or six pieces, and roll each to the size of the pan on which they will be stored. A 10 × 15-inch or 12 × 18-inch pan is the best choice. Dividing the batch of puff pastry into four pieces will yield sheets about ¼ inch thick; six pieces will yield sheets about 3/16 inch thick.

PUFF PASTRY

Dough

2½ CUPS UNBLEACHED ALL-PURPOSE FLOUR, ABOUT 12½ OUNCES

¾ CUP CAKE FLOUR, ABOUT 3 OUNCES

1 STICK BUTTER, 4 OUNCES, COLD

1½ TEASPOONS SALT

1 CUP PLUS 2 TABLESPOONS VERY COLD WATER

Butter

¼ CUP UNBLEACHED ALL-PURPOSE FLOUR, ABOUT 1¼ OUNCES

4 STICKS BUTTER, 1 POUND, COLD

Mixing the Dough. Place the all-purpose flour in a 3-quart bowl and sift the cake flour over it. Thoroughly stir together the two flours. Slice the butter into thin pieces and add to the bowl.

Rub in the butter by hand, tossing and squeezing it in. The butter should be completely mixed with the flour so that no visible pieces of butter remain. Stir the salt into the water to dissolve it. Make a well in the flour-butter mixture and add the water. Using a rubber spatula, scrape across the bottom of the bowl through the center of the dough. Turn the bowl and continue scraping

until a ropy dough is formed. Do not apply any pressure to the dough with the spatula. If the dough seems dry, add more water, 1 tablespoon at a time, to complete moistening. Cover the bowl and set it aside while preparing the butter.

Preparing the Butter. Pour the ¼ cup flour in a mound on the work surface and coat the 1 pound of butter with it. If the butter is in sticks, unwrap each stick and pound separately. If the butter is in a solid block, cut the block into four or five thin pieces for the pounding. Pound the butter with a rolling pin to make it malleable and plastic, but still cool. By hand, squeeze the butter into a solid mass, then shape it into a square, 1 inch thick.

Forming the Package of Dough. Lightly flour the work surface and dough. Press the dough into a rough square about 1 inch thick. Do not be concerned if the dough is not holding together smoothly. Roll out the four corners of the dough into flaps, about ¼ inch thick. Place the square of butter on the dough, aligning it so that the corners of the square are between the flaps. Fold the flaps over the butter without stretching them. Make sure that no butter is exposed. If some shows through,

seal the dough around it by pinching the dough together.

Rolling. Lightly flour the work surface and the dough. Gently press the dough with a rolling pin, giving the dough a series of horizontal strokes, very close together, beginning with the edge of the dough closest to you and working toward the far end. Continue pressing the dough in this fashion until it is about ⅜ inch thick. During the pressing, check to see that the surface and dough are adequately dusted with flour; add more flour as needed to prevent sticking. Roll over the dough again along the length with an even pressure, once or twice, to make it ¼ inch thick. Take care during the pressing and rolling that the corners remain 90-degree angles.

Folding. Fold both ends of the dough in toward the center, then fold them again, to

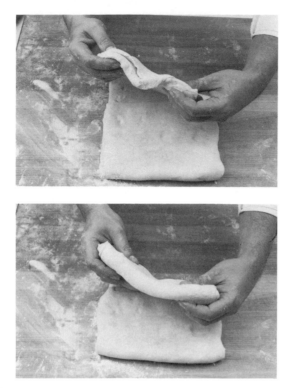

make four layers. The folded package of dough will resemble a book, with a spine on one side and the covers opening opposite it. Position the package of dough so that the spine is on the left.

Lightly flour the work surface and dough and repeat the pressing as before. Roll the dough along the length as before, then roll several times along the width to form a rectangle approximately 9 × 24 inches. Check the corners again and fold the dough, both ends in toward the center, then over again as before.

Resting. Wrap the dough in plastic wrap and refrigerate it. The ideal resting time is about 1 hour. The dough may be left longer if necessary, up to 24 hours.

Completing the Turns. Lightly flour the work surface and dough. Position the dough with the spine at the left of the surface. If the dough has rested more than 1 hour, it will be very hard. Allow it to soften slightly, until the butter feels flexible when the dough is pressed hard with the fingertips.

Press the dough as before, dusting with flour under and on the dough, then roll it. Keep the corners even. Fold the dough again so that both ends meet in the center; fold over again to make four layers. Position the dough with the spine on the left, then repeat the pressing, rolling and folding once more.

Resting the Dough Before Use. Wrap the dough in plastic wrap, then refrigerate it at least 4 hours or overnight. During this time the gluten will relax and the dough will be less elastic and easier to roll.

Holding. The dough can be refrigerated for about 3 days. If you do not intend to use all of the dough at once, double-wrap the remaining dough in plastic wrap and freeze it for up to 1 month. Defrost the dough in the refrigerator overnight before using it.

If you prepare a batch of the dough and do not intend to use it within 3 days, divide the dough into six pieces, each about ½ pound, wrap and freeze.

Yield. About 3 pounds

A Note about Rolling Puff Pastry and Scraps

Always be as accurate as possible when rolling puff pastry into a shape. Work with a ruler to verify the exact dimensions specified in the recipe. Rolling the dough too large and trimming it to the desired size will probably not affect the outcome of the recipe adversely (the thickness of the dough may vary by as much as ⅛ inch, depending on the recipe), but will generate scraps of dough. Also, some recipes like the Gâteau Pithiviers and both Apple Tartelettes, since they are round, also generate scraps of dough.

Save all scraps of puff pastry, pressing them together in a thin horizontal layer, rather than piling the scraps on top of each other. Wrap well in plastic wrap and refrigerate any scraps overnight. Use the scraps to make Palmiers, Paillettes or even a Mille Feuille layer. They are not suitable for use in a pastry where the dough must rise very high. If the scraps are used for a recipe that generates more scraps, discard them.

QUICK PUFF PASTRY

This fast version of puff pastry considerably shortens the time spent in preparing the dough. Quick puff pastry is best used for pastries where the light delicacy of puff pastry is desired, but not the dramatic height.

1¼ CUPS UNBLEACHED ALL-PURPOSE FLOUR, ABOUT 6¼ OUNCES

⅓ CUP CAKE FLOUR, ABOUT 1¼ OUNCES

2 STICKS BUTTER, ½ POUND, COLD

½ TEASPOON SALT

½ CUP VERY COLD WATER

Mixing the Dough. Place the all-purpose flour in a 2-quart bowl and sift the cake flour over it. Thoroughly stir together the two flours. Slice 2 tablespoons of the butter into thin

pieces and add to the bowl. Rub in the butter by hand, tossing and squeezing in the butter until there are no longer any visible pieces of butter. Cut the remaining butter into ½-inch cubes. (The best way to do this with stick butter is to cut each stick in quarters, lengthwise, then into ½-inch slices.) Add the butter cubes to the flour mixture. Toss with a rubber spatula just to separate and distribute the butter. Do not rub the butter into the flour.

Stir the salt into the water to dissolve it. Make a well in the flour-butter mixture and add the water. Toss gently with the spatula until the dough is evenly moistened. Tilt the bowl to isolate any unmoistened flour and add drops of water, if necessary, to complete the moistening. Press and squeeze dough in bowl to form a rough cylinder.

Turning. Lightly flour the work surface and the dough. Using the palm of your hand, press down on the dough three or four times to shape the dough into a rough rectangle. Press and pound the dough with the rolling pin to form an even rectangle about ½ inch thick. Roll the dough back and forth along the length once or twice until it is an even rectangle about ¼ inch thick. At this stage, pieces of butter are likely to stick to the surface. If the dough does stick, loosen it with a long spatula or a scraper. Clean the surface to minimize further sticking.

Folding. Fold both ends of the dough in toward the center, then fold them again to make four layers. The folded package of dough will resemble a book, with a spine on one side and the covers opening opposite it.

Position the package of dough so that the spine is on the left.

Lightly flour the work surface and the dough and repeat the pressing as before. Roll the dough along the length as before, then roll several times along the width to form a rectangle approximately 6 × 18 inches. Check the corners again and fold the dough, both ends in toward the center, then over again as before. Repeat the process once more so that the dough will have three double turns.

Resting. Wrap the dough well in plastic and chill it at least 1 hour before using it.

Holding. The dough can be refrigerated for about 3 days. If you do not intend to use all of the dough at once, double-wrap the remaining dough in plastic wrap and freeze it for up to 1 month. Defrost the dough in the refrigerator overnight before using it.

If you prepare a batch of the dough and do not intend to use it within 3 days, divide the dough into four pieces, each about five ounces, wrap and freeze.

Yield. About 1¼ pounds

QUICK CHOCOLATE PUFF PASTRY

A variation on traditional puff pastry, this chocolate version uses a combination of semisweet chocolate and cocoa powder to flavor the dough. Be careful that the dough keeps cool during the preparation or it may soften and become difficult to handle.

2 OUNCES SEMISWEET CHOCOLATE, FINELY CUT

⅔ CUP WATER, APPROXIMATELY

2 CUPS UNBLEACHED ALL-PURPOSE FLOUR,
ABOUT 10 OUNCES

¾ TEASPOON SALT

2 TABLESPOONS SUGAR, ABOUT 1 OUNCE

4 TABLESPOONS BUTTER, 2 OUNCES, COLD

2 STICKS BUTTER, 8 OUNCES, COLD

3 TABLESPOONS COCOA POWDER, ABOUT ½
OUNCE

Preparing the Chocolate. Place the chocolate in a small heatproof bowl over a pan of hot but not simmering water. Melt the chocolate, stirring it often. Once melted, stir 4 tablespoons hot water into it and whisk to combine. Then stir 6 tablespoons cold water into the mixture. Pour the chocolate/water into a glass measuring cup. There should be ¾ cup liquid. If not, add cold water to make ¾ cup.

Mixing the Dough. Stir together the flour, sugar and salt in a bowl. Rub the 2 ounces butter into the flour mixture with the fingertips until there are no longer any visible pieces of butter. Keep the mixture powdery and cool and not pasty.

Make a well in the flour/butter mixture and add the chocolate water. Mix the liquid into the flour with a rubber spatula, folding it in, scraping the inside of the bowl and tossing the dough with the spatula rather than cutting through it or pressing the dough. Squeeze the dough together two or three times, cover with plastic wrap and refrigerate while preparing the butter.

Preparing the Butter. Sift the cocoa powder on the work surface; unwrap and place the ½ pound of butter on it. Turn the butter around in the cocoa to coat it. Pound the butter with a rolling pin to make it malleable and plastic.

Squeeze the butter and cocoa together to mix them to a smooth but still firm and cool consistency. Do not be concerned if the butter does not absorb every bit of the cocoa—there will not be much left over.

Forming the Package of Dough and Butter. Lightly flour the work surface and dough. Press the dough into a rectangle about 6 × 12 inches. Take 1-tablespoon bits of the butter and press them to about ¼ inch thick. Evenly distribute the butter over the bottom two thirds of the dough, leaving a slight margin around the outside. Fold the top, unbuttered portion of the dough over the center, buttered portion. Fold the bottom, buttered portion upward over the center. This will make a package of five layers of alternating dough and butter.

Rolling and Folding the Dough. Position the dough on the work surface so that the fold is at the left and the open portion of the package of dough faces right. Lightly flour the work surface and dough. Press it with a rolling pin in horizontal strokes to flatten it into a rectangle about 6 × 12 inches. Gently roll over the dough several times until it is about ¼ inch thick, and forms a rectangle about 8 × 18 inches.

Fold both ends of the dough in toward the center, then fold over again to make four layers. Revolve the dough a quarter turn so that the fold is on the left and the open part of the dough is in the right. Press and roll the dough as before and fold it again, both ends in toward the center, then over again to make four layers.

On the second rolling the dough may become too soft to roll. If so, refrigerate the dough, wrapped in plastic, and continue rolling later, after the dough has become firm.

After folding the dough the second time, wrap it in plastic and refrigerate it at least 2 hours or until firm before attempting to use the dough.

Holding. The dough can be refrigerated for about 3 days. If you do not intend to use all of the dough at once, double-wrap the remaining dough in plastic wrap and freeze it for up to 1 month. Defrost the dough in the refrigerator overnight before using it.

If you prepare a batch of the dough and do not intend to use it within 3 days, divide the dough into four pieces, each about 7½ ounces, wrap and freeze.

Yield. About 1 pound 14 ounces

STRAWBERRY PUFF PASTRY SHORTCAKES WITH VANILLA SAUCE

Using Quick Puff Pastry to replace the more traditional shortcake biscuit produces a light, delicate dessert. The strawberries in the recipe can be replaced with raspberries, blackberries or blueberries, or a combination.

½ BATCH QUICK PUFF PASTRY (PAGES 185–186), ABOUT 10 OUNCES

Whipped Cream
1 CUP HEAVY WHIPPING CREAM
2 TABLESPOONS SUGAR, ABOUT 1 OUNCE
1 TABLESPOON LIQUEUR

Berries
2 PINTS FRESH STRAWBERRIES

Vanilla Sauce
¾ CUP HEAVY WHIPPING CREAM
¾ CUP MILK
⅓ CUP SUGAR, ABOUT 2½ OUNCES
½ VANILLA BEAN, SPLIT
4 EGG YOLKS
1 TABLESPOON LIQUEUR

CONFECTIONERS' SUGAR
MINT LEAVES FOR DECORATING

Preparing the Dough and Fillings. Lightly flour the work surface and the dough, then roll the pastry to a rectangle, 10 × 15 inches. Slide onto a pan and refrigerate about 1 hour, until firm and rested. Whip the cream with the sugar and liqueur. Rinse, hull and slice the berries into a bowl. Set cream and berries aside refrigerated.

Dock the dough well and place on a parchment paper–lined 10 × 15-inch pan. Cover with another piece of paper and another pan and bake at 350°F about 30 minutes, turning dough often and watching its progress, until it is golden and baked through. Remove from the oven and cool between the pans to prevent warping. Using a 2½-inch cutter, cut the pieces of baked pastry into disks.

Preparing the Vanilla Sauce. Combine cream, milk, sugar and vanilla bean in a saucepan and bring to a boil over medium heat. Whisk yolks in a bowl until liquid. Whisk one quarter of the boiling liquid into the yolks. Then return the remaining liquid to a boil and whisk in the yolk mixture. Continue whisking until the cream thickens, about 30 seconds. Remove from heat while still beating, strain into a bowl and cool over ice water, stirring occasionally. Remove, rinse and reserve vanilla bean for another use. Stir in the liqueur.

Assembling. Place half the pastry disks on a pan. Using a pastry bag fitted with a ½-inch star tube, pipe a large rosette of whipped cream on each. Divide the berries among the shortcakes, pressing them into the cream. Top with the remaining pastry disks and dredge them with confectioners' sugar.

Place each on a dessert plate and pour the Vanilla Sauce around it. Decorate with more berries or mint leaves.

Holding. Prepare all the components up to 1 day in advance, but assemble the shortcakes immediately before serving.

Yield. 12 portions

PEACH AND RASPBERRY COBBLER

Another recipe where Quick Puff Pastry replaces the more substantial shortcake dough. Use other combinations of fruits, if you desire. Apricots and cherries, sweet or sour; apples and blackberries or blueberries; or even equal parts of blueberries and raspberries all make delicious variations.

Cobbler Filling

3 POUNDS RIPE PEACHES, ABOUT 10 TO 12
3 TABLESPOONS FLOUR, ABOUT 1 OUNCE
¾ CUP SUGAR, ABOUT 5¾ OUNCES
PINCH NUTMEG
½ PINT FRESH RASPBERRIES *OR* 1 CUP
    I.Q.F. RASPBERRIES
¼ TEASPOON ALMOND EXTRACT
1 TEASPOON VANILLA EXTRACT
2 TABLESPOONS LEMON JUICE
3 TABLESPOONS BUTTER, 1½ OUNCES

½ BATCH QUICK PUFF PASTRY (PAGES 185-186), ABOUT 10 OUNCES

Egg Wash
1 EGG
PINCH SALT

CRÈME FRAICHE OR LIGHTLY WHIPPED CREAM

Preparing the Filling. Cut an "x" in the blossom end of each peach. Immerse two or three at a time in a pan of boiling water and blanch for 30 seconds. Immediately remove to a large bowl of ice water. Skin the peaches after they are blanched—the skin should peel away easily if the peaches are ripe. If not, touch up with a paring knife to remove remaining skin. Halve, pit and slice each peach into eight or ten wedges.

Combine the flour, sugar and nutmeg in a bowl. Butter a 1½- to 2-quart baking dish and strew the bottom of the dish with ¼ cup of the flour/sugar. Toss the remaining flour/sugar into the peaches and carefully fold in the raspberries so as not to bruise them. Pour into the prepared baking dish. Sprinkle with the extracts and the lemon juice. Dot with the butter.

Rolling. Lightly flour the work surface and the dough. Roll the dough to a ⅛ inch thick rectangle about as long and twice as wide as the baking dish. Cut the pastry into 1-inch strips in the width. Beat together the egg and salt and paint the strips using a flexible pastry brush.

Adhere half the strips diagonally on the surface of the filling, leaving about ½ inch between each strip. Finish with the remaining strips adhering them at a 45° angle to the first strips to form a lattice. Chill 1 hour to rest the dough and prevent it from shrinking.

Baking. Bake the cobbler on the middle rack of the oven at 375°F about 30 minutes, until the top crust is a deep golden and the filling is just beginning to bubble. Cool on a rack and serve warm or at room temperature with crème fraiche or lightly whipped cream.

Holding. Serve the cobbler on the day it is baked.

Yield. About 8 portions

PALMIERS

Perhaps the simplest puff pastry, Palmiers are known and loved in many countries. Called palm leaves, butterflies, pig's ears and elephant ears, they best reflect both the delicate flavor and texture of the puff pastry. The quantity of sugar seems large, but it is necessary for the Palmiers to caramelize sufficiently.

1 CUP SUGAR, ABOUT 7½ OUNCES
¼ BATCH PUFF PASTRY, ABOUT 12 OUNCES (PAGES 182–185), OR ½ BATCH QUICK PUFF PASTRY, ABOUT 10 OUNCES (PAGES 185-186)

Spread half the sugar on the work surface and place the dough on it. Spread the remaining sugar on the dough. Press the dough in successive firm strokes in both directions with the rolling pin to flatten it and make the sugar stick to it. Move the dough frequently and redistribute the sugar evenly underneath and on top of it.

Evenly roll the dough to an 8 × 12-inch rectangle. Strew any sugar which has not adhered to the dough evenly on the surface.

Fold both the 12-inch ends of the dough over half the way toward the middle—about 2 inches. Fold both ends in toward the middle again, to make a piece of dough 4 × 12

inches. Fold over again at the middle, to make six layers about 2 × 12 inches. Cut the strip of dough into two 2 × 6-inch lengths. Wrap each piece of dough in plastic wrap and chill about 1 hour until firm. Reserve the remaining sugar for another use, but not for beating egg whites, since the sugar is greasy from the dough.

Unwrap the strips of dough and cut into ½-inch slices, using a sharp knife. Dip one of the cut surfaces of each into sugar. Place the Palmiers, 2 inches apart all around, on paper-lined baking pans, sugared-side down.

Baking. Bake at 400°F in the bottom third of the oven for about 10 to 15 minutes. During the baking, the Palmiers will expand horizontally and the sugar on the sides against the pan will melt and caramelize. Check frequently during baking to make sure that some do not caramelize too quickly. If necessary, remove some from the pan and allow the others to continue baking until sufficiently caramelized.

Cool on a rack, caramelized sides up.

Holding. Keep the Palmiers in a tin, making sure that they do not take on any moisture, which would make them soggy and also cause the sugar to melt. Palmiers, like all puff pastries, are always best on the day they are baked, when the butter in the pastry retains its fresh flavor.

Yield. About 2 dozen

PAILLETTES

These "little straws" are not a dessert, but are one of the best known and best loved puff pastries. Traditionally served with clear soups, they are also an excellent cocktail pastry. Only the best Parmesan cheese and Hungarian paprika (the word "Szeged" appears on the label) should be used to complement the delicate flavor of the puff pastry.

¼ BATCH PUFF PASTRY, ABOUT 12 OUNCES (PAGES 182–185), OR ½ BATCH QUICK PUFF PASTRY, ABOUT 10 OUNCES (PAGES 185 186)

Egg Wash
1 EGG
PINCH SALT

¾ CUP FINELY GRATED PARMESAN CHEESE
2 TEASPOONS HUNGARIAN PAPRIKA

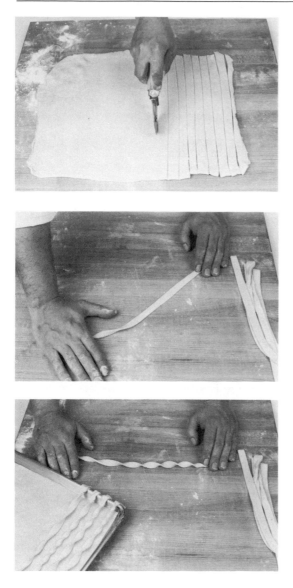

Preparing the Dough. Lightly flour the work surface and the dough. Press the dough in successive firm strokes in both directions with a rolling pin. Move the dough frequently and renew the flour under and on it. Roll evenly to approximately a 12-inch square.

Beat the egg and salt together, then paint the surface of the dough, using a flexible pastry brush. Cover half of the dough (a 6 × 12-inch rectangle) with an even layer of the cheese, then paprika. Fold the other half of the dough over it and press to adhere the dough together. If the dough is soft or resistant, slide it onto a pan and chill briefly to firm it. Roll the dough back to a 12-inch square. Chill until firm.

Cut the chilled dough into ½ × 12-inch strips. Twist the strips, one at a time, into corkscrew shapes: Position the strip at a 45-degree angle to left edge of the surface. Hold down the left end of the strip with the left hand. With the right hand, roll the right end of the strip until the strip is parallel to the edge of the surface, forming a corkscrew shape. Place on a paper-lined 10 × 15-inch or 12 × 18-inch pan, pressing the edges to the rim of the pan to prevent the Paillettes from unraveling during baking.

Baking the Paillettes. Bake the Paillettes at 400°F in the middle level of the oven for about 10 to 12 minutes, or until they are a deep golden color. Immediately remove to a cutting board and trim off the ends; cut the Paillettes into 4- to 6-inch lengths. Cool on a rack.

Holding. Store in a tightly covered tin.

Yield. About 4 to 6 dozen, depending on the length they are cut after baking

Sacristains

A sweet version of the Paillettes, where sugar and ground nuts are substituted for the cheese and paprika.

Preparation and baking are the same. Use ⅔ CUP GRANULATED SUGAR, ⅔ CUP GROUND NUTS (almonds or pecans are best) and ½ TEASPOON GROUND CINNAMON mixed together and strewn on half the dough.

CHOCOLATE WALNUT STRAWS

These tender straws are a variation of the classic Sacristain, usually made with plain puff pastry and almonds. Although almonds—or even pecans or hazelnuts—work well, the flavor of the walnuts complements the chocolate best.

⅓ CUP WALNUT PIECES, ABOUT 1¼ OUNCES

¼ CUP SUGAR, ABOUT 1¾ OUNCES

½ BATCH QUICK CHOCOLATE PUFF PASTRY, ABOUT 1 POUND (PAGES 186-188)

Preparing the Walnut and Sugar Mixture. Combine the walnuts and sugar in the bowl of a food processor and pulse to finely chop the walnuts, but not to a powder—less than 30 seconds.

Rolling. Lightly flour the work surface and the dough. Press the dough with the rolling pin to soften it slightly. If the dough is extremely hard, let it soften 30 minutes at a cool room temperature before attempting to roll it. Roll the dough to a rectangle about 6 × 12 inches.

Filling the Dough. Paint the dough with cold water using a flexible pastry brush and scatter the walnut mixture on half the dough. Fold the other half of the dough over to cover the walnut mixture and press to adhere. If the dough is still cool and firm, roll the dough to a rectangle about 8 × 12 inches. If not, slide the dough onto a cookie sheet and refrigerate until firm, then roll it.

Cutting and Shaping. Before beginning to cut the straws, trim the 12-inch ends of the dough straight and even, using a cutting wheel. Cut the dough into twelve ½ × 12-inch strips. Twist each strip into a corkscrew shape and place it on a 10 × 15-inch or 12 × 18-inch jelly-roll pan lined with parchment paper. Press the ends of the straws on the rim of the pan to prevent the straws from unraveling during baking. Refrigerate the straws about 1 hour before baking.

Baking. Bake at 375°F until they feel firm and the sugar is beginning to caramelize, about 15 minutes. Remove from the oven, trim away the edges and cut into 6-inch lengths with a sharp knife. Remove from the pan and cool them on a rack.

Holding. Store the straws in a tightly covered, airtight container, up to 5 days.

Yield. 2 dozen

FLEURONS

In classic French cooking, a Fleuron is a crisp little crescent of puff pastry used to garnish foods served in delicate cream sauces: vegetables, such as asparagus; eggs; variety meats, such as sweetbreads; fish and shellfish. Nowadays, other shapes are also popular; a little puff pastry fish may accompany a fish dish, or a puff pastry mushroom may accompany a dish of wild mushrooms. I have used Fleurons effectively for simple desserts, too. A pear-shaped Fleuron may accompany a simple poached pear with Crème Anglaise; a strawberry-shaped Fleuron can dress up a simple portion of Strawberry Bavarian Cream—the possibilities abound.

Use cutters, such as a star or heart, or make a pattern from stiff paper or cardboard and use a sharp paring knife to cut the shapes.

For best results let the dough rest and dry, as stated in the recipe. The resting will prevent the shapes from distorting while they are baking; the drying ensures ease in cutting the dough and a beautifully glazed surface.

The yolk is added to the egg wash for a darker, richer finish.

¼ BATCH PUFF PASTRY, ABOUT 12 OUNCES
   (PAGES 182-185)

Egg Wash
   1 EGG
   1 EGG YOLK
   PINCH SALT

Rolling, Marking and Egg Washing the Dough. Lightly flour the work surface and the dough. Press the dough in successive firm strokes in both directions with a rolling pin. Move the dough frequently to renew the flour under and on it. Roll to a 12-inch square. Slide the dough onto a floured pan.

Beat the egg, yolk and salt together until very liquid; strain. Paint the dough with an even coat of the egg wash. Dip the tines of a fork in the remaining egg wash and streak the surface of the dough with the back of the fork, drawing the fork toward you at a 45-degree angle to the dough, in a series of vertical lines, close together, so the entire surface of the dough is covered with evenly spaced stripes. If you wish, make a second set of streaks, diagonal to the first ones. Paint again with the egg wash so that the streaks are filled with the egg wash. Refrigerate the dough, uncovered, to firm it and to dry the egg wash, at least two hours, or longer if necessary.

Cutting Out the Shapes. For the classic crescent shape, use a plain or fluted round cutter, about 2½ to 3 inches in diameter. Remove the dough from the refrigerator and slide it onto a cutting board or a sheet of parchment

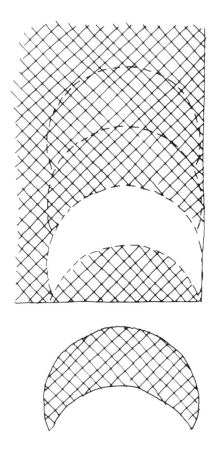

paper. Position the dough so that the stripes are perpendicular to the edge of the work surface facing you. Position the cutter at the edge of the dough closest to you, so that the edge of the dough falls along the diameter of the cutter. Cut out a half disk of the dough. Position the far end of the cutter about 2 inches behind the first curved cut, and cut again to make a crescent shape. Continue cutting out all the dough in the same manner. If the egg wash is not completely dry, the edge of the cutter may become caked with flour and egg wash. Rinse it occasionally under warm water and dry before continuing to cut.

To freeze raw Fleurons, line them on a pan and place in the freezer for an hour; quickly arrange the frozen Fleurons in a tin or other container with a tight-fitting cover and return to the freezer for up to several weeks. Do not defrost before baking.

Transfer the Fleurons to a baking pan lined with parchment paper, as they are cut.

Baking. Bake the Fleurons at 375°F about 15 to 20 minutes, until they are well risen and a deep golden color. Transfer the pan to a rack and cool the Fleurons on the pan.

Holding. The Fleurons are best baked the day they are served. Keep Fleurons loosely covered, at room temperature. For advance preparation, follow the procedure for freezing, above.

Yield. About 2 dozen

CROUSTADES

This recipe represents one of many systems for preparing an empty puff pastry case. Although the traditional French *Vol au Vent* is round, I like the more tailored appearance of this square pastry. Although a Croustade may be made in any size—just remember that the piece of dough must be square—the one in this recipe is perfect for either a substantial appetizer, light main course or dessert.

Fill the Croustades with any mixture of sauced meat, fish or shellfish as an appetizer or main course. Reheat the Croustades briefly at 350°F before filling. For a dessert, fill with a dab of pastry cream and mixed fruit or berries. Or, make a more impressive presentation by filling with fruit or berries and surrounding the Croustade on the plate with a contrasting flavor Crème Anglaise—the possibilities are limitless.

⅓ BATCH PUFF PASTRY, ABOUT 1 POUND
(PAGES 182-185)

Egg Wash
1 EGG
PINCH SALT

Rolling the Dough. Lightly flour the work surface and the dough. Press the dough in successive firm strokes in both directions with a rolling pin. Move the dough frequently to renew the flour under and on it. Roll the dough to a 15 × 20-inch rectangle. Flour the dough and fold it in half without pressing the crease and slide it onto a floured pan or cookie sheet. Cover loosely with plastic wrap and refrigerate at least an hour.

Forming Croustades. Remove the dough from the refrigerator and place on a cutting board or sheet of parchment paper. Gently unfold the dough and press it flat with the palm of your hand. Using a ruler as a guide, cut the dough into twelve 5-inch squares with a sharp pastry wheel or thin-bladed knife. Transfer the squares of dough to two parchment paper–lined cookie sheets or 12 × 18-inch pans.

Fold over each square of dough to form a triangle and make a cut over the fold on either side, ½ inch from the cut edge, to within ½ inch of the point of the triangle, as in the illustration, below.

Unfold the triangles back into squares and dock the inside squares well with a fork. Beat together the egg and salt and paint the inside squares with the egg wash. Fold the outer corners over to the opposite inside corners, one at a time, as in the illustration, below.

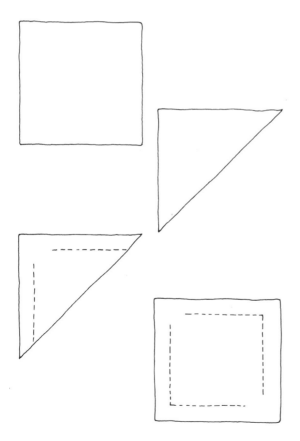

Press the borders of the Croustades well with fingertips to adhere. Indent the outside edges with the back of a knife at ¼-inch intervals. Finally, egg wash the borders, taking care not to let any drip down the sides.

Baking. Bake at 375°F about 25 minutes, until the Croustades are well puffed and golden. Remove the pan from the oven and empty out the inside squares: Use a fork to loosen the sides of the inner square and lift it out. If there is a large quantity of raw dough on the inside, carefully remove it with the fork, taking care not to pierce the bottom of the Croustades. Discard the underdone dough. If you wish to save the inner squares, removed first, to use as covers for the filling, line them up on the pan if there is room, or place on a separate parchment paper–lined pan. Return the Croustades and the covers, if used, to the oven for five minutes. Cool the

Croustades on the pan, on a rack.

If you are using the Croustades for a savory filling, reheat at 350°F about 7 or 8 minutes, before filling with the hot mixture. Serve immediately.

Holding. The Croustades are best on the day they are baked. You may form them the day before and keep them refrigerated, loosely covered with plastic wrap, until baked. If you must bake the Croustades in advance, store them in the refrigerator, tightly covered, and reheat at least 10 minutes at 350°F or they will be soggy.

Yield. 12 Croustades

PETITS TARTELETTES AUX FRUITS ROUGES

Fill these delicate tartelettes with any combination of sliced raw or cooked fruit. The berries make a colorful presentation. Since this recipe generates a lot of scraps, let them rest for a day and then use them for a batch of Palmiers, straws or a small mille feuille.

½ BATCH PUFF PASTRY, ABOUT 1½
  POUNDS (PAGES 182–185)

Egg Wash
  1 EGG
  PINCH SALT

Pastry Cream
  1 CUP MILK
  ⅓ CUP SUGAR, ABOUT 2½ OUNCES
  2 TABLESPOONS CORNSTARCH, ABOUT ½
    OUNCE

  3 EGG YOLKS
  2 TABLESPOONS BUTTER, 1 OUNCE, SOFTENED
  2 TEASPOONS VANILLA EXTRACT

Whipped Cream
  1 CUP HEAVY WHIPPING CREAM
  2 TABLESPOONS SUGAR, ABOUT 1 OUNCE
  1 TEASPOON VANILLA EXTRACT

Berries
  3 CUPS MIXED BERRIES: SLICED
    STRAWBERRIES, RASPBERRIES, BLUEBERRIES,
    RED CURRANTS, PITTED CHERRIES

Vanilla Sauce
  1 CUP MILK
  1 CUP HEAVY WHIPPING CREAM
  ⅓ CUP SUGAR, ABOUT 2½ OUNCES
  ½ VANILLA BEAN, SPLIT
  6 EGG YOLKS

Raspberry Sauce
  TWO 10-OUNCE PACKAGES FROZEN
    RASPBERRIES
  ⅔ CUP SUGAR, ABOUT 5 OUNCES
  1 TABLESPOON LEMON JUICE
  2 TABLESPOONS FRAMBOISE

Rolling. Divide dough in half. Lightly flour the work surface and the dough. Press the dough in successive firm strokes in both directions with a rolling pin. Move the dough frequently to renew the flour under and on it. Roll out each half ³⁄₁₆ inch thick, into a rectangle 12 × 16 inches; place each on a paper-lined pan. Allow dough to rest in refrigerator about 1 hour.

Forming and Baking. Remove dough from the refrigerator, dock well, and cut into twenty-four 4-inch disks, using a plain cutter. Place half the disks on a paper-lined pan. Cut a 2½-inch opening in the center of each of the remaining disks. Whisk the egg and salt together and paint the disks on the pan with the egg wash. Center the rings on the disks and firmly press them into place. Dock the rings with the point of a paring knife at ½ inch intervals. Bake at 375°F about 25 minutes, until well risen and deep golden. Cool the tartelettes on a rack.

Preparing the Pastry Cream. Bring ¾ cup milk and the sugar to a boil in a small saucepan. Beat the cornstarch into tl.e remaining milk; beat in the yolks. Beat one third of the boiling milk into the yolk mixture. Return the remaining milk to a boil and beat in the yolk mixture. Beat constantly until the Pastry Cream thickens and returns to a full boil; continue beating it about 1 minute. Remove from heat; beat in the butter and vanilla and pour into a clean, dry bowl. Chill with plastic wrap directly on the surface.

Whipping the Cream. Combine the cream, sugar and vanilla and whip until the cream holds its shape. Fold one quarter of the cream into the cooled Pastry Cream.

Preparing the Vanilla Sauce. Combine the milk, cream, sugar and vanilla bean in a medium saucepan and bring to a boil over medium heat. Beat the yolks in a bowl until liquid. Beat one third of the boiling mixture into the yolks. Then return the remaining milk/cream to a boil and beat in the yolk mixture. Continue beating until the cream thickens, about 30 seconds. Remove from heat while still beating, strain into a bowl and cool it over ice water, stirring occasionally. Remove and reserve vanilla bean for another use.

Preparing the Raspberry Sauce. Combine the raspberries and sugar in a saucepan over me-dium heat. Bring to a boil and simmer until slightly thickened, about 10 minutes. Puree in food processor, strain to remove seeds and cool. Stir in the lemon juice and liqueur.

Assembling. Cover twelve large dessert plates with the two sauces, swirling them together in a pattern. Place a tartelette in the center of each plate. Pipe the Pastry Cream in the opening and fill the center with the mixed berries, allowing the berries to spill over slightly. Pipe a rosette of whipped cream on the berries.

Holding. Prepare all the components up to 1 day in advance, but assemble the tartelettes immediately before serving.

Yield. 12 portions

INDIVIDUAL CHOCOLATE FEUILLETTÉS WITH RASPBERRIES

The flakiness of the chocolate puff pastry is a perfect contrast to the smooth richness of the White Chocolate Chantilly and the slight tartness of the raspberries. The tops of the feuillettés are finished with confectioners' sugar and a caramelized design.

Chocolate Feuillettés
    ½ BATCH QUICK CHOCOLATE PUFF PASTRY
        ABOUT 1 POUND (PAGES 186–188)

White Chocolate Chantilly
    5 OUNCES WHITE CHOCOLATE, FINELY CUT
    8 OUNCES HEAVY WHIPPING CREAM
    1 TABLESPOON FRAMBOISE OR RASPBERRY
        LIQUEUR

Raspberry Sauce

2 ½-PINT BASKETS FRESH RASPBERRIES *OR* 1
10-OUNCE PACKAGE FROZEN RASPBERRIES

⅓ CUP SUGAR, ABOUT 2½ OUNCES

1 TABLESPOON FRAMBOISE OR RASPBERRY
LIQUEUR

1 ½-PINT BASKET FRESH RASPBERRIES
CONFECTIONERS' SUGAR

Preparing the Feuillettés. Position a rack in the center of the oven. Line a cookie sheet with parchment paper. Lightly flour the work surface and the dough. Press the dough with the rolling pin to soften it slightly. If the dough is extremely hard, let it soften 30 minutes at a cool room temperature before attempting to roll it. Roll to a rectangle approximately 13 × 17 inches. Slide the dough onto the paper-lined cookie sheet and chill about 1 hour, or until firm. Preheat the oven to 350°F.

Using a sharp cutting wheel, cut the dough into twelve 4-inch squares (during baking the squares will shrink slightly so that the finished feuillettés will be approximately 3 to 3½ inches square). Remove any scraps of dough from the pan.

Bake the feuillettés until they are risen and are beginning to feel crisp, about 15 minutes. Lower the heat to 300°F and continue baking another 10 minutes until they are dry and very light. Slide the parchment paper with the feuillettés on it to a rack to cool.

Making the Chantilly. Place the white chocolate in a bowl. Bring ⅓ cup of the cream to a simmer in a small saucepan over medium heat and pour over the chocolate. Allow to stand for 2 or 3 minutes so that the chocolate melts, then whisk until smooth. Cool it to room temperature. Whip the remaining ⅔

cup cream until it holds soft peaks. Whip in the liqueur, then fold into the white chocolate mixture.

Preparing the Raspberry Sauce. Combine the fresh or frozen raspberries with the sugar in a saucepan over medium heat. Bring to a boil and simmer until slightly thickened about 10 minutes. Puree the sauce in a food processor, strain to remove the seeds and cool. Stir in the liqueur.

Assembling. Pipe half the White Chocolate Chantilly on six of the cooled squares using a ½-inch star tube. Divide the raspberries equally among the feuillettés, pressing them gently into the White Chocolate Chantilly. Pipe the remaining chantilly on the raspberries. Invert the other six squares on the chantilly, pressing very gently to adhere. The sides of the assembled feuillettés should be neat and not require smoothing. Sift confectioners' sugar neatly over the tops to make an even ⅛-inch coating. Heat a skewer or an old knife in the flame of a gas range or on the element of an electric range until it is red-hot. Pick up the skewer or knife with several thicknesses of a dry towel and mark the tops of the feuillettés with 2 diagonal lines to form an X. To caramelize the tops neatly, approach the skewer or knife as close as possible to the sugar without actually touching it. Reheat the skewer or knife as needed to finish the remaining feuillettés. Place each feuilletté in the center of a dessert plate and spoon the Raspberry Sauce around it.

Holding. Prepare all the components up to 1 day in advance, but assemble the feuillettés no more than 2 or 3 hours ahead.

Yield. 6 Feuillettés

PINEAPPLE COCONUT TART

The buttery delicacy of the puff pastry contrasts nicely with the coconut's sweetness and the pineapple's slight acidity. Poaching the pineapple reduces the acidity and makes even an underripe one palatable. Use this recipe for other combinations of fruit—mixed berries with a cream flavored with toasted almonds would make a lovely variation.

¼ BATCH PUFF PASTRY, ABOUT 12 OUNCES (PAGES 182–185)

Pastry Cream
1 CUP MILK
⅓ CUP SUGAR, ABOUT 2½ OUNCES
2 TABLESPOONS CORNSTARCH, ABOUT ½ OUNCE
3 EGG YOLKS
2 TABLESPOONS BUTTER, 1 OUNCE, SOFTENED
2 TEASPOONS VANILLA EXTRACT
1 TABLESPOON LIGHT RUM OR KIRSCH
1 CUP UNSWEETENED SHREDDED COCONUT, TOASTED, ABOUT 3 OUNCES

Poached Pineapple
1 RIPE PINEAPPLE, ABOUT 3 POUNDS
1 CUP SUGAR, ABOUT 7½ OUNCES
½ VANILLA BEAN OR 2 TEASPOONS VANILLA EXTRACT

Egg Wash
1 EGG
PINCH SALT

Apricot Glaze
½ CUP APRICOT PRESERVES
1 TABLESPOON WATER OR POACHING SYRUP FROM THE PINEAPPLE

Rolling the Dough. Lightly flour the work surface and the dough. Press the dough in successive firm strokes in both directions with a rolling pin. Move the dough frequently to renew the flour under and on it. Roll the dough about ⅛ inch thick, to a rectangle 12 × 16 inches; place on a parchment paper–lined pan. Allow to rest in the refrigerator about 1 hour.

Preparing the Pastry Cream. Bring ¾ cup milk and the sugar to a boil in a small saucepan. Whisk the cornstarch into the remaining milk; whisk in the yolks. Whisk one third of the boiling milk into the yolk mixture. Return the remaining milk to a boil and beat in the yolk mixture. Whisk constantly until the Pastry Cream thickens and returns to a full boil; continue whisking about 1 minute. Remove from heat; whisk in the butter and vanilla and pour into a clean, dry bowl. Chill with plastic wrap directly on the surface. Stir in the liquor and half the coconut.

Poaching the Pineapple. Peel, quarter, core and slice the pineapple. Place in a 2½-quart saucepan, sprinkle with the sugar and add the vanilla bean or vanilla. Pour in cold water to cover. Bring to a boil over medium heat and simmer until tender, about 5 to 10 minutes. Cool the pineapple in the syrup.

Forming. Cut the dough into a 12-inch square and four 1 × 12-inch strips. Place the square of dough on a parchment paper–lined pan and dock it. Beat together the egg and salt. Brush the edges of the dough with the egg wash and adhere the strips to the square, overlapping them at the corners. Firmly press the strips with a fingertip; make indentations around the perimeter of the shell, at ½-inch intervals, using the back of a knife. Dock the tops of the strips with the point of a knife at ½-inch intervals. Paint the top edge of the strips with the egg wash.

Baking. Bake at 400°F until well risen and beginning to color, about 15 minutes. Lower oven temperature to 350°F. Continue baking 10 to 15 minutes longer, or until the tart shell is well colored and dry. Cool on a rack.

Preparing the Apricot Glaze. Bring the preserves and water to a boil, strain into another saucepan and reduce, simmering, until the glaze coats the back of a spoon.

Assembling. Place the tart shell on a board or a serving platter and spread the Pastry Cream in it, using a metal spatula.

Drain the pineapple slices and overlap in rows, beginning each row at opposite ends of the tart, to cover the Pastry Cream. Reheat the Apricot Glaze, if necessary, and brush over the pineapple. Strew the remaining toasted coconut around the edges of the tart.

Holding. Keep 1 to 2 hours at a cool room temperature, or refrigerate, loosely covered with aluminum foil, up to 6 to 8 hours before serving.

Yield. About 10 portions

CARAMELIZED APPLE TARTELETTES

These delicate tartelettes are well worth the little extra work to prepare them. A baked disk of puff pastry is spread with a Calvados-flavored Pastry Cream, then covered with poached apple slices. Finally the tartelettes are dredged with sugar, then caramelized.

½ BATCH PUFF PASTRY, ABOUT 1½ POUNDS (PAGES 182–185)

Calvados Pastry Cream

1 CUP MILK
⅓ CUP SUGAR, ABOUT 1¾ OUNCES
2 TABLESPOONS CORNSTARCH, ABOUT ½ OUNCE
3 EGG YOLKS
2 TABLESPOONS BUTTER, 1 OUNCE, SOFTENED
1 TEASPOON VANILLA EXTRACT
1 TABLESPOON CALVADOS

3 POUNDS GOLDEN DELICIOUS APPLES, ABOUT 5 TO 6 MEDIUM
1 CUP SUGAR, ABOUT 7½ OUNCES
3 TO 4 CUPS WHITE WINE
1 STRIP LEMON ZEST

⅓ CUP SUGAR, ABOUT 2½ OUNCES

Rolling the Dough. Lightly flour the work surface and the dough. Press the dough in successive firm stokes in both directions with a rolling pin. Move the dough frequently to renew the flour under the dough and on it. Roll to a rectangle about 16 × 21 inches. Slide the dough onto a floured pan and chill it until it is firm.

Cutting the Bases for Tartelettes. Place the dough on a lightly floured work surface and dock well with a fork. Cut into twelve 5-inch disks. Place on one or two parchment paper–lined baking pans and allow them to rest, refrigerated, several hours.

Baking. Bake at 400°F until golden and well

risen, about 10 to 15 minutes. Slide from the pan and cool on a rack.

Preparing the Pastry Cream. Bring ¾ cup milk and the sugar to a boil in a saucepan. Whisk the cornstarch into the remaining milk; whisk in the yolks. Whisk half the boiling milk into the yolk mixture. Return the remaining milk to a boil and whisk in the yolk mixture. Whisk constantly, until the Pastry Cream thickens and returns to a full boil; continue whisking about 1 minute. Remove from heat; whisk in butter and vanilla and pour into a clean, dry bowl. Chill with plastic wrap directly on the surface. Stir the Calvados into the cold Pastry Cream.

Cooking the Apples. Peel, halve, core and slice the apples as for a tart, across the core into ¼-inch slices, keeping the halves intact. Place in a pan that will just hold them and sprinkle with the sugar. Add white wine to cover and lemon zest. Cover with a piece of parchment or wax paper with a small hole cut in the center. Cook over medium heat until the wine begins to simmer. Simmer very gently 5 minutes. Lift the apples out of the syrup with a slotted spoon and drain on a paper-towel-lined pan. Cool and refrigerate.

Assembling. Beat the Pastry Cream by hand to soften it slightly. Spread about 1 tablespoon on the center of each base, mounding it slightly. Arrange the apple slices overlapping, all around the base. Overlap two or three slices in the center to cover the area where the slices meet, and sprinkle lightly with the sugar.

Lift the tartelettes onto buttered baking pans and run them under a very hot broiler, watching constantly, until the apples caramelize to a deep golden color. Remove immediately from the hot pans to a rack to cool (the caramelized sugar might cause them to stick if they cool).

Holding. Keep loosely covered at a cool room temperature no more than 5 or 6 hours before serving.

Yield. 12 Tartelettes

MILLE FEUILLES

Among the most light and delicate of all desserts, the Mille Feuille is always popular and well received. It is really a type of layer cake, where the layers are baked sheets of puff pastry and the filling is usually flavored pastry cream, often combined with fruit and whipped cream. The Mille Feuille may be presented in a variety of shapes and finished in different ways. The recipes that follow illustrate many of the techniques for preparing differently shaped and filled Mille Feuilles.

Review the following details for maximum success.

Layers

Roll the dough to an even thickness. Thin spots will burn before the rest of the dough bakes through. Refrigerate the rolled sheets of dough well covered with plastic wrap, on a floured cookie sheet or jelly roll pan, at least an hour, or overnight, to minimize shrinkage and distortion during baking. Before baking, dock the layers well so that they remain flat during baking. Bake the layers sandwiched between two pans, inverting them several times during baking, so that the layers bake evenly on both sides. Cool the layers between the pans, on a rack, so they remain flat and straight after cooling. Cut into the desired shape as soon as the layers are cool enough to handle. If the layers are completely cooled they may be so crisp that they will shatter easily when cut; if a layer shatters, ignore it, and just reassemble the pieces when assembling the Mille Feuille—if possible, use the shattered layer in the middle, where the breaks will not be obvious.

Cut the layers into any shape—use most of the baked puff pastry sheets or the quantity of filling will be too much.

Bake and cut the layers in advance if desired. Stack between cardboards of the same size as the layers, double-wrap tightly

with plastic wrap, then freeze up to 1 month. Unwrap, place on a cookie sheet, reheat in a 375°F oven about 5 minutes and cool before preparing the Mille Feuille.

Glaze

Always glaze the layers to waterproof them, using a flavor that will blend well with the flavor of the Mille Feuille. Any jelly or

strained preserves will make a good glaze—reduce until a drop of the glaze is no longer sticky on its surface after it cools. If you use a neutral glaze, like apple jelly, add a tablespoon or two of an *eau de vie* or liqueur that will blend well with the flavor of the filling.

Filling

I like to use a layer of flavored pastry cream (add a little of the same *eau de vie* or liqueur that is in the glaze), a layer of fruit and a layer of sweetened whipped cream. The total depth of the filling on the layer should not exceed three-quarters of an inch. The fruit makes the

Mille Feuille less rich and provides important structural support, helping to cut down on the pastry cream and whipped cream oozing out of it when cut.

Finishing

Save any scraps from cutting the baked sheets, crush and use them to finish the sides of the Mille Feuille. Smooth the sides with a metal spatula, then press the crumbs against the side with the palm of your hand. If you don't have enough scraps to do this, substitute crushed, toasted sliced almonds.

Finish the top of the Mille Feuille with a dusting of confectioners' sugar. Trace a lattice pattern in the sugar with the point of a knife, or burn the lattice pattern into the sugar with

the back of an old knife, heated on the stove. Or, cover the whole outside, side and top with a minutely thin layer of whipped cream, and press crumbs or crushed, toasted sliced almonds all over; dust the Mille Feuille, top and side, with a light coating of confectioners' sugar. Or, glaze the top with fondant, as in the recipe for the Mille Feuille aux Fraises, pages 205–206. Review the techniques for making Fondant Icing, pages 25-26, before glazing the Mille Feuille. If you use the fondant, finish the sides last to cover any icing drips.

Holding

Assemble no more than 3 or 4 hours in advance, and refrigerate, loosely covered with plastic wrap or aluminum foil. After too long a wait, even the glaze will not prevent the layers from softening.

Cutting

You *must* use a very sharp, long, serrated knife. A dull knife will have the same effect on the Mille Feuille as a hammer would. Hold the knife straight with the blade perpendicular to and touching the top. Saw back and forth, cutting through the top pastry layer only. Wipe the knife blade on a damp towel between each cut. If iced with fondant, rinse the knife blade in running warm water and wipe it lightly between each cut. After dividing the top into portions, hold the knife at a 45-degree angle to the top and cut through, beginning at the far side, cutting toward you. Support the far side of the Mille Feuille with the palm of your other hand to minimize the back and forth motion that would rock the layers apart. If you are finishing the top with confectioners' sugar, cut the top layer into portions before placing it on the Mille Feuille.

MILLE FEUILLE AUX FRAISES

The Mille Feuille, literally "1,000 leaves," is one of the most interesting uses of puff pastry. In most cases puff pastry is used because of its dramatic rising ability. Here, the dough is deliberately prevented from rising, through docking and weighting the dough while it is baking. The result is thin, fragile layers which are then stacked with a delicate fruit and cream filling. The technique of using half circles of dough for the middle layer of the Mille Feuille economizes on the quantity of dough needed to prepare it.

½ BATCH PUFF PASTRY, ABOUT 1½ POUNDS (PAGES 182–185)

Pastry Cream
1 CUP MILK
⅓ CUP SUGAR, ABOUT 2½ OUNCES
2 TABLESPOONS CORNSTARCH, ABOUT ½ OUNCE
3 EGG YOLKS
1 TABLESPOON BUTTER, ½ OUNCE, SOFTENED
2 TEASPOONS VANILLA EXTRACT

Raspberry Glaze
1 CUP RASPBERRY PRESERVES
3 TABLESPOONS WATER

Filling
1 CUP HEAVY WHIPPING CREAM
¼ CUP SUGAR, ABOUT 1¾ OUNCES
1 PINT STRAWBERRIES, ABOUT 2 CUPS

¼ CUP CONFECTIONERS' SUGAR

Rolling the Dough and Forming the Layers. Lightly flour the work surface and the dough. Press the dough in successive firm strokes in both directions with a rolling pin. Move the dough frequently to renew the flour under and on it. Roll the dough to a 12 × 16-inch rectangle. Divide the dough in half, to make two rectangles, each 8 × 12 inches. Refrigerate one of the rectangles on a floured pan while rolling the other. Roll the first rectangle to a 12 × 16-inch rectangle, slide onto a floured pan, cover with plastic wrap and refrigerate several hours. Repeat with the other rectangle.

After the dough has rested, dock well, turn over and dock the other side. Arrange each piece of dough on a 10 × 15-inch pan lined with parchment papaer. Top each piece of dough with another piece of paper and pan of the same size.

Bake at 375°F about 15 minutes. Turn the layers over (merely invert the sandwich of pan-dough-pan) and continue baking until the pastry layers are a deep gold and baked through, up to another 15 to 20 minutes, checking the layers several times by removing one of the pans. If you must use two different racks in the oven, change the position of the pans often from one rack to the other, so that the layers bake evenly.

When baked, remove to racks to cool, leaving the layers between the pans so they cool flat and straight.

Cutting the Layers. Cut two 10-inch disks from cardboard to use as patterns to cut the dough. Leave one of the patterns intact and cut the other one in half. As soon as the baked layers are cool enough to handle, transfer them to a cutting board. Place the disk and half disk on each piece of dough and cut around them with the point of a sharp paring knife. Place the two 10-inch disks and the two half disks on a pan. Reserve the scraps, crush to crumbs and use to finish the side of the Mille Feuille.

Preparing the Pastry Cream. Bring 1 cup milk and the sugar to a boil in a saucepan. Whisk the cornstarch into the remaining milk; whisk in the yolks. Whisk one third of the boiling milk into the yolk mixture. Return the remaining milk to a boil and whisk in the yolk mixture. Whisk constantly until the Pastry Cream thickens and returns to a full boil; continue whisking about 1 minute. Remove from heat. Whisk in the butter and vanilla and pour into a clean, dry bowl. Chill with plastic wrap directly on the surface. Stir the Kirsch into the cold Pastry Cream.

Preparing the Raspberry Glaze. Bring the preserves and water to a boil, strain into another saucepan and reduce, simmering until the glaze coats the back of the spoon.

Preparing the Whipped Cream. Combine the cream and the sugar in a bowl. Whip until it holds firm peaks. Fold about one quarter of the cream into the Pastry Cream, reserving the remainder.

Preparing the Strawberries. Rinse, hull and slice the berries into a small bowl.

Assembling. Place one of the pastry disks on a cardboard and brush with the Raspberry Glaze. Brush the two half-disks with the glaze. Let the glaze cool and set for a minute before continuing or it will cause the filling spread on it to melt. Spread half the Pastry Cream on the layer and strew with half the strawberries. Spread half the whipped cream on the strawberries. Place the two glazed half-disks on the whipped cream. Repeat with the remaining Pastry Cream, strawberries and whipped cream. Top with the last pastry disk. Using a light cake pan, press the top layer, so that the top of the dessert is level and the layers adhere.

Finishing. Using a metal spatula, smooth the sides with any filling that oozes out. Press the reserved crumbs against the sides of the dessert, using the palm of the hand or the tip of the metal spatula.

Sift confectioners' sugar neatly over the top to make an even $1/8$-inch coating. Heat a skewer or an old knife in the flame of a gas range or on the element of an electric range until it is red-hot. Pick up the skewer or knife with several thicknesses of a dry towel and mark a lattice pattern on the top: Make five or six lines vertically, then another five or six on a diagonal to the first ones. To caramelize the top neatly, bring the skewer or knife as close as possible to the sugar without actually touching it. Reheat the skewer or knife as necessary to finish the remaining lines.

Holding. Serve within an hour or refrigerate, loosely covered with plastic wrap, for no more than 3 or 4 hours. The glaze seals the layers and prevents the pastry from becoming soggy, but this cannot be prevented indefinitely.

Yield. About 10 to 12 portions

CHEESE AND ALMOND HEART

In this variation on the classic Mille Feuille, crisp puff pastry is layered with a Sabayon-based cream cheese mousse flavored with dark rum and dotted with toasted almonds. Substitute plumped raisins or currants for the almonds, if you wish.

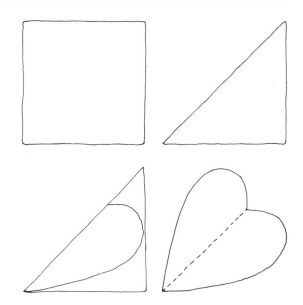

½ BATCH PUFF PASTRY, ABOUT 1½ POUNDS (PAGES 182–185)

Cheese Filling

4 EGG YOLKS

¼ CUP DARK RUM

½ CUP SUGAR, ABOUT 3¾ OUNCES

1 ENVELOPE UNFLAVORED GELATIN, 2½ TEASPOONS

¼ CUP WATER

1 POUND CREAM CHEESE WITHOUT VEGETABLE GUM, AT ROOM TEMPERATURE

1 TEASPOON VANILLA EXTRACT

¾ CUP HEAVY WHIPPING CREAM

½ CUP TOASTED SLICED ALMONDS, ABOUT 1½ OUNCES

CONFECTIONERS' SUGAR

Making the Heart-Shaped Templates. Prepare a heart-shaped pattern from a piece of stiff paper such as a manila folder: Trim the paper to a 9-inch square, then fold it diagonally. Mark and cut the paper as illustrated.

Rolling the Dough and Forming the Layers. Lightly flour the work surface and the dough. Press the dough in successive firm strokes in both directions with a rolling pin. Move the

dough frequently to renew the flour under and on it. Roll the dough to a 12 × 16-inch rectangle. Divide the dough in half, to make two rectangles, each 8 × 12 inches. Refrigerate one of the rectangles on a floured pan while rolling the other. Roll the first rectangle to a 12 × 16-inch rectangle, slide onto a floured pan, cover with plastic wrap and refrigerate several hours. Repeat with the other rectangle.

After the dough has rested, dock well, turn over and dock the other side. Arrange each piece of dough on a 10 × 15-inch pan lined with parchment paper. Top each piece of dough with another piece of paper and pan of the same size.

Bake at 375°F about 15 minutes. Turn the layers over (merely invert the sandwich of pan-dough-pan) and continue baking until the pastry layers are a deep gold and baked through, up to another 15 to 20 minutes, checking the layers several times by removing one of the pans. If you must use two different racks in the oven, change the position of the pans often from one rack to the other, so that the layers bake evenly.

When baked, remove to racks to cool, leaving the layers between the pans so they cool flat and straight.

Cutting the Layers. As soon as the baked layers are cool enough to handle, transfer them to a cutting board. Place the template on one baked sheet as per the illustration below and cut a heart shape using the point of a sharp paring knife. Fold the template vertically and cut a half-heart from the remaining dough. Put the cut layer aside and cut the remaining baked layer. Reserve the scraps, crush to crumbs and use to finish the side of the Mille Feuille.

Making the Cheese Filling. Prepare a Sabayon by whisking the yolks and rum. Whisk in the sugar in a slow stream. Whisk constantly over simmering water until very thick. Whisk on medium speed until cool.

Sprinkle the gelatin on the surface of the water in small heatproof bowl. Allow the gelatin to soften for 5 minutes. Place the bowl over a pan of simmering water to clear and melt the gelatin, about 5 minutes. Remove the bowl from the water.

Place the cream cheese in the mixer bowl. Beat with the paddle on medium speed until smooth, scraping the bowl and beater several times. Beat in the Sabayon in three additions, scraping the bowl and beater between each addition. Beat in the vanilla. Remove the bowl from the mixer. Whisk about ½ cup of the cream-cheese Sabayon into the dissolved gelatin. Quickly and vigorously, whisk the gelatin mixture into the remaining cream cheese mixture. Clean the sides of the bowl with a rubber spatula and reserve the mixture at room temperature.

Finishing. Whisk the cream until it holds a firm peak and fold it into the cream cheese mixture along with the almonds. At this point, the filling should be firm enough to spread. If it is not, allow it to stand at a cool room temperature until it firms up. If the filling is very thin, refrigerate it, stirring frequently with a rubber spatula to prevent lumps from forming.

Assembling. Using the template as a guide, cut a base from a piece of stiff, corrugated cardboard. With a palette knife, spread 1 tablespoon of the cheese filling in the center of the base. Place one of the pastry hearts on this, pressing so it adheres. Reserve ½ cup of the filling for finishing the sides of the dessert.

Spread half of the remaining filling on the first pastry heart. Place the two half hearts on this, joining them at the center. Carefully spread with the remaining filling. Top with the last pastry layer. Using a light cake pan, press the top layer so that the top of the dessert is level and the layers adhere.

Finishing. Using a metal spatula, smooth the sides with any filling that oozes out and the reserved ½ cup of filling. Press the reserved crumbs against the sides of the dessert, using the palm of the hand or the tip of the metal spatula. Reserve the remaining crumbs in a covered container in a cool place for up to one week, or discard them. Sift confectioners' sugar over the top of the dessert.

Holding. Keep 1 to 2 hours at a cool room temperature, or refrigerate it, loosely covered with aluminum foil, up to 6 to 8 hours before serving. If the dessert has been refrigerated, bring it to room temperature about 1 hour (less in a warm room) before serving it.

Yield. About 10 to 12 portions

PEAR MILLE FEUILLE

Use the system in this recipe to make a Mille Feuille in any shape and vary the filling to suit that shape. For an apple, fill with poached apple slices and Calvados flavored pastry cream, as in the Apple and Calvados Tart, page 141. Try a strawberry filled with sliced strawberries and a Kirsch pastry cream, as in the round Mille Feuille aux Fraises, pages 205–206.

This Mille Feuille uses only two layers of puff pastry to make the process of cutting the pear-shaped layers and assembling the dessert less complicated. Remember that you will have two 10 × 15-inch layers of baked puff pastry—cut them in any shape you desire, making sure that the shape you choose maximizes the use of the layer. Choose a shape that will not leave many scraps after cutting or there will be too much filling for the layers.

Use a mat cutting knife for making the stiff cardboard pattern. It is safer and more efficient than using a razor blade or ruining a good kitchen knife.

½ BATCH PUFF PASTRY, ABOUT 1½ POUNDS (PAGES 182–185)

Pastry Cream
1 CUP MILK
⅓ CUP SUGAR, ABOUT 2½ OUNCES
2 TABLESPOONS CORNSTARCH, ABOUT ½ OUNCE
3 EGG YOLKS
1 TABLESPOON BUTTER, ½ OUNCE, SOFTENED
2 TEASPOONS VANILLA EXTRACT

Whipped Cream
1 CUP HEAVY WHIPPING CREAM
1 TABLESPOON PEAR ALCOHOL OR DARK RUM

Poached Pears
2 CUPS WATER
1 CUP ICE
JUICE OF 1 LEMON
1½ POUNDS FIRM RIPE BARTLETT OR BOSC PEARS, 4 OR 5 PEARS
¾ CUP SUGAR, ABOUT 5¾ OUNCES
½ VANILLA BEAN OR 2 TEASPOONS VANILLA EXTRACT

Pear Glaze
½ CUP APPLE JELLY
¼ CUP PEAR POACHING SYRUP

CONFECTIONERS' SUGAR

Making a Cardboard Pattern. On a piece of stiff paper such as a manila folder, about 10 × 15 inches, draw a pear shape, including a stem and a leaf. Cut out the pear, stem and leaf and reserve them for cutting the puff pastry later.

Rolling the Dough and Forming the Layers. Lightly flour the work surface and the dough. Press the dough in successive firm strokes in both directions with a rolling pin. Move the dough frequently to renew the flour under and on it. Roll the dough to a 12 × 16-inch rectangle. Divide the dough in half, to make two rectangles, each 8 × 12 inches. Refrigerate one of the rectangles on a floured pan while rolling the other. Roll the first rectangle to a 12 × 16-inch rectangle, slide onto a floured pan, cover with plastic wrap and refrigerate several hours. Repeat with the other rectangle.

After the dough has rested, dock well, turn over and dock the other side. Arrange each piece of dough on a 10 × 15-inch pan lined with parchment paper. Top each piece of dough with another piece of paper and another pan of the same size.

Bake at 375°F about 15 minutes. Turn the layers over (merely invert the sandwich of pan-dough-pan) and continue baking until the pastry layers are a deep gold and baked through, up to another 15 to 20 minutes, checking the layers several times by removing one of the pans. If you must use two different racks in the oven, change the position of the pans often from one rack to the other, so that the layers bake evenly.

When baked, remove to racks to cool, leaving the layers between the pans so they cool flat and straight.

Cutting the Pear Shapes. Place the pattern on each baked sheet and cut out two pears, two leaves and two stems using the point of a small sharp paring knife. Crumble and reserve scraps.

Preparing the Pastry Cream. Bring ¾ cup milk and the sugar to a boil in a small saucepan. Whisk the cornstarch into the remaining milk; whisk in the yolks. Whisk one third of the boiling milk into the yolk mixture. Return the remaining milk to a boil and whisk in the yolk mixture. Whisk constantly until the Pastry Cream thickens and returns to a full boil; continue whisking about 1 minute. Remove from heat; whisk in the butter and vanilla and pour the Pastry Cream into a clean, dry bowl. Chill with plastic wrap directly on the surface.

Poaching the Pears. Combine the water, ice and lemon juice in a 2½-quart saucepan. Peel, halve and core the pears and immediately plunge into the water. When all the pears are in the water, remove the ice and enough water to leave the pears covered by an inch. Add the sugar and vanilla bean or vanilla. Cover with a disk of parchment paper with a hole in the center. Bring the pears to a boil over medium heat; lower the heat and simmer until tender. Remove from the syrup and drain, cut-side down, on a paper-towel-lined pan. Refrigerate until cold. Slice each pear half across the core into ¼-inch slices, keeping the pear halves intact.

Preparing the Fillings. Combine the cream and the pear alcohol or rum; whip the cream until it holds firm peaks. Fold one quarter of the cream into the Pastry Cream, reserving the remainder.

Preparing the Glaze. Combine the apple jelly and poaching syrup, bring to a boil and simmer until the glaze coats the back of a spoon.

Assembling. Using the pear, stem and leaf patterns, cut a piece of stiff corrugated cardboard and place one of the pear-shaped pieces of dough on it with the stem and leaf at the top. Paint the layer with the hot glaze and cool. Spread Pastry Cream on the glazed layer. Fan out the sliced pear halves on the Pastry Cream, placing some on the stem and the leaf also. Evenly cover the pears with the whipped cream, gently spreading with an spatula. Top each piece with the second puff pastry layer. Using a light-weight cookie sheet, press the top layer so that the top of the dessert is level.

Finishing. Smooth the sides with any cream which oozes out, using a palette knife. Press the reserved crumbs to the sides, using the palm of the hand or the tip of the metal spatula. Dust confectioners' sugar over the top. Arrange the pear on a platter.

Holding. Keep the dessert 1 to 2 hours at a cool room temperature, or refrigerate, loosely covered with aluminum foil, up to 3 to 4 hours before serving.

Yield. About 10 to 12 portions

APPLE TARTELETTES

These simple tartelettes point out one of the most interesting features of puff pastry—the the dough will rise up around an area that has been weighted. Here, apples are placed on disks of dough. The dough under the apples will not rise, but the dough around the apples will rise up to form a border around the apples, resembling a miniature tart shell. Because the tartelettes are made from raw fruit and raw dough, it is important to watch the baking carefully, making sure that the dough is sufficiently baked through before removing the tartelettes from the oven. In case the ap-

ples are coloring too much, loosely cover the tartelettes with aluminum foil, lower the position of the pan in the oven and continue baking until the pastry is baked through.

¼ BATCH PUFF PASTRY, ABOUT 12 OUNCES (PAGES 182–185)
2 TO 2½ POUNDS GOLDEN DELICIOUS APPLES, 4 TO 5 APPLES
2 TABLESPOONS BUTTER, 1 OUNCE, MELTED

Cinnamon Sugar
2 TABLESPOONS SUGAR, ABOUT 1 OUNCE
¼ TEASPOON CINNAMON

Egg Wash
1 EGG
PINCH SALT

Apricot Glaze
¾ CUP APRICOT PRESERVES
2 TABLESPOONS WATER

½ CUP CHOPPED TOASTED WALNUTS OR CRUSHED TOASTED SLICED ALMONDS, ABOUT 2 OUNCES

Rolling the Dough. Lightly flour the work surface and the dough. Press the dough in successive firm strokes in both directions with a rolling pin. Move the dough frequently to renew the flour under and on it. Roll the dough ⅛ inch thick, to approximately a 12-inch square. Place on a floured pan. Allow to rest in refrigerator about 1 hour.

Preparing the Apples. Peel, halve and core the apples, and slice each half into ¼-inch slices across the core, leaving the halves intact. Line up the apple halves on a pan or plate and brush them with the melted butter. Combine the cinnamon and sugar and sprinkle evenly over the apples.

Forming the Tartelettes. Using a round cutter, cut the dough into eight or nine 4-inch disks. Transfer the disks to a paper-lined baking pan and dock them carefully to avoid distorting their shape, leaving about ½-inch margin around the circumference of the disk undocked.

Beat together the egg and salt. Egg wash the disks carefully. Center an apple half on each disk.

Baking. Bake at 375°F until the apples are cooked and the pastry is baked through, about 30 minutes. Remove from the pan to a rack; cool.

Preparing the Apricot Glaze. Bring the preserves and water to a boil, strain into another saucepan, and reduce, simmering, until the glaze coats the back of a spoon.

Finishing. Brush the apples and the edge of the pastry with the glaze. Press the nuts around the edge of the tartelettes, being sure not to cover the apples.

Holding. Keep at room temperature for up to 12 hours, or refrigerate for up to a day. Reheat at 350°F about 10 minutes before serving.

Yield. About 8 or 9

BANDE AUX FRUITS

The Bande or strip is a common type of French fruit tart. It is popular because it retains a neat, tailored appearance even after several portions are cut from it. It is also useful to precut the portions and reform the strip on a platter or long, narrow board. Any fruit that doesn't darken once cut is appropriate to use on the Bande. Some, such as apples, pears, and peaches, are better used for the Bande aux Pommes which follows. Any berries, kiwi, slices of orange or pineapple (the last two are very juicy and should not be used if the tart is to stand for a long time) will make a lovely Bande. The fruit is arranged in rows, the length of the Bande, alternating one type of fruit per row. Or use one type of fruit, such as raspberries, filling the Bande generously with them.

¼ BATCH PUFF PASTRY, ABOUT 12 OUNCES (PAGES 182–185)

Egg Wash
1 EGG
PINCH SALT

Pastry Cream
1 CUP MILK
⅓ CUP SUGAR, ABOUT 2 OUNCES
2 TABLESPOONS CORNSTARCH, ABOUT ½ OUNCE
3 EGG YOLKS
1 TABLESPOON BUTTER, ½ OUNCE, SOFTENED
2 TEASPOONS VANILLA EXTRACT

Neutral Glaze
1 CUP APPLE JELLY

ABOUT 3 CUPS ASSORTED FRUIT: STRAWBERRIES, RASPBERRIES, SLICED KIWI, ORANGE SEGMENTS OR SLICES

¼ CUP TOASTED, SLICED ALMONDS, ABOUT ¾ OUNCE

Rolling and Forming the Dough. Lightly flour the work surface and the dough. Press the dough in successive firm strokes in both directions with a rolling pin. Move the dough frequently to renew the flour under and on it. Roll the dough 3/16 inch thick into a rectangle, approximately 8 × 16 inches. Flour a baking pan and place the dough on it. Loosely cover with plastic wrap and refrigerate about 1 hour

or until firm. Remove from the refrigerator and slide it off the pan onto a lightly floured surface.

Using a sharp cutting wheel, cut dough into two 1-inch strips and one 6-inch strip. Place the 6-inch strip on a paper-lined baking pan and dock. Beat together the egg and salt. Paint the long edges with egg wash. Pick up the 1-inch strips of dough without stretching them. (A long spatula is useful for this.) Apply to the long sides, pressing very hard with fingertips; indent the sides of the strip with the back of a knife at 1/2-inch intervals; dock the top of the narrow strips with the point of a knife at a 45-degree angle to the edge, every 1/2 inch. Do not trim the narrow ends of the strip until after baking.

Baking. Bake at 400°F until pastry is well colored and interior is no longer damp, about 20 to 25 minutes. Slide onto a rack and cool to room temperature.

Preparing the Pastry Cream. Bring 3/4 cup milk and the sugar to a boil in a saucepan. Whisk the cornstarch into the remaining milk; whisk in the yolks. Whisk one third of the boiling milk into the yolk mixture. Return the milk to a boil and whisk in the yolk mixture. Whisk constantly until the Pastry Cream thickens and returns to a full boil; continue whisking about 1 minute. Remove from heat. Whisk in the butter and vanilla. Pour into a clean, dry bowl. Chill with plastic wrap directly on the surface.

Preparing the Neutral Glaze. Reduce the apple jelly in a small saucepan over medium heat until it coats the back of a spoon.

Finishing. Thinly spread Pastry Cream over central area of strip. (Only about half the cream will be needed.) Refrigerate the leftover Pastry Cream and use within a day or two for another Bande or in the base of a tart. Arrange fruit, such as strawberries, sliced kiwis, raspberries and orange slices, overlapping, in lengthwise rows over the Pastry Cream. Brush with the glaze. The edges of the Bande outside the first and last rows of fruit may be glazed and sprinkled with a thin row of toasted, sliced almonds or chopped, blanched pistachios. Trim the short ends of the Bande.

Holding. Keep at a cool room temperature for no more than 3 hours before serving.

Yield. About 8 to 10 portions

BANDE AUX POMMES

This variation of the Bande has a bit of almond filling spread on the raw dough before the fruit is arranged over it. Any fruit which will stand up to baking such as apples, pears, apricots, or firm peaches may be used here.

¼ BATCH PUFF PASTRY, ABOUT 12 OUNCES
(PAGES 182–185)

Egg Wash
1 EGG
1 PINCH SALT

Almond Frangipane
2 OUNCES ALMOND PASTE
2 TABLESPOONS SUGAR, ABOUT 1 OUNCE
2 EGG YOLKS
1 TEASPOON GRATED LEMON ZEST
2 TABLESPOONS BUTTER, 1 OUNCE
2 TABLESPOONS UNBLEACHED ALL-PURPOSE
FLOUR, ABOUT ½ OUNCE

1½ TO 2 POUNDS GOLDEN DELICIOUS
APPLES, ABOUT 3 TO 4
2 TABLESPOONS BUTTER, 1 OUNCE, MELTED

Apricot Glaze
¾ CUP APRICOT PRESERVES
2 TABLESPOONS WATER

2 TABLESPOONS TOASTED SLICED ALMONDS,
ABOUT ½ OUNCE
CONFECTIONERS' SUGAR

Rolling and Forming the Dough. Lightly flour the work surface and the dough. Press the dough in successive firm strokes in both directions with a rolling pin. Move the dough frequently to renew the flour under and on it. Roll the dough ³⁄₁₆ inch thick into a rectangle, approximately 8 × 16 inches. Flour a baking pan and place the dough on it. Loosely cover with plastic wrap and refrigerate about 1 hour, or until firm. Remove the dough from the refrigerator and slide it off the pan onto a lightly floured surface.

Using a sharp cutting wheel, cut dough into two 1-inch strips and one 6-inch strip. Place the 6-inch strip on a paper-lined baking pan and dock. Beat together the egg and salt. Paint the long edges with egg wash. Pick up the 1-inch strips of dough without stretching them. (A long spatula is useful for this.) Apply to the long sides, pressing very hard with fingertips; indent the sides of the strip with the back of a knife at ½-inch intervals; dock the top of the narrow strips with the point of a knife at a 45-degree angle to the edge, every ½ inch. Do not trim the narrow ends of the strip until after baking.

Mixing the Frangipane. Break the almond paste into 1-inch pieces and place in the bowl of an electric mixer with the sugar, one of the egg yolks and the lemon zest. Beat with the paddle on medium speed until smooth. With a rubber spatula, scrape bowl and beaters. Add the butter and continue beating until smooth and light. Scrape down again and beat in the other yolk until it is absorbed. Scrape down again and beat until smooth. Beat in the flour just until it disappears.

Assembling. Spread the frangipane in the central area of the strip. Peel, core, and halve the apples and slice ⅛ inch thick; fan halves slightly. Arrange, overlapping, on frangipane. Brush with melted butter.

Baking. Bake at 400°F for 20 minutes, then lower temperature to 350°F and continue baking, until the apples are cooked and the pastry is baked through, about 20 minutes longer. Slide onto a rack and cool to room temperature.

Preparing the Apricot Glaze. Bring preserves and water to a boil, strain into another saucepan and reduce, simmering, until the glaze coats the back of a spoon.

Finishing. Brush the apples and the edges of the Bande with the glaze. Strew the almonds between the apples and the edges of the Bande. Dust the almonds with the confectioners' sugar.

Holding. The Bande will hold well for half a day at a cool room temperature. Or, refrigerate the baked, cooled, but unglazed Bande up to two days, well covered with plastic wrap. Reheat at 350°F for about 15 minutes and cool on a rack. Then finish with the glaze, almonds and confectioners' sugar.

Yield. About 8 to 10 portions

GÂTEAU PITHIVIERS

Long renowned as one of France's most beloved pastries, the Gâteau Pithiviers is also one of the most flattering uses for Puff Pastry, since the dough rises to dramatic heights during baking. In his wonderful *Hundred Glories of French Cooking,* Robert Courtine describes Pithiviers, south of Paris, where the pastry originated, as a good-food center famous for its duck terrine, honey and a hay-wrapped cheese named for it. He also suggests that the original filling for the Pithiviers may have been made from filberts, since the town was formerly a center for their cultivation.

When I prepare Almond Frangipane in large quantities, I use about 12 ounces of it for the filling of a 10-inch Gâteau Pithiviers. You may use the recipe for the Almond Frangipane, page 155; or the following filling, made with whole almonds and sugar. Substitute other nuts—hazelnuts (omit the almond extract), or even pistachios—for a less classic, but equally delicious Pithiviers.

½ BATCH PUFF PASTRY, ABOUT 1½ POUNDS (PAGES 182–185)

Ground Almond Frangipane
⅔ CUP WHOLE BLANCHED ALMONDS, ABOUT 3½ OUNCES
½ CUP SUGAR, ABOUT 3¾ OUNCES
6 TABLESPOONS BUTTER, 3 OUNCES, SOFTENED
½ TEASPOON ALMOND EXTRACT
1 TEASPOON GRATED LEMON ZEST
1 TABLESPOON DARK RUM
3 EGG YOLKS
⅓ CUP UNBLEACHED ALL-PURPOSE FLOUR, ABOUT 1¾ OUNCES

Egg Wash

    1 EGG
    PINCH SALT

Rolling the Dough. Lightly flour the work surface and the dough. Press the dough in successive firm strokes in both directions with a rolling pin. Move the dough frequently to renew the flour under and on it. Roll the dough ³⁄₁₆ inch thick to a rectangle, approximately 11 × 22 inches. Cut into two 11-inch squares. Flour two baking pans or cookie sheets, slide a piece of dough onto each pan, cover loosely with plastic wrap and refrigerate an hour or two.

Preparing the Filling. Combine the almonds and sugar in the bowl of a food processor fitted with the steel blade. Pulse the mixture on and off at one-second intervals, about fifteen times, to grind very finely. Cream the butter by machine on medium speed and beat in the ground almond and sugar mixture. Beat in the almond extract, lemon zest and rum and continue beating until light, about 3 minutes longer. Beat in the yolks, one at a time, beating smooth between each addition, scraping the bowl and beaters between each yolk. Scrape again and beat in the flour, just until it is absorbed.

Assembling. Place one of the squares on a parchment-lined baking pan or cookie sheet. Using a dull knife, mark a 10-inch circle, then a 4-inch circle in its center on the dough. Spread the filling on the 4-inch circle, piling it high. Beat together the egg and salt. Brush the egg wash between the filling and the edge of the 10-inch circle. Place the second square of dough on top; lightly flour the dough.

Press the dough down well all around the filling. Invert a pan or bowl that is 6 inches in diameter in the center and press down firmly to seal in the filling. Repeat with an 8-inch pan or bowl. Finally, place a 10-inch pan or bowl on the dough, but do not press. Using a sharp pastry wheel or a thin knife, cut around the pan or bowl. Remove the scraps.

Indent the side of the pastry deeply at 1½-inch intervals, using the back of a knife. Dock the area between the 6-inch and 8-inch circles with the point of a paring knife: Hold the knife perpendicular to the top of the pastry, at a 45-degree angle to the outer circle, to make a series of diagonal slashes, pressing the knife downward until it touches the pan. Repeat, reversing the direction of the angle on

each slash, to make each into an "x." Cut a vent hole in the top center: With your fingers, pinch the dough and lift upward; cut straight across, parallel to the pastry, with a small, sharp knife. Chill the pastry, loosely covered with plastic wrap, about 1 hour.

Immediately before baking, make a series of curved slashes on the mound of filling, using a small, sharp knife. Hold the knife at a 30-degree angle to the top, at the vent hole, and make a curved slash out to the 6-inch circle, cutting no more than halfway into the dough. Make about twelve slashes over the filling in this way. Brush the entire outside of the pastry very carefully with the egg wash, being careful to avoid making the egg wash accumulate in puddles.

Baking. Bake at 400°F about 20 minutes. Lower temperature to 350°F and continue baking until the pastry is well colored, risen and the interior is no longer damp, 40 to 45 minutes longer. Slide the Gâteau Pithiviers off the pan to a rack to cool.

Holding. This is best only a few hours after it has been baked. Leftovers reheat successfully—store covered with plastic wrap at room temperature, for up to two days. For advance preparation, form the Pithiviers and refrigerate up to two days before baking.

Yield. About 10 portions

9

CAKE LAYERS

The recipes in this section cover different types of cake layers. All the layers are meant to be finished with creams, mousses and other types of fillings and coverings. None of these cake layers is meant to function on its own as a plain cake.

The cake layers are different types of sponges—cakes that rely on the air beaten into eggs for their lightness and ability to rise during baking. The *Génoise* is a delicate sponge made with whole eggs; *Génoise Mousseline* is a richer version with extra yolks and butter; *Biscuit* is a sponge made with separated eggs and usually piped into ladyfingers and disk-shaped layers; the *Nut Sponge* is also made with separated eggs but incorporates ground nuts for richness and flavor.

GÉNOISE

Sometimes referred to as Génoise Ordinaire, this is one of the most versatile dessert prepa-

rations. Used as a base for many different layered and rolled cakes, the Génoise is not extremely exciting on its own. But the flavored moistening syrup used during finishing more than makes up for the cake's rather bland taste.

A classic example of an egg-foam batter, the Génoise derives all its lightness and ability to rise during baking from the air beaten into the eggs during whipping. To assure a high volume of air, eggs and sugar are first combined and heated; this makes it possible to whip the eggs to a greater volume.

A machine is always used to sufficiently aerate the egg foam. Whipping the egg foam on a table-model mixer with the balloon whip attachment usually takes 4 to 5 minutes on the highest speed. Whipping with a hand-held rotary mixer will take approximately 7 to 10 minutes on the highest speed, moving the mixer in a wide circular motion in the bowl to maximize the amount of air beaten into the egg foam.

To test for maximum whipping, look for "ribboning": Withdraw the whip from the foam and watch the consistency of the ribbon which forms on the foam's surface as it drops back into it. It should be very light, not at all liquid, and remain intact for about 20 seconds before dissolving into the foam.

The dry ingredients are then incorporated by gentle folding. A combination of cake flour and cornstarch provides enough starch to easily set the batter and give the finished Génoise a fine texture and tight grain. The cake flour and cornstarch are mixed together and sifted several times, then folded into the egg foam in several additions. The folding must be accomplished both gently and quickly to retain the maximum amount of air in the batter. If the dry ingredients are folded in too roughly, the friction of the folding will knock air out of the foam. If the folding is not thorough enough the finished Génoise will be riddled with lumps of unincorporated starch or, worse, will fall because of insufficient starch mixed into the egg foam to bind and set it.

To fold the dry ingredients into the egg foam, sift about one third on the foam's surface, using a sifter or a small strainer. With a rubber spatula, cut through the center of the foam, inserting the spatula at the far end of the bowl, scraping through the foam, all the way down to the bottom of the bowl, and bringing the spatula out at the end of the bowl closest to you. Quickly revolve the bowl about 30 degrees and repeat the folding process. Then pour the batter into a buttered and paper-lined pan.

Since the air in the egg foam tends to dissipate on standing, the time from the point where the egg foam is sufficiently whipped to the point where the batter is in the oven must be kept to a minimum, no longer than 4 or 5 minutes.

The Génoise may be baked as a round layer or a rectangular sheet. As a round layer, it will take about 30 minutes to bake.

A rectangular layer, 1 inch thick, will take only 10 or 15 minutes to bake, since it is so much shallower. The signs of doneness are a marked rising—usually about a 100 percent increase in volume; a good deep golden crust color; a firmness when pressed with the flat palm of the hand; and a slight shrinkage away from the side of the pan. Once baked, the Génoise must be removed from the oven and the pan immediately. Overbaking will cause it to shrink so that the top is much smaller than the bottom. Leaving the Génoise in the pan after baking will cause the outside to become extremely dry and brittle. This is especially crucial where rectangular layers are concerned, since they are frequently used to make rolled cakes and will not roll successfully if dry and brittle.

To remove the round Génoise layer from the pan, loosen it by inserting a paring knife between the edge of the Génoise and the side of the pan. Push the knife blade all the way down until it touches the bottom of the pan. Then, loosen the Génoise from the side of the pan by scraping the blade of the knife against the pan, not into the Génoise, which would scar the side of it. Immediately invert the Génoise onto the work surface and, using a wide spatula, reinvert it onto a rack to cool. If the Génoise has overbaked slightly, cool it directly against the work surface. This will trap the condensation which develops between the surface and the Génoise, maximizing the layer's moisture. For the rectangular layer, loosen it with a paring knife as above, then lift one edge of the Génoise by the paper. Grasping the corners of the paper, pull the Génoise layer out of the pan and cool it directly against the work surface. The thin, rectangular Génoise is always cooled in this way to retain maximum moisture.

To store any Génoise, double-wrap in plastic wrap and refrigerate it for up to 3 or 4 days. The Génoise also freezes very well, for up to 1 month. In all cases do not remove the paper until you are ready to finish the Génoise, for ease of handling.

PLAIN GÉNOISE (GÉNOISE ORDINAIRE)

The round layer is split and used as a layer cake; the rectangular layer is used for a rolled cake or a square or rectangular cake.

4 EGGS

PINCH SALT

⅔ CUP SUGAR, ABOUT 5 OUNCES

½ CUP CAKE FLOUR, ABOUT 2 OUNCES

3 TABLESPOONS CORNSTARCH, ABOUT ¾ OUNCE

Preparing the Pan. For a round layer, use a 9-inch diameter × 2½- to 3-inch-deep springform pan. (A 10-inch diameter × 2-inch-deep layer pan can also be used.) For a rectangular layer, use a 10 × 15-inch jelly-roll pan. (A 12 × 18-inch half-sheet pan can also be used.) Butter the pan and line the bottom with a piece of parchment or wax paper, cut to fit.

Preheating the Oven. Heat the oven to 350°F. Adjust the oven rack to the middle level.

Mixing the Egg Foam. Break the eggs into the bowl of an electric mixer or into a 4- to 5-quart stainless steel bowl if a hand mixer is to be used. Whisk until liquid. Beat in the salt,

then the sugar, in a stream.

Warming the Egg Foam. Place the bowl over, not in, a pan of simmering water and stir constantly with a hand whip to keep the eggs from setting and scrambling. Heat the egg mixture to about 100 to 110°F. The egg mixture should just feel lukewarm.

Whipping the Egg Foam. Immediately remove the bowl from the pan of water and whip the egg mixture on maximum speed with the balloon whip until it is cool and increased in volume, about 4 to 5 minutes. The egg foam should increase about five times its original

volume and become very pale yellow in color. If using a hand mixer, the process should take 7 to 10 minutes.

Mixing the Dry Ingredients. While the egg foam is beating, mix the cake flour and cornstarch together on a piece of wax paper. Sift onto another piece of paper and sift back and forth three times to thoroughly mix.

Testing the Egg Foam. When the egg foam seems sufficiently beaten, remove it from the mixer and test for a good ribbon.

Folding in the Dry Ingredients. Sift one third of the dry ingredients onto the egg foam. Fold the dry ingredients into the foam with a rubber spatula. Continue sifting and folding in the remaining dry ingredients, adding them in two more stages.

Molding the Batter. The batter should be poured into the prepared pan immediately after it is made. Pour the batter into the prepared pan, scraping the last batter out of the bowl with a rubber spatula. For a round layer, immediately tilt the pan in a circular motion so that the batter reaches the top of the pan all around. This will help the batter rise

evenly and keep the top of the baked Génoise flat, rather than domed in the center. Drop the pan onto the surface from a distance of about 3 inches to settle the contents.

For a rectangular layer, carefully spread the batter with an offset spatula, held at an angle. Do not push the blade of the spatula too deeply into the batter or the batter may lose air. Evenly spread the batter into the corners of the pan since the corners tend to dry and become brittle if they are too thin. Immediately place the filled pans in the oven.

Baking. Bake in the preheated 350°F oven, for about 30 minutes for the round layer and about 10 to 15 minutes for the rectangular layer.

Testing for Doneness. After half the baking time the Génoise should be rising and only beginning to color on the top. If the top is burning, lower the oven temperature to 300°F. The Génoise is sufficiently baked when its top is deep gold and feels firm when the center is gently pressed with a flat palm. The Génoise will also slightly shrink away from the sides of the pan.

Unmolding. Immediately remove from the oven and loosen with a small, sharp knife. For the round layer, invert it onto the work surface and immediately turn right-side up, using a wide spatula or grasping it firmly on either side and inverting it onto a rack to cool. For the rectangular layer, lift one of the short edges and grasp both corners of the paper to slide the layer out of the pan. Cool the rectangular layer directly against the work surface to conserve its moisture. Do not remove the paper.

Holding. Double wrap in plastic wrap and refrigerate or freeze it. Place the wrapped round layer back in the cleaned pan so that it does not become dented during storage. Slide the rectangular layer back into a clean pan of the same size or larger before wrapping it. The Génoise will keep well in the refrigerator for 4 to 5 days, or in the freezer for up to 1 month. Defrost at room temperature for about 1 hour before using.

Yield. One 9- or 10-inch round or one 10 × 15-inch or 12 × 18-inch rectangle

Chocolate Génoise

The procedure for the Chocolate Génoise is identical to that of the Plain Génoise. The ingredients vary slightly: The quantities of the cake flour and cornstarch are reduced to allow for the cocoa powder. A small amount of baking soda is also added to the batter not to leaven it but to counteract the acidity and possible heaviness of the cocoa powder. Be especially careful in sifting together the dry ingredients. Sometimes, even after sifting, small lumps remain in the cocoa powder; these lumps can weigh down the batter and prevent it from rising to its fullest during baking.

4 EGGS
PINCH SALT
2/3 CUP SUGAR, ABOUT 5 OUNCES
1/3 CUP CAKE FLOUR, ABOUT 1 1/2 OUNCES
1/3 CUP CORNSTARCH, ABOUT 1 1/2 OUNCES
3 TABLESPOONS UNSWEETENED COCOA POWDER, ABOUT 1/2 OUNCE
2 PINCHES BAKING SODA

Follow instructions for Plain Génoise (pages 220–223), sifting the cocoa powder and baking soda together with the cake flour and cornstarch.

RICH GÉNOISE (GÉNOISE MOUSSELINE)

A rich and dense version of the Génoise which has recently become popular, the Génoise Mousseline has extra egg yolks and butter to enrich it. Since the butter makes a fairly dense cake which cannot be rolled without cracking, the Génoise Mousseline is only prepared in round layers. The method for incorporating the butter is interesting—it was probably developed by the famed French pastry chef Gaston Le Nôtre, perhaps the single most influential force in modern pastrymaking. To prevent the batter from falling from the addition of the butter, a small portion of the batter is removed, the butter is stirred into it, then it is carefully folded back into the remaining batter.

½ STICK BUTTER, 2 OUNCES

3 EGGS

3 EGG YOLKS

PINCH SALT

½ CUP SUGAR, ABOUT 3¾ OUNCES

⅓ CUP CAKE FLOUR, ABOUT 1½ OUNCES

¼ CUP CORNSTARCH, ABOUT 1 OUNCE

Preparing the Pan. Use a 9-inch diameter × 2½- to 3-inch-deep springform pan.

Preheating the Oven. Heat the oven to 350°F. Adjust the oven rack to the middle level.

Preparing the Butter. Melt the butter in a small saucepan over low heat. Do not allow the butter to sizzle or take on any color. After the butter has melted, leave it over the lowest heat possible so that it bubbles up slightly and the water in the butter evaporates, about 1 to 2 minutes. Remove from the heat and allow to cool.

Mixing the Egg Foam. Whisk the eggs and yolks with a hand whip until liquid. Whisk in the salt, then the sugar, in a stream.

Warming the Egg Foam. Place the bowl over, not in, a pan of simmering water and stir with a hand whip to keep the eggs from setting and

scrambling. Heat the egg mixture to about 100 to 110°F. The egg mixture should just feel lukewarm.

Whipping the Egg Foam. Immediately remove the bowl and whip the egg mixture on maximum speed with the mixer balloon whip until it is cool and increased in volume, about 4 to 5 minutes. The egg foam should increase about five times over its original volume and become very pale yellow in color. If using a hand mixer, the process should take 7–10 minutes.

Mixing the Dry Ingredients. While the egg foam is whipping, mix the cake flour and cornstarch together.

Testing the Egg Foam. When the egg foam seems sufficiently whipped, remove it from the mixer and test for a firm ribbon. The egg foam for Génoise Mousseline is firmer than that for a Plain Génoise because of the extra yolks. It should be possible to draw a line with your fingertip, about ¼ inch deep, across the diameter of the egg foam, and the line should hold without the egg foam moving back together to obliterate it.

Folding in the Dry Ingredients. Sift one third of the dry ingredients onto the egg foam. Fold the dry ingredients into the egg foam with a rubber spatula. Continue sifting and folding in the remaining dry ingredients, adding them in two more stages.

Folding in the Butter. Remove about 1 cup of the Génoise batter to a small bowl, add the cooled, melted butter, and stir it in, gently but thoroughly. Quickly fold the buttered batter back into the remaining batter, being careful not to overmix.

Molding the Batter. Pour the batter into the prepared pan. Immediately tilt the pan in a circular motion so that the batter reaches the top of the pan all around. Drop the pan onto the surface from a distance of about 3 inches to settle the contents.

Baking. Bake in the preheated 350°F oven for about 30 minutes.

Testing for Doneness. After half the baking time, the Génoise Mousseline should be rising and only beginning to color on the top. If the top is burning, lower the oven temperature to 300°F. The Génoise Mousseline is sufficiently baked when its top is deep gold and it feels firm when the center is gently pressed with a flat palm. The Génoise Mousseline will also slightly shrink away from the side of the pan.

Unmolding. Immediately remove from the oven and loosen with a small, sharp knife. Invert the pan onto the work surface and immediately turn the Génoise right-side up again, using a wide spatula or grasping it firmly on either side and inverting it on a rack to cool. Leave the paper under the Génoise.

Holding. Double-wrap in plastic wrap, place it back in the pan, and refrigerate or freeze it. The Génoise Mousseline will keep well in the refrigerator for 4 to 5 days, or in the freezer for up to 1 month. Defrost at room temperature for 1 hour before using.

Yield. 1 9-inch round layer

BISCUIT BATTER

Unlike the Génoise batter which is made with whole eggs, biscuit batter is made with separated eggs. For maximum aeration, the yolks and the whites are beaten separately, then combined. Cake flour is folded into the egg mixture to bind it. Biscuit batter is normally piped into finger shapes or disks which are for desserts such as Charlottes—rich fillings surrounded by sponge fingers. The batter may also be baked in a pan, although I prefer a Génoise for this type of cake layer.

Aeration is the most important consideration. The maximum amount of air must be beaten into both the yolks and the whites to ensure a greater density after they are combined. Since the quantity of flour is proportionately greater than in a Génoise batter, it is especially important to fold in the flour gently, without dissipating too much air. After the addition of the flour, the batter must still hold its shape well or the fingers and disks will not rise enough, making them dense and heavy.

Folding the cake flour into the batter should be done in three or four stages, sifting over a little at a time and folding it in gently but quickly. Once ready, the batter should be piped. It is best to have the paper-lined pans, the pastry bag and the tube ready before mixing the batter. For baking the fingers, a shaker or a fine strainer with confectioners' sugar should also be ready. The fingers are thickly dusted with confectioners' sugar to dry the surface during baking. This is important when unmolding desserts lined with the fingers; if not sufficiently dry, the fingers will stick to the mold and look sloppy. For this reason, many desserts using an exterior of sponge fingers are surrounded by a ribbon—the ribbon conceals the unsightly surface of the fingers.

Be careful not to overbake the sponge fingers or disks or they will be dry and hard. They will turn a deep golden color during baking and should have the same type of texture as a baked Génoise, feeling firm when pressed with a fingertip. Immediately remove the paper containing the sponge fingers or disks from the pan to prevent them from becoming too dry from the heat retained by the pan.

The sponge fingers and disks keep very well for a few days in the refrigerator, left on the parchment paper, stacked on a pan and tightly closed in a plastic bag. They may also be frozen, double-bagged to combat the freezer's drying effects. The chocolate and spiced biscuit batters that follow are prepared in the same way as the plain biscuit batter. The chocolate batter is not dusted with the confectioners' sugar so that its darker color shows.

SPONGE FINGERS

4 EGGS, SEPARATED
PINCH SALT
1 TEASPOON VANILLA EXTRACT
½ CUP SUGAR, ABOUT 3¾ OUNCES
¾ CUP CAKE FLOUR, ABOUT 3 OUNCES
CONFECTIONERS' SUGAR FOR DUSTING

Preparing. Use two 10 × 15-inch rectangular pans. (Two 12 × 18-inch pans or cookie sheets can also be used.) Line the pans with parchment paper, cut to fit. Place a ½-inch plain tube in a pastry bag. Have the confectioners' sugar and a fine strainer or shaker ready for dusting.

Preheating the Oven. Heat the oven to 350°F. Adjust the oven rack to the middle level.

Whipping the Yolks. Whip the yolks in a 2-quart bowl or the bowl of an electric mixer until liquid. Whip in half the sugar in a slow stream, then the vanilla, until the yolks and sugar have become very light and lemon-colored, at least 5 minutes. The sugar will substantially dissolve and the yolks will increase almost three times over their original volume. Set the yolk mixture aside.

Whipping the Whites. Whip the whites and the salt on medium speed with a mixer until they are white, opaque and begin to hold their shape. Increase the speed to the maximum and whip in the remaining sugar in a slow stream. When all the sugar has been added, the whites should stand straight up in a firm peak.

Combining the Yolks and Whites. Fold the yolk mixture into the beaten whites gently but thoroughly, making sure that they are well mixed and that no lumps of egg white remain. Be careful not to deflate any air out of the mixture.

Folding in the Cake Flour. Sift one quarter of the cake flour over the egg mixture and fold in with a rubber spatula, cutting repeatedly through the center of the bowl and keeping the spatula against the side of the bowl, scraping all the way down to the bottom. Revolve the bowl about 30 degrees every time the spatula goes through it. Repeat with the remaining cake flour, occasionally scraping the side of the bowl to prevent the cake flour from sticking and forming lumps in the bat-

ter. Using a rubber spatula, transfer the batter to the pastry bag.

Shaping. Holding the bag at a 45-degree angle to the paper-lined pan, pipe out about thirty 3-inch fingers, touching the end of the tube to the paper and pulling it away slowly, continuing to squeeze the bag and maintaining contact with the paper. Generously dredge the confectioners' sugar over the fingers so it does not melt on the surface before they are baked.

Baking. Bake in the preheated 350°F oven for about 15 minutes. Test for doneness by checking the color—it should be deep gold. The sponge fingers should also feel firm and springy to the touch when pressed with a fingertip.

Cooling. Slide the papers from the pans to racks to cool. Shake off the excess confectioners' sugar after the fingers have cooled.

Holding. Stack the cooled fingers, still adhering to the paper, on a baking pan and slide the pan into a large plastic bag. Seal the bag well and refrigerate for up to 3 days. Or double-bag the pan and freeze for up to 1 month.

Yield. Approximately thirty to thirty-six 3-inch fingers

The baking, cooling and holding procedures are the same as for the Sponge Fingers.

Yield: Two 8- to 9-inch disks

Sponge Disks

The sponge disks use the same ingredients and batter preparation as the Sponge Fingers, although they are not dusted with confectioners' sugar.

Preparing the Pans and Batter. Use two 10 × 15-inch rectangular pans. (Two 12 × 18-inch pans or cookie sheets can also be used.) Line the pans with parchment paper, cut to fit. Trace an 8-inch disk on each piece of paper with a pencil, then invert. Place a ½-inch plain tube in a pastry bag. Prepare the biscuit batter as in the Sponge Fingers above.

Piping. Starting in the center of one of the disks, pipe the batter in a continuous spiral to the outer edge. Hold the pastry bag perpendicular to the pan and about 1 inch above it so that a stream of batter as large as the opening in the tube continuously flows from it. The motion should come more from swinging the entire upper body in a light circular movement, rather than trying to move only the wrist or arm. Repeat with the remaining batter for the second disk.

Sponge Fingers and Disk

The biscuit batter may also be used to prepare about twenty-four 3-inch sponge fingers and one 8-inch disk, following the above procedures. The fingers and disk will be sufficient for any of the Charlotte recipes.

Spiced Sponge Fingers

Proceed exactly as above, adding ½ TEASPOON CINNAMON and ¼ TEASPOON NUTMEG to the cake flour and sifting them together several times to mix. These are excellent for fall and holiday desserts and are an important part of the Caramelized Apple Charlotte.

Chocolate Biscuit Batter

Although the method is exactly the same, the Chocolate Biscuit Batter has slightly different proportions, to make up for the heaviness of the cocoa powder. Both the extra egg white and the pinch of baking soda provide additional lightness. The chocolate sponge fingers should not be dredged with the confectioners' sugar.

4 EGG YOLKS
5 EGG WHITES
PINCH SALT
1 TEASPOON VANILLA EXTRACT
½ CUP SUGAR, ABOUT 3¾ OUNCES
½ CUP CAKE FLOUR, ABOUT 2 OUNCES
3 TABLESPOONS COCOA POWDER, ABOUT ½
    OUNCE
PINCH BAKING SODA

Proceed as for the biscuit batter, sifting together the cake flour, cocoa powder and baking soda, and substituting that mixture for the cake flour in the Sponge Fingers recipe.

NUT ROLL SPONGE

This is a moist and flexible version of a biscuit batter, suitable for rolling. The texture of the baked sponge is light and not at all rubbery as this type of sponge often can be. Assembled like the Sponge Fingers, the Nut Roll Sponge must be carefully watched to avoid overbaking, since it would lose its flexibility and ability to be rolled.

1 CUP WHOLE ALMONDS OR HAZELNUTS (ABOUT
    5½ OUNCES) OR 1⅓ CUPS PECAN
    OR WALNUT HALVES (ABOUT 5½ OUNCES)
⅓ CUP CAKE FLOUR, ABOUT 1½ OUNCES
4 EGGS
⅔ CUP SUGAR, ABOUT 5 OUNCES
PINCH SALT

Preparing the Pan. Use a 10 × 15-inch jelly-roll pan. (A 12 × 18-inch half-sheet pan can also be used.) Butter the pan and line the bottom with a piece of parchment paper, cut to fit.

Preheating the Oven. Heat the oven to 350°F. Adjust the oven rack to the middle level.

Preparing the Dry Ingredients. Place the nuts in the bowl of a food processor fitted with the steel blade and finely grind them. Pulse on and off at one-second intervals about ten or twelve times to grind the nuts to the consistency of cornmeal. Be careful not to let the ground nuts cake up at the bottom edge of the bowl; scrape with a spatula several times during the grinding. Place in a small bowl and sift over the cake flour. When preparing a chocolate nut roll, be sure to sift the cocoa powder carefully to remove any lumps, sifting it over the cake flour and ground nuts in the bowl.

Stir together briefly so that the flour and nuts are not evenly mixed. This allows the batter to absorb the cake flour evenly rather than only that which clings to the outside of the ground nuts. Set aside.

Whipping the Yolks. Whisk the yolks in a 3-quart bowl until liquid. Whisk in half the sugar in a slow stream and continue whipping, by hand or by machine, until the yolks and sugar have become very light and lemon-colored, about 5 minutes. The sugar will substantially dissolve and the yolks will increase almost three times over their original volume. Set the yolk mixture aside.

Whipping the Egg Whites. Whip the whites and the salt until they are white, opaque and beginning to hold their shape. Increase the speed and whip in the remaining sugar in a slow stream. When all the sugar has been added, the whites should stand straight up in a firm peak.

Combining the Yolks and Whites. Fold the yolk mixture into the beaten whites gently but thoroughly, making sure that they are well mixed and that no lumps of egg white remain. Be careful not to deflate any air out of the mixture.

Folding in the Dry Ingredients. Scatter one quarter of the dry ingredients over the egg mixture and fold in with a rubber spatula, cutting through the center of the bowl and keeping the spatula against the side of the bowl, scraping all the way down to the bottom. Revolve the bowl about 30 degrees every time the spatula goes through it. Repeat with the remaining dry ingredients, occasionally scraping the side of the bowl to prevent them from sticking and forming lumps in the batter.

Molding the Batter. Pour the batter into the prepared pan and spread evenly, using an offset spatula.

Baking. Bake in the preheated 350°F oven for about 15 minutes. It should color to a light gold during baking and feel firm but moist when pressed with a flat palm.

Unmolding. Loosen the sponge around the edge with a paring knife and pull out of the pan by grasping the corners of the paper on one of the short ends. Cool the sponge directly against the work surface for maximum retention of moisture. Do not remove the paper.

Holding. Slide the completely cooled sponge back into the pan and double-wrap in plastic, or slide into a large plastic bag and tightly seal the bag. The Nut Roll Sponge will keep for several days in the refrigerator. To freeze, slide it back into the pan and double-bag it to minimize the drying effects of the freezer. Defrost covered at room temperature for about 1 hour before finishing it. Ideally, for maximum flexibility during rolling, the cake should be used as fresh as possible.

Yield. One 10 × 15-inch or 12 × 18-inch cake layer

Chocolate Nut Roll Sponge

In place of the cake flour, use a combination of 3 TABLESPOONS CAKE FLOUR and 3 TABLESPOONS COCOA POWDER.

ALMOND SPONGE

This recipe for a delicate almond sponge uses blanched almonds, but I have successfully used many different types of nuts in the recipe, including hazelnuts, pecans, walnuts and pistachios. I usually vary the flavoring according to the type of nut used, adding some grated lemon zest or cinnamon, or some almond extract to accentuate the flavor of the nut. See the variations that follow the recipe for flavoring suggestions.

Use this recipe for a round layer, to be split for preparing layer cakes; or as a flat sheet, to be used in the construction of square and rectangular cakes.

1 CUP WHOLE, BLANCHED ALMONDS, ABOUT 5½ OUNCES
¾ CUP CAKE FLOUR, ABOUT 3 OUNCES
4 EGGS, SEPARATED
¾ CUP GRANULATED SUGAR, DIVIDED, ABOUT 5¾ OUNCES
1 TEASPOON GRATED LEMON ZEST
¼ TEASPOON ALMOND EXTRACT
PINCH SALT

Preparing the Pan. For a round layer, use a 9-inch diameter $\times$ $2\frac{1}{2}$- to 3-inch-deep springform pan. (A 10-inch diameter $\times$ 2-inch-deep layer pan can also be used.) For a rectangular layer, use a 10 $\times$ 15-inch jelly-roll pan. (A 12 $\times$ 18-inch half-sheet pan can also be used.) Butter the pan and line the bottom with a piece of parchment paper, cut to fit.

Preheating the Oven. Heat the oven to 350°F. Adjust the oven rack to the middle level.

Grinding the Almonds. Place the almonds in the work bowl of a food processor and pulse at one-second intervals about ten or twelve times to grind the almonds to the consistency of cornmeal. There should be just over 1 cup. Place in a small bowl and sift the cake flour over them. Stir together briefly, so that they are not evenly mixed. This allows the batter to absorb the cake flour evenly later on rather than absorbing only the cake flour that clings to the outside of the ground nuts. Set aside.

Whipping the Yolks and Sugar. Whisk the yolks together. Whisk in half the sugar in a stream, the lemon zest and almond extract and whip on medium speed for about 2 to 3 minutes, until it is light and forms a slowly dissolving ribbon when the beater is withdrawn. Or whisk by hand, for about 5 minutes.

Whipping the Egg Whites. Whip the egg whites and salt until they are white, opaque and beginning to hold their shape. Increase the speed and whip in the remaining sugar in a slow stream. Continue whipping until the egg whites hold a firm peak.

Mixing the Batter. Quickly fold the yolk mixture into the whites, then fold in the nut-flour mixture in three or four additions, mixing thoroughly with a rubber spatula.

Molding the Batter. Pour the batter into the prepared pan and spread it evenly, using an offset spatula.

Baking. Bake in the preheated 350°F oven, for about 30 minutes for the round layer or about 15 minutes for the rectangular layer. When baked, the layer will be an even deep golden color, will feel firm when pressed with the palm of the hand and will shrink slightly from the side of the pan.

Unmolding. Loosen with a small sharp knife. For a round layer, invert it onto the work surface and immediately turn right-side up, using a wide spatula or grasping it firmly on either side and inverting it onto a rack to cool. For a rectangular layer, slide a knife or spatula under one of the short edges then grasp both corners of the paper to slide the layer out of the pan. Cool the layer directly against the surface to conserve its moisture. Do not remove the paper.

Holding. Double-wrap in plastic wrap, place it back in the pan and refrigerate several days or freeze for up to 1 month. If frozen, defrost covered at room temperature before using.

Yield. 1 9-inch round or 10 $\times$ 15-inch layer

Hazelnut Sponge

Substitute 1 CUP BLANCHED OR UNBLANCHED HAZELNUTS for the almonds; omit the almond extract.

Pecan Sponge

Substitute $1\frac{1}{4}$ CUPS PECAN HALVES OR PIECES for the almonds; omit the lemon zest and almond extract and use 1 TEASPOON VANILLA EXTRACT and $\frac{1}{2}$ TEASPOON GROUND CINNAMON.

Walnut Sponge

Proceed as for Pecan Sponge, substituting 1 ¼ CUPS WALNUT HALVES OR PIECES for the pecans.

Pistachio Sponge

Substitute 1 CUP BLANCHED PISTACHIOS for the almonds; use the lemon zest and almond extract as for the Almond Sponge.

Chocolate Nut Sponge

Substitute ½ CUP CAKE FLOUR sifted with 3 TABLESPOONS COCOA POWDER for the ¾ cup cake flour in the Almond Sponge. Omit the grated lemon zest. Use with any type of Nut Sponge.

10

CAKES

A cake usually marks a festive occasion. Birthdays, anniversaries, weddings and most other milestones are celebrated with cakes. Although difficult to define specifically, cakes (*gâteaux* in French and *Torten* in German) are made from baked batters. Some plain cakes are left unadorned, but the most popular cakes are rolled, layered or molded with a filling. These more elaborate cakes are usually referred to as *entremets* (desserts) in French, signaling their delicacy and richness.

Cake making has always been one of the most popular branches of baking. The creativity possible when combining different layers, flavors, fillings, glazes, finishes and decorations opens virtually limitless possibilities for variations.

The recipes in this chapter serve as models for different techniques of assembling different styles of cakes. Each is followed by suggestions for variations in flavor and presentation.

In creating your own combinations, choose flavors which harmonize well and enhance them with liqueurs or extracts. Keep the combinations simple, limiting them to two or three per cake. Nothing is worse than a cake overburdened with too many discordant flavors.

ROLLED CAKES

A rolled cake, sometimes referred to as a log or a roulade, is a thin, rectangular cake layer spread with a filling and rolled to form a cylinder with an attractive spiral pattern of the filling.

Rolled cakes have the advantage of retaining a neat appearance even after a few portions have been cut. A popular shape, the roll is the basis for the traditional French Bûche de Noël, or Christmas log. The recipes in this section feature several fillings, but the procedure for handling and assembling the roll is as detailed below.

General Technique for Rolled Cakes

Preparing the Layer for Filling. For easy handling, the layer should remain attached to the paper on which it was baked. Slide a baking pan or cookie sheet under the layer, cover the layer with a clean sheet of parchment or wax paper, then another pan or cookie sheet. Grasping the pans, invert them, with the layer between. Remove the top pan and carefully peel away the paper attached to the baked layer. Replace with a clean piece of paper and pan and invert. Remove top pan and paper and slide the layer off the bottom pan, leaving it on the fresh paper.

The procedure sounds more complicated than it really is. Using the pans to support the layer makes it possible to easily handle it without accidentally breaking or tearing it.

Filling the Layer. Evenly position the layer on the fresh paper. Using an offset spatula, evenly spread the filling, about ⅜ inch thick. Uneven spreading of the filling will result in an uneven roll.

Rolling the Layer. Fold over 1 inch of the near, long end of the layer, making sure that it remains folded. Grasping the paper under the

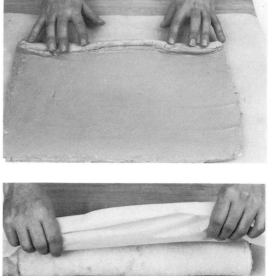

layer, lift the paper to roll the layer. The layer will continue to roll easily after the initial fold. Roll slowly, with the paper close to the layer so that there are no gaps. After the layer is completely rolled, move it to the center of the paper, keeping the seam on the bottom.

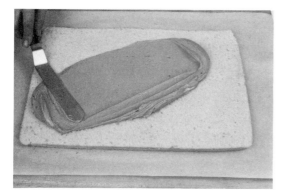

Wrapping the Layer. Fold the paper over the roll in the length. Roll the cake in the paper so that it is completely wrapped. Twist the ends of the paper tightly, close to the ends of the cake.

Chilling the Cake. Refrigerate for several hours so that the filling sets and the roll can be handled easily. For a whipped cream filling, place the cake in the freezer for several hours to firm.

Finishing the Cake. Remove the cake from the refrigerator or freezer and unwrap. Cut a piece of stiff cardboard to fit under the cake and place the cake on it seam-side down. Roughly spread the outside of the cake with the covering material (buttercream, ganache, etc.). Smooth with an offset spatula, starting at the bottom of the roll and smoothing up to the top. The covering should be no more than 1/4 inch thick. Finish according to the particular recipes.

Decorating the Cake. For nuts or chocolate shavings, evenly distribute them along the length of a sheet of parchment or wax paper longer than the cake, making a line at each side of the paper in the length. Place the roll on the paper between the two lines of nuts or chocolate and press them to the sides using the palms of your hands or a spatula. Slide a long spatula under the cake and remove it to the back of a pan. Chill the cake to set.

For a glaze, chill the cake after masking it with the covering material. Place on a rack over a pan to catch the drippings (the cardboard under the cake makes it easy to move by sliding a long spatula under the cardboard) and pour the glaze over it. Make sure that the glaze entirely covers the sides since it is easy to miss the sides at the bottom where they curve in. Use some of the glaze in the pan to patch any bare areas with a spatula. Leave the cake on the rack and pan and chill until the glaze is set. Carefully loosen the cake from the rack with the tip of a paring knife. Slide a large spatula under the cake and remove it to a work surface or a cutting board. Trim the edges of the roll, cutting diagonally with a sharp knife that has been run under hot water and dried. Cut through the cake and the cardboard. The roll should then exhibit a tight, even spiral of the filling inside the cake.

STRAWBERRY MERINGUE ROLL

The richness of the strawberry and cream filling of this cake is tempered by the lightness of the meringue covering. The roll may be prepared in advance and refrigerated up to the point of covering it with the meringue. After coating with the meringue, the dessert should be served within 6 hours.

Plain Génoise
  4 EGGS
  PINCH SALT
  2/3 CUP SUGAR, ABOUT 5 OUNCES
  1/2 CUP CAKE FLOUR, ABOUT 2 OUNCES
  3 TABLESPOONS CORNSTARCH, ABOUT 3/4
    OUNCE

Strawberry and Cream Filling
  1 PINT STRAWBERRIES, ABOUT 2 CUPS
  3 TABLESPOONS SUGAR, ABOUT 1 1/2 OUNCES
  1 TABLESPOON KIRSCH OR LIQUEUR
  1 CUP HEAVY WHIPPING CREAM

Swiss Meringue Covering
> 4 EGG WHITES
> PINCH SALT
> ¾ CUP SUGAR, ABOUT 5¾ OUNCES
>
> CONFECTIONERS' SUGAR

Preparing the Génoise. Combine and warm the eggs, salt and sugar and whip on high speed until cool and increased in volume. Sift together the flour and cornstarch and fold into the egg foam. Pour the batter into a buttered and paper-lined 10 × 15-inch or 12 × 18-inch pan and spread evenly. Bake at 350°F about 10 to 15 minutes. Immediately remove layer from pan and cool.

Strawberry and Cream Filling. Rinse, hull and slice the berries and combine with the sugar. Cover and refrigerate an hour or so. Whip the cream with the liqueur until it holds its shape well. Immediately before spreading the filling on the cake layer, drain and fold in the sliced berries.

Assembling. Remove the paper from the bottom of the Génoise and position on a clean paper. Trim ¼ inch or any dry areas off the edges and evenly spread the filling over the layer. Roll up the cake and filling in the paper and chill it at least 2 hours. Or, place in the freezer half an hour to firm it.

Preparing the Meringue. Combine and warm the egg whites, salt and sugar, whisking gently over simmering water until the egg whites are hot and the sugar dissolved. Whip on medium speed until cool and increased in volume, about 4 to 5 minutes. Do not overwhip or the meringue will be dry.

Covering the Roll. Unwrap the roll and position it on a piece of cardboard that just fits under it. Evenly spread the meringue over the surface of the roll. Pipe a decoration along the top of the roll, using a star tube, then dredge with confectioners' sugar. Place on a cookie sheet or the back of a pan and place it in a preheated 400°F oven about 5 minutes to color the meringue. Cool briefly and refrigerate. After it is cold, trim the edges off the roll diagonally with a sharp knife.

Holding. Refrigerate, loosely covered with plastic wrap, no more than 6 hours.

Yield. About 10 portions

Variations

Substitute an ALMOND ROLL SPONGE for the plain Génoise.

Substitute 1 PINT RASPBERRIES for the strawberries and a CHOCOLATE GÉNOISE for the plain.

Lightly poached sour cherries would also be good with a Chocolate Génoise.

HAZELNUT MOCHA ROLL

The combination of the moist hazelnut sponge and the coffee flavored buttercream makes a rich but surprisingly light dessert. The flavors combine well and the slight crunch of the hazelnuts contrasts with the smoothness of the buttercream.

Hazelnut Roll Sponge
> 1 CUP WHOLE HAZELNUTS, ABOUT 5½ OUNCES
> ⅓ CUP CAKE FLOUR, ABOUT 1½ OUNCES
> 4 EGGS, SEPARATED

⅔ CUP SUGAR, ABOUT 5 OUNCES
PINCH SALT

Mocha Sabayon Buttercream

6 EGG YOLKS

½ CUP SUGAR, ABOUT 3¾ OUNCES

½ CUP STRONG BREWED ESPRESSO COFFEE
   OR 3 TABLESPOONS INSTANT COFFEE
   DISSOLVED IN ⅓ CUP HOT WATER AND
   COOLED

3 STICKS BUTTER, 12 OUNCES, SOFTENED

1 TO 2 TABLESPOONS DARK RUM, OPTIONAL

½ CUP TOASTED AND SKINNED HAZELNUTS,
   COARSELY CHOPPED OR CRUSHED, ABOUT
   2 OUNCES

Preparing the Hazelnut Roll Sponge. Butter a 10 × 15-inch jelly-roll pan and line the bottom with a piece of parchment paper, cut to fit. Process the hazelnuts in a food processor until very fine, then sift the flour over them in a bowl. Whip the yolks, then whip in half the sugar in a stream until light in color and aerated. Whip the whites and salt on medium speed until they are white and opaque. Increase the speed and whip in the remaining sugar in a slow stream until the whites hold a firm peak. Fold the yolks into the whites, then scatter over and fold in the hazelnut mixture in several additions. Scrape the batter into the prepared pan and spread evenly. Bake at 350°F about 15 minutes. Loosen the layer around the inside edges of the pan with a paring knife and slide, pulling on the edge of the paper, off the pan to the work surface to cool.

Preparing the Buttercream. Whisk the yolks. Whisk in the sugar, then the coffee. Place the bowl over simmering water and whisk constantly until thickened. Whip on medium speed until cool and increased in volume, about 5 or 6 minutes. Whip in the butter in several additions until the buttercream is smooth. Whisk in the optional rum.

Assembling. Remove the paper from the bottom of the sponge and position on a clean paper. Trim ¼ inch or any dry areas off the edges and evenly spread half the filling over the layer. The filling should be no more than ⅜ inch thick. Roll up the cake and filling in the paper and chill it at least 1 hour. Or, place in the freezer for half an hour or so to firm it.

Finishing and Decorating. Unwrap the roll and position it on a piece of cardboard that just fits under it. Evenly spread a little more than half the remaining buttercream over the surface of the roll. Place the crushed hazelnuts on a piece of paper, making two long lines at the edge of the paper. With the palm of the right hand or a spatula, lift the hazelnuts and adhere them against the sides of the roll, one side at a time so that the hazelnuts cover about halfway up each side. To mark each portion, pipe the remaining buttercream on the top of the roll in a series of twelve large rosettes. Slide the roll onto a cookie sheet or the back of a pan and chill to firm the buttercream, about 1 hour. Finally, trim the edges diagonally with a sharp knife.

Holding. Refrigerate, loosely covered with plastic wrap, up to 12 hours in advance. Keep away from any foods that may give it an off taste.

Yield. About 12 portions

Variations

Substitute one of the other NUT ROLL SPONGES for the hazelnut. Almond, walnut and pecan would all work well here. If substituting the sponge, use the same nuts on the outside of the roll.

CHOCOLATE CHOCOLATE ROLL

This roll uses a Chocolate Génoise filled and covered with a whipped ganache, then covered with a shiny Ganache Glaze. A few rosettes of the whipped ganache piped on the glaze will give the sheen a beautiful definition.

Chocolate Génoise

4 EGGS
PINCH SALT
2/3 CUP SUGAR, ABOUT 5 OUNCES
1/3 CUP CAKE FLOUR, ABOUT 1 1/2 OUNCES
1/3 CUP CORNSTARCH, ABOUT 1 1/2 OUNCES
1/3 CUP COCOA POWDER, ABOUT 1 OUNCE
2 PINCHES BAKING SODA

2 TABLESPOONS ORANGE OR RASPBERRY LIQUEUR, OPTIONAL

Rich Ganache Filling

1 POUND BITTERSWEET OR SEMISWEET CHOCOLATE, FINELY CUT
1 1/3 CUPS HEAVY WHIPPING CREAM
2 TABLESPOONS ORANGE OR RASPBERRY LIQUEUR, OPTIONAL

Ganache Glaze

8 OUNCES BITTERSWEET OR SEMISWEET CHOCOLATE, FINELY CUT
1 CUP HEAVY WHIPPING CREAM

Preparing the Chocolate Génoise. Butter a 10 × 15-inch jelly-roll pan and line the bottom with a piece of parchment paper, cut to fit. Combine and warm the eggs, salt and sugar and whip on high speed until cool and increased in volume. Sift the flour, cornstarch, cocoa and baking powder several times; sift over the egg foam several times; and fold in. Pour batter into the prepared pan and spread evenly. Bake at 350°F about 10 to 15 minutes. Immediately remove layer from pan and cool.

Preparing the Rich Ganache. Place the chocolate in a bowl. Bring the cream to a boil and pour over the chocolate. Allow to stand 2 minutes, whisk, then strain into a clean, dry bowl. Cool to room temperature to set.

Preparing the Glaze. Place the chocolate in a bowl. Bring the cream to a boil and pour over the chocolate. Allow to stand 2 minutes, then whisk and strain into a clean, dry bowl. Cool at room temperature until it is no longer warm to the touch, before pouring over the roll. If the room is cool, do not prepare the glaze more than 1 hour before pouring it.

Assembling. Remove the paper from the bottom of the Génoise and position on a clean paper. Trim 1/4 inch or any dry areas off the edges. Sprinkle the Génoise with the optional liqueur, distributing it evenly. Beat the Rich Ganache on medium speed until light, about 1 to 1 1/2 minutes, beating in the optional liqueur after the Ganache has lightened. Evenly spread half the Ganache over the layer. The filling should be no more than 3/8 inch thick. Roll up the cake and filling in the paper and chill it at least 1 hour. Or, place in the freezer for half an hour or so to firm it.

Finishing. Position the roll on a piece of cardboard that just fits under it. Smoothly spread all but about ½ cup of the remaining Ganache around the outside of the roll. Slide onto a cookie sheet or the back of a pan and chill about ½ hour to set the Ganache. Remove the roll from the refrigerator and place on a rack over a pan. Pour the cooled glaze through a fine strainer held close to the roll. Refrigerate to set the glaze.

Decorating. Loosen the bottom of the roll from the rack with the point of a paring knife. Slide a spatula under the cardboard and remove it to the work surface. Place the remaining Rich Ganache (warm it slightly over warm water and rewhip it by hand if it has set firm) in a pastry bag fitted with a star tube. Pipe a series of twelve large rosettes on the top of the roll in a row, one to mark each portion. Trim the ends of the roll diagonally with a sharp knife. Remove the roll to a platter and refrigerate.

Holding. Refrigerate, loosely covered with plastic, up to 12 hours in advance. Keep it away from foods that may give it an off taste.

Yield. About 12 portions

Variations

For a beautiful contrast between layer and filling, substitute a PLAIN GÉNOISE for the chocolate.

Or use one of the NUT ROLL SPONGES using DARK RUM or COGNAC instead of the orange or raspberry liqueur.

LEMON MARZIPAN ROLL

The richness of the Almond Roll Sponge and the Lemon Buttercream complement the smooth sweetness of the marzipan. Nothing can give a dessert the same type of tailored finish as a coating of marzipan. To retain a neat cylindrical shape, have the filled roll well chilled before attempting to cover it with the marzipan.

Almond Roll Sponge

1 CUP WHOLE ALMONDS, ABOUT 5½ OUNCES

⅓ CUP FLOUR, ABOUT 1½ OUNCES

4 EGGS, SEPARATED

⅔ CUP SUGAR, ABOUT 5 OUNCES

PINCH SALT

BUTTER

Lemon Buttercream

4 EGG WHITES

PINCH SALT

1 CUP SUGAR, ABOUT 7½ OUNCES

3 STICKS BUTTER, 12 OUNCES, SOFTENED

1 TABLESPOON GRATED LEMON ZEST

⅓ CUP STRAINED LEMON JUICE, 2 MEDIUM LEMONS

1 TABLESPOON KIRSCH OR WHITE RUM, OPTIONAL

Marzipan

8 OUNCES ALMOND PASTE

2 CUPS CONFECTIONERS' SUGAR, ABOUT 8½ OUNCES

3 TO 5 TABLESPOONS LIGHT CORN SYRUP

1 TO 2 DROPS YELLOW FOOD COLORING

1 OUNCE BITTERSWEET OR SEMISWEET CHOCOLATE, FINELY CUT

Preparing the Almond Roll Sponge. Butter a 10 × 15-inch jelly-roll pan and line the bottom with a piece of parchment paper, cut to fit. Process the almonds in a food processor until very fine. Place in a bowl, then sift the flour over the almonds. Whip the yolks, then whip in half the sugar until light in color and aerated. Whip the whites and salt on medium speed until they are white and opaque. Increase the speed and whip in the remaining sugar in a slow stream until the egg whites hold a firm peak. Fold the yolks into the whites, then scatter over and fold in the almond mixture in several additions. Scrape the batter into the prepared pan and spread evenly. Bake at 350°F about 15 minutes. Loosen the layer around the inside edges of the pan with a paring knife and slide, pulling on the edge of the paper, off the pan to the work surface to cool.

Preparing the Lemon Buttercream. Combine and warm the egg whites, salt and sugar until the egg whites are hot and the sugar is dissolved. Whip on medium speed until cool and increased in volume. Beat in the butter in several additions until the buttercream is smooth. Beat in the lemon juice a tablespoon at a time. Beat in the optional liqueur.

Preparing the Marzipan. Combine the almond paste with the sugar and beat on low speed until reduced to very fine crumbs. Beat in half the corn syrup and test a handful: If it kneads smooth and is not dry, enough has been added. If dry, continue adding corn syrup. Pour the marzipan on the work surface. Add color to it and knead until smooth, about one quarter at a time, then knead it all together. Keep it well wrapped in several layers of plastic wrap until used.

Assembling. Remove the paper from the bottom of the sponge and position on a clean paper. Trim ¼ inch or any dry areas off the edges and evenly spread half the filling over the layer. The filling should be no more than ½ inch thick. Roll up the cake and filling in the paper and chill at least 1 hour. Or, place in the freezer for half an hour or so to firm it.

Finishing. Unwrap the roll and position it on a piece of cardboard that just fits under it. Evenly spread a little more than half the remaining buttercream over the surface of the roll. Slide the roll onto a cookie sheet or the back of a pan and chill it to firm the buttercream, about 1 hour.

Covering with the Marzipan. Lightly dust the surface and the marzipan with confectioners' sugar. Roll the marzipan into a rectangle about 10 × 18 inches, moving it often and dusting it and the surface with the sugar to prevent sticking. Remove the roll from the refrigerator and position it, right-side up, with the cardboard still under it at the near long end of the marzipan. Using the cardboard under the roll, invert it so that the top of the roll rolls over and is in the center of the marzipan rectangle. Lift the marzipan, from the far side, up over the roll, then trim in a straight line in the middle of the bottom of the roll. Lift the near end of the marzipan to meet it and evenly trim so that the marzipan does not overlap. Place the cardboard on the seam and invert the roll back onto the cardboard. Trim the ends of the roll diagonally with a sharp knife.

Decorating. Place the chocolate in a small bowl over hot water, and stir occasionally to melt. Make a cone from a piece of parchment paper and pipe streaks of chocolate on the marzipan, parallel with the ends of the roll so that it is streaked with diagonal lines.

Holding. Refrigerate the roll to set the chocolate streaks. Keep refrigerated, loosely covered with plastic wrap, up to 12 hours. Keep away from any foods that may give it an off taste.

Yield: About 12 portions

Variations

Substitute a RASPBERRY BUTTERCREAM for the lemon and cover with natural color marzipan. Pipe a design of the buttercream on the marzipan.

Or, use a CHOCOLATE GÉNOISE with the RASPBERRY BUTTERCREAM and cover the roll with CHOCOLATE MARZIPAN—add ¼ CUP WELL-SIFTED COCOA POWDER at the beginning when preparing the marzipan with the sugar and almond paste. It may need 2 or 3 tablespoons corn syrup since the cocoa powder will make the marzipan dry. Be careful not to use too much confectioners' sugar when rolling the marzipan.

BÛCHE DE NOËL

The traditional French Christmas log exists in many variations of flavor and presentation. I like this one because the chocolate cake and coffee buttercream are not an excessively sweet combination. Also, the marzipan decorations can be prepared well in advance and kept loosely covered until needed.

Chocolate Génoise

4 EGGS
⅔ CUP SUGAR, ABOUT 5 OUNCES
PINCH SALT
⅓ CUP CAKE FLOUR, ABOUT 1½ OUNCES
⅓ CUP CORNSTARCH, ABOUT 1½ OUNCES
3 TABLESPOONS COCOA POWDER, ABOUT ½ OUNCE
2 PINCHES BAKING SODA

Coffee Meringue Buttercream

4 EGG WHITES, ½ CUP
1 CUP SUGAR, ABOUT 7½ OUNCES
3 STICKS BUTTER, 12 OUNCES, SOFTENED
2 TABLESPOONS INSTANT ESPRESSO
2 TABLESPOONS RUM OR BRANDY

Marzipan

8 OUNCES ALMOND PASTE
2 CUPS CONFECTIONERS' SUGAR, ABOUT 8½ OUNCES
3 TO 5 TABLESPOONS LIGHT CORN SYRUP

COCOA POWDER
FOOD COLOR

CONFECTIONERS' SUGAR

Preparing the Chocolate Génoise. Butter a 10 × 15-inch jelly-roll pan and line the bottom with a piece of parchment paper, cut to fit. Combine and warm the eggs, sugar and salt, then whip on high speed until cool and increased in volume. Sift together the remaining Génoise ingredients several times, sift over the egg foam and fold in. Pour the batter into the prepared pan and spread evenly. Bake at 350°F for 15 minutes. Immediately remove from the pan and cool on the work surface.

Preparing the Buttercream. Combine and warm the egg whites and sugar until the sugar is dissolved and the egg whites are hot. Whip on medium speed until cool and increased in volume. Beat in the butter until the buttercream is smooth. Combine the instant coffee and liquor and beat into the buttercream.

Remove the paper from the bottom of the Génoise and position on a clean paper. Trim ¼ inch or any dry areas off the edges and evenly spread with half the buttercream. Roll up the cake and filling in the paper and chill at least 1 hour. Or, place in the freezer for half an hour to firm.

Preparing the Marzipan. Combine the almond paste and the sugar and beat on low speed until reduced to very fine crumbs. Beat in half the corn syrup, then test a handful: If it kneads smooth and is not dry, enough has been added. If dry, continue adding the corn syrup. Pour the marzipan on the work surface and knead until smooth.

Marzipan Mushrooms. Roll a third of the marzipan into a cylinder and cut into 1-inch lengths. Roll half the lengths into spheres. Press the cylinders against the spheres to make mushrooms. Smudge with cocoa powder.

Holly Leaves. Add green color to a third of the marzipan and roll into a long cylinder. Flatten with the back of a spoon and loosen with a spatula. Cut into diamonds to make leaves, or use a leaf-shaped cutter.

Holly Berries. Add red color to a tiny piece of marzipan. Roll into tiny spheres.

Pine Cones. Add cocoa powder to the remaining marzipan and form two cone shapes. Slash sides of cones with the point of scissors.

Finishing. Trim the edges of the cake diagonally, cutting one edge about 2 inches away from the end. Position the larger cut piece on the Bûche about two-thirds across the top.

Cover the Bûche with the remaining buttercream, making sure to curve around the protruding branch on the top. Streak the buttercream with a fork or decorating comb. Transfer to a platter and add the marzipan decorations. Sprinkle the platter and Bûche sparingly with confectioners' sugar "snow."

Holding. Refrigerate, loosely covered with plastic wrap, up to 12 hours. Keep away from any foods that may give it an off taste.

Yield. About 12 portions

LAYER CAKES

Nothing makes for a more festive dessert than a layer cake. Traditionally used to commemorate life's important events, a layer cake conveys that it's a special occasion. Old-fashioned American layer cakes were made from three or more separate layers resulting in a rather tall and substantial cake. The layer cakes that follow are all made from one layer, which in most cases is then cut into separate layers. The resulting cake is not as tall or as substantial.

Although cutting the layers requires some skill, success depends most on using a long, sharp serrated knife, an essential piece of equipment for this type of work. For spreading the filling and masking the cake, an offset spatula does an exceptionally good job. It works on the same principle as a mason's trowel and makes it easy to spread the outside of the cake smoothly.

Finally, if you are not satisfied with the smoothness of the cake after it has been masked, use ground nuts, shaved chocolate, a glaze or cover the cake with a thinly rolled piece of marzipan to achieve a smooth, professional looking finish.

General Technique for Layer Cakes

Preparing the Layer. Invert the cake onto the work surface and carefully peel away the paper on which it was baked. If a springform pan was used to bake the layer, use the metal disk from the pan to assemble the cake on. (Since there is a rim on the top of the disk which will make it difficult to cut the finished cake, invert the disk.) If the springform bottom is not available, use a bakers' corrugated cardboard circle, or cut a circle from stiff or corrugated cardboard to use as the base of the cake. If cutting the cardboard, use the bottom of the cakepan as a guide.

With a sharp, serrated knife, trim the crust from the top of the cake. The layer may be slightly domed in the center; if so, trim it flat by cutting straight across the top of the cake from one side to the other.

Dividing into Separate Layers. Hold the knife perpendicular to the side of the cake at the point where the cut is to be made, about one third down from the top. Use the blade of the knife to mark the line to be cut all around the cake, revolving the cake against the knife. Do not cut deeply into the cake, but make a thin line about ⅛ inch deep, concentrating on keeping the line straight. Then revolve the cake against the knife, keeping the knife positioned at the line. The knife will penetrate more deeply into the layer so that after two revolutions, the layer will be separated from

the cake. Slide a cardboard disk or a flat plate under the layer and remove it. Repeat with the remaining part of the cake, making the next cut in the center between the top and bottom to make three layers of even thickness.

Assembling the Cake. Place the bottom layer— the bottom of the original layer—on the cardboard or pan bottom. Using a brush, moisten it with a flavored syrup. Dip the brush into the syrup and lightly press it into the surface of the layer. Do not use a painting motion or the layer will not absorb enough of the syrup. (Place the syrup in a measuring cup to gauge the right amount for each layer.) Do not overmoisten the bottom layer or the cake will have an unstable foundation.

Spread the layer with one third of the fill-

Position the top layer as with the second one and brush with the syrup. If the side of the cake seems dry, brush it also with the syrup. Before attempting to mask the cake with the remaining filling or other covering material, clean the work area to make sure that it is free of all crumbs and syrup.

Masking the Outside of the Cake. Holding the cake with the left hand positioned under the cake, mask the side of the cake with the covering material. Pick up about a tablespoon of it on the offset spatula and press it into the side of the cake. Hold the spatula at a strict right angle to the cake, pressing it against the cardboard or pan bottom. Avoid angling the spatula inward toward the top or the side of the cake will not be straight. Then use the spatula to spread the covering material over a

ing called for in the particular recipe. Transfer the filling to the center of the layer using a rubber spatula. Then, use an offset spatula to spread the filling evenly over the layer. Keep the rubber spatula in the remaining filling to avoid picking up crumbs and mixing them into the filling. The offset spatula is best held àt a slight angle to the layer so that the side edge of the blade does most of the spreading. The filling should be about ¼ inch thick.

Position the middle layer evenly on the filling. Line up the far edge of the second layer to the far edge of the first one, keeping the second layer on the plate or cardboard. Carefully withdraw the plate or cardboard and the layer will fall evenly into place. Repeat the moistening and filling as on the first layer.

small area. Repeat, revolving the cake on the left hand until the entire side of the cake is covered. Do not attempt to spread the side smoothly at this point.

Place the cake on the work surface and transfer most of the remaining covering material to it, as in filling the layers. Spread it from the center outward in all directions, to the edge of the cake. Be especially careful to avoid picking up crumbs with the spatula. Clean the spatula and pick up the cake again in the left hand. Smooth the side of the cake with the spatula in one smooth movement, revolving the cake against the spatula.

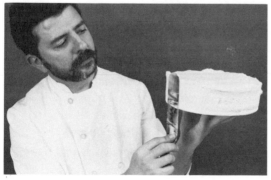

Place the cake on the work surface and smooth the top. Using the side edge of the spatula as in filling the layers, draw the cover-

ing material that has accumulated on the edge of the cake in toward the center, sweeping the spatula against the top of the cake toward the center in repeated motions from the edge inward. After a little practice it is easy to achieve a smooth, even finish on the outside of the cake. If the cake will be glazed, it should be refrigerated at this point.

Finishing the Outside of the Cake. If the cake is to have ground nuts or chocolate shavings on the side, adhere them immediately after masking the cake, before chilling it. Ground nuts are adhered by holding the cake in the left hand and pressing a handful of the nuts carefully against the side of the cake with the right hand. Use the same method for adhering chocolate shavings but press them against the

cake, holding a wide spatula in the right hand to transfer the shavings. They would melt too easily on contact with the palm of the hand.

Decorating the Cake. To decorate the top of the cake simply, place the remaining covering material in a pastry bag fitted with a star tube. Pipe a border around the top edge of the cake. Avoid piping a design in the center of the cake, or the cake will look sloppy after a few portions have been cut from it and the center design is partially cut away.

Glazing the Cake. If the cake is to have a glaze poured over it, refrigerate the cake after masking it to set the outside. Place the chilled, masked cake on a rack over a pan and pour the glaze evenly and slowly over the cake in a spiral from the center outward.

Refrigerate the cake, still on the rack and pan, to set the glaze. Loosen the cake around the bottom edge with a small paring knife and transfer it to a platter. A border of buttercream can be very effective against a dark chocolate glaze.

CHOCOLATE WALNUT CAKE

Sometimes I call this cake a *Grenoblois*—from Grenoble—the center of France's walnut producing area. It is one of the most tailored-looking cakes I know, with its dark chocolate glaze and its sugared walnut halves. The addition of the chopped walnuts to the glaze adds an extra dimension to the appearance of the cake.

Walnut Sponge
    1¼ CUPS WALNUT HALVES, ABOUT 5½ OUNCES
    ¾ CUP CAKE FLOUR, ABOUT 3 OUNCES
    4 EGGS, SEPARATED
    ¾ CUP SUGAR, DIVIDED, ABOUT 5¾ OUNCES
    PINCH SALT

Rum Syrup
    ½ CUP WATER
    ¼ CUP SUGAR, ABOUT 1¾ OUNCES
    2 TABLESPOONS DARK RUM
    ½ TEASPOON VANILLA EXTRACT

Walnut-Rum Sabayon Buttercream
    6 EGG YOLKS
    ½ CUP DARK RUM OR STRONG COFFEE
    ½ CUP SUGAR, ABOUT 3¾ OUNCES
    3 STICKS BUTTER, 12 OUNCES
    ¾ CUP CHOPPED WALNUTS, LIGHTLY TOASTED, ABOUT 3 OUNCES

Ganache Glaze
    8 OUNCES BITTERSWEET OR SEMISWEET CHOCOLATE, FINELY CUT
    1 CUP HEAVY WHIPPING CREAM

¾ CUP CHOPPED WALNUTS, LIGHTLY
    TOASTED, ABOUT 3 OUNCES

10 OR 12 WALNUT HALVES, LIGHTLY DUSTED
    WITH CONFECTIONERS' SUGAR

Preparing the Walnut Sponge. Butter a 9-inch diameter × 2½- to 3-inch-deep springform pan and line the bottom with a piece of parchment paper, cut to fit. Process the walnuts in a food processor until very fine. Sift the cake flour over the walnuts and combine. Whip the yolks, then whip in half the sugar until light in color and aerated. Whip the egg whites and salt on medium speed until white and opaque. Increase the speed and whip in the remaining sugar. Continue whipping until the whites hold a firm peak. Fold the yolks into the whites, then scatter over and fold in the walnut and flour mixture in several additions. Pour the batter into the prepared pan. Bake at 350°F about 30 minutes. Remove from the pan and cool on a rack, on the paper.

Preparing the Syrup. Combine the sugar and water in a small saucepan and bring to a boil over medium heat. Pour into a small bowl, cool to room temperature and stir in the rum.

Preparing the Buttercream. Whisk the yolks, then whisk in the rum or coffee and sugar. Place the bowl over simmering water and whisk constantly until thickened. Whip on medium speed until cool and increased in volume, 5 to 7 minutes. Whip in the butter until the buttercream is smooth.

Remove half the buttercream from the bowl and set aside for finishing the cake. Stir the chopped walnuts into the remaining buttercream for the filling.

Preparing the Glaze. Place the chocolate in a small bowl. Bring the cream to a boil and pour over the chocolate. Allow to stand 2 minutes to melt, whisk, then strain into a clean dry bowl.

Cool at room temperature until it is no longer warm to the touch before pouring it over the finished cake. If the room is cool, do not prepare the glaze more than 1 hour before pouring it.

Preparing the Decorations. Lightly dust the walnut halves with confectioners' sugar and set aside.

Assembling. Using a sharp, serrated knife, slice the Walnut Sponge into three layers. Place the bottom layer on a cardboard or inverted springform base and moisten with a third of the syrup. Spread with half of the Walnut-Rum Sabayon Buttercream. Repeat with the second layer, syrup and buttercream. End with the top layer and moisten with the remaining syrup. Mask the outside of the cake with the plain rum buttercream, reserving some for decorations. Place the cake on a platter and refrigerate about 1 hour to firm the buttercream.

Glazing. Remove the cake from the refrigerator and place on a rack over a pan. Pour the cooled glaze over the cake through a strainer held close to the cake. Refrigerate to set the glaze.

Decorating. Place the reserved buttercream in a pastry bag fitted with a small star tube and make ten or twelve rosettes around the border of the cake. Top each with a sugared walnut half.

Holding. Refrigerate, loosely covered with plastic wrap, up to 12 hours before serving. Let stand at room temperature about 1 hour before serving.

Yield. About 10 to 12 portions

Chocolate Walnut Cake with Chocolate Buttercream

Substitute a CHOCOLATE GÉNOISE layer for the Walnut Sponge. Add 4 OUNCES BITTERSWEET OR SEMISWEET CHOCOLATE melted with ¼ CUP WATER to the rum buttercream. Omit the glaze and decorate the cake with the sugared walnut halves.

GÂTEAU PRUDENCE

This cake is named in honor of my friend Prudence Hilburn from Piedmont, Alabama. Prudence and I became friends in 1984 when she kept the books at Peter Kump's school and I first started teaching there. When Prudence left to return home to Alabama, I made this cake for a farewell party we had for her and her husband, Huey. Since that day, it has become one of Peter Kump's favorite cakes.

The cake is composed of a chocolate Génoise layer split in half, with a chocolate meringue layer between the layers of Génoise. The filling is a Ganache Praliné with butter.

Chocolate Meringue
1½ TABLESPOONS COCOA POWDER, ABOUT ½ OUNCE
½ CUP SUGAR, ABOUT 3¾ OUNCES
2 EGG WHITES, ¼ CUP
PINCH SALT

Chocolate Génoise
4 EGGS
PINCH SALT
⅔ CUP SUGAR, ABOUT 5 OUNCES
⅓ CUP CAKE FLOUR, ABOUT 1½ OUNCES
⅓ CUP CORNSTARCH, ABOUT 1½ OUNCES
3 TABLESPOONS COCOA POWDER, ABOUT ½ OUNCE
2 PINCHES BAKING SODA

Rum Syrup
⅓ CUP WATER
3 TABLESPOONS SUGAR, ABOUT 1½ OUNCES
3 TABLESPOONS DARK RUM

Ganache Beurré Praliné
1 POUND BITTERSWEET OR SEMISWEET CHOCOLATE, FINELY CUT
1⅓ CUPS HEAVY WHIPPING CREAM
6 TABLESPOONS BUTTER, 3 OUNCES, SOFTENED
½ CUP PRALINE PASTE (PAGES 48–49), ABOUT 4½ OUNCES

2 OUNCES BITTERSWEET OR SEMISWEET CHOCOLATE

Preparing the Meringue. Sift the cocoa powder with ¼ cup of the sugar. Whip the egg whites on medium speed with the salt until white and opaque, increase the speed to maximum and whip in the remaining sugar in a stream, until the egg whites hold a firm peak. Sift the cocoa and sugar mixture over the beaten egg whites and fold in with a rubber spatula. Line a cookie sheet with parchment paper; draw a 9-inch circle on the paper and turn the paper over. Using a pastry bag fitted with a ½-inch plain tube, pipe the meringue in a disk on the paper: Hold the bag about 1 inch above the pan, perpendicular to it, and pipe a continuous spiral from the center of the circle to the edge. If there is a little meringue left over, pipe some fingers on the same pan to use as cookies. Bake the meringue layer at 300°F in the middle of the oven about 30 minutes, until dry and crisp, being careful it does not burn. Place the pan on a rack to cool.

Preparing the Chocolate Génoise. Butter a 9-inch diameter × 2½- to 3-inch-deep springform pan and line the bottom with a piece of parchment paper, cut to fit. Combine and warm the eggs, salt and sugar and whip on high speed until cool and increased in volume. Sift together the cake flour, cornstarch, cocoa powder and baking soda several times, then sift over and fold into the egg foam. Pour the batter into the prepared pan. Bake at 350°F about 30 minutes. Remove from pan and cool on a rack.

Preparing the Syrup. Bring the sugar and water to a boil in a small saucepan. Cool and stir in the rum.

Preparing the Ganache. Place the chocolate in a bowl. Bring the cream to a boil and pour over the chocolate. Let stand 2 minutes, whisk, then strain into a clean, dry bowl. Cool to room temperature until it sets.

Just before assembling the cake, beat the butter and Praline Paste together on medium speed until smooth. Add the set Ganache all at once and continue beating to lighten. If the Ganache is very hard, warm it slightly over hot water before adding it to the butter mixture.

Shave the chocolate with a vegetable peeler or by drawing a small, round cutter across its surface. Refrigerate if the room is warm.

Assembling. Trim the meringue disk to an even 9-inch diameter. Trim the top of the Génoise and cut into two layers, each about 1 inch thick. Place one Génoise layer on a cardboard or the inverted springform bottom. Moisten the layer with half the syrup, then spread with a third of the Ganache. Top with the meringue layer and spread with another third of the Ganache. Top with the other Génoise layer and moisten with the remaining syrup. Spread the side and top of the cake smooth with the remaining Ganache. Use any leftover Ganache to pipe a border of rosettes on the top of the cake, using a pastry bag fitted with a small star tube. Press the chocolate shavings against the side of the cake with a spatula.

Holding. Wrap the cake loosely in plastic wrap and refrigerate. The cake will keep well for at least three days. Allow the cake to come to room temperature before serving.

Yield. About 12 portions

QUADRUPLE CHOCOLATE CAKE

I first made this cake for the opening menu at the student-run restaurant at the New York Restaurant School in May 1981. Though it has several components, all may be easily prepared in advance and the cake itself, once assembled, will keep for several days in the refrigerator. I like it better after it has had a chance to mellow because the meringue layers soften slightly.

Although this cake uses a Chocolate Génoise layer and a Ganache filling like the Gâteau Prudence, it is different in appearance and texture. The Génoise and meringue are reversed, so the cake is composed of two chocolate nut meringue layers and a thin layer of Génoise between them. The Ganache used here is lighter with a deeper chocolate flavor.

Chocolate Génoise

4 EGGS

PINCH SALT

⅔ CUP SUGAR, ABOUT 5 OUNCES

⅓ CUP CAKE FLOUR, ABOUT 1½ OUNCES

⅓ CUP CORNSTARCH, ABOUT 1½ OUNCES

3 TABLESPOONS COCOA POWDER, ABOUT ½ OUNCE

2 PINCHES BAKING SODA

Chocolate Nut Meringue

1 CUP SUGAR, ABOUT 7½ OUNCES

⅔ CUP WHOLE ALMONDS OR HAZELNUTS OR A COMBINATION, ABOUT 3½ OUNCES

2 TABLESPOONS COCOA POWDER, ABOUT ¼ OUNCE

4 EGG WHITES, ½ CUP

PINCH SALT

Rum Syrup

⅓ CUP WATER

3 TABLESPOONS SUGAR, ABOUT 1½ OUNCES

3 TABLESPOONS DARK RUM

Rich Ganache

12 OUNCES BITTERSWEET OR SEMISWEET CHOCOLATE, FINELY CUT

1 CUP HEAVY WHIPPING CREAM

2 TO 3 OUNCES BITTERSWEET OR SEMISWEET CHOCOLATE

Preparing the Chocolate Génoise. Butter a 9-inch diameter × 2½- to 3-inch-deep springform pan and line the bottom with a piece of parchment paper, cut to fit. Combine and warm the eggs, salt and sugar and whip on high speed until cool and increased in volume. Sift together the cake flour, cornstarch, cocoa powder and baking soda several times, then sift over and fold into the egg foam. Pour the batter into the prepared pan. Bake at 350°F about 30 minutes. Immediately remove from pan and cool on a rack.

Preparing the Meringue. Line two cookie sheets or rectangular pans with parchment paper and trace a 9-inch circle on each piece of paper, then invert the paper. Combine half the sugar, the nuts and the sifted cocoa powder in a food processor and grind very finely. Whip the egg whites and salt on medium speed until opaque and beginning to hold their shape. Increase the speed and whip in the remaining sugar in a slow stream, until the whites hold a very stiff peak. Fold in the nut mixture, in three or four additions. Place in a pastry bag fitted with a ½-inch plain tube and pipe the meringue in two disks on the prepared pans. Bake at 300°F until they are crisp and almost dried through, about 30 minutes. Cool on the pans.

Preparing the Syrup. Bring the sugar and water to a boil in a small saucepan. Cool and stir in the rum.

Preparing the Ganache. Place the chocolate in a bowl. Bring the cream to a boil and pour over the chocolate. Let stand 2 minutes, beat, then strain into a clean dry bowl. Cool at cool room temperature until it sets.

Just before assembling the cake, beat the set Ganache on medium speed and continue beating to lighten it.

Shave the chocolate with a vegetable peeler or by drawing a round cookie cutter across its surface. Refrigerate if the room is warm.

Assembling. Trim each meringue disk to an even 9-inch diameter with the point of a sharp paring knife. Trim the top of the Génoise and cut into two layers, each about ¾ inch thick. Wrap and reserve one of the layers for another use, such as a Trifle.

Place a dab of the Ganache on a cardboard or springform base and press one of the meringue layers on it, flat-side down. Spread with one third of the Ganache. Moisten the top of the Génoise with half the syrup and invert onto the Ganache, then moisten the other side of the Génoise with the remaining syrup. Spread with one third of the Ganache and place the other meringue layer on it, flat-side down. Spread the remaining Ganache around the side of the cake, being careful not to get any on the top of the cake. Adhere the chocolate shavings (or pulverized meringue trimmings) to the Ganache on the side of the cake, using a spatula.

Holding. Wrap the cake in plastic wrap and refrigerate. It will keep very well for about 3 days.

Yield. About 10 to 12 portions

Variations

Substitute a flavored buttercream for the Ganache: liqueur, orange, raspberry, praline. Vary the nuts in the meringue—hazelnuts would be better when using a praline buttercream.

Use a plain instead of a Chocolate Génoise for contrast with the chocolate-nut meringue layers.

Use almond or hazelnut layers with a plain

Génoise. A raspberry buttercream and syrup would be striking with this combination.

CHOCOLATE CHESTNUT CAKE

This is a perfect cake for the holiday season. The rich chestnut flavor perfectly complements the chocolate and the Kirsch and the buttercream brings out the sweetness of the chestnuts. When buying the chestnut spread or *Crème de Marrons,* which is already sweetened, do not confuse it with chestnut puree, which contains no sugar and will not mix smoothly with the butter for the filling.

Chocolate Génoise

    4 EGGS
    PINCH SALT
    ⅔ CUP SUGAR, ABOUT 5 OUNCES
    ⅓ CUP CAKE FLOUR, ABOUT 1½ OUNCES
    ⅓ CUP CORNSTARCH, ABOUT 1½ OUNCES
    3 TABLESPOONS COCOA POWDER, ABOUT ½
        OUNCE
    2 PINCHES BAKING SODA

Kirsch Syrup

    ½ CUP WATER
    ¼ CUP SUGAR, ABOUT 1¾ OUNCES
    ½ TEASPOON VANILLA EXTRACT
    2 TABLESPOONS KIRSCH

Chestnut Buttercream

    2 STICKS BUTTER, 8 OUNCES
    1 CUP CHESTNUT SPREAD, OR SWEETENED
        CHESTNUT PUREE, PAGE 45
    2 TABLESPOONS KIRSCH

Ganache Glaze

1 CUP HEAVY WHIPPING CREAM

8 OUNCES BITTERSWEET OR SEMISWEET
CHOCOLATE, FINELY CUT

CRYSTALLIZED VIOLETS *OR MARRONS GLACÉS*
(CANDIED CHESTNUTS)

Preparing the Chocolate Génoise. Butter a 9-inch diameter × 2½- to 3-inch-deep springform pan and line the bottom with a piece of parchment paper, cut to fit. Combine and warm the eggs, salt and sugar and whip until cool and increased in volume. Sift together the cake flour, cornstarch, cocoa powder and baking soda several times then sift over and fold into the egg foam. Pour the batter into the prepared pan. Bake at 350°F about 30 minutes. Immediately remove from pan and cool on a rack.

Preparing the Syrup. Bring the sugar and water to a boil in a small saucepan. Pour into a small bowl and cool. Stir in the vanilla and Kirsch.

Preparing the Chestnut Buttercream. Beat the butter until soft and light. Beat in the chestnut spread until smooth, then beat in the Kirsch. Keep covered at a cool room temperature until needed.

Preparing the Glaze. Place the chocolate in a small bowl. Bring the cream to a boil and pour over the chocolate. Allow to stand 2 minutes, beat, then strain into a clean dry bowl. Cool at room temperature until it is no longer warm to the touch before pouring it over the finished cake. If the room is cool, do not prepare the glaze more than 1 hour before pouring it.

Preparing the Decorations. Crush the crystallized violets slightly if they are very large. If using the candied chestnuts, drain well on paper towels (do not rinse them) and cut or break them into ½-inch pieces.

Assembling. Using a sharp, serrated knife, slice the Génoise into three layers. Place the bottom layer on a cardboard or inverted springform base and moisten with one third of the syrup. Spread the layer with a third of the chestnut buttercream. Repeat with the second layer, syrup and buttercream. End with the top layer and moisten with the remaining syrup. Mask the outside of the cake with half the remaining buttercream, reserving the rest for decorations. Place the cake on a platter and refrigerate about 1 hour to firm the buttercream.

Glazing. Remove the cake from the refrigerator and place on a rack over a pan. Pour the cooled glaze over the cake through a strainer held close to the cake. Refrigerate to set the glaze.

Decorating. Place the remaining buttercream in a pastry bag fitted with a small star tube and make ten or twelve rosettes around the border of the cake. Top each with a piece of crystallized violet or candied chestnut.

Holding. Refrigerate, loosely covered with plastic wrap, up to 12 hours before serving it. Let stand at room temperature about 1 hour before serving.

Yield. About 10 to 12 portions

PEACH MERINGUE CAKE

This is an extremely light layer cake. The Génoise is filled with a slightly thickened and not-too-sweet peach mixture and covered with a light meringue. Do not prepare the meringue in advance; it must be spread on the cake immediately after it is made. The dessert is satisfying in its combination of flavors, but is neither rich nor heavy.

Plain Génoise
4 EGGS
PINCH SALT
⅔ CUP SUGAR, ABOUT 5 OUNCES
½ CUP CAKE FLOUR, ABOUT 2 OUNCES
3 TABLESPOONS CORNSTARCH, ABOUT ¾ OUNCE

Peach Filling
2½ POUNDS RIPE FREESTONE PEACHES, YELLOW OR WHITE, ABOUT 5 TO 6 MEDIUM
⅓ CUP SUGAR, ABOUT 5 OUNCES
2 TABLESPOONS LEMON JUICE
3 TABLESPOONS LIGHT RUM
2 TABLESPOONS CORNSTARCH, ABOUT ½ OUNCE

Rum Syrup
½ CUP WATER
¼ CUP SUGAR, ABOUT 1¾ OUNCES
2 TABLESPOONS LIGHT RUM
1 TEASPOON VANILLA EXTRACT

Swiss Meringue
4 EGG WHITES
¾ CUP SUGAR, ABOUT 5¾ OUNCES

½ CUP SLICED, BLANCHED ALMONDS, ABOUT 1½ OUNCES
½ CUP CONFECTIONERS' SUGAR, APPROXIMATELY

Preparing the Plain Génoise. Butter a 9-inch diameter × 2½- to 3-inch-deep springform pan and line the bottom with a piece of parchment paper, cut to fit. Combine and warm the eggs, salt and sugar and whip on high speed until cool and increased in volume. Sift together the flour and cornstarch several times, then sift again over the egg foam and fold in. Pour the batter into the prepared pan. Bake the layer at 350°F about 30 minutes. Immediately remove layer from pan and cool.

Preparing the Peach Filling. Cut a cross in the blossom end of each peach and plunge into boiling water for about 30 seconds. Remove with a slotted spoon to a bowl of ice water. Peel the peaches using the point of a paring knife to pull away the skin. If they do not peel easily, use the paring knife remove the skin. Halve the peaches and cut each half into five or six wedges. Combine the peach wedges, sugar and lemon juice in a 2-quart saucepan. Cover and cook over low heat about 5 minutes, until a lot of the juice has exuded from the peaches.

Uncover the pan and continue cooking the peaches over low heat until the juices are somewhat reduced, about 5 to 10 minutes more. Combine the rum and cornstarch in a small bowl, stirring until smooth. Beat some of the peach juices into the starch mixture to warm it, then stir into the simmering peach mixture. Stir gently and continue cooking about 3 to 4 minutes. Pour into a bowl, cover with plastic wrap and refrigerate until cold.

Preparing the Syrup. Combine the sugar and water in a small saucepan. Bring to a boil over medium heat. Cool and stir in the rum and vanilla.

Assembling. Using a sharp, serrated knife, slice the cake into three layers. Place the bottom layer on a cardboard or inverted spring-form bottom and moisten it with a third of the syrup. Spread the layer with half the filling. Repeat with the second layer, syrup and remaining filling. End with the last layer and moisten the top and side of the cake with the remaining syrup. Refrigerate the cake briefly while preparing the meringue. Or wrap and refrigerate the cake until the next day before finishing the cake.

Preparing the Meringue. Combine and warm the egg whites and the sugar over simmering water, stirring until the egg whites are hot and the sugar dissolved. Whip on medium speed until cool and increased in volume.

Finishing. Evenly spread the meringue around the outside of the cake, using an offset spatula. Pipe a lattice of the meringue on top, using a pastry bag fitted with a ¼-inch plain or star tube. Then pipe a border around the top edge. Slightly crush the sliced almonds with your hands and press them around the side. Sprinkle a few pinches of the almonds on the top. Dredge the cake all over with confectioners' sugar; place on the back of a pan or a cookie sheet and into a preheated 400°F oven for about 5 minutes to color the meringue. Remove from the oven and cool it at room temperature.

Holding. Refrigerate, loosely covered with plastic wrap, no more than 6 hours before serving.

Yield. About 10 to 12 portions

Pineapple Coconut Cake

Prepare the filling, substituting about 4 CUPS PARED AND FINELY SLICED FRESH PINEAPPLE for the peaches. Substitute COCONUT for the sliced almonds on the outside of the cake.

Variations

Substitute an ALMOND SPONGE for the plain one. Strew the peach filling with a few FRESH RASPBERRIES after spreading it on each layer. Or stir some SLICED STRAWBERRIES into the filling before spreading it on the layers.

BOURBON PECAN CAKE

This was a popular dessert at Windows on the World in the winter of 1983–84. The Pecan Sponge and the caramel buttercream are a good background for the bourbon.

Pecan Sponge
    1¼ CUPS PECAN HALVES, ABOUT 5½
       OUNCES
    ¾ CUP CAKE FLOUR, ABOUT 3 OUNCES
    ¼ TEASPOON CINNAMON
    4 EGGS, SEPARATED
    ¾ CUP SUGAR, DIVIDED, ABOUT 5¾
       OUNCES
    PINCH SALT

Bourbon Syrup
    ½ CUP WATER
    ¼ CUP SUGAR, ABOUT 1¾ OUNCES
    2 TABLESPOONS BEST BOURBON
    ½ TEASPOON VANILLA EXTRACT

Caramel Bourbon Buttercream

6 EGG YOLKS

¾ CUP SUGAR, ABOUT 5¾ OUNCES

½ TEASPOON LEMON JUICE

¼ CUP HOT WATER

3 STICKS BUTTER, 12 OUNCES

2 TABLESPOONS BEST BOURBON

1½ CUPS PECAN HALVES, ABOUT 6 OUNCES

Preparing the Pecan Sponge. Butter a 9-inch diameter × 2½- to 3-inch-deep springform pan and line the bottom with a piece of parchment paper, cut to fit. Process the pecans in a food processor until very fine. Sift the cake flour over the pecans, add the cinnamon and combine. Whip the yolks, then whip in half the sugar until light in color and aerated. Whip the egg whites and salt on medium speed until white and opaque. Increase the speed and whip in the remaining sugar. Continue whipping until the egg whites hold a firm peak. Fold the yolks into the whites, scatter over then fold in the pecan and flour mixture in several additions. Pour the batter into the prepared pan. Bake the layer at 350°F about 30 minutes. Remove from the pan and cool on a rack, on the paper.

Preparing the Syrup. Combine the sugar and water in a small saucepan and bring to a boil over medium heat. Pour into a small bowl, cool to room temperature and stir in the bourbon and vanilla.

Preparing the Buttercream. Whip the yolks on medium speed while preparing the caramel. Combine the sugar and lemon juice in a small saucepan and stir to a consistency of wet sand. Place over medium heat and allow to begin melting. Stir the sugar occasionally so that it melts evenly. Cook the sugar to a deep amber caramel, being careful not to overcook or it will be bitter. Carefully pour in the hot water in a stream, since the caramel can splatter as the liquid is added. Allow the diluted caramel to return to a boil, and to boil for 1 minute. Pour the boiling caramel syrup over the yolks, while they are whipping. Continue whipping the yolks and caramel until the mixture is aerated and cool. Whip in the butter, incorporating it in five or six additions. Whip the buttercream until smooth, then whip in the bourbon very slowly. Hold the buttercream at room temperature.

Preparing the Garnish. Process the pecans in a food processor until coarsely chopped.

Toast the chopped pecans in a 350°F oven about 5 to 10 minutes, stirring often, until they are golden. Reserve at room temperature.

Assembling. Using a sharp, serrated knife, slice the sponge into three layers. Place the bottom layer on a cardboard or inverted springform base and moisten it with one third of the syrup. Spread the layer with a third of the Caramel Bourbon Buttercream. Repeat with the second layer syrup and buttercream. End with the top layer and moisten with the remaining syrup. Mask the outside of the cake with the remaining buttercream. Lift the cake on one hand and adhere the chopped pecans all around the outside of the cake, first on the sides, then on the top. Use an offset spatula to spread the top of the cake flat, sweeping away any excess chopped pecans at the same time.

Holding. Refrigerate, loosely covered with plastic wrap, up to 12 hours before serving it. Let stand at room temperature about 1 hour before serving.

Yield. About 10 to 12 portions

TRIPLE ORANGE CAKE

This was a popular cake in the early eighties, back in the days of the Total Heaven Baking Company, which I owned in partnership with Peter Fresulone and Bill Liederman. Although it is fairly sweet, the combination of the fresh orange flavor and the orange liqueur works well. Try adding a squeeze of lemon or lime juice along with the orange juice and change the orange liqueur to white rum for a lively variation.

   Covering the outside of the cake entirely with toasted sliced almonds is a quick, easy way to give a tailored looking finish.

Plain Génoise
   4 EGGS
   PINCH SALT
   2/3 CUP SUGAR, ABOUT 5 OUNCES
   1/2 CUP CAKE FLOUR, ABOUT 2 OUNCES
   3 TABLESPOONS CORNSTARCH, ABOUT 3/4
      OUNCE

Orange Syrup
   1/2 CUP WATER
   1/4 CUP SUGAR, ABOUT 1 3/4 OUNCE
   2 TABLESPOONS STRAINED ORANGE JUICE
   2 TABLESPOONS ORANGE LIQUEUR

Orange Buttercream
   1/2 CUP SUGAR, ABOUT 3 3/4 OUNCES
   3 TABLESPOONS WATER
   2 TEASPOONS LIGHT CORN SYRUP *OR* 1/8
      TEASPOON CREAM OF TARTAR
   6 EGG YOLKS
   3 STICKS BUTTER, 12 OUNCES
   1 TABLESPOON GRATED ORANGE ZEST

   2 TABLESPOONS STRAINED ORANGE JUICE
   2 TO 3 TABLESPOONS ORANGE LIQUEUR

   1/4 CUP ORANGE MARMALADE

   1 CUP BLANCHED, SLICED ALMONDS, VERY
      LIGHTLY TOASTED, ABOUT 3 OUNCES

   1/4 CUP CONFECTIONERS' SUGAR

Preparing the Plain Génoise. Butter a 9-inch diameter × 2 1/2- to 3-inch-deep springform pan and line the bottom with a piece of parchment paper, cut to fit. Combine and warm the eggs, salt and sugar and whip on high speed until cool and increased in volume. Sift together the flour and cornstarch; sift over and fold into the egg foam. Pour the batter into the prepared pan. Bake the layer at 350°F about 30 minutes. Immediately remove from pan and cool.

Preparing the Syrup. Combine the sugar and water in a small saucepan. Bring to a boil over medium heat. Cool and stir in the orange juice and orange liqueur.

Preparing the Buttercream. Combine sugar, water and corn syrup or cream of tartar in a 1-quart saucepan. Heat to boiling, wiping the inside of the pan with a brush dipped in cold water. Insert a candy thermometer and cook to the soft ball stage, 238°F. For such a small quantity of syrup, it may be difficult to ascertain the temperature on a candy thermometer. About 3 minutes of boiling should bring this quantity of syrup to the proper temperature. When the syrup begins to boil, whip the yolks on medium speed until the syrup reaches the desired temperature, then pour the syrup in a stream down the side of the bowl, avoiding the whip. Continue whipping on medium speed until cool, about 5 minutes.

Whip in the butter, then the orange zest. Whip in the orange juice very slowly, then the orange liqueur, also very slowly, until smooth.

Assembling. Using a sharp serrated knife, divide the Génoise into three layers. Place the bottom layer on a cardboard or inverted springform bottom, and moisten with one third of the syrup. Thinly spread with half of the marmalade. Spread a third of the buttercream evenly on the layer. Repeat with the second layer, syrup, marmalade and buttercream. End with the top layer and moisten with the remaining syrup. Mask the outside of the cake with the remaining buttercream, spreading it very thinly.

Finishing. Lift the cake on one hand and adhere the cooled, toasted sliced almonds, first to the side of the cake and then strew them evenly over the top of the cake to cover the buttercream entirely. Chill the cake to set the buttercream so that the almonds remain adhered to it. Dredge the cake very lightly with confectioners' sugar immediately before serving.

Holding. Refrigerate, well wrapped in plastic, a day or two before serving. Allow to stand at room temperature ½ hour before serving.

Yield. Approximately 10 to 12 portions

Variations

Substitute an ALMOND SPONGE OR CHOCOLATE GÉNOISE for the plain one. If using the Chocolate Génoise, cover the outside of the cake with CHOCOLATE SHAVINGS instead of almonds.

With an almond sponge or plain Génoise, substitute a LEMON BUTTERCREAM for the orange, flavor the syrup with LEMON JUICE AND KIRSCH instead of orange juice and orange liqueur, and substitute RASPBERRY PRESERVES for the orange marmalade.

PUNSCHTORTE (RUM PUNCH CAKE)

One of the most popular cakes in the Viennese repertoire, the *Punschtorte* is made from a Génoise-like sponge layer, moistened with a syrup flavored with lemon and orange juices, dark rum and vanilla—the *Punsch* (punch) referred to in the name.

For the cake to absorb as much syrup as possible, I like to split the cake into layers and moisten each layer for even absorption, then reassemble the layers with some apricot glaze. The glaze is not a filling, but helps to hold the cake together.

In Vienna, *Punsch* goods—cakes, squares, balls and slices—are vehicles for utilizing fresh trimmings and cake scraps. For a cake like this one, the top and bottom layers would be made from a fresh cake layer, the middle layer from scraps moistened with plenty of syrup and loosely pressed into a layer shape.

Normally a *Punschtorte* is covered with a pink fondant icing; this version uses a marzipan covering, a little less sweet and more tailored looking.

The Viennese spongecake layer used here is very similar to a Génoise in technique, but has a firmer texture to absorb large amounts of syrup.

Viennese Spongecake

5 EGGS

1 TEASPOON GRATED LEMON ZEST

½ CUP SUGAR, ABOUT 3¾ OUNCES

1 CUP CAKE FLOUR, ABOUT 4 OUNCES

Punch Syrup

½ CUP WATER

⅓ CUP SUGAR, ABOUT 2½ OUNCES

¼ DARK RUM

¼ CUP ORANGE JUICE

2 TABLESPOONS LEMON JUICE

1 TEASPOON VANILLA EXTRACT

Apricot Glaze

1½ CUPS APRICOT PRESERVES

¼ CUP WATER

Marzipan

8 OUNCES ALMOND PASTE

2 CUPS CONFECTIONERS' SUGAR, ABOUT 8½ OUNCES

3 TO 5 TABLESPOONS LIGHT CORN SYRUP

1 OUNCE SEMISWEET CHOCOLATE, MELTED

RED FOOD COLORING

CORNSTARCH

Preparing the Spongecake Layer. Butter a 9-inch diameter × 2½- to 3-inch-deep springform pan and line the bottom with a piece of parchment paper, cut to fit. Combine and warm the eggs, lemon zest and sugar and whip on high speed until cool and increased in volume. Sift cake flour over the egg foam and fold in. Pour into the prepared pan and bake at 350°F about 30 minutes. Unmold and cool the layer right-side up on a rack.

Preparing the Syrup. Bring the sugar and water to a boil in a saucepan. Cool and stir in the remaining syrup ingredients.

Preparing the Apricot Glaze. Combine the preserves and water and bring to a boil over medium heat, stirring occasionally. Strain into another pan and simmer until the glaze coats the back of a spoon.

Preparing the Marzipan. Combine the almond paste with the sugar and beat on slow speed until the sugar is reduced to very fine crumbs. Beat in half the corn syrup, then test a handful: If it kneads smooth and is not dry, enough has been added. If dry continue adding corn syrup. Pour on the work surface and knead until smooth. Remove a small piece and wrap in plastic. Add a drop of the coloring to the remaining marzipan to tint it a pale pink. Wrap in plastic.

Assembling. Using a sharp, serrated knife, divide the cake into three layers and place the bottom layer on a platter or cardboard. Moisten with a third of the syrup and brush with a third of the glaze. Repeat with the remaining layers. Brush the entire cake with the glaze.

Lightly dust the work surface and pink marzipan with confectioners' sugar and roll thinly. Cover the cake with it and trim away the excess. Use the excess to make a rope to finish the bottom of the cake. Pipe a chocolate design on the cake with the melted chocolate, using a paper cone. Make a flower or other decoration from the white marzipan, for the center of the cake.

Holding. Keep, at room temperature, up to 2 days.

Yield. About 12 to 15 portions

CHOCOLATE RASPBERRY CAKE

This cake and the orange variation that follows never fail to elicit compliments. The slight acidity of the fruit is good with the chocolate and the richness of the Ganache is offset by the lightness of the Génoise. Although the recipe does not include it, the cake may be glazed with Ganache (as in the Chocolate Chestnut Cake) after being masked with the whipped Ganache. If you glaze the cake, save some of the whipped Ganache to pipe a simple border or decoration on the glaze.

Chocolate Génoise

4 EGGS

PINCH SALT

⅔ CUP SUGAR, ABOUT 5 OUNCES

⅓ CUP CAKE FLOUR, ABOUT 1½ OUNCES

⅓ CUP CORNSTARCH, ABOUT 1½ OUNCES

3 TABLESPOONS COCOA POWDER, ABOUT ½ OUNCE

2 PINCHES BAKING SODA

Framboise Syrup

½ CUP WATER

¼ CUP SUGAR, ABOUT 1¾ OUNCES

2 TABLESPOONS FRAMBOISE OR RASPBERRY LIQUEUR

1 TEASPOON VANILLA EXTRACT

Rich Ganache

1 POUND BITTERSWEET OR SEMISWEET CHOCOLATE, FINELY CUT

1⅓ CUPS HEAVY WHIPPING CREAM

2 TO 3 TABLESPOONS FRAMBOISE OR RASPBERRY LIQUEUR

¼ CUP SEEDLESS RASPBERRY PRESERVES OR ⅓ CUP RASPBERRY PRESERVES, STRAINED TO REMOVE SEEDS

2 TO 3 OUNCES BITTERSWEET OR SEMISWEET CHOCOLATE FOR SHAVINGS

FRESH RASPBERRIES, OPTIONAL

Preparing the Chocolate Génoise. Butter a 9-inch diameter × 2½- to 3-inch-deep springform pan and line the bottom with a piece of parchment paper, cut to fit. Combine and warm the eggs, salt and sugar and whip on high speed until cool and increased in volume. Sift together the cake flour, cornstarch, cocoa powder and baking soda several times. Sift over egg foam and fold in. Pour the batter into the prepared pan. Bake at 350°F about 30 minutes. Immediately remove from pan and cool on a rack.

Preparing the Syrup. Bring the sugar and water to a boil in a small saucepan. Cool and stir in the liqueur and the vanilla.

Preparing the Ganache. Place the chocolate in a bowl. Bring the cream to a boil and pour over the chocolate. Let stand 2 minutes. Beat and strain it into a clean dry bowl. Cool to room temperature until the Ganache sets. Just before assembling the cake, beat the Ganache to lighten it, then beat in the liqueur 1 tablespoon at a time.

Strain the preserves if necessary and reserve in a small bowl. Shave the chocolate with a cookie cutter or vegetable peeler onto a piece of wax paper. Refrigerate in a small bowl if the room is warm.

Assembling. Using a sharp, serrated knife, divide into three layers. Place the bottom layer on a cardboard or inverted springform base and moisten with a third of the syrup.

Spread the layer with half the preserves, then a third of the Ganache. Repeat with the second layer, preserves, syrup and Ganache. End with the top layer and moisten with the remaining syrup. Mask the outside of the cake with half the remaining Ganache. Press the chocolate shavings against the side of the cake using a metal spatula. Place the remaining Ganache in a pastry bag fitted with a star tube and pipe a decoration on the cake. Top with the fresh raspberries. Refrigerate to set the Ganache.

Holding. Refrigerate, loosely covered with plastic wrap, up to 12 hours before serving. Let stand at room temperature about 1 hour before serving.

Yield. About 10 to 12 portions

Variations

For a Chocolate Orange Cake, substitute OR-ANGE MARMALADE for the raspberry preserves and ORANGE LIQUEUR for the raspberry liqueur. A plain Génoise can be substituted for the chocolate.

LEMON SUCCÈS CAKE

The combination of Succès, an old-fashioned name for the almond meringue layers, and the lemon filling successfully contrasts sweetness and tartness. The inspiration for this dessert is a classic Swiss pastry called the *Zuger Kirschtorte,* a Kirsch cake from Zug, a city south of Zürich in the heart of the cherry-growing area. The original pairs almond meringue with a Kirsch-flavored syrup and buttercream.

Plain Génoise
4 EGGS
PINCH SALT
2/3 CUP SUGAR, ABOUT 5 OUNCES
1/2 CUP CAKE FLOUR, ABOUT 2 OUNCES
3 TABLESPOONS CORNSTARCH, ABOUT 3/4 OUNCE

Almond Meringue
3/4 CUP WHOLE ALMONDS, ABOUT 4 OUNCES
1/2 CUP SUGAR, ABOUT 3 3/4 OUNCES
2 TABLESPOONS CORNSTARCH, ABOUT 1/2 OUNCE
4 EGG WHITES, 1/2 CUP
PINCH SALT
1/2 CUP SUGAR, ABOUT 3 3/4 OUNCES

Lemon Syrup
1/3 CUP WATER
3 TABLESPOONS SUGAR, ABOUT 1 1/2 OUNCES
2 TABLESPOONS STRAINED LEMON JUICE
2 TABLESPOONS WHITE RUM

Lemon Sabayon Buttercream
4 EGG YOLKS
1/3 CUP STRAINED LEMON JUICE
1/2 CUP SUGAR, ABOUT 3 3/4 OUNCES
2 STICKS BUTTER, 8 OUNCES, SOFTENED
1 TABLESPOON WHITE RUM

Preparing the Plain Génoise. Butter a 9-inch diameter × 2 1/2- to 3-inch-deep springform pan and line the bottom with a piece of parchment paper, cut to fit. Combine and warm the eggs salt and sugar and whip on high speed until cool and increased in volume. Sift together the flour and cornstarch several times; sift over the egg foam and fold in. Pour the batter into the prepared pan. Bake it at 350°F about 30 minutes. Immediately remove layer from the pan and cool.

Preparing the Succès. Finely grind the almonds and the ½ cup sugar in a food processor. Stir in the cornstarch. Whip the the egg whites and salt until white and opaque. Increase the speed, whip in the other ½ cup sugar, and continue whipping until the egg whites hold a firm peak. Fold in the almond mixture by hand.

Thinly spread in two 9-inch disks on paper-lined pans. Bake at 300°F about 30 minutes.

Preparing the Syrup. Bring the sugar and water to a boil. Cool. Add lemon juice and rum.

Preparing the Buttercream. Whisk the yolks. Whisk in the lemon juice, then the sugar. Place the bowl over simmering water and beat constantly until thickened. Whip on medium speed until cool and increased in volume, about 5 minutes. Whip in the butter gradually and continue whisking until the buttercream is smooth. Whisk in the rum.

Assembling. Trim the crust from the top and sides of the Génoise. Cut a 9-inch disk from cardboard. Using the disk as a guide, trim the Almond Meringue layers to an even 9-inch diameter. Reserve and crush the trimmings.

Place a dab of the buttercream on the cardboard and place one of the Succès disks on it. Spread it with a third of the buttercream. Moisten the Génoise layer with half the syrup, invert it on the buttercream, then moisten with the remaining syrup. Spread the Génoise with another third of the buttercream and place the second Almond Meringue layer on it. Spread the remaining buttercream only around the sides of the cake.

Adhere the Succès crumbs to the buttercream and dust the top of the cake with confectioners' sugar.

Holding. Chill to set the buttercream. Keep loosely covered with plastic in the refrigerator up to 8 hours. Remove from refrigerator about 1 hour before serving.

Yield. About 10 to 12 portions

CHOCOLATE PISTACHIO ORANGE CAKE

This striking and unusual dessert utilizes three flavors which harmonize beautifully in taste and appearance.

Pistachio Sponge
   1 CUP BLANCHED PISTACHIOS, ABOUT 5½ OUNCES
   ¾ CUP CAKE FLOUR, ABOUT 3 OUNCES
   4 EGGS, SEPARATED
   ¾ CUP SUGAR, DIVIDED, ABOUT 5½ OUNCES
   1 TEASPOON GRATED LEMON ZEST
   ¼ TEASPOON ALMOND EXTRACT
   PINCH SALT

Orange Ganache
   12 OUNCES BITTERSWEET OR SEMISWEET CHOCOLATE, FINELY CUT
   1 CUP HEAVY WHIPPING CREAM
   2 TABLESPOONS ORANGE LIQUEUR

Orange Syrup
   ½ CUP WATER
   ¼ CUP SUGAR, ABOUT 1¾ OUNCES
   3 TABLESPOONS ORANGE LIQUEUR

Candied Orange Filling

½ CUP CANDIED ORANGE PEEL, ABOUT 2
    OUNCES
2 TABLESPOONS ORANGE LIQUEUR

Whipped Cream

1½ CUPS HEAVY WHIPPING CREAM
2 TABLESPOONS SUGAR, ABOUT 1 OUNCE
2 TABLESPOONS ORANGE LIQUEUR

SHAVED MILK CHOCOLATE
CANDIED ORANGE PEEL
BLANCHED PISTACHIOS
CONFECTIONERS' SUGAR

Preparing the Sponge. Butter a 9-inch diameter × 2½- to 3-inch-deep springform pan and line the bottom with a piece of parchment paper, cut to fit. Process the nuts in a food processor until very fine. Sift the cake flour over the nuts and combine. Whip the yolks, then whip in half the sugar until light in color and aerated. Whip the egg whites and salt on medium speed until white and opaque. Increase the speed and whip in the remaining sugar. Continue whipping the whites until the whites hold a firm peak. Fold the yolks into the whites, then fold in the pistachio mixture in two or three additions. Pour the batter into the prepared pan. Bake at 350°F about 30 minutes. Remove from the pan and cool on a rack, on the paper.

Preparing the Ganache. Place the chocolate in a bowl. Bring the cream to a boil and pour over the chocolate. Let stand 2 minutes, then whisk smooth and strain into another bowl. Refrigerate, whisking often until cool, but not set.

Preparing the Syrup. Combine the water and sugar in a small pan and bring to a boil. Cool and stir in the orange liqueur.

Preparing the Filling. Finely chop the peel and combine with the liqueur.

Preparing the Whipped Cream. Combine the cream, sugar and liqueur and whip on medium speed until firm.

Assembling. Using a sharp serrated knife, divide the Pistachio Sponge into two layers and place one on a cardboard. Moisten with half the syrup and spread with most of the Ganache, reserving some for a decoration. Drain the candied peel and distribute evenly on the Ganache. Cover with a layer of whipped cream. Place the second layer on the cream and moisten with the remaining syrup. Cover the outside of the cake with the whipped cream and press the shavings against the side of the cake. Make a border of rosettes around the edge of the cake with the remaining Ganache and decorate the rosettes with cutouts of candied peel and some pistachios. Place some chopped pistachios in the center and dust them lightly with confectioners' sugar.

Holding. Refrigerate the cake for up to 6 hours before serving.

Yield. About 12 portions

GÂTEAU MENTONNAIS

Named for the first French town over from the Italian border on the Côte d'Azur, this dessert combines a light Génoise with a delicate lemon-perfumed pastry cream. The cake is covered and decorated with a meringue and quickly colored in the oven. The name derives from the fact that Menton grows a large crop of native lemons every year.

Lemon Génoise

4 EGGS

PINCH SALT

2/3 CUP SUGAR, ABOUT 5 OUNCES

1 TABLESPOON FINELY GRATED LEMON ZEST

1/2 CUP CAKE FLOUR, ABOUT 2 OUNCES

3 TABLESPOONS CORNSTARCH, ABOUT 1/2 OUNCE

Lemon Pastry Cream

1 CUP MILK

1/3 CUP SUGAR, ABOUT 2 1/2 OUNCES

2 LEMONS, GRATED ZEST AND STRAINED JUICE

2 TABLESPOONS CORNSTARCH

4 EGG YOLKS

3 TABLESPOONS BUTTER, 1 1/2 OUNCES

Rum Syrup

1/2 CUP WATER

1/4 CUP SUGAR, ABOUT 3 3/4 OUNCES

3 TABLESPOONS WHITE RUM

Meringue

4 EGG WHITES, 1/2 CUP

3/4 CUP SUGAR, ABOUT 5 3/4 OUNCES

3/4 CUP BLANCHED, SLICED ALMONDS, ABOUT 2 1/4 OUNCES

1/2 CUP CONFECTIONERS' SUGAR, ABOUT 2 1/4 OUNCES

Preparing the Génoise. Butter a 9-inch diameter × 2½- to 3-inch-deep springform pan and line the bottom with a piece of parchment paper, cut to fit. Combine and warm the eggs, salt, sugar and the lemon zest. Whip on high speed until cool and increased in volume. Sift together the flour and cornstarch several times. Sift over the egg foam and fold in. Pour the batter into the prepared pan. Bake at 350°F about 30 minutes. Immediately remove from pan and cool.

Preparing the Pastry Cream. Bring milk and sugar to a boil. Whisk the cornstarch with the juice. Whisk in the yolks. Whisk half the boiling milk into the egg mixture. Whisk the egg mixture into the remaining milk, whisking constantly until the cream thickens and returns to a boil. Remove from the heat and whisk in the butter. Pour into a small bowl, place plastic wrap against the surface of the cream and chill until firm and cold.

Preparing the Syrup. Bring sugar and water to a boil. Cool and stir in rum.

Preparing the Meringue. Combine and warm the egg whites and sugar over a pan of simmering water, stirring until the sugar is dissolved and the egg whites are hot (130°F). Whip on medium speed until cool and increased in volume. Do not prepare the meringue until ready to spread it on the cake or it will lose volume while waiting.

Assembling. Using a sharp, serrated knife, divide the Génoise into three layers. Place the first layer on a cardboard disk or serving platter and moisten it with a third the syrup. Spread with half the lemon cream. Repeat with the second layer, syrup and cream. End with the last layer and brush with the remaining syrup.

Finishing. Prepare the meringue and mask the cake with it, using an offset spatula. Pipe a decorative pattern with the meringue around the outside of the cake and on the top, using a pastry bag fitted with a star tube. Or, adhere the almonds all over the top and side of the cake. Dust with the confectioners' sugar and color the meringue in a hot oven—400°F for 5 minutes, turning the cake so that it colors evenly. Cool and chill before serving it.

Holding. Refrigerate, loosely covered with plastic wrap, for up to 6 hours before serving.

Yield. About 12 portions

RECTANGULAR CAKES

A rectangular cake, sometimes called a pavé (cobblestone), has a very tailored and elegant appearance. Any of the layer cakes in the previous section can be made into rectangular cakes by baking the batter in a 10 × 15-inch or 12 × 18-inch pan instead of the round pan. The quantities of the filling and covering materials remain the same, since these cakes have the filling spread between the layers and on top, but usually the sides, rather than being covered, are left exposed and trimmed straight after the cake has set in the refrigerator.

General Technique for Rectangular Cakes

Preparing the Layer for Filling. Follow the procedure for rolled cakes (pages 234–235).

Cutting the Layer into Separate Layers. Using a sharp, serrated knife, cut the layer into three layers of equal size in the length. Or cut the layer in half in the width, depending on the cake being prepared.

Assembling the Cake. Cut a piece of stiff or corrugated cardboard the same size as one of the cut layers. Place one of the layers on the cardboard and moisten with a third of the syrup using a brush. Press the moistened brush lightly into the layer, rather than use a painting motion or the layer will be insufficiently moistened.

Spread the layer with a third of the filling using an offset spatula. Spread the filling back and forth on the layer; do not let the filling run over the edges of the layer. (Since the cake will not be covered on the sides, any of the filling that protrudes between the layers will be trimmed away later.) The filling should be ¼ to ⅜ inch thick.

To place the second layer on easily, slide it onto a cookie sheet or the back of a rectangular pan the same size as the one it was baked in. Let the layer hang about 1 inch over the edge of the cookie sheet or pan back and line it up with the far edge of the first filled layer. Press to adhere the edge and slide away the cookie sheet or pan, allowing the layer to fall into place on the filling.

Repeat the moistening and filling. Follow the same procedure for the third layer, covering it with the filling.

Chilling the Cake to Set It. Slide the cake on its cardboard onto a cookie sheet or the back of a pan and chill approximately 1 hour until the filling is set and firm.

Trimming the Edges of the Cake. Remove the cake from the refrigerator and leave it on the cookie sheet or pan back. Trim the sides of the cake straight and even using a sharp serrated knife run under hot water and wiped dry. Repeat the heating and drying of the knife for each side of the cake.

CHOCOLATE HAZELNUT LOAF

The combination of the hazelnut cake layer and the Praline Paste–flavored Ganache is a rich but delicate one. Sometimes, for a sleek finish, I like to cover the outside of this cake with Ganache Glaze. In that case, omit the hazelnuts on the outside of the cake.

Hazelnut Sponge

1 CUP WHOLE HAZELNUTS, ABOUT 5½ OUNCES
¾ CUP CAKE FLOUR, ABOUT 3 OUNCES
4 EGGS, SEPARATED
¾ CUP SUGAR, DIVIDED, ABOUT 3¾ OUNCES
PINCH SALT

Rum Syrup

½ CUP WATER
¼ CUP SUGAR
3 TABLESPOONS DARK RUM

Ganache Praliné

18 OUNCES BITTERSWEET OR SEMISWEET CHOCOLATE, FINELY CUT
1½ CUPS HEAVY WHIPPING CREAM
1 STICK BUTTER, 4 OUNCES, SOFTENED
⅔ CUP PRALINE PASTE (PAGES 48–49), ABOUT 6 OUNCES

1½ CUPS HAZELNUTS, TOASTED, SKINNED AND COARSELY CHOPPED, ABOUT 6 OUNCES

Preparing the Sponge. Butter a 10 × 15-inch jelly-roll pan and line the bottom with a piece of parchment paper, cut to fit. Process the hazelnuts in a food processor until very fine. Sift the cake flour over the hazelnuts and combine. Beat the yolks, then beat in half the sugar until light in color and aerated. Beat the egg whites and salt on medium speed until white and opaque. Increase the speed and beat in the remaining sugar. Continue beating until the whites hold a firm peak. Fold the yolks into the whites, then scatter over and fold in the nut and flour mixture in several additions. Spread the batter evenly in the prepared pan. Bake at 350°F about 15 minutes. Remove from the pan and cool on a rack, on the paper.

Preparing the Syrup. Bring the sugar and water to a boil in a small saucepan. Remove from heat. Cool and stir in the rum.

Preparing the Ganache. Place the chocolate in a bowl. Bring the cream to a boil and pour over the chocolate. Allow to stand 2 minutes, then stir smooth. Cool until it begins to set. Beat the butter and Praline Paste together by machine until smooth, then beat in the Ganache. Continue beating 1 to 2 minutes until well combined and very light.

Assembling. Cut the Hazelnut Sponge into three 3 × 15-inch layers, depending on the size pan used. Place one layer on a piece of cardboard. Moisten the layer with a third of the syrup. Spread the layer with about a third of the Ganache. Repeat with the second layer, syrup and Ganache. End with the top layer and moisten with the remaining syrup. Use about half of the remaining Ganache to mask the top and sides of the cake evenly.

Finishing. Pipe a border around the top of the cake with the remaining Ganache, using a small star tube. Adhere the hazelnuts to the sides of the cake, using a spatula. Slide a long spatula under the cake and transfer it to a platter.

Holding. Refrigerate, loosely covered with plastic wrap, up to one day before serving.

Yield. About 12 to 15 portions

Variations

Substitute another nut sponge, using the same nut on the outside of the cake.
A plain or chocolate Génoise also works well with this recipe.

RASPBERRY WHITE CHOCOLATE PAVÉ

The white chocolate's sweetness contrasts nicely with the raspberries' slight acidity. Lightly poached and well drained sour cherries or cranberries are also good with the white chocolate filling. For a modernized version of the famous Black Forest cake—usually made from a chocolate cake layer with Kirsch, sour cherries, chocolate shavings and whipped cream—substitute a Chocolate Génoise sheet for the Almond Sponge.

Almond Sponge

1 CUP WHOLE BLANCHED ALMONDS, ABOUT
   5½ OUNCES
¾ CUP CAKE FLOUR, ABOUT 3 OUNCES
4 EGGS, SEPARATED
¾ CUP SUGAR, DIVIDED, ABOUT 5¾
   OUNCES
1 TEASPOON GRATED LEMON ZEST
¼ TEASPOON ALMOND EXTRACT
PINCH SALT

Framboise Syrup

½ CUP WATER
¼ CUP SUGAR, ABOUT 1¾ OUNCES
3 TABLESPOONS FRAMBOISE OR RASPBERRY
   LIQUEUR

White Chocolate Ganache

18 OUNCES WHITE CHOCOLATE, FINELY CUT
1 STICK BUTTER, 4 OUNCES
1 CUP HEAVY WHIPPING CREAM, CHILLED

TWO ½-PINTS FRESH RASPBERRIES
¾ CUP SHAVED WHITE CHOCOLATE

Preparing the Sponge. Use a 10 × 15-inch jelly-roll pan or a 12 × 18-inch half-sheet pan. Butter the pan and line the bottom with a piece of parchment paper, cut to fit. Process the almonds in a food processor until very fine. Sift the cake flour over the almonds and combine. Whip the yolks, then whip in half the sugar until light in color and aerated.

Whip the egg whites and salt on medium speed until white and opaque. Increase the speed and whip in the remaining sugar. Continue beating until the egg whites hold a firm peak. Fold the yolks into the whites, then scatter over and fold in the almond and flour mixture in several additions. Spread the batter on the prepared pan. Bake at 350°F about 15 minutes. Remove from the pan and cool on a rack, on the paper.

Preparing the Syrup. Bring the sugar and water to a boil in a small saucepan. Cool and stir in the Framboise.

Preparing the Ganache. Combine the white chocolate with the butter in a bowl. Melt, stirring constantly over a pan of hot, not simmering, water. Remove from the water and stir in the cream in six or eight additions. Refrigerate, covered, until set.

Assembling. Cut the layer in half widthwise to make two 7½ × 10-inch layers. Place one layer on a piece of cardboard. Moisten the layer with half of the syrup. Evenly spread the layer with a third of the Ganache. Arrange the raspberries close together on the Ganache, reserving five or six for decoration.

Place the second layer on the work surface and spread it with a third of the Ganache. Invert the layer onto the raspberries, so that the side spread with the Ganache is against the raspberries. Press the layer very gently to adhere it to the raspberries without crushing them. Moisten with the syrup and evenly spread with the Ganache. Strew the white chocolate shavings evenly over the Ganache. Slide the cake onto the back of a pan or cookie sheet and chill the cake to set the Ganache.

Finishing. Remove the cake from the refrigerator and trim about ¼ inch from each side so that the sides are perfectly straight and the filling is exposed. Rinse the knife under hot water and wipe it off before cutting each side.

Holding. Refrigerate, loosely covered. Serve the cake on the day it is made or the raspberries may begin to bleed.

Yield. About 10 to 12 portions

Variations

Use a CHOCOLATE GÉNOISE.
Or, substitute 2 TO 3 CUPS FIRM, WELL- DRAINED SLICED POACHED PEACHES for the raspberries.

PAVÉ AUX FRAISES

The name of this dessert derives from the French word for cobblestone. Although the shape is reminiscent of the typical French paving device, all similarities end there! Extremely striking in appearance, the Pavé is light and refreshing in taste.

Almond Sponge
- 1 CUP WHOLE BLANCHED ALMONDS, ABOUT 5½ OUNCES
- ¾ CUP CAKE FLOUR, ABOUT 3 OUNCES
- 4 EGGS, SEPARATED
- ¾ CUP SUGAR, DIVIDED, ABOUT 5¾ OUNCES
- 1 TEASPOON GRATED LEMON ZEST
- ¼ TEASPOON ALMOND EXTRACT
- PINCH SALT

Crème Mousseline with Kirsch
- 2 CUPS MILK
- ⅔ CUP SUGAR, ABOUT 5 OUNCES
- ¼ CUP CORNSTARCH
- 6 EGG YOLKS
- 2 TEASPOONS VANILLA EXTRACT
- 3 STICKS BUTTER, 12 OUNCES, SOFTENED
- 2 TABLESPOONS KIRSCH

Kirsch Syrup
- ½ CUP WATER
- ¼ CUP SUGAR, ABOUT 1¾ OUNCES
- 3 TABLESPOONS KIRSCH

Marzipan

8 OUNCES ALMOND PASTE

2 CUPS CONFECTIONERS' SUGAR, ABOUT 8½ OUNCES

3 TO 5 TABLESPOONS LIGHT CORN SYRUP

RED OR GREEN FOOD COLORING

3 OUNCES BITTERSWEET OR SEMISWEET CHOCOLATE, MELTED

4 PINTS STRAWBERRIES, RINSED, HULLED AND DRAINED

Preparing the Sponge. Use a 10 × 15-inch jelly-roll pan or a 12 × 18-inch half-sheet pan. Butter the pan and line the bottom with a piece of parchment paper, cut to fit. Process the almonds in a food processor fitted with a steel blade until very fine. Sift the cake flour over the almonds and combine. Whip the yolks, then whip in the lemon zest, almond extract and half the sugar until light in color and aerated. Whip the egg whites with the salt on medium speed until white and opaque. Increase the speed and whip in the remaining sugar. Continue whipping until the whites hold a firm peak. Fold the yolks into the whites, then scatter over and fold in the nut mixture in several additions. Spread the batter in the prepared pan. Bake at 350°F about 5 minutes. Immediately remove from the pan and cool on the work surface.

Preparing the Crème Mousseline. Bring 1½ cups of the milk to a boil with the sugar. Whisk cornstarch with remaining milk. Whisk in the yolks. Whisk a quarter of the boiling milk into the egg mixture. Whisk the egg mixture into the remaining milk, whisking constantly until the cream thickens and returns to a boil. Boil, whisking constantly, 30 seconds. Whisk in the vanilla off the heat. Scrape into a clean bowl or pan, cover surface with plastic wrap and refrigerate until cold. Beat butter until soft and light. Beat in cold Crème Mousseline all at once and continue beating until very smooth, then beat in the Kirsch, a little at a time.

Preparing the Syrup. Bring the sugar and water to a boil in a small saucepan. Cool and stir in the Kirsch.

Preparing the Marzipan. Combine the almond paste and sugar and beat on low speed until reduced to very fine crumbs. Beat in half the corn syrup, then test a handful: If it kneads smooth and is not dry, enough has been added. If dry, continue adding corn syrup. Pour the marzipan on the work surface, add color and knead until smooth. Double-wrap in plastic until needed.

Assembling. Cut the almond layer in half, making two 9 × 12-inch layers. Invert one layer on the back of a pan, paint with the melted chocolate and refrigerate to set. Invert the layer chocolate-side down on a cardboard or platter. Moisten with half the syrup and spread with a ¼-inch layer of the Crème Mousseline. Place the whole berries, points up, on the filling, then cover with most of the remaining Crème Mousseline, spreading it well in the spaces between the berries to make an even layer. Invert the other layer on the berries, moisten with the remaining syrup and spread the top with a thin layer of the remaining Crème Mousseline. Chill the cake several hours, loosely covered with plastic wrap.

Finishing. On a surface lightly dusted with cornstarch, thinly roll the marzipan. Position the marzipan on the cake and trim away the excess with scissors. Trim the edges of the cake straight with a sharp, serrated knife, exposing the centers of the strawberries. Decorate the top of the cake with a marzipan flower or a few berries.

Holding. Keep the cake refrigerated up to 8 hours before serving.

Yield. About 15 portions

SYMPHONIE

A variation of the now-classic Opéra, this dessert combines two rich fillings with a surprisingly light result. Often served in tiny squares, the Symphonie has a stark, tailored appearance so characteristic of these modern French pastries.

Hazelnut Sponge
- 1½ CUPS WHOLE, UNBLANCHED HAZELNUTS, ABOUT 8 OUNCES
- 1 CUP AND 2 TABLESPOONS CAKE FLOUR, ABOUT 4½ OUNCES
- 6 EGGS, SEPARATED
- 1 CUP AND 2 TABLESPOONS SUGAR, DIVIDED, ABOUT 8 OUNCES
- PINCH SALT

Rum Syrup
- ½ CUP WATER
- ¼ CUP SUGAR, ABOUT 1¾ OUNCES
- 3 TABLESPOONS DARK RUM
- 1 TEASPOON VANILLA EXTRACT

Ganache
- 1 POUND BITTERSWEET OR SEMISWEET CHOCOLATE, FINELY CUT
- 1⅓ CUPS HEAVY WHIPPING CREAM

Praliné Buttercream
- 4 EGG YOLKS
- ¼ CUP DARK RUM
- ⅓ CUP SUGAR, ABOUT 2½ OUNCES
- ½ CUP PRALINE PASTE (PAGES 48–49)
- 2 STICKS UNSALTED BUTTER, 8 OUNCES, SOFTENED

- 4 OUNCES BITTERSWEET OR SEMISWEET CHOCOLATE, MELTED

Preparing the Sponge. Butter two 10 × 15-inch jelly-roll pans and line the bottom of each with a piece of parchment paper, cut to fit. Beat the yolks, then beat in the vanilla and half the sugar until light and aerated. Combine the hazelnuts and flour and set aside. Beat the egg whites with the salt on medium speed until white and opaque. Increase the speed and beat in the remaining sugar. Continue beating until the whites hold a firm peak. Fold the yolks into the whites, then scatter over and fold into the nut mixture in several additions.

Divide the batter between the prepared pans and spread evenly. Bake at 350°F about 10 minutes. Immediately remove from the pans and cool directly on the work surface.

Preparing the Syrup. Bring the sugar and water to a boil in a small saucepan. Cool and stir in the rum and vanilla.

Preparing the Ganache. Place the chocolate in a bowl. Bring the cream to a boil and pour over the chocolate. Let stand 2 minutes, then whisk until smooth. Cool at room temperature until set. Immediately before using, beat by machine until lightened, about 2 minutes.

Preparing the Buttercream. Whisk the yolks with the rum, then the sugar. Place the bowl over simmering water and whisk constantly until thickened. Whip on medium speed until cool and increased in volume, about 5 minutes. Whip in the butter, then the Praline Paste. Beat the buttercream smooth.

Assembling. Cut each cake layer into a 10-inch square and a 5 × 10-inch rectangle. Invert one of the square layers onto the back of a pan and paint with the melted chocolate and allow to set. Invert the layer chocolate side down on a cardboard or platter. Moisten the layer with a third of the syrup, then spread the layer with two thirds of the Ganache. Invert the two half-layers on the Ganache. Moisten with the syrup and spread with the buttercream. Repeat with the other square layer, syrup and Ganache. Streak the top of the cake with a serrated knife or decorating comb. Chill, loosely covered with plastic wrap, to set the fillings.

Finishing. Trim the sides straight and even with a sharp, serrated knife dipped in hot water and wiped. Fill a paper cone with melted chocolate and write "Symphonie" on the top. Decorate with shreds of gold leaf.

Holding. Keep the cake refrigerated, loosely covered with plastic wrap, up to 12 hours before serving.

Yield. About 15 to 20 portions

DARK AND WHITE CHOCOLATE PAVÉ WITH STRIPED FILLING

This striking dessert is actually much easier to prepare than it looks. The "checkerboard" effect of the filling is really simple to achieve.

Chocolate Génoise

4 EGGS

PINCH SALT

2/3 CUP SUGAR, ABOUT 5 OUNCES

1/3 CUP CAKE FLOUR, ABOUT 1 1/2 OUNCES

1/3 CUP CORNSTARCH, ABOUT 1 1/2 OUNCES

3 TABLESPOONS COCOA POWDER, ABOUT 1/2 OUNCE

2 PINCHES BAKING SODA

Rich Ganache

1 POUND BITTERSWEET OR SEMISWEET CHOCOLATE, FINELY CUT

1 1/3 CUPS HEAVY WHIPPING CREAM

White Ganache

18 OUNCES WHITE CHOCOLATE, FINELY CUT

6 TABLESPOONS BUTTER, 3 OUNCES

1/4 CUP HEAVY WHIPPING CREAM

Cognac Syrup

1/2 CUP WATER

1/4 CUP SUGAR, ABOUT 1 3/4 OUNCES

3 TABLESPOONS COGNAC

DARK CHOCOLATE SHAVINGS
WHITE CHOCOLATE SHAVINGS

Preparing the Chocolate Génoise. Butter a 10 × 15-inch jelly-roll pan and line the bottom with a piece of parchment paper, cut to fit. Combine and warm the eggs, salt and sugar and whip on high speed until cool and increased in volume. Sift remaining Génoise ingredients together several times; sift over the egg foam and fold in. Pour the batter onto the prepared pan and spread evenly. Bake at 350°F about 15 minutes. Immediately remove from the pan and cool on a rack.

Preparing the Rich Ganache. Place the chocolate in a bowl. Bring the cream to a boil and pour over the chocolate. Let stand 2 minutes, then whisk smooth. Cool at room temperature to set.

Preparing the White Ganache. Combine the chocolate with the butter in a bowl. Melt, stirring constantly over a pan of hot, but not simmering, water. Remove from water and stir in cream in five or six additions. Refrigerate, covered, until set.

Preparing the Syrup. Combine the sugar and water in a small pan and bring to a boil. Cool and stir in the Cognac.

Assembling. Divide the Génoise sheet in three 3 × 15-inch layers. Place the first layer on a cardboard and moisten with a third of the syrup. Beat each Ganache separately to lighten. Fill a pastry bag fitted with a ½-inch plain tube with each. Pipe the white Ganache diagonally from the top left corner to the bottom right one. Alternate diagonal stripes of each Ganache to cover the layer. Place the second layer on the layer of Ganache and moisten it. Pipe a diagonal line of the Rich Ganache on the layer and alternate the Ganaches in diagonal stripes.

Place the last layer on and moisten with the remaining syrup. Pipe the Ganaches as on the first layer. Chill the cake to set the Ganache.

With a warm knife, trim the sides of the Pavé even to expose the pattern of the fillings.

Holding. Cover the Pavé loosely with plastic wrap and refrigerate it for up to one day. Remove from the refrigerator about thirty minutes before serving—long enough to take the chill off it, but not long enough to begin to soften the filling.

Yield. About 12 to 15 portions

CHARLOTTES

There is a good deal of controversy about the origin of the Charlotte. Usually made of sponge fingers which enclose a light filling such as a mousse or Bavarian cream, Charlottes have been popular since the time of Carême at the beginning of the nineteenth century.

Several possibilities exist for the origin of the name: It may commemorate Queen Charlotte of England, the wife of King George III, or the heroine of Goethe's novel *Die Leiden des Jungen Werthers*—the Sufferings of Young Werther—about an extremely sentimental young man hopelessly in love with a married woman called Lotte—a shortened form of Charlotte. The third possibility is that it derives in conception from the Chartreuse, a dish of poultry, usually partridge, baked in a mold lined with cabbage and vegetables, much the same way that the Charlotte is lined with sponge fingers.

Traditionally the Charlotte is made in a Charlotte mold, smaller in diameter at the base than at the top. The Charlottes that follow are molded in a straight-sided springform pan. Aside from the easier availability of this pan, the Charlotte is shorter, less substantial and easier to cut into portions.

General Technique for Charlottes

For a Charlotte 9 to 10 inches in diameter, prepare a sponge disk 8 to 9 inches in diameter and 24 to 30 sponge fingers.

Trimming the Base. Depending on the size of the pan used, trim the sponge disk 1 inch smaller in diameter, using a pan or a cardboard pattern as a guide. If the base is too wide, it will be impossible to fit the fingers in around it. If it is too narrow, the fingers will not stand straight while the pan is being lined and the filling may seep out around the bottom edge after it is poured into the lined pan.

Trimming the Sponge Fingers. Trim the bottom off one of the sponge fingers so that it is no taller than the side of the pan. Use it as a pattern, placing it on the remaining sponge fingers one at a time, and trim to the same height. Then trim the sides of the fingers straight, shaving off as little as possible so that the sides are perfectly straight. This is important since there can be no gaps between the fingers or the filling may seep out.

Lining the Pan. Place the sponge disk in the bottom of the springform pan and position it in the center with an even space all around it. Fit the trimmed sponge fingers into the space, rounded-sides out. Fit them closely together in between the edge of the base and the inside of the pan.

Filling the Charlotte. Pour the filling into the lined pan and loosely cover with plastic wrap.

Refrigerate at least 4 hours (overnight is best) to set the filling.

Unmolding the Charlotte. Release the spring in the side of the pan and remove the side. Leave the Charlotte on the springform bottom, or carefully slide it onto a platter, using a wide spatula to ease it off the pan bottom.

CHARLOTTE AUX FRAMBOISES

Use this recipe as a model for any type of Charlotte filled with a berry Bavarian cream, substituting different berries and an appropriately flavored berry alcohol or liqueur for the raspberries and Framboise. Strawberries and Kirsch or black currants and Crème de Cassis are two possibilities.

All the basic Bavarian cream recipes yield the correct amount to fill a Charlotte of this size.

Sponge Disk and Fingers

    4 EGGS, SEPARATED
    ½ CUP SUGAR, ABOUT 3¾ OUNCES
    PINCH SALT
    1 TEASPOON VANILLA EXTRACT
    ¾ CUP CAKE FLOUR, ABOUT 3 OUNCES
    CONFECTIONERS' SUGAR

Raspberry Bavarian Cream

    4 HALF-PINTS RASPBERRIES, ABOUT 4 CUPS,
        OR 2 10-OUNCE PACKAGES FROZEN
        RASPBERRIES
    ¾ CUP SUGAR, ABOUT 5¾ OUNCES
        (REDUCE SUGAR TO ½ CUP FOR FROZEN
        RASPBERRIES)
    2 TABLESPOONS FRAMBOISE OR RASPBERRY
        LIQUEUR
    2 TABLESPOONS LEMON JUICE
    1½ ENVELOPES UNFLAVORED GELATIN,
        ABOUT 1 TABLESPOON PLUS 1 TEASPOON
    2 CUPS HEAVY WHIPPING CREAM

    ¾ CUP HEAVY WHIPPING CREAM
    1 TABLESPOON SUGAR
    FRESH RASPBERRIES

Preparing the Sponge Disk and Fingers. Line two 10 × 15-inch jelly-roll pans with parchment paper. Fit a pastry bag with a ½-inch plain tube.

Whisk the yolks, then whisk in half the sugar and the vanilla until light and aerated. Whip the egg whites and salt on medium speed until white and opaque. Increase the speed and beat in the remaining sugar. Continue beating until the whites hold a firm peak. Fold the yolks into the whites, then sift over and fold in the cake flour in several additions.

Fill the pastry bag with the batter. Pipe one 8-inch disk onto one of the prepared pans, then pipe the remaining batter into 2½- to 3-inch fingers, 1½ inches apart. Dredge the fingers with confectioners' sugar. Bake at 350°F about 15 minutes. Remove from the pans to a rack and cool completely.

Preparing the Raspberry Bavarian Cream. Combine raspberries and sugar in a saucepan. Bring to a boil, stirring occasionally. Simmer for 5 to 10 minutes, until slightly thickened. Cool and puree in a food processor. Strain.

Pour the Framboise and lemon juice into a small bowl and sprinkle gelatin on the surface to soften. Place over simmering water, stirring, until gelatin is clear. Remove the bowl from the water and whisk in ½ cup of the raspberry puree. Whisk the gelatin mixture into the remaining puree. Whip the cream until it holds its shape and fold into the raspberry mixture.

Assembling. Trim the sponge disk to an even 8-inch diameter and place in the bottom of a 9-inch springform pan. Evenly trim the sides and bottoms of the sponge fingers. Fit the fingers inside the pan, rounded-sides out. Pour the Raspberry Bavarian into the lined pan and chill to set.

Unmolding. Remove the side of the pan and slide the Charlotte off the springform base onto a platter.

Finishing. Whip the ¾ cup cream with the sugar until firm. Pipe a border of rosettes on top of the Charlotte with a star tube. Decorate with fresh raspberries.

Holding. Refrigerate, loosely covered with plastic wrap, up to 12 hours before serving.

Yield. About 10 to 12 portions

CHARLOTTE PRALINÉE

The decoration of Nougatine diamonds is a striking one, but may be omitted to save time.

Sponge Disk and Fingers
4 EGGS, SEPARATED
½ CUP SUGAR, ABOUT 3¾ OUNCES
PINCH SALT
1 TEASPOON VANILLA EXTRACT
¾ CUP CAKE FLOUR, ABOUT 3 OUNCES
CONFECTIONERS' SUGAR

Nougatine
1¼ CUPS SLICED ALMONDS, ABOUT 4
    OUNCES
1 CUP SUGAR, ABOUT 7½ OUNCES
1 TEASPOON LEMON JUICE

Pralin Bavarian Cream
¾ CUP MILK
2¾ CUPS HEAVY WHIPPING CREAM, DIVIDED
⅓ CUP SUGAR, ABOUT 2½ OUNCES
4 EGG YOLKS
1½ ENVELOPES UNFLAVORED GELATIN, 1
    TABLESPOON PLUS 1 TEASPOON
⅓ CUP LIQUEUR, DARK RUM OR BRANDY
¾ CUP PRALIN POWDER, MADE FROM THE
    SCRAPS OF THE NOUGATINE

¾ CUP HEAVY WHIPPING CREAM
1 TABLESPOON SUGAR, ABOUT ½ OUNCE

Preparing the Sponge Disk and Fingers. Line two 10 × 15-inch jelly-roll pans with parchment paper. Fit a pastry bag with a ½-inch plain tube.

Whisk the yolks, then whisk in half the sugar and the vanilla until light and aerated. Whip the egg whites and salt on medium speed until white and opaque. Increase the speed and whip in the remaining sugar. Continue whipping until the whites hold a firm peak. Fold the yolks into the whites, then sift over and fold in the cake flour in several additions.

Fill the pastry bag with the batter. Pipe one 8-inch disk onto one of the prepared pans, then pipe the remaining batter into 2½- to 3-inch fingers, 1½ inches apart. Dredge the fingers with confectioners' sugar. Bake at 350°F about 15 minutes. Remove from the pans to a rack and cool completely.

Preparing the Nougatine. Toast the almonds at 350°F for about 10 minutes. Combine the sugar and lemon juice in a small saucepan over medium heat to begin melting. Stir the caramel occasionally. When it reaches a light amber color, remove from the heat and stir in the almonds. Pour the Nougatine on an oiled marble and turn it over on itself several times. Quickly roll into a long strip using an oiled rolling pin. With an oiled knife, cut out twelve small diamonds and set aside on an oiled pan to cool. Allow the scraps to harden, then pulverize in a food processor to make Pralin Powder.

Preparing the Pralin Bavarian Cream. Bring the milk, ¾ cup of the cream and sugar to a boil. Whisk the yolks. Whisk a third of the hot milk mixture into the yolk mixture. Then return the remaining milk mixture to a boil; whisk the yolk mixture into the boiling liquid, beating constantly until the cream thickens. Strain and set aside. Sprinkle the gelatin on the liqueur in a small bowl and allow the gelatin to soften. Stir the softened gelatin into the hot custard cream. Allow to cool at room temperature, or stir it over cold water to hasten the cooling. Whip the remaining 2 cups cream until it holds its shape, then fold into the custard cream with the Pralin Powder.

Assembling. Trim the sponge disk to an even 8-inch diameter and place in the bottom of a 9-inch springform pan. Evenly trim the sides and bottoms of the sponge fingers. Fit the fingers inside the pan, rounded-sides out. Pour the Pralin Bavarian Cream into the lined pan and chill to set.

Unmolding. Remove the side of the pan and slide the Charlotte off the springform base onto a platter.

Finishing. Whip the ¾ cup cream with the sugar until firm. Pipe a border of rosettes on top of the Charlotte with a star tube. Decorate with the Nougatine diamonds.

Holding. Refrigerate, covered loosely, up to two hours before serving. To keep longer, prepare it up to 1 day in advance and refrigerate, still in the mold and undecorated, covered with plastic wrap. Unmold and finish as above.

Yield. About 10 to 12 portions

LEMON CHARLOTTE WITH MERINGUE

One of my favorite combinations. Note that the temperature for coloring the meringue is higher in this recipe so it colors quickly and the filling doesn't melt.

Sponge Disk and Fingers
4 LARGE EGGS, SEPARATED
½ CUP SUGAR, ABOUT 3¾ OUNCES
PINCH SALT
1 TEASPOON VANILLA EXTRACT
¾ CUP CAKE FLOUR, ABOUT 3 OUNCES
CONFECTIONERS' SUGAR

Lemon Mousse
6 EGG YOLKS
¾ CUP SUGAR, ABOUT 5½ OUNCES
½ CUP STRAINED LEMON JUICE
1½ ENVELOPES UNFLAVORED GELATIN,
    ABOUT 1 TABLESPOON PLUS 1 TEASPOON
¼ CUP WATER
2 TABLESPOONS WHITE RUM, OPTIONAL
2 CUPS HEAVY WHIPPING CREAM

Meringue
4 EGG WHITES, ½ CUP
¾ CUP SUGAR, ABOUT 5½ OUNCES

¼ CUP CONFECTIONERS' SUGAR, ABOUT 1
    OUNCE
⅓ CUP SLICED ALMONDS, OPTIONAL, ABOUT
    1 OUNCE

Preparing the Sponge Disk and Fingers. Line two 10 × 15-inch jelly-roll pans with parchment paper. Fit a pastry bag with a ½-inch plain tube.

Whisk the yolks, then whisk in half the sugar and the vanilla until light and aerated. Whip the egg whites and salt on medium speed until white and opaque. Increase the speed and beat in the remaining sugar. Continue beating until the whites hold a firm peak. Fold the yolks into the whites, then sift over and fold in the cake flour in several additions.

Fill the pastry bag with the batter. Pipe one 8-inch disk onto one of the prepared pans, then pipe the remaining batter into 2½- to 3-inch fingers, 1½ inches apart. Dredge the fingers with confectioners' sugar. Bake at 350°F about 15 minutes. Remove from the pans to a rack and cool completely.

Preparing the Lemon Mousse. Whisk the yolks, sugar and the lemon juice. Place over simmering water, whisking constantly until the mixture thickens. Whip until cool.

Sprinkle the gelatin over the water and optional rum in a small bowl. Allow to soften, then place over simmering water until clear. Whisk ½ cup of the lemon mixture into the dissolved gelatin. Whip the gelatin mixture into the remaining lemon mixture. Beat the cream until it begins to hold its shape and fold in.

Assembling. Trim the disk to an even 8-inch diameter and place in the bottom of a 9-inch springform pan. Evenly trim the sides and bottoms of the sponge fingers. Fit the fingers into the the pan, rounded-side out. Pour the Lemon Mousse into the lined pan and chill until set. Freeze ½ hour before finishing with meringue. Or, place in the freezer to hasten the setting so that the outside will be very stiff when it is placed in the oven to color the meringue.

Preparing the Meringue. Combine and warm the egg whites and sugar until the egg whites are hot and the sugar is dissolved. Whip on medium speed until cool and increased in volume.

Finishing. Remove the Charlotte from the freezer. Place the meringue in a pastry bag fitted with a large star tube and pipe the meringue in a series of large rosettes all over the mousse on top of the Charlotte. Be sure that the meringue touches the edges of the sponge fingers to prevent it from sliding. Strew the meringue with the optional sliced almonds and lightly dredge with confectioners' sugar. Place in a preheated 500°F oven until light golden, about 1 to 2 minutes. Remove from the oven and refrigerate immediately. Unmold just before serving.

Holding. Refrigerate no more than 3 or 4 hours before serving. Or prepare the Charlotte the day before and keep it tightly wrapped in the refrigerator. Finish and unmold 3 to 4 hours before serving.

Yield. About 10 to 12 portions

LOW-CALORIE RASPBERRY CHARLOTTE

This is a satisfying but light low-calorie dessert. Each portion contains about 230 calories. The raspberry mousse derives its richness from low-fat ricotta instead of heavy cream and its lightness from a Swiss meringue.

Sponge Disk and Fingers

4 EGGS, SEPARATED
½ CUP SUGAR, ABOUT 3¾ OUNCES

PINCH SALT
1 TEASPOON VANILLA EXTRACT
¾ CUP CAKE FLOUR, ABOUT 3 OUNCES
CONFECTIONERS' SUGAR

Raspberry Mousse

2 10-OUNCE PACKAGES FROZEN RASPBERRIES
  IN LIGHT SYRUP, DEFROSTED
⅓ CUP WATER
1½ ENVELOPES UNFLAVORED GELATIN,
  ABOUT 1 TABLESPOON PLUS 1 TEASPOON
1 15-OUNCE CONTAINER LOWFAT RICOTTA
5 EGG WHITES, ⅔ CUP
¾ CUP GRANULATED SUGAR, ABOUT 5¾
  OUNCES

Preparing the Sponge Disk and Fingers. Line two 10 × 15-inch jelly-roll pans with parchment paper. Fit a pastry bag with a ½-inch plain tube.

Whisk the yolks, then whisk in half the sugar and the vanilla until light and aerated. Whip the egg whites and salt on medium speed until white and opaque. Increase the speed and whip in the remaining sugar. Continue whipping until the whites hold a firm peak. Fold the yolks into the whites, then sift over and fold in the cake flour in several additions.

Fill the pastry bag with the batter. Pipe one 8-inch disk onto one of the prepared pans, then pipe the remaining batter into 2½- to 3-inch fingers, 1½ inches apart. Dredge the fingers with confectioners' sugar. Bake at 350°F about 15 minutes. Remove from the pans to a rack and cool completely.

Assembling. Trim the disk to an even 8-inch diameter and place in the bottom of a 9-inch springform pan. Evenly trim the bottoms and sides of the fingers. Fit the fingers into the

pan, rounded-sides out.

Preparing the Mousse. Puree the raspberries in a food processor and strain. Bring remaining liquid to a boil, simmer and reduce to 1½ cups. Cool. Sprinkle the gelatin over the water in a small bowl, allow to soften, then place over simmering water until clear. Place ricotta in food processor and process until smooth. Add cooled raspberry puree, then gelatin and process. Pour into a large bowl.

Preparing the Meringue. Combine and warm the egg whites and sugar until the egg whites are hot and the sugar is dissolved. Whip on medium speed until cool and increased in volume. Fold the meringue into the raspberry mixture and pour the mousse into the prepared pan.

Holding. Refrigerate about 6 hours or overnight to set. To unmold, remove side of springform and slide onto a platter.

Yield: 12 portions

CHARLOTTE AUX POIRES

Desserts surrounded with sponge fingers always appear festive. This Charlotte is surrounded by sponge fingers streaked with chocolate for an especially striking presentation.

Sponge Disk and Fingers

4 EGGS, SEPARATED
½ CUP SUGAR, ABOUT 3¾ OUNCES
PINCH SALT
1 TEASPOON VANILLA EXTRACT
¾ CUP CAKE FLOUR, ABOUT 3 OUNCES
1 TEASPOON COCOA POWDER

Poached Pears

2 CUPS ICE

3 CUPS WATER

2 TABLESPOONS LEMON JUICE

4 POUNDS FIRM, RIPE PEARS, SUCH AS
BARTLETT OR COMICE, ABOUT 7 OR 8
MEDIUM

½ VANILLA BEAN

1 CUP SUGAR, ABOUT 7½ OUNCES

Pear Bavarian Cream

2 CUPS PREPARED PEAR PUREE FROM THE
POACHED PEARS, ABOVE

¼ CUP PEAR ALCOHOL OR PEAR LIQUEUR

1 TABLESPOON LEMON JUICE

1½ ENVELOPES UNFLAVORED GELATIN,
ABOUT 1 TABLESPOON PLUS 1 TEASPOON

2 CUPS HEAVY WHIPPING CREAM

Apricot Glaze

¾ CUP APRICOT PRESERVES

2 TABLESPOONS WATER

Preparing the Sponge Disk and Fingers. Line three 10 × 15-inch jelly-roll pans with parchment paper; butter two of the pans. Fit a pastry bag with a ½-inch plain tube.

Whisk the yolks, then whisk in half the sugar and the vanilla until light and aerated. Whip the egg whites and salt on medium speed until white and opaque. Increase the speed and whip in the remaining sugar. Continue whipping until the whites hold a firm peak. Fold the yolks into the whites, then sift over and fold in the cake flour in several additions.

Remove ¼ cup of the batter to a small bowl. Sift in cocoa powder and stir.

Place chocolate batter in a small paper cone and streak the prepared pans with it. Pipe the plain batter on the streaked pans in 3-inch fingers, using the pastry bag. On a separate paper-lined pan, pipe an 8-inch disk of the batter to form a base. Bake fingers and disk at 350°F about 10 to 15 minutes. Remove fingers from pan to cool on rack.

Preparing the Pears. Place ice, water and lemon juice in a large saucepan. Peel, halve and core the pears and immediately plunge into the water. After all the pears are pared, remove ice and add the vanilla bean and sugar. Cover with a disk of parchment paper cut to fit with a hole in the center. Bring pears to a boil over medium heat; lower heat and simmer pears until tender. Remove six halves to use as a garnish and refrigerate on a plate covered with plastic wrap. Continue cooking the remaining pears until they are very soft. Drain, cool and puree in the food processor. Refrigerate the puree.

Preparing the Bavarian Cream. Pour the pear alcohol and lemon juice into a small bowl and sprinkle the gelatin on the surface to soften. Place over simmering water, stirring until the gelatin is clear. Remove the bowl from the water and whisk in ½ cup of the pear puree. Whisk the gelatin mixture into the remaining puree. Whip the cream until it holds its shape and fold into the puree.

Preparing the Glaze. Combine preserves and water in a small saucepan. Bring to a boil over medium heat, stirring occasionally. Strain into another pan and boil until the glaze coats the back of a spoon. Reserve.

Assembling. Trim the disk to an even 8-inch diameter and place in the bottom of a 9-inch springform pan. Evenly trim the sides and bottoms of the sponge fingers. Fit the fingers inside the pan, streaked- (bottom) side out.

Pour the Bavarian into the lined pan and chill to set.

Finishing. Thinly slice the reserved pears across the core. Arrange the sliced pear halves, fanned out, on the top of the Bavarian. Reheat the glaze and allow it to cool. Glaze the pears with a flexible brush. Chill to set the glaze. Remove the side of the pan before serving.

Holding. Refrigerate uncovered up to 2 hours before serving. To keep longer, prepare it up to 1 day in advance and refrigerate, still in the mold and undecorated, covered with plastic wrap. Unmold and finish as above.

Yield. About 10 to 12 portions

LIGHT CHOCOLATE CHARLOTTE

The combination of the chocolate sponge fingers, chocolate mousse and chocolate shavings makes an intensely flavored but still light dessert.

Chocolate Sponge Disk and Fingers
½ CUP CAKE FLOUR, ABOUT 2 OUNCES
3 TABLESPOONS COCOA POWDER, ABOUT ½ OUNCE
PINCH BAKING SODA
4 EGG YOLKS
½ CUP SUGAR, ABOUT 3¾ OUNCES
5 EGG WHITES, ⅔ CUP
PINCH SALT
1 TEASPOON VANILLA EXTRACT

Light Chocolate Mousse
½ CUP BOILING WATER OR HOT COFFEE
12 OUNCES SEMISWEET OR BITTERSWEET CHOCOLATE, FINELY CUT
1 ENVELOPE UNFLAVORED GELATIN, ABOUT 2½ TEASPOONS
¼ CUP WATER
6 EGG YOLKS
½ CUP SUGAR, ABOUT 3¾ OUNCES
3 TABLESPOONS WATER
2 TEASPOONS LIGHT CORN SYRUP OR ⅛ TEASPOON CREAM OF TARTAR
3 TABLESPOONS LIQUEUR, OPTIONAL
2 CUPS HEAVY WHIPPING CREAM

CHOCOLATE SHAVINGS

Preparing the Chocolate Sponge Disk and Fingers. Sift together the cocoa, cake flour and baking soda and set aside. Line two 10 × 15-inch jelly-roll pans with parchment paper. Fit a pastry bag with a ½-inch plain tube.

Whisk the yolks, then whisk in half the sugar and the vanilla until light and aerated. Whip the egg whites and salt on medium speed until white and opaque. Increase the speed and whip in the remaining sugar. Continue whipping until the whites hold a firm peak. Fold the yolks into the whites, then sift over and fold in the flour mixture in several additions.

Fill the pastry bag with the batter. Pipe one 8-inch disk onto one of the prepared pans, then pipe the remaining batter into 2½- to 3-inch fingers, 1½ inches apart. Bake at 350°F about 15 minutes. Remove from the pans to a rack and cool completely.

Preparing the Mousse. Pour the boiling water or coffee over the chocolate. Let stand 2 minutes, then stir to melt. Let cool.

Sprinkle the gelatin over the ¼ cup of water in a small bowl to soften. Place bowl over simmering water and stir until the gelatin is clear. Whip the egg yolks. Heat the sugar, water, and corn syrup or cream of tartar to 238°F. Whip hot syrup into yolks. Whip until cool.

Whip the cream until it holds its shape. Fold the egg yolk mixture into the melted chocolate. Whisk in the optional liqueur. Whip about a quarter of the chocolate mixture into the gelatin, then whisk the gelatin mixture into the remaining chocolate. Fold in the whipped cream.

Assembling. Pour the mousse into the lined pan, sprinkle chocolate shavings in a border around the top of the mousse and cover loosely with plastic wrap. Refrigerate until set. Release the spring on the pan and remove the side of the pan.

Holding. Refrigerate, covered with plastic wrap, up to 1 or 2 days before serving.

Yield. About 10 to 12 portions

Variation

Substitute WHITE CHOCOLATE in the mousse recipe, reducing sugar by half.

STRAWBERRY CHARLOTTE

Sponge Disk and Fingers
4 EGGS, SEPARATED
½ CUP SUGAR, ABOUT 3¾ OUNCES
PINCH SALT
1 TEASPOON VANILLA EXTRACT
¾ CUP CAKE FLOUR, ABOUT 3 OUNCES
CONFECTIONERS' SUGAR

Strawberry Bavarian Cream
2 PINTS STRAWBERRIES
¾ CUP SUGAR, ABOUT 5¾ OUNCES
1 TABLESPOON LEMON JUICE
2 TABLESPOONS KIRSCH
¼ CUP WATER
1½ ENVELOPES UNFLAVORED GELATIN,
  ABOUT 1 TABLESPOON PLUS 1 TEASPOON
2 CUPS HEAVY WHIPPING CREAM
¾ CUP HEAVY WHIPPING CREAM
2 TABLESPOONS SUGAR, ABOUT 1 OUNCE
1 PINT FRESH STRAWBERRIES

Preparing the Sponge Disk and Fingers. Line two 10 × 15-inch jelly-roll pans with parchment paper. Fit a pastry bag with a ½-inch plain tube.

Whisk the yolks, then whisk in half the sugar and the vanilla until light and aerated. Whip the egg whites and salt on medium speed until white and opaque. Increase the speed and beat in the remaining sugar. Continue beating until the whites hold a firm peak. Fold the yolks into the whites, then sift over and fold in the cake flour in several additions.

Fill the pastry bag with the batter. Pipe one 8-inch disk onto one of the prepared pans, then pipe the remaining batter into 2½- to 3-inch fingers, 1½ inches apart. Dredge the fingers with confectioners' sugar. Bake at 350°F about 15 minutes. Remove from the pans to a rack and cool completely.

Preparing the Bavarian Cream. Rinse, hull and thinly slice the berries. Place into a 3-quart saucepan with the sugar and stir to combine.

Bring to a boil on medium heat, then simmer until the mixture thickens slightly, about 5 minutes. Puree, then cool. Stir in the Kirsch and lemon juice.

Pour the water into a 1-quart bowl, sprinkle the gelatin on the surface and let soften. Place over simmering water, stirring, until gelatin is clear. Remove the bowl from the water and whisk in ½ cup of the strawberry puree. Whisk the gelatin into the remaining puree.

Whip the cream until it holds its shape and fold into the strawberry mixture.

Assembling. Trim the disk to an even 8-inch diameter and place in the bottom of a 9-inch springform pan. Evenly trim the sides and bottoms of the sponge fingers. Fit the fingers inside the pan, rounded-side out. Pour the Strawberry Bavarian Cream into the lined pan and chill to set. Release the spring on the pan and remove the side of the pan.

Finishing. Whip the ¾ cup cream and the sugar until firm. Pipe out a border of rosettes around the top edge of the Charlotte using a pastry bag fitted with a star tube. Rinse the strawberries, halve lengthwise through hulls and place, cut-side up, on rosettes.

Holding. Refrigerate uncovered up to 2 hours before serving. To keep longer, prepare it up to 1 day in advance and refrigerate, still in the mold and undecorated, covered with plastic wrap. Unmold and finish as above.

Yield. About 10 to 12 portions

Variations

Use any of the other fruit Bavarian creams in Chapter 4 as a Charlotte filling, decorating the outside with more of the same fruit.

MOLDED LAYER CAKES

Molded layer cakes are of fairly recent origin. Using mousses and Bavarian creams as fillings, they are part of the recent trend toward lighter desserts. Since the fillings are lighter than the buttercreams and ganaches of traditional cakes, they are used more generously. Much of the beauty of these molded layer cakes derives from the perfectly even alternating layers of the Génoise Mousseline layers and the filling, making a striking contrast in color.

One of the most popular of all molded layer cakes is the Miroir. Literally "mirror," the cake is made from alternating layers of Génoise Mousseline and vividly colored berry Bavarian cream. The only decoration on the cake is a perfectly clear shiny glaze made from the same fruit as the filling. Berry flavors are popular for Miroirs because of their bright color.

In preparing a molded cake using a Bavarian cream made from hard or stone fruit, it is striking to cover the top of the cake with poached slices of the same fruit and brush the fruit with a neutral or apricot glaze.

One-Layer Cakes

There is an almost minimalist version of the molded cake in which a filling covers one layer of a sponge disk. This type of cake is fast and easy to prepare and looks tailored and neat.

General Technique for Molded Layer Cake

Since the layers of both cake and filling are of equal thickness in these cakes, only two layers of each are used. The Génoise Mousseline is used here because of its firmness and ability to hold moisture well. It is normal for a mousse or Bavarian cream to seep a little liquid after it has stood for a while and the Génoise Mousseline is capable of absorbing this liquid without becoming soggy.

Preparing the Layer. Invert the cake onto the work surface and carefully peel away the paper on which it was baked. With a sharp, serrated knife, trim the crust from the top of the cake. The layer may be slightly domed in the center; if so, trim it flat by cutting straight across the top of the cake from one side to the other.

Dividing the Cake Layer into Separate Layers. Hold the knife perpendicular to the side of the cake at the point where the cut is to be made, about ½ inch down from the top. Follow the procedure for dividing into separate layers (page 243). Repeat with the remaining part of the cake, cutting another ½-inch layer, for the molded cake. There should be another thin layer about ½ to ¾ inch thick left over. Reserve it to use as the base of a Charlotte instead of a sponge disk or in one of the one-layer molded cakes which follow. Trim the two layers to be used for the molded cake to an even diameter about 1 inch smaller than the pan to be used as a mold.

In filling the cake with the mousse or Bavarian cream, the filling will run down around the layer, completely enclosing it. When the cake is unmolded, only the mousse or Bavarian will be visible and the cake layers will not be seen until the dessert is cut.

Assembling. Place one of the trimmed layers of Génoise Mousseline in the bottom of the pan to be used as a mold. Moisten it with half the syrup in the recipe using a brush. Pour half the filling over the layer, smoothing it evenly with a small offset spatula, making sure that the sides of the layer are well cov-

ered and that the filling has filled the area between the layer and the mold.

Place the second layer on the filling, making sure it is centered, rests on the filling, and does not sink into it. Carefully moisten the layer; do not push it into the filling. Or, place the layer on a tart pan bottom or flat plate, moisten it, then slide it onto the filling. Fill the mold, covering the layer and the area

around it with the remaining filling. Spread the top as smoothly as possible with a long, straight spatula.

Refrigerate the cake until the filling is set, about 4 hours or overnight. Avoid covering the dessert until it has begun to set or the filling may wrinkle from contact with the plastic wrap. This is especially important in the case of a Miroir where the glaze would reflect any unevenness in the top of the filling.

Finishing the Cake (Only for Miroirs). If the cake is a Miroir, remove it from the refrigerator and pour the cooled but still liquid glaze over the top of the cake through a strainer held close to the top of the cake. Tilt the cake in all directions to cover the top completely with the glaze. Refrigerate to set the glaze, about 1 hour.

Unmolding the Cake. Warm the side of the pan with a cloth dipped in hot water and wrung out. Insert a sharp, thin knife between the inside of the pan and the cake and run the knife around the inside of the pan. Be careful to scrape the blade of the knife into the pan rather than the cake. Release the spring and carefully lift off the side of the pan without allowing it to touch the cake. Leave the cake on the pan bottom and place it on a platter.

Decorating the Cake. Cover the top of the cake with a decoration according to the individual recipe. Slices of poached fruit, meringue or a piped decoration of whipped cream may be used. The side of the cake may be left unadorned (as in a Miroir) or finished with nuts or chocolate shavings.

For a one layer molded cake, the procedure is the same as above. Smooth the top carefully since any irregularities would be all the more noticeable in such a short cake.

MIROIR FRAMBOISE

The mirror (miroir) refers to the shiny glaze atop the dessert.

Rich Génoise
   ½ STICK BUTTER, 2 OUNCES
   3 EGGS
   3 YOLKS
   PINCH SALT
   ½ CUP SUGAR, ABOUT 3¾ OUNCES
   ⅓ CUP CAKE FLOUR, ABOUT 1½ OUNCES
   ¼ CUP CORNSTARCH, ABOUT 1 OUNCE

Raspberry Puree

4 HALF PINTS RASPBERRIES *OR* 3 10-OUNCE
PACKAGES FROZEN RASPBERRIES IN SYRUP
¾ CUP SUGAR, ABOUT 5¾ OUNCES

Raspberry Bavarian Cream

2 CUPS RASPBERRY PUREE
2 TABLESPOONS FRAMBOISE *OR* RASPBERRY
LIQUEUR
2 TABLESPOONS LEMON JUICE
1½ ENVELOPES UNFLAVORED GELATIN,
ABOUT 1 TABLESPOON PLUS 1 TEASPOON
2 CUPS HEAVY WHIPPING CREAM

Framboise Syrup

½ CUP WATER
¼ CUP SUGAR, ABOUT 1¾ OUNCES
½ TEASPOON VANILLA EXTRACT
3 TABLESPOONS FRAMBOISE

Raspberry Glaze

⅓ CUP RASPBERRY PUREE, ABOVE
½ CUP CURRANT JELLY
2 TABLESPOONS FRAMBOISE
1 ENVELOPE UNFLAVORED GELATIN, 2 ½
TEASPOONS

Preparing the Rich Génoise. Butter a 9-inch diameter × 2½- to 3-inch-deep springform pan and line the bottom with a piece of parchment paper, cut to fit. Melt the butter over low heat. Do not allow it to sizzle or take on any color. Leave it over the lowest heat possible so that it bubbles up slightly and the water in the butter evaporates. Remove from the heat and cool.

Combine and warm the eggs, yolks, salt and sugar and whip on high speed until cool and increased in volume. Sift together the flour and cornstarch several times. Sift over the egg foam and fold in. Remove a cup of the batter to a bowl, stir in the butter, then fold into the remaining batter. Pour the batter into the prepared pan. Bake at 350°F for about 30 minutes. Remove from the pan immediately and cool on a rack.

Preparing the Raspberry Puree. Combine raspberries and sugar and in a saucepan. Bring to a boil, stirring occasionally. Simmer for 5 to 10 minutes until slightly thickened. Cool and puree in a food processor. Strain.

Preparing the Syrup. Combine sugar and water in a small pan and bring to a boil. Cool and add the vanilla and Framboise.

Preparing the Raspberry Glaze. Melt the Raspberry Puree and the jelly in a small saucepan over low heat. Combine the gelatin and the Framboise and allow to stand for several minutes. Stir the softened gelatin into the raspberry mixture and return to a boil. Strain.

Preparing the Raspberry Bavarian Cream. Pour the Framboise and lemon juice into a small bowl and sprinkle the gelatin on the surface to soften. Place over simmering water, stirring, until the gelatin is clear. Remove the bowl from the water and whisk in ½ cup of the Raspberry Puree. Whisk the gelatin mixture into the remaining puree. Whip the cream until it holds its shape, then fold into the raspberry mixture.

Assembling. Slice the Génoise and make two layers. Place one layer in the bottom of a 10-inch springform pan and moisten it with half the syrup, then pour in half the Bavarian cream. Repeat with the other layer, syrup and remaining Bavarian cream. Chill until set.

Heat the glaze to melt it and allow to cool slightly. Pour a thin layer through a strainer over the Bavarian cream. Chill to set the glaze. Dip a thin knife in hot water and run it around the inside of the pan. Release the spring and lift it off. Smooth the sides with a wet spatula if necessary.

Holding. Keep the Miroir refrigerated, loosely covered with aluminum foil (not touching the glaze), up to 8 hours before serving. To prepare a day in advance, keep it covered with plastic wrap in the refrigerator, but only glaze it on the day it is to be served.

Yield. About 12 portions

DÉLICE AU CALVADOS

This Calvados "delight" may be made with applejack to give it an American flavor. A striking presentation, the *Delice* is decorated with poached apple slices.

Rich Génoise

½ STICK BUTTER, 2 OUNCES
3 EGGS
3 EGG YOLKS
PINCH SALT
½ CUP SUGAR, ABOUT 3¾ OUNCES
⅓ CUP CAKE FLOUR, ABOUT 1½ OUNCES
¼ CUP CORNSTARCH, ABOUT 1 OUNCE

Apple Puree

2 POUNDS McINTOSH OR GOLDEN
DELICIOUS APPLES, ABOUT 4 TO 5
MEDIUM
¾ CUP SUGAR, ABOUT 5¾ OUNCES
½ CUP WATER
½ TEASPOON CINNAMON

Apple Bavarian Cream

⅓ CUP CALVADOS
1 TABLESPOON LEMON JUICE

1½ ENVELOPES UNFLAVORED GELATIN,
ABOUT 1 TABLESPOON PLUS 1 TEASPOON
2 CUPS APPLE PUREE
2 CUPS HEAVY WHIPPING CREAM

Calvados Syrup

½ CUP WATER
¼ CUP SUGAR, ABOUT 1¾ OUNCES
1 TEASPOON VANILLA EXTRACT
3 TABLESPOONS CALVADOS

Apple Slices Cooked in White Wine

3 FIRM APPLES, SUCH AS GOLDEN
DELICIOUS, ABOUT 1½ POUNDS
½ CUP SUGAR, ABOUT 3¾ OUNCES
2 CUPS WHITE WINE
1 STRIP LEMON ZEST

Apricot Glaze

¾ CUP APRICOT PRESERVES
2 TABLESPOONS WATER

½ CUP HEAVY WHIPPING CREAM
2 TABLESPOONS TOASTED SLICED ALMONDS

Preparing the Rich Génoise. Melt the butter over low heat. Do not allow it to sizzle or take on any color. Leave it over the lowest heat possible so that it bubbles up slightly and the water in the butter evaporates. Remove from the heat and cool.

Combine and warm the eggs, yolks, salt and sugar and whip on high speed until cool and increased in volume. Sift together the flour and cornstarch and fold into the egg mixture. Remove a cup of the batter to a bowl, stir in the butter, then fold into the batter. Pour the batter into a buttered and paper-lined 9-inch springform pan and bake at 350°F for about 30 minutes. Immediately remove from the pan and cool on a rack.

Preparing the Apple Puree. Peel, core and slice the apples into a saucepan. Add sugar and water and cook over medium heat until the apples are reduced to a very thick puree, stirring often. Process apples in a food processor and cool.

Preparing the Apple Bavarian Cream. Pour the Calvados and lemon juice into a small bowl and sprinkle the gelatin on the surface to soften. Place over simmering water, stirring, until the gelatin is clear. Remove the bowl from the water and whisk in ½ cup of the Apple Puree. Whisk the gelatin mixture into the remaining puree. Whip the cream until it holds its shape and fold into the apple mixture.

Preparing the Apple Brandy Syrup. Bring the sugar and water to a boil over medium heat. Cool and add the vanilla and the Calvados.

Preparing the Apple Slices Cooked in White Wine. Peel, core and slice the apples as for a tart, keeping the halves intact. Place the apple halves in a pan that will just hold them and sprinkle with the sugar. Add white wine to cover and the lemon zest; cook over medium heat until they begin to simmer. Simmer for 5 minutes. Lift the apples out of the syrup and cool on a plate.

Preparing the Apricot Glaze. Combine the preserves and water in a small saucepan and bring to a boil, stirring occasionally. Strain into another pan and boil until the glaze coats the back of a spoon.

Assembling. Slice the Génoise and make two layers. Place one layer in the bottom of a 10-inch springform pan. Brush the layer with half the syrup. Pour half the Bavarian cream over the layer. Repeat with the other layer, syrup and Bavarian cream. Chill to set.

Finishing. Unmold and arrange the apple slices, overlapping, at the outer edge. Brush with the glaze. Whip the cream until it holds its shape. Pipe rosettes of the cream with a star tube to fill in the center. Strew the rosettes with the toasted sliced almonds.

Holding. Keep the Délice refrigerated, loosely covered with aluminum foil (not touching the whipped cream), up to 8 hours before serving. To prepare a day in advance, keep it covered with plastic wrap in the refrigerator, but only decorate it on the day it is to be served.

Yield. About 10 to 12 portions

ONE-LAYER MOLDED CAKES

Everyone who works with pastry nowadays owes a great debt of gratitude to Yves Thuries, author of the magnificent *Livre de Recettes d'un Compagnon de Tour de France,* a wonderful set of books that records both classic and modern French desserts. It was here that I first saw one-layer cakes—molded cakes composed of one thin layer of biscuit or Génoise, covered with a rich filling. Simple to prepare, these desserts manage to remain light because their richness is not in excessive quantity.

Use this technique with a plain or chocolate Génoise layer or a nut sponge, though you will need only half the layer; freeze the remainder for another dessert of this type to be made later or for a Trifle, pages 293–294.

PEAR AND CHOCOLATE CAKE

A good fall dessert in which the poached pears complement the texture of the filling perfectly.

Chocolate Sponge Disk
¼ CUP CAKE FLOUR, ABOUT 1 OUNCE
1½ TABLESPOONS COCOA POWDER, ABOUT
    ¼ OUNCE
2 EGGS, SEPARATED
½ TEASPOON VANILLA EXTRACT
¼ CUP SUGAR, ABOUT 2 OUNCES
PINCH SALT

Pears Poached in Vanilla Syrup
2½ POUNDS RIPE PEARS, ABOUT 5
    BARTLETT OR COMICE
1 CUP SUGAR, ABOUT 7 ½ OUNCES
2 TABLESPOONS LEMON JUICE
½ VANILLA BEAN

Chocolate Chantilly
1½ CUPS HEAVY WHIPPING CREAM
1 POUND SEMISWEET CHOCOLATE, FINELY
    CUT

Pear Syrup
⅓ CUP POACHING SYRUP
3 TABLESPOONS PEAR WILLIAMS OR PEAR
    LIQUEUR

Preparing the Chocolate Biscuit. Sift cake flour and cocoa powder together and set aside. Whisk the yolks then whisk in the vanilla and half of the sugar until light and aerated. Whip the whites and salt on medium speed until white and opaque. Increase the speed and add the remaining sugar until the whites hold a firm peak. Fold the yolks into the whites and sift the cake flour/cocoa powder over the batter and fold it in.

Using a plain tube with a 1½-inch opening, pipe out the batter onto paper-lined baking pan, forming an 8-inch disk. Bake at 350°F 10 to 15 minutes. Slide paper to rack to cool.

Preparing the Pears Poached in Vanilla Syrup. Place ice, water and lemon juice in a large pan. Peel, halve and core the pears and immediately plunge into the water. Drain away all but enough water to cover the pears and add the sugar and vanilla bean. Cover with a disk of paper with a hole in the center. Bring to a boil over medium heat. Simmer the pears until tender. Drain and cool.

Preparing the Pear Syrup. Combine the syrup and the liqueur.

Preparing the Chocolate Chantilly. Heat ½ cup of the cream, remove from the heat, add the chocolate, let stand 2 minutes and whisk smooth. Strain into a bowl and cool. Whip the remaining cream and quickly fold into the chocolate mixture.

Assembling. Trim the biscuit layer to an even 8-inch diameter. Place it in the bottom of a 9-inch springform. Moisten with the syrup. Drain the pear halves reserving one for a decoration. Thinly slice and arrange on the biscuit, leaving a 1-inch margin. Pour the chocolate cream over the pears and smooth it to cover them. Wrap and chill.

Run a thin knife around the inside of the springform and release the spring. Smooth the sides and decorate with the remaining pear half.

Holding. Keep the cake refrigerated, loosely covered with plastic wrap, up to 8 hours before serving. To prepare a day in advance, keep it covered with plastic wrap in the refrigerator, but only unmold on the day it is to be served.

Yield. About 12 portions

CRANBERRY MIROIR

A light and tangy dessert perfect for the finale of a rich holiday meal, the Cranberry Miroir is simple to prepare and beautiful to behold.

Sponge Disk
2 EGGS
1/4 CUP SUGAR, ABOUT 1 3/4 OUNCES
PINCH SALT
6 TABLESPOONS CAKE FLOUR, ABOUT 1 1/2 OUNCES

Cranberry Puree
2 12-OUNCE BAGS CRANBERRIES
1 CUP SUGAR, ABOUT 7 1/2 OUNCES
1/3 CUP WATER

Orange Syrup
1/4 CUP WATER
1/4 CUP SUGAR, ABOUT 1 3/4 OUNCES
2 TABLESPOONS ORANGE LIQUEUR

Cranberry Bavarian Cream
2 CUPS CRANBERRY PUREE
1 TABLESPOON GRATED ORANGE ZEST
1/3 CUP ORANGE JUICE
1 ENVELOPE UNFLAVORED GELATIN, ABOUT 2 1/2 TEASPOONS
2 CUPS HEAVY WHIPPING CREAM

Cranberry Glaze
1/3 CUP CRANBERRY PUREE
1/2 CUP CURRANT JELLY
2 TABLESPOONS WATER
1 ENVELOPE UNFLAVORED GELATIN, ABOUT 2 1/2 TEASPOONS

Sugared Pecans
1 CUP PECAN HALVES, ABOUT 4 OUNCES
1 TABLESPOON EGG WHITE
1/2 CUP SUGAR, ABOUT 3 3/4 OUNCES

Preparing the Cranberry Puree. Rinse and pick over the cranberries and combine with the sugar and water in a large saucepan. Bring to a boil over medium heat, lower heat and simmer until slightly reduced, about 5 to 10 minutes. Puree, strain and chill.

Preparing the Sponge Disk. Whisk the yolks with half the sugar until very light and aerated. Whip the whites and salt on medium speed until white and opaque. Increase the speed and add the remaining sugar until the whites hold a firm peak. Fold the yolks into the whites, then sift over and fold in the cake flour. Pipe the batter with a 1/2-inch plain tube to make an 8-inch disk on a paper-lined baking pan. Bake the layer at 350°F about 10–15 minutes. Slide the paper to a rack to cool.

Preparing the Syrup. Bring the sugar and water to a boil. Cool and stir in the orange liqueur.

Preparing the Sugared Pecans. Place the pecan halves in a small roasting pan. Coat well with the egg white, then toss in the sugar. Bake at 325°F, stirring every 5 minutes, until they are golden and dry, about 30 minutes. Cool.

Preparing the Cranberry Bavarian Cream. Place the Cranberry Puree in a large bowl and stir in the grated zest. Place the orange juice in a small bowl and sprinkle the gelatin on the surface to soften. Place over simmering water to melt. Whisk some of the Cranberry Puree into the gelatin mixture, then whisk the gelatin into the remaining puree. Whip the cream until it holds its shape and fold into puree.

Assembling. Trim the Biscuit layer to an even 8-inch diameter and place in the bottom of a 9-inch springform pan. Moisten it well with the orange syrup. Pour the Cranberry Bavarian over and smooth the top. Chill to set.

Preparing the Glaze. Soak the gelatin in the water. Combine the Cranberry Puree and the jelly and bring to a boil. Add the gelatin and return to a boil. Pass through a very fine strainer and cool at room temperature. Pour the cooled glaze through a strainer onto the Bavarian cream and tilt to cover the surface. Chill to set.

Finishing. Insert a small, sharp knife between the Bavarian cream and the mold and loosen it. Lift off the side of the mold. Decorate with the cooled Sugared Pecans.

Holding. Keep the Miroir refrigerated, loosely covered with aluminum foil (not touching the glaze), up to 8 hours before serving. To prepare a day in advance, keep it covered with plastic wrap in the refrigerator, but only glaze it on the day it is to be served.

Yield. About 12 portions

NOISETTE

French for "hazelnut," the Noisette captures the essence of fragrant, buttery hazelnuts. The richness of the hazelnut filling is tempered by the crunch of the crushed, toasted hazelnuts used to decorate it.

Sponge Disk

2 EGGS, SEPARATED
¼ CUP SUGAR, ABOUT 1¾ OUNCES
PINCH SALT
1 TEASPOON VANILLA EXTRACT
6 TABLESPOONS CAKE FLOUR, ABOUT 1½ OUNCES

Praliné Mousse

¾ CUP PRALINE PASTE (PAGES 48–49)
1½ STICKS BUTTER, 6 OUNCES, SOFTENED
4 EGG WHITES, ½ CUP
¾ CUP SUGAR, ABOUT 5½ OUNCES

Cognac Syrup

¼ CUP WATER
2 TABLESPOONS SUGAR, ABOUT 1 OUNCE
2 TABLESPOONS COGNAC

1 CUP TOASTED, BLANCHED, CHOPPED HAZELNUTS, ABOUT 4 OUNCES

Preparing the Sponge Disk. Whisk the yolks, then whisk in half the sugar until light and aerated. Whip the egg whites and salt on medium speed until white and opaque. Increase the speed and whip in the remaining sugar. Continue whipping until the whites hold a firm peak. Fold the yolks into the whites, then fold in the cake flour in three or four additions.

Using a pastry bag with a ½-inch plain tube, pipe one 8-inch circle onto paper-lined pans. Bake at 350°F about 15 minutes. Remove from the pans to a rack to cool.

Preparing the Cognac Syrup. Bring sugar and water to boil. Cool and add the cognac.

Preparing the Mousse. Beat the Praline Paste on medium speed to soften. Beat in the butter and continue beating until smooth. Set aside.

Combine and warm the egg whites and sugar until the whites are hot and sugar dissolves. Whip until cool and increased in volume. Fold into the praline mixture.

Assembling. Trim the biscuit layer to an even 8-inch diameter. Place it in the bottom of a 9-inch springform pan. Moisten the layer with the syrup. Spread the mousse over the biscuit, smoothing the top. Chill.

Finishing. Insert a thin knife around the inside of the springform and loosen. Remove the side. Decorate the outside with the hazelnuts.

Holding. Keep the dessert refrigerated up to 1 day.

Yield. About 8 to 10 portions

COFFEE ALMOND CAKE

Another light, elegant one-layer cake, with contrasting flavors and textures.

Sponge Disk

2 EGGS, SEPARATED
¼ CUP SUGAR, ABOUT 1¾ OUNCES
PINCH SALT
1 TEASPOON VANILLA EXTRACT
6 TABLESPOONS CAKE FLOUR, ABOUT 1½ OUNCES

Coffee Syrup

2 TABLESPOONS SUGAR, ABOUT 1 OUNCE
¼ CUP COFFEE
2 TABLESPOONS BRANDY OR DARK RUM

Coffee Mousse

4 EGG YOLKS
⅓ CUP HOT COFFEE
3 TABLESPOONS INSTANT ESPRESSO
⅓ CUP SUGAR, ABOUT 2½ OUNCES
⅓ CUP BRANDY OR DARK RUM
1½ ENVELOPES UNFLAVORED GELATIN, ABOUT 1 TABLESPOON PLUS 1 TEASPOON
1½ CUPS HEAVY WHIPPING CREAM

Sugared Almonds

1 CUP SLICED ALMONDS, ABOUT 3 OUNCES
1 TABLESPOON EGG WHITE
½ CUP SUGAR, ABOUT 3¾ OUNCES

Preparing the Biscuit Base. Whisk the yolks, then whisk in half the sugar until light and aerated. Whip the egg whites and salt on medium speed until white and opaque. Increase the speed and whip in the remaining sugar. Continue whipping until the whites hold a firm peak. Fold the yolks into the whites, then fold in the cake flour in three or four additions.

Using a pastry bag with a ½-inch plain tube, pipe one 8-inch circle onto paper-lined pans. Bake at 350°F about 15 minutes. Remove from the pan to a rack to cool.

Preparing the Coffee Syrup. Stir the sugar into the hot coffee and dissolve it. Cool and add the brandy.

Preparing the Mousse. Combine the coffee, yolks and sugar. Place the bowl over simmering water and beat constantly until the mixture thickens. Beat until cool. Meanwhile, soften the gelatin in the brandy and dissolve it over hot water. When the coffee mixture is cool, beat about 1 cup of it into the dissolved gelatin, then beat the gelatin mixture into the remaining coffee mixture. Whip the cream until it holds its shape and fold into the coffee mixture.

Assembling. Trim the biscuit layer to an even 8-inch diameter. Place it in the bottom of a 9-inch springform pan and moisten with the syrup. Pour the mousse over and smooth it. Chill to set.

Preparing the Sugared Almonds. Place the sliced almonds in a small roasting pan. Coat well with the egg white, then toss in the sugar. Bake at 325°F for about 20 to 30 minutes, stirring them frequently. Cool the almonds.

Finishing. Run a thin, sharp knife around the inside of the springform. Remove the sides. Decorate the top of the dessert with sugared almonds.

Holding. Keep the dessert refrigerated up to 1 day.

Yield. About 8 to 10 portions

CHOCOLATE CHANTILLY

Perhaps the simplest fancy chocolate dessert, the Chocolate Chantilly has a delicate, sophisticated flavor. Dress it up with some Chocolate Plastic ruffles and ribbons, pages 308–310, if you have time.

Sponge Disk
2 EGGS, SEPARATED
¼ CUP SUGAR, ABOUT 1¾ OUNCES
PINCH SALT
1 TEASPOON VANILLA EXTRACT
6 TABLESPOONS CAKE FLOUR, ABOUT 1½ OUNCES

Rum Syrup
2 TABLESPOONS SUGAR, ABOUT 1 OUNCE
¼ CUP WATER
2 TABLESPOONS DARK RUM

Chocolate Chantilly
1½ CUPS HEAVY WHIPPING CREAM
1 POUND SEMISWEET CHOCOLATE, FINELY CUT

1 CUP CHOCOLATE SHAVINGS
CONFECTIONERS' SUGAR

Preparing the Sponge. Whisk the yolks, then whisk in half the sugar until light and aerated. Whip the egg whites and salt on medium speed until white and opaque. Increase the speed and whip in the remaining sugar. Continue whipping until the whites hold a firm peak. Fold the yolks into the whites, then fold in the cake flour in three or four additions.

Using a pastry bag with a ½-inch plain tube, pipe one 8-inch circle onto paper-lined pans. Bake at 350°F about 15 minutes. Remove from the pans to a rack to cool.

Preparing the Rum Syrup. Bring sugar and water to a boil. Cool and add the rum.

Preparing the Chocolate Chantilly. Heat ½ cup of the cream, remove from heat, add the chocolate and whisk smooth. Strain into a bowl and cool. Whip the remaining cream and quickly fold into the chocolate mixture.

Assembling. Trim the sponge disk to an even 8-inch diameter. Place it in the bottom of a 9-inch springform pan and moisten with the syrup. Spread the Chocolate Chantilly over the disk, smoothing the top. Chill.

Finishing. Run a thin sharp knife around the inside of the springform and remove the sides. Decorate the outside of the dessert with fine chocolate shavings. Dust lightly with confectioners' sugar.

Holding. Keep the dessert refrigerated up to 1 day.

Yield. About 8 to 10 portions

CHOCOLATE MOUSSE CAKE

Unlike the other one- and two-layer molded cakes in this chapter, this cake needs to be finished after unmolding.

Use this as a base recipe with any of the cake layer and mousse recipes.

Chocolate Génoise

4 EGGS
PINCH SALT
2/3 CUP SUGAR, ABOUT 5 OUNCES
1/3 CUP CAKE FLOUR, ABOUT 1 1/2 OUNCES
1/3 CUP CORNSTARCH, ABOUT 1 1/2 OUNCES
3 TABLESPOONS COCOA POWDER, ABOUT 1/2 OUNCE
2 PINCHES BAKING SODA

Moistening Syrup

1/2 CUP WATER
1/4 CUP SUGAR, ABOUT 2 1/2 OUNCES
3 TABLESPOONS LIQUEUR OR STRONG COFFEE

Chocolate Mousse

12 OUNCES SEMISWEET CHOCOLATE, FINELY CUT
1/2 CUP BOILING WATER OR HOT COFFEE
6 EGG YOLKS

1/3 CUP GRANULATED SUGAR, ABOUT 2 1/2 OUNCES
1/3 CUP LIQUEUR OR STRONG COFFEE
1 ENVELOPE UNFLAVORED GELATIN, ABOUT 2 1/2 TEASPOONS
1/4 CUP WATER
2 CUPS HEAVY WHIPPING CREAM

1 CUP HEAVY WHIPPING CREAM
1 CUP CHOCOLATE SHAVINGS

Preparing the Chocolate Génoise. Combine and warm the eggs, salt and the sugar and whip on high speed until cool and increased in volume. Sift the remaining Génoise ingredients and fold into the egg foam in three or four additions. Pour the batter onto a buttered and paper-lined 9-inch springform pan and tilt the pan so that the batter reaches to the top all around. Bake at 350°F about 30 minutes. Unmold and cool on paper on a rack.

Preparing the Syrup. Bring the water and sugar to a boil. Cool and stir in the liqueur or coffee.

Preparing the Chocolate Mousse. Combine the chocolate with the water or coffee over hot water and stir occasionally to melt the chocolate. Remove from the water and cool. Combine and warm the yolks, sugar and liqueur or coffee. Whisk constantly until the mixture thickens. Beat on medium speed about 5 minutes, until cooled and thick. Sprinkle the gelatin on the water in a small bowl and allow to stand 2 minutes to soften. Place in a pan of gently simmering water to melt.

Remove the yolk mixture from the mixer and whisk in the dissolved gelatin. Whisk in the cooled chocolate mixture. Whip the cream until it holds a soft peak and fold into the chocolate mixture.

Assembling. Cut the Génoise layer horizontally into three thin layers. Place one layer in the bottom of a 9-inch springform pan and moisten it with a third of the syrup. Pour half the mousse on the layer. Repeat with the second layer, syrup and remaining mousse. End with the top layer and moisten with the remaining syrup. Wrap the pan in plastic and refrigerate the dessert at least 6 hours to set the mousse. May be prepared up to 3 days in advance up to this point.

Finishing. Whip the cream until it holds a firm peak. Using a cookie cutter or a melon ball scoop, make the chocolate shavings by dragging the tool across the surface of the chocolate. Run a small, sharp knife around the inside of the pan. Remove the side of the pan and lift it off. Spread the outside of the dessert with the whipped cream, using an offset spatula. Press the chocolate shavings against the side of the dessert, using a clean spatula. Pipe the remaining whipped cream in a series of rosettes, using a pastry bag fitted with a medium size star tube, around the top border of the dessert. Sprinkle some chocolate shavings in the center of the top and a pinch on each rosette.

Holding. Keep the finished dessert refrigerated, loosely covered, up to 6 hours before serving.

Yield. About 10 to 12 portions

STRAWBERRY TRIFLE

The Trifle is the perfect vehicle for using cake layer trimmings and those few extra leftover sponge fingers. I keep the trimmings in a tightly closed plastic bag in the freezer, for no longer than a month or so, and make a Trifle as soon as the trimmings accumulate to a sufficient quantity.

The Trifle may be made completely in advance (even the day before), tightly covered with plastic wrap and refrigerated. Finish the top of the Trifle with the whipped cream, strawberries and sliced almonds several hours before serving.

Feel free to vary any of the ingredients: Substitute other berries or fruit; a different wine; or a different flavor preserves—a Trifle, as its name indicates, is not a solemn dessert.

ONE 9- OR 10-INCH GÉNOISE LAYER OR ABOUT 4 CUPS FRESH OR FROZEN GÉNOISE TRIMMINGS, MIXED WITH LEFTOVER SPONGE FINGERS, IF DESIRED

Pastry Cream
2 CUPS MILK
2/3 CUP SUGAR, ABOUT 5 OUNCES
1/4 CUP CORNSTARCH, ABOUT 1 OUNCE
6 EGG YOLKS
2 TABLESPOONS BUTTER, 1 OUNCE
2 TEASPOONS VANILLA EXTRACT
2 TABLESPOONS KIRSCH, OTHER *EAU DE VIE,* OR LIQUEUR

Whipped Cream
1 1/2 CUPS HEAVY WHIPPING CREAM
2 TABLESPOONS SUGAR, ABOUT 1 OUNCE
1 TEASPOON VANILLA EXTRACT

2 PINTS FRESH STRAWBERRIES, ABOUT 4 CUPS
3/4 CUP SWEET SHERRY, OR OTHER SWEET FORTIFIED WINE, SUCH AS MADEIRA OR MARSALA

¾ CUP TOASTED, SLICED ALMONDS, ABOUT
  2¼ OUNCES
⅔ CUP STRAWBERRY PRESERVES

Preparing the Cake Layer. Cut the cooled Génoise layer into vertical slices, about ¼ inch thick. Set aside, covered, at room temperature. If using frozen scraps, unwrap and place on a paper-lined baking pan or cookie sheet to defrost, covered, at room temperature.

Preparing the Pastry Cream. Bring 1½ cups of the milk and the sugar to a boil in a 2-quart saucepan. Meanwhile whisk together the remaining milk and the cornstarch in a 2-quart bowl until smooth. Whisk in the yolks. Whisk one third of the boiling milk into the yolk mixture. Return the remaining milk to a boil and whisk in the tempered yolk mixture. Whisk constantly until the pastry cream thickens and returns to a boil. Beat in the butter. Pour the Pastry Cream into a bowl and press plastic wrap against the surface; refrigerate until cold.

Whipping the Cream. Combine the cream with the sugar and whip it on medium speed until it holds its shape, but is not too stiff. Cover and refrigerate.

Preparing the Strawberries. Reserve the six best-looking strawberries in the refrigerator to serve as a decoration. Rinse, hull and slice the remaining strawberries into a bowl. Sprinkle with the Kirsch, cover and refrigerate.

Preparing the filling. Remove the Pastry Cream from the refrigerator and gently stir in the vanilla and Kirsch. Fold in about one third of the whipped cream.

Assembling. Make a layer of the cake slices or trimmings in the bottom of a 2- to 3-quart glass bowl. Sprinkle with one quarter of the sherry and the sliced almonds and one third of the preserves and strawberries; spread with one third of the filling. Make two more layers in the same manner. Top with a last layer of cake, then sprinkle with the remaining sherry. Spread the top with the remaining whipped cream (check that it has not liquefied; rewhip if necessary). Rinse the reserved strawberries and halve them, leaving the hull intact and cutting through it. Arrange, cutside up, around the inside edge of the bowl, on the Trifle. Scatter the remaining sliced almonds in the center.

Holding. Loosely cover with plastic wrap and refrigerate several hours. For longer advance preparation, make the Trifle the day before, cover tightly with plastic and refrigerate. Finish with the whipped cream, strawberries and almonds several hours before serving.

Yield. About 12 portions

11

DECORATING

More excesses have been committed in the name of cake decorating than in any other branch of the culinary arts. "Decorated" cakes are often heavily burdened with butter-cream ornaments in deep, vibrant colors. Sometimes plastic effigies of cartoon characters or seasonal figures like Santas and bunnies are added.

Most of these well-meaning attempts at making desserts more appealing stem from the traditions of food presentation developed in the early nineteenth century. In the days of Carême, banquets for the great households—imperial, royal and noble—where he was employed took the form of elaborately decorated buffets, where all the food was presented at one time. Even the simplest dishes were placed atop immense pediments made from tallow or sugar, sculpted and finished in elaborate borders and decorations that vied in beauty with the work of gold- and silversmiths. Cakes in the shape of ruined temples, Chinese pagodas and rustic pavilions were the rule at these gatherings and the habit persisted well into the twentieth century.

Although Escoffier's great words of advice, *"faites simple"* (do it simply), represented a great streamlining and simplification of these presentations about ninety years ago, it must be remembered that Escoffier himself was the author of a volume entitled *Les Fleurs en Cire* (Wax Flowers). These flowers were meant to be used as decorations of buffet food, not necessarily confined to desserts.

The decorating tradition is one that is strongly allied to the presentation of desserts. Delicate, frivolous creations such as birthday and wedding cakes are appropriate backgrounds for decorations as ephemeral as their contents. But to burden a delicate dessert with loud colors and heavy ornament all but defeats the purpose of decorating any food, that is, to make its appearance as appetizing as its eventual flavor.

The types of decorations presented here are simple in both appearance and execution. In working with decorations for desserts keep the following principles in mind:

1. *Neatness and precision count.* Practice the decoration before executing it on the dessert.

A simply finished, neat-looking dessert is infinitely more appetizing than one which is covered with poorly executed, more elaborate decorations.

2. *Practice.* No one has yet been born with an innate ability to make marzipan flowers or chocolate ribbons. These techniques have taken time to perfect in all who can do them. It is much better to hold off on these more elaborate effects until they have been perfected with a bit of practice. And keep in mind that none of these techniques is so difficult as to be impossible to master—or no one would be able to do them.

3. *Strive for simplicity and subtlety more than striking effects.* The cake that has a perfectly executed border of minute shells or stars or a smooth, even covering of marzipan or Chocolate Plastic is infinitely more desirable than one which is covered with large mounds of confusedly piped buttercream or an entire garden's worth of marzipan or chocolate flowers. A single flower is a far more striking decoration than a dozen.

4. *Use restraint in coloring.* Although most professional decorators use paste colors, I prefer the liquid ones. More easily obtained, the liquid colors are not as strong and leave a greater margin for error. Nothing can be done to remedy the overuse of paste color short of starting over with a fresh batch of marzipan and adding the too-deeply-colored batch to it.

Although the liquid colors do not come in the range of shades that the paste colors do, it is easier to achieve a pale, delicate shade with them. When using color, start with *very* little and add more, drop-by-drop, to make a very pale pastel shade. Although dark or bright colors may be appropriate in some types of specialty work (making cakes in the shape of everything from golf courses and vacation homes to the heads of movie stars is a thriving, if not widespread, business) it is not within the realm of this book to approach that subject.

The techniques presented in the following pages cover the use of the pastry bag and different shaped tips for piping borders and other decorations from whipped cream, meringue, buttercream and Ganache. The use of the cornet for piping liquid chocolate is also illustrated.

There is also a whole range of "solid" decorations made from marzipan, chocolate and Chocolate Plastic. These can be used to cover an entire dessert such as a layer cake or roulade, or merely to fashion small decorations such as leaves and flowers to accent a more simply presented one.

Delicacy and restraint are the guiding principles of good decorating.

TECHNIQUES FOR PIPED DECORATIONS

The Pastry Bag

Using a pastry bag and tubes or tips in conjunction with it is one of the easiest ways to decorate a dessert. Whether piping a simple row of rosettes of whipped cream on an unmolded ring of Bavarian cream or finishing the top border of a layer cake with a row of delicate shells, the use of a bag and tubes accomplishes this work neatly and symmetrically.

Bear the following considerations in mind when using a pastry bag:

1. *Plastic-coated canvas bags are the best for all-purpose decorating use.*

2. *For piping large quantities of whipped cream or batter, a large bag, 14 or 16 inches long, is the most efficient.* For piping small quantities of buttercream or Ganache, choose smaller bags, 8 or 10 inches long.

3. *For piping whipped cream or meringue always choose a tube with a fairly large opening—approximately ⅜ to ½ inch.* Forcing whipped cream through too small a tube has the same effect as overwhipping it and will cause water to drain from it after it has been piped on the dessert. Piping meringue with too small a tube will force air out of it and cause the meringue to fall and liquefy.

When using a star tube for whipped cream or meringue, choose one that has five or six large triangular teeth rather than a tube with small, fine teeth. The fine teeth are too small to make a lasting imprint; the design will be somewhat blurred.

4. *Conversely, for buttercream or Ganache, either type of star tube may be used, the finer teeth making a good impression in the greater density of these two creams.*

5. *Simple geometric designs made with a plain tube also can be very effective.* They give a dessert a more tailored, stark appearance as opposed to the frilliness of decorations with the star tubes.

6. *Always mark the cake top where the designs are to fall.* If the design is to cover a large area, such as the entire top border of the cake, proceed slowly so that the shells, rosettes, etc., are all the same size.

7. *When piping a border of buttercream or Ganache, by all means practice it first.* Unless the creams are really abused, they can stand being piped once or twice before being applied to the cake. Practice the design on a clean piece of parchment paper or wax paper with an outline the same size as the cake top drawn on it. Or practice on a clean plate or the back of a cake pan. The cream can then be scraped off easily with a spatula and applied to the cake.

8. *Only fill the pastry bag by a third at the most, to have the best control in piping small designs.* A bag that is too full is unwieldy and brings the controlling hand too far from the design to be able to exert the best movement.

9. *Learn to pipe using a steady rhythm,* so that the cadence from one squeeze to the next takes over and helps each design which flows from the bag to be uniform.

10. *Remove the tube from bag and rinse both the tube and bag in hot water immediately after each use.* Dry the tube—tin plated tubes that begin to wear can rust if not dried immediately. Avoid rancid bags by washing them with kitchen laundry in the washing machine with detergent and bleach. Air dry bags as opposed to using the dryer which might melt the plastic coating.

11. *Piping requires practice.* Make up a batch of buttercream and practice the designs in the following samplers. Practicing with the buttercream by piping it on a clean surface, such as parchment paper, and scraping it up and repiping it several times, will not render it unusable in a dessert later on.

The Cornet

The cornet, or paper cone, was one of the original methods of decorating. Since the use of the pastry bag and tubes dates from only the last quarter of the nineteenth century, previous to that time most decorating was accomplished with the cornet.

Mostly used now for fine line piping, the opening of the cornet can also be trimmed in different ways to pipe leaves and other shapes. Although this can be a quick way to achieve different effects with the same cornet, it is simpler and more reliable to use the pastry bag and tubes for this.

Parchment paper is the best material for cornets. In an emergency I have used waxed paper and even typing paper, but the parchment paper gives the best results.

There are a couple of different methods for making the cones. The following illustrations outline the method that I find most efficient.

Observe these rules when using the cornet for best results:

1. *Make sure that the end of the cornet is completely closed before filling it.* Any opening will expand during piping. If the end is closed, it is easier to cut an opening of the desired size and it will remain constant during piping.

2. *Do not overfill the cornet.* A 3- to 4-inch cornet holds about a teaspoon or two of chocolate. Since the line piped is so fine, the material goes a long way.

3. *Fold and close the wide end of the cornet very tightly.* If the cornet is not overfilled and the wide end is well closed, you will avoid having the material flow out both ends at the same time.

4. *A steady, even pressure at the top of the cornet makes an even line that holds without breaking.*

5. *Moving with a flowing as opposed to abrupt gesture keeps the line even and prevents it from breaking.*

6. *Make curves and loops in the piped line by slowing down the flow as opposed to moving the cornet in a different direction.* The unbroken flow of the icing or chocolate will curve and loop automatically when the flow is slowed down.

Different Tubes and Decorations They Make

1. SMALL PLAIN TUBE

Dots:

Dots of graduated sizes:

Interlocking curves:

2. LARGE PLAIN TUBE
Large dots:

Geometric designs:

3. SMALL STAR TUBE, NARROW TEETH
Shell border:

Alternating shell border:

Rosettes:

4. SMALL STAR TUBE, WIDE TEETH
Shell border:

Alternating shell border:

Rosettes:

5. ST.-HONORÉ TUBE

Alternating egg shapes:

MARZIPAN

Probably medieval in origin, marzipan is made from almonds and sugar worked to a paste. In Europe, marzipan is often made in a pastry shop from freshly blanched almonds combined with sugar cooked to the soft ball stage—really a combination of fondant and almonds—and crushed through granite rollers until very smooth. Unfortunately the blade in a food processor or blender does not accomplish the same degree of fineness and would leave the mixture rather gritty. For this reason marzipan in the United States is usually made from commercially prepared almond paste along with confectioners' sugar and corn syrup. The extra sugar dries out the very moist almond paste and also lightens its color. The corn syrup then returns the marzipan to a workable consistency. It can be rolled to cover a cake or be made into flowers and leaves or decorative shapes.

Mixing marzipan is a gradual process; add the corn syrup carefully, since too much can over moisten and make it soft and sticky, rendering it useless. If this happens, knead more confectioners' sugar into the marzipan by hand.

Sometimes marzipan is tinted with food coloring. Professional decorators use paste colors. Liquid colors are more practical for home use since they are not as strong and leave a greater margin for error in coloring the marzipan.

½ POUND ALMOND PASTE, 1 SMALL CAN

2 CUPS CONFECTIONERS' SUGAR, ABOUT 8½ OUNCES

3 TO 5 TABLESPOONS LIGHT CORN SYRUP

Mixing the Marzipan in a Heavy-Duty Mixer

Break the almond paste into 1-inch pieces and place in the bowl of a heavy-duty electric mixer. Sift the confectioners' sugar to remove any lumps, add half and mix with the paddle on lowest speed until the mixture is dry and powdery. Add the remaining sugar slowly, continuing to mix on lowest speed. Add half the corn syrup and continue mixing about 2 minutes.

Testing the Moistening. Stop the mixer and remove a small handful of the mixture. Attempt to knead it smooth. If dry and crumbly, return the sample to the mixer, add half the remaining corn syrup, mix 2 minutes and test again.

Kneading the Marzipan. When sufficiently moistened, the marzipan will still appear dry and crumbly in the mixer. A heavy-duty home mixer does not have sufficient strength to mix the ingredients to a smooth dough. Pour the mixture out on a clean, smooth work

store in a plastic bag at room temperature or in the freezer. If you freeze it, defrost at room temperature and allow to warm to room temperature before working with it.

Yield. About 18 ounces

Mixing the Marzipan in the Food Processor

Cut the almond paste into 1-inch pieces, and combine with all the confectioners' sugar and half the corn syrup in the bowl of a food processor fitted with the steel blade. Pulse the machine on and off for 2 seconds at a time, about ten or twelve times. Test the consistency, as above. Add more corn syrup, as necessary, until the marzipan kneads smooth easily, pulsing the processor at 2-second intervals, three or four times. Knead and wrap as above.

Be careful not to overmix the marzipan or it will be oily. The food processor subjects the ingredients to greater friction than the mixer, and the almond paste can exude the oil more easily.

Coloring the Marzipan

For all one color, add a drop of coloring to the crumbly mixture as it comes from the mixer or processor so the coloring kneads in evenly. Or, add coloring to the kneaded marzipan, just before using. Liquid food coloring works best since it does not color the marzipan too vividly. Be careful not to add too much color; use the tiniest drop possible. The safest way is to squeeze a drop of color onto a small plate

surface and knead smooth. Do this in batches, keeping the unkneaded marzipan covered with a towel to prevent it from drying. As the marzipan is kneaded, cover the kneaded pieces with a towel. Finally, knead the entire mass together and shape into a thick cylinder.

Holding. Double-wrap in plastic wrap and

and use a toothpick to transfer it, a little at a time, as needed to achieve the desired shade.

Chocolate Flavored Marzipan

Knead ¼ CUP OF COCOA POWDER, sifted through a very fine strainer, into the marzipan as it comes from the mixer or into the kneaded marzipan. If coloring only part of a batch, use less cocoa powder proportionately. If the marzipan becomes dry, knead in a drop or two of water. One of my favorite decorating techniques uses chocolate marzipan variegated with plain for marbelized leaves and flowers.

Covering a Cake with Marzipan

One batch of marzipan will cover a 10-inch cake easily. Spread the surface of the cake with buttercream, Ganache or another smooth frosting to make the marzipan adhere. Whipped cream is not suitable, since it would soak into the marzipan and cause it to disintegrate. Reduced apricot or raspberry glaze is fine if brushed on the cake while hot and allowed to cool.

Unwrap the marzipan, plain or colored, and knead smooth. Shape into a disk, about 1 inch thick. Lightly dust a smooth, clean work surface and the marzipan with confectioners' sugar. Roll the marzipan back and forth with a rolling pin, without rolling over the ends. Revolve the disk about 45 degrees and roll again. Continuing to move the marzipan every time you roll over it will prevent it from sticking to the surface and the rolling pin. Dust very lightly with cornstarch when nec-

essary. Avoid using too much cornstarch or its taste will be apparent and the marzipan's surface will be dry and cracked.

For a 9- or 10-inch cake, roll the marzipan to a disk, approximately 14 to 16 inches in diameter. Position the rolling pin at the edge of the disk closest to you and gently roll the marzipan on the rolling pin, without pressing, or the marzipan will stick to itself. Position the rolling pin on the edge of the cake farthest from you, allow the marzipan to unroll so that about ½ inch is on the work surface under the cake, and quickly unroll the marzipan over the cake. Smooth the top of the cake by pressing gently with the palm of the hand, then gently press the marzipan against the side of the cake, so that there are *no* creases. Trim away the excess at the bottom and re-

serve it for finishing the edge. Knead the scraps back together and roll with the palms of both hands into a rope as long as the circumference of the cake. Place the cake on a platter, carefully lift the rope of marzipan and position it at the bottom edge of the cake. Overlap the ends where they meet and make

a diagonal cut with a small knife. Remove the excess and press the ends together. Press a series of diagonal lines in the rope with the back of a small knife.

Marzipan Leaves

Knead a drop of green color into one eighth a batch of marzipan. Roll the marzipan into a rope about 12 inches long. Flatten the rope with the palm of the hand and smooth it with the bowl of a spoon: Run the bowl of the spoon back and forth in the length of the marzipan, pressing gently, until the marzipan is about $3/16$ inch thick and about 1 inch wide. Run the blade of a knife or a spatula under the ribbon of marzipan to detach it from the surface.

Cut the ribbon diagonally at $1\frac{1}{4}$-inch intervals, making even-sided diamonds. Pick up one leaf at a time and press in slightly with a fingertip at one side in the width to soften the angle into a curve. Vein the leaves with the back of a knife, or leave them plain. Prop the leaves at different angles against the side of a jelly-roll pan, so they dry in different positions. Let some of the leaves dry straight, too. (See illustration on page 306.)

Marzipan Carnations

Knead a drop of red or yellow color into one eighth a batch of marzipan. Roll into a rope about 12 inches long. Flatten the rope with the palm of the hand and smooth it with the bowl of a spoon: Run the bowl of the spoon back and forth in the length of the marzipan, pressing gently, until the marzipan is about

³⁄₁₆ inch thick and about 1 inch wide. Burnish the end closest to you so the edge is thinner than the rest of the ribbon. Run the blade of a knife or spatula under the ribbon to loosen it from the work surface.

To make a fringe, make a series of ½-inch slashes, ¼ inch apart along the thinner edge of the ribbon using the point of a small knife. Beginning at one end, roll up the fringe, keeping it straight at the slashed edge to make a brushlike form. Pick up the brush from the unslashed edge, slashes upward, and pinch inward, under the slashes, gently at first, revolving the flower and pinching repeatedly, to make the petals unfurl. Finally, pinch away the excess rolled, unslashed marzipan at the base. Cut the base of the carnation straight and even with the point of a small knife. Stand the carnation on a pan to dry. If desired, dip the edge of a pastry brush in a drop or two of food coloring, position the brush, bristles upward, close to the carnation, and with a fingertip, flick back the bristles to spray droplets of the coloring on the petals, for a dappled effect.

Variegated Carnations

Start with three pieces of marzipan, leaving two white, and adding coloring to the third. Roll each into a 12-inch rope, as above, then twist the three ropes together. Roll the rope, cut into four pieces, roll each piece to a thin rope, and twist together again. Roll to a smooth rope and cut into three pieces. Roll each to a 12-inch rope and make carnations as above. Use the scraps to make more carnations where the marbling will be more subtle, to make a range of shades in the flowers.

Marzipan Roses

For each rose, cut off one sixteenth of the batch of marzipan. Knead smooth and roll into a rope about 4 inches long. Cut the rope into seven equal pieces. Fashion one piece into a cone, about 1¼ inches high, and set aside to be the base for the flower. Roll each piece into a sphere, then press against the work surface with the palm of the hand to make a disk. Work with the pieces a couple at a time, keeping the rest under a towel to prevent them from drying.

Using the bowl of a spoon, flatten the disk to make it paper-thin at the edge, leaving it thicker in the center. Use light pressure with the spoon, beginning in the center of the disk, moving the spoon in an ever-widening circle, increasing the pressure as the spoon reaches the edge of the disk, so that the edge is very thin and smooth. Form petals that are 2 to 2½ inches in diameter and about ³⁄₁₆ inch thick at the center. Make three petals in this way to be the center bud of the rose. Arrange the first three petals on the work surface and make a ½-inch slash, perpendicular to the edge, in the least attractive edge of each. Pick up and pleat each petal at the slash, sliding one cut edge under and the other over the petal, pressing to adhere, so that the petal is now concave. Repeat with the other two petals.

To form the center bud, place the cone-shaped base against one of the petals (keep the slashed edges of the petals at the bottom so the slashes will not be visible in the finished rose), slightly to the left of the center and about ⅛ inch below the edge of the petal. Curve the left edge of the petal around the base. Insert the left side of the second

Marzipan Roses, continued

petal between the base and the first petal, to the right of the base. Curve the second petal to the left around the base, then insert the third petal between the base and the second. At this point, the three petals around the base should appear as a "Y" from above. Pinch the base of the bud gently to adhere the petals at the bottom, then curve the upper edges of the petals back slightly, to give a natural expression to the bud.

To make a larger rose, prepare three more petals like the first three. Holding each between thumb and first finger at the slash, use the other hand to curve back the edge of each, pinching the edge of the petal in two or three places. Adhere the outside petals, one at a time, to the bud, pressing against the bud at the very bottom, and arranging them equidistant around the bud. To make a very full open rose, make five more petals and adhere them around the rose.

CHOCOLATE DECORATIONS

Chocolate decorations are among the richest and most festive looking of all possible cake decorations. From the simple continuous lines of piped chocolate, to elaborate ruffles and ribbons made of Chocolate Plastic, nothing dresses up a cake or dessert more.

Use the chocolate decorations with chocolate desserts. Although a chocolate filigree border is appropriate on any dessert, use the more substantial decorations like chocolate shavings and plastic only on desserts where the chocolate flavor will not clash with the main dessert flavor. I would not use chocolate shavings on a dessert made of a plain Génoise with lemon buttercream, although I would use them with a chocolate Génoise and chestnut buttercream. The same is true for covering a cake with ruffles and ribbons made from Chocolate Plastic.

Piping Chocolate with the Cornet

Finely cut 1 to 1½ ounces semisweet or bittersweet chocolate and place in a small heatproof bowl; set over a pan of hot, but not simmering water. Stir to melt the chocolate. Add ½ teaspoon vegetable oil to the chocolate, stirring it in thoroughly, if it seems very thick. Cool until the chocolate is just warm to the touch.

Fill a cornet half full of chocolate and fold the top down several times to close it. Cut a small hole in the end of the cornet with sharp scissors.

Hold the cornet in the thumb and first two fingers of the hand you use to write, with the thumb on one side of the top and the 2 fingers on the other, fairly perpendicular to the surface to be decorated. Squeeze with an even, medium pressure, as hard as you would pinch a leaf of parsley to pull it away from the stem. To begin piping, start with the cornet close to the paper or cake, let the flow of chocolate begin, then lift the cornet away from the surface and allow the stream of chocolate to drop slowly from a height of an inch or two. Some people like to steady the wrist of the piping hand by resting it on the open palm of the other hand. I like to use the first finger of my left hand to steady the side of the cornet, which I hold in my right hand.

Use the cornet to make any of the designs on pages 299–300. Practice using the cornet by making straight lines on a piece of paper. Then copy some of the designs onto a piece of white paper with a dark pencil. Place a piece of wax paper on the paper and use them as a guide for practice.

Chocolate Shavings

These make good decorations for all types of desserts. Good chocolate shavings are large, thin and well curled. When possible, choose milk or white chocolate for shaving—try a combination of these along with dark chocolate for a pretty effect. Choose a large piece of chocolate if you can, such as a piece cut from a large (10 or 11 pound) block of chocolate. Or, use a 3 or 4 ounce bar, rather than a 1 ounce square. Leave the chocolate at a warm room temperature for 30 minutes before attempting to shave it—keep the chocolate in the kitchen while the oven is on, and it will soften very slightly, so it shaves easily.

Place the bar or block of chocolate on a jelly-roll pan lined with parchment or wax paper. Use any of the following implements to shave the chocolate: a melon ball scoop, a small paring knife, a tiny tartelette pan or a round cookie cutter.

Draw the implement, at a 45-degree angle, across the bar of chocolate, toward you, using a gentle pressure, especially if you are using a thin bar of chocolate. Several times, remove the bar from the paper, and bend the paper, removing it from the pan, sliding the chocolate shavings into a bowl. Refrigerate the shavings until time to use them. Continue shaving the remaining chocolate. As long as you are preparing the shavings, prepare a lot, and keep in a sealed plastic container at a cool room temperature or in the refrigerator.

Another technique is to use a vegetable peeler on the side of the chocolate bar—this works well if the chocolate is fairly soft. If not, the pressure needed to shave from the side usually shatters the thin chocolate bar.

Always use a fairly gentle pressure, especially if the chocolate is firm—too much pressure will detach rough, heavy shards of chocolate instead of shavings.

To cover a cake with chocolate shavings, use a spatula to press the chocolate against the cake covered with Ganache, buttercream, or whipped cream. If you use your hands to press the shavings in place they will melt.

To cover the top of a cake with the shavings scatter them thickly on the cake, then use a spatula to level the top and sweep off the excess. A light dusting of confectioners' sugar makes the shavings stand out.

CHOCOLATE PLASTIC

This decorating paste—similar to marzipan in some ways it is used—makes lovely, dramatic decorations for cakes. Use it to envelop an entire layer or rolled cake, as you would marzipan, or fashion ruffles and ribbons for delicate decorations.

The different quantities of corn syrup below reflect the different composition of the chocolates—the semisweet has a higher sugar content and is a bit softer, necessitating less corn syrup.

8 OUNCES SEMISWEET CHOCOLATE

¼ CUP LIGHT CORN SYRUP

OR

8 OUNCES BITTERSWEET CHOCOLATE

⅓ CUP LIGHT CORN SYRUP

Finely cut the chocolate and place in a small, heatproof bowl set over a pan of hot, not simmering, water. Stir to melt the chocolate. Remove the bowl from the pan and cool until the chocolate is just lukewarm to the touch.

Add the corn syrup, scraping out the measuring cup with a small rubber spatula. Stir into the chocolate, making sure to scrape the side of the bowl well, to avoid lumps.

The mixture will thicken somewhat and appear dull—do not overmix or the fat may separate from the chocolate, ruining the preparation. Scrape the mixture onto a piece of plastic wrap so it is about ½ inch thick, and fold the plastic over it to enclose. Slide the package onto a plate and refrigerate it until very firm, about 2 hours. Or place the Chocolate Plastic in the freezer for ½ hour to firm.

Yield. 10–11 ounces, enough to cover a 9- or 10-inch cake with ruffles and ribbons

Working with Chocolate Plastic

Remove from the refrigerator and unwrap. Lightly dust the work surface and Chocolate

Plastic with sifted cocoa powder. Pound the Chocolate Plastic with a rolling pin to soften and make pliable, then divide into four pieces. Shape each into a cylinder and flatten with the rolling pin or heel of the hand. Lightly dust again with the sifted cocoa powder and roll them into thin ribbons. Or, use a pasta machine to roll the ribbons thinly, passing them in order through every other setting, ending with the next to last. (If it is extremely cool in the room, you may be able to pass the ribbons through the last setting, resulting in a wonderfully thin ribbon that is almost transparent.)

Use the ribbons to surround a cake. Pleat some of the ribbons into ruffles and cover the entire top of a cake with concentric rows of them, for a beautiful effect.

Or, mass the entire batch of Chocolate Plastic together and use it to cover a cake or roll, rolling it out, dusting it and the surface lightly with sifted cocoa powder, as you would for marzipan.

To make *leaves* from the chocolate plastic, roll with the rolling pin or pasta machine, cut into 1¼-inch-wide ribbons and proceed as for marzipan leaves. For *carnations,* roll the Chocolate Plastic with rolling pin or machine, and proceed as for marzipan carnations.

For *roses,* proceed as above, rolling ribbons, then use a round cutter about 2 to 2½ inches in diameter to cut the petals. Make the conical rose bases from the scraps, pressing them together, then proceed as for marzipan roses. Try making the edges thinner with the back of a spoon, before shaping the petals, but the spoon technique is not well suited to the Chocolate Plastic since it causes it to soften excessively.

DECORATIONS FROM TEMPERED CHOCOLATE

Shiny decorations from tempered chocolate make elegant adjuncts to cakes. Although the system for tempering the chocolate, pages 40-41, can be complicated, you can achieve fine results even if the chocolate does not temper perfectly.

Chocolate Cutouts

Use to decorate the top or side of a cake, placing on, or touching the cake at one point and at an angle to it, to give height.

Line a cookie sheet with parchment paper. Spread 8 ounces of tempered chocolate in a 12-inch square on the paper. Allow the chocolate to stand at room temperature until it begins to set—it will no longer look wet.

With a sharp, pointed knife, cut the square into 1-inch strips, then cut again diagonally at 1-inch intervals to make diamonds. Chill briefly, then detach the cutouts from the paper. Vary the size of the cutouts, if desired. Try using a cookie cutter to make different shapes. A fluted round cutter makes attractive disks. Halve and use on the side of a cake, positioning them with the straight edge uppermost, making a scalloped border around the cake.

GLOSSARY

Aged Spirits—Neutral spirits or brandies aged in wood. Their tawny color is acquired from the inside of the barrel. Scotch, bourbon, applejack, Calvados, brandy, Cognac.

Almond Paste—A commercial product made from almonds and sugar, available in cans.

Bavarian—A type of cream made from crème anglaise or sweetened fruit puree bound with gelatin and lightened with whipped cream.

Baking Blind—Baking a pastry crust without a filling.

Beating—Mixing ingredients or batter vigorously with a wooden spoon or the paddle attachment of a table-model mixer.

Biscuit—(Pronounced BEES QUEE) A type of batter used to make sponge fingers. Also indicates a kind of sponge cake in which the yolks and whites are beaten separately.

Bloom—A grayish film on chocolate that develops when the chocolate has been exposed to a warm temperature. Bloom does not affect the chocolate's performance.

Bombe—A two-layered, semi-spherical ice cream dessert. The outer layer is ice cream or sherbet and the inner layer is made from a pâte à bombe with flavoring and whipped cream added.

Brandies—Distilled spirits which may or may not be aged, made from fermented fruits or wine, such as apples for Calvados, raspberries for Framboise.

Buttercream—A spreading, filling and covering cream made from butter combined with crème anglaise, sabayon, pâte à bombe or meringue.

Caramel—The stage in sugar cooking before the sugar burns completely.

Caramelize—To brown a meringue or other preparation.

Chantilly—Lightly whipped, sweetened and vanilla-flavored cream. Also used to describe the texture of lightly whipped cream even when it hasn't been sweetened.

Choux—Small round or spherical puffs made from pâte à choux, often filled with whipped cream or crème pâtissiere.

Cinnamon—Spice made from the outer bark of the *Cinnamomum cassia*.

Clove—The dried, unopened buds of the evergreen tree *Eugenia carophyllata.*

Cognac—An aged brandy distilled from wine in the Cognac region of France.

Creaming—The process of beating butter to soften it to a light, aerated state. Also refers to beating the creamed butter with sugar and possibly other ingredients to lighten and aerate them.

Crème—Literally "cream"; refers to custardy mixtures like pastry cream, Bavarian cream and buttercream.

Crème Anglaise—Literally "English cream"; a delicate custard cream made only from milk or milk and cream, sugar and egg yolks. Used as a sauce or base for Bavarian cream or buttercream.

Crème Pâtissière—Literally "pastry cream"; a starch-thickened pastry cream used as a filling.

Crystallize—The process whereby a solution of dissolved or melted sugar reverts to the state it was in before melting due to mishandling. May refer to candied or sugar-coated flowers, such as violets, lilacs and roses.

Cutting in—Incorporating butter into dry ingredients for a pastry dough so that it remains in distinguishable pieces.

Docking—Piercing holes at intervals in a pastry dough to prevent it from rising or distorting during baking.

Feuilletté—A pastry or dessert made from puff pastry. Literally "leaved," referring to the leaves of puff pastry dough.

Flavoring Extracts (lemon, orange, etc.)—Made from alcohol combined with an essential oil.

Fruit Brandies *(Eaux de Vie)*—Spirits distilled from different fruits and berries. Usually not aged. Framboise is made from raspberries, Kirsch from cherries.

Fruit Liqueurs—Thick, sweet preparations made from alcohol, fruit juice or puree, and sugar syrup. Grand Marnier is made from oranges, Crème de Cassis from black currants.

Fraisage—Process of smearing a pastry dough to complete the mixing. A classic French technique.

Frangipane—An almond filling or batter.

Ganache—A preparation made from chocolate and cream used for spreading, filling, and covering or glazing depending on the concentration of chocolate.

Gâteau—"Cake" in French.

Génoise—Literally French for "Genoese," meaning from Genoa. A type of sponge cake in which whole eggs and sugar are beaten together to aerate the batter.

Génoise Ordinaire—Literally ordinary or plain génoise composed of eggs, sugar and starch (cake flour and cornstarch).

Génoise Mousseline—A rich génoise with added egg yolks and butter.

Ginger—The root or tuber of *Zingiber officinale.* Used in both fresh and powdered (dry) forms.

Glazing—Pouring or brushing a substance such as ganache or reduced preserves over a dessert to give it a finished sheen.

Grease—A confectioner's term for the interferent, added to a sugar syrup, to help prevent crystallization, such as cream of tartar, corn syrup, lemon juice or vinegar.

Herb—The leaves and stems of aromatic plants.

Herb Liqueurs—Like fruit liqueurs, these are made from alcohol infused with different herbs and then combined with a sugar syrup, for example, Chartreuse, Benedictine.

Interferent—See *Grease.*

Lattice—A series of lines crisscrossed with a second set of diagonal lines; can be piped in buttercream, or made with strips of dough.

Liaison—Binding technique whereby two elements of disparate temperature or consistency are combined.

Mace—The outer bark of nutmeg.

Marzipan—A combination of almond paste, sugar and corn syrup used as a decoration or confection.

Meringue—A combination of egg white and sugar baked or used as a base for mousse or buttercream.

Mousse—Literally "foam" in French, a preparation of aerated eggs, yolks or whites, with flavoring and gelatin and whipped cream, usually bound with gelatin.

Nougatine—Combination of caramel and usually toasted sliced almonds, rolled out while still hot and cut into decorative shapes.

Nutmeg—The nut or inside of a fruit of the *Myristica fragrans* tree.

Panade—A cooked mixture of water, butter and flour or other starch, even breadcrumbs.

Pâte Brisée—Literally "bruised" paste or dough; a rich, flaky, buttery dough, especially suited to being baked blind.

Pâte Sablée—Literally "sandy" paste or dough; a cookie dough.

Pâte Sucrée—Literally "sweet dough"; a less delicate cookie dough than the pâte sablée.

Pie—A pastry with bottom crust and filling, and often a top crust, baked in a sloping-sided pan.

Pralin—Crushed nougatine.

Praline—A pecan candy from New Orleans.

Praliné(e)—French name for praline paste or an adjective used to describe something flavored with Praline Paste or with Pralin Powder.

Praline Paste—A flavoring paste made from caramel and almonds and/or hazelnuts crushed together to a paste.

Puree—Cooked fruit reduced to a paste.

Rest—To allow dough to stand, usually in the refrigerator, before more rolling, shaping or baking.

Roulade—Literally "roll"; a cylindrical cake where the filling is rolled inside a rectangular cake layer.

Rubbing—See *Cutting in.*

Sabayon—Mixture of egg yolks, flavoring and usually sugar heated over simmering water while beaten until thick, then beaten until cool.

Spices—The seeds, bark and sometimes roots of tropical plants.

Sponge—A type of very aerated cake, like a biscuit or Génoise.

Succès—A type of nut meringue, baked and used as cake layers.

Syrup—A liquid sugar, like corn syrup or glucose, or a solution of granulated sugar dissolved in water or other liquid.

Tart—A straight-sided pastry with the bottom and sides made of dough, with a filling.

Tempering—The process of bringing chocolate to the temperature where it is stable and will set properly after melting, or incorporating a fragile substance such as egg yolks or dissolved gelatin into another by stirring some of the first substance into the egg yolks or gelatin before adding them to it.

Torte—German for "cake."

Turn, Single, Double, Half—Refers to the process of folding a dough such as puff pastry and then changing the position before rolling it out again.

Wash (Egg Wash)—Beaten eggs or egg yolks used to adhere layers of dough together or to help it color to a deep sheen during baking.

Whipping—The process of agitating a mixture with a wire whip or the balloon whip of a table-model mixer to incorporate air.

Wines, fortified—Wines to which flavoring, alcohol, and sometimes sugar are added, to flavor and preserve them. For example, Madeira, Sherry, Marsala.

SOURCES OF SUPPLY

The following is a list of suppliers for particular ingredients, equipment and assorted other goods. It is by no means a complete list of suppliers for these items. Check local phone books for grocery wholesalers—friendly ones will usually allow you to order small amounts if you pay cash and pick up the goods at their, rather than your, convenience. If you have trouble locating a local supplier, check with a local cooking school or bakery—a friendly bakery may even sell you parchment paper, cardboards, boxes and difficult-to-find ingredients.

EQUIPMENT

Check the phone book for your local restaurant supply store, a good source for high quality knives, pans (especially the commercial 12 × 18-inch half sheets), and assorted tools like strainers, bench scrapers and whisks. Hardware, department and variety stores supply basic equipment like cookie sheets, layer pans and springforms.

General Kitchen Equipment

Bridge Kitchenware
214 East 52 Street
New York, NY 10022
Telephone (212) 688-4220
No catalog

Fred Bridge, dean of imported cookware suppliers, carries a complete line of pastry and dessert supplies: pans of every size and description, including removable-bottom tart pans, commercial half-sheet pans and 2-inch-deep layer pans. Also, pastry bags and tubes, cutters and rolling pins. Since he carries a vast amount of stock, try to be specific if you phone for a particular piece of equipment.

Decorating Supplies

Maid of Scandinavia
3244 Raleigh Avenue
Minneappolis, MN 55416
Telephone (800) 328-6722
Catalog available

Write or call for a very complete catalog of all sorts of decorating supplies, from bags and tubes to more elaborate equipment used by dedicated decorators. They also offer a full line of colors, many prepared decorations, books on decorating and baking and domestic and imported chocolate in bulk.

The Chocolate Gallery
135 West 50 Street
New York, NY 10019
Telephone (212) 582-3510
No catalog

Joan Mansour carries a full line of decorating equipment as well as being New York's most talented teacher of cake decorating. Aside from specialized decorating needs, there are also pans, cardboards and wedding cake supplies.

SPECIALTY FOODS

Van Rex
530 West 25 Street
New York, NY 10001
Telephone (212) 675-7777
Price list available

Rachel and Marcel Akselrod supply New York's and the country's best restaurants and hotels with imported food products. Exquisite French Praline Paste, and magnificent Valrhona chocolate, chestnut spread, and crystallized flowers are all available here.

BIBLIOGRAPHY

Amendola, Joseph. *The Bakers' Manual for Quantity Baking and Pastry Making.* Rochelle Park, N.J.: Hayden, 1972.

Barker, William. *The Modern Patissier.* New York: Arco, 1978.

Barrows, A.B. *Everyday Productions of Baked Goods.* Boston: Cahners Books, 1975.

Bernachon, Maurice et Jean-Jaques. *La Passion du Chocolat.* Paris: Flammarion, 1985.

Chaboissier, D. *Le Compagnon Patissier.* 2 vols. Paris: Editions Jerome Villette, 1983.

Courtine, Robert. *The Hundred Glories of French Cooking.* New York: Farrar, Straus, Giroux, 1977. Translated by Derek Coltman.

Darenne, E. & E. Duval. *Traité de Pâtisserie Moderne.* Paris: Flammarion, 1974.

Del Soldo, Marco. *Il Manuale Del Pasticciere Moderno.* Milan: DeVecchi, 1973.

D'Ermo, Dominique. *The Modern Pastry Chef's Guide to Professional Baking.* New York: Harper & Row, 1962.

Fance, Wilfred James. *The New International Confectioner.* London and Coulsdon, England: Virtue & Company, 1981.

————. *The Students' Technology of Breadmaking and Flour Confectionary.* London: Routledge & Keegan Paul, 1976.

Franchiolo, P.J. *L' Art Chez le Pâtissier Confisseur-Glacier.* Paris: 1958.

Herisse, Emile, and C. Herman Senn. *Pastry-Making and Confectionery.* London: Ward, Lock, n.d.

Hillman, Howard. *The Cook's Book.* New York: Avon, 1981.

Kollist, E.J. *The Complete Patissier.* London: MacLaren & Sons, n.d.

Lacam, Pierre. *Le Memorial Historique et Géographique de la Pâtissiere.* Paris, 1895.

Langseth-Christensen, Lillian, and Carol Sturm Smith. *The Complete Kitchen Guide.* New York: Grosset & Dunlap, 1968.

Layton, T.A. *Cheese and Cheese Cookery.* Cleveland: The Wine and Food Society in Association with World Publishing, 1967.

Mayer, Eduard. *Wiener Suss-Speisen.* Linz, Austria: Trauner Verlag, 1982.

McGee, Harold. *On Food and Cooking.* New York: Charles Scribner's Sons, 1984.

Pancoast, Harry M., W. Ray and B.A. Junk. *Hand-*

book of Sugars. Westport, CT: AVI, 1980.

Pasquet, Ernest. *La Pâtisserie Familiale.* Paris: Flammarion, 1974.

Phillips, Bert J. *The Pastry Chef.* New York: Bonanza Books, 1965.

Richards, Paul. *Cakes for Bakers.* Chicago: Baker's Helper Company, 1932.

Richards, Paul. *Paul Richards' Pastry Book.* Chicago: Hotel Monthly Press, n.d.

Schneider, Elizabeth. *Uncommon Fruits and Vegetables.* New York: Harper and Row, 1986.

Sultan, William J. *Modern Pastry Chef.* Vols 1 & 2. Westport, Ct.: AVI, 1977.

Sultan, William, J. *Practical Baking.* Westport, Ct.: AVI, 1982.

Teubner, Christian, et al. *Das Grosse Buch Der Kuchen and Torten.* D-8958 Fussen, 1983.

Teubner, Christian and Sybil Grafin Schonfeldt. *The Great Dessert Book.* New York: Hearst Books, 1983.

Thuries, Yves. *Le Livre de Recettes d'un Compagnon du Tour de France.* 3 vols. Gaillac, France: Societé Editar, 1980, 1982, 1979 (Vols. 1, 2, 3).

Vitalis, M. *Les Bases de la Pâtisserie, Confiserie, Glacerie.* Paris: Editions J. Lamore, 1979.

Weber, J.M. Erich. *Schule und Praxis des Konditors.* Radebeul-Dresden, Germany: Internationaler Fachverlag J.M. Erich Weber, 1927.

Matt, Werner, and Walter Glocker. *Erlesenes aus Osterreiches Kuche.* Linz, Austria: Rudolf Trauner Verlag, 1982.

Witzelsberger, Richard. *Das Oesterreichische Mehlspeisen Kochbuch.* Vienna: Verlag Kremayr & Scheriau, 1979.

INDEX